World Intellectual Property Indicators 2022

WIPO
WORLD
INTELLECTUAL PROPERTY
ORGANIZATION

Suggested citation: World Intellectual Property Organization (WIPO) (2022). *World Intellectual Property Indicators 2022.* Geneva. WIPO. DOI:10.34667/tind.47082

First published 2022

World Intellectual Property Organization
34, chemin des Colombettes, P.O. Box 18
CH-1211 Geneva 20, Switzerland

ISBN: 978-92-805-3462-7 (print)
ISBN: 978-92-805-3463-4 (online)
ISSN: 2709-5193 (print)
ISSN: 2709-5207 (online)

Cover: WIPO

Contents

Foreword

Daren Tang, Director General,
World Intellectual Property
Organization (WIPO)

This year's *World Intellectual Property Indicators* (*WIPI*) report reveals strong growth in intellectual property (IP) filings in 2021, as entrepreneurship, technology, innovation and digitalization continue to drive forward national and global growth.

Patent applications grew by 3.6% last year. Trademark and industrial design filing activity grew by even more – 5.5% and 9.2%, respectively. And worldwide IP filings reached an all-time high, with 3.4 million patent applications, 13.9 million trademark applications (specifying 18.1 million classes) and applications for 1.5 million designs filed last year.

This is consistent with the fact that 2021 was a year of robust recovery in many parts of the world. The global economy grew by 6% last year, the fastest rate of increase in more than four decades.

It also reflects the multi-faceted consequences of the COVID-19 crisis. On the one hand, the pandemic triggered extreme disruption across large swathes of the global economy. On the other hand, it proved to be a potent and powerful accelerator of certain economic sectors and trends. This was especially true when it came to new and frontier technologies, with businesses and governments around the world identifying digitalization and innovation as key avenues of future growth.

To underscore this, the report finds that even at the height of the pandemic in 2020 patent filings relating to computer technology grew by over 13%, cementing this area as the most frequently featured technology in published patent applications worldwide. Indeed, taken together, the five largest fields for patent applications – computer technology, electrical machinery, measurement, digital communications and medical technology – now account for a third of all applications globally, up five percentage points from a decade ago.

Similarly, research and technology is the top sector in which applicants sought trademark protection abroad last year, accounting for one in five global non-resident filings. Next are health, clothing and accessories, and leisure and education, all areas where the relationship between brands and consumers is being reshaped by the digital acceleration.

By illuminating key growth sectors and headline indicators, as well as providing a whole range of analysis relating to IP activities, we hope that the report's rich dataset will function as a practical tool for policymakers, IP professionals, industry, academia, and other stakeholders around the world.

Robust and reliable data has always been the bedrock of effective policymaking and has a direct bearing on the ability of governments and authorities to design and implement measures that help make IP a powerful catalyst for growth. Such data takes on added importance during periods of global economic turbulence, serving as an invaluable tool for charting a course through powerful headwinds.

Therefore we are grateful to our partners in 150 national and regional IP offices for supporting this report and our work at WIPO. We hope that this year's *WIPI* will help Member States navigate an uncertain global environment while continuing to generate economic and social impact through innovation, creativity and IP.

Acknowledgments

World Intellectual Property Indicators 2022 was prepared under the direction of Daren Tang (Director General) in the IP and Innovation Ecosystems Sector led by Marco Aleman (Assistant Director General), and supervised by Carsten Fink (Chief Economist). The report was prepared by Kyle Bergquist, Mosahid Khan, Ryan Lamb, Bruno Le Feuvre and Hao Zhou, all from the Department for Economics and Data Analytics. Peter Button and Ariane Besse of the International Union for the Protection of New Varieties of Plants (UPOV) provided comments and suggestions for the plant varieties section. Alexandra Grazioli and Matteo Gragnani of the Brands and Designs Sector provided comments and suggestions for the geographical indications section. Gratitude is also due to Enrico Turrin of the Federation of the European Publishers for sharing some of the creative economy data.

Samiah Do Carmo Figueiredo and Jovana Stojanović provided administrative support. Gratitude is also due to the Information and Digital Outreach Division for the editing and design and to staff in the Printing Plant for their services.

Further information

Online resources

The electronic version of this report and the underlying data can be downloaded at *www.wipo.int/ipstats*. This webpage also provides a link to the IP Statistics Data Center, offering access to WIPO's statistical data.

Contact information

Statistics and Data Analytics Division
Website: *www.wipo.int/ipstats*
e-mail: *ipstats.mail@wipo.int*

Key numbers

Patents	2020	2021	Growth rate (%)	Share of world total (%)
Applications worldwide	**3,281,900**	**3,401,100**	**3.6**	**100.0**
China	1,497,159	1,585,663	5.9	46.6
US	597,172	591,473	–1.0	17.4
Japan	288,472	289,200	0.3	8.5
Utility models				
Applications worldwide	**3,000,100**	**2,924,490**	**–2.5**	**100.0**
China	2,926,633	2,852,219	–2.5	97.5
Germany	12,318	10,576	–14.1	0.4
Russian Federation	9,195	9,079	–1.3	0.3
Trademarks				
Application class counts worldwide	**17,193,800**	**18,145,100**	**5.5**	**100.0**
China	9,345,710	9,454,794	1.2	52.1
US	870,276	899,678	3.4	5.0
EUIPO (EU office)	438,469	497,542	13.5	2.7
Industrial designs				
Application design counts worldwide	**1,387,800**	**1,515,200**	**9.2**	**100.0**
China	770,362	805,710	4.6	53.2
EUIPO (EU office)	113,195	117,049	3.4	7.7
UK	32,733	74,781	128.5	4.9
Plant varieties				
Applications worldwide	**22,620**	**25,340**	**12.0**	**100.0**
China	8,960	11,195	24.9	44.2
Community Plant Variety Office (EU)	3,427	3,480	1.5	13.7
US	1,432	1,902	32.8	7.5

Source: WIPO Statistics Database, September 2022.

Patents

Highlights

Global patent applications returned to pre-Covid-19 levels in 2021

Innovators around the world filed 3.4 million patent applications in 2021, slightly higher than the pre-COVID peak of 3.3 million filed in 2018 (figure 1.1). Patent applications worldwide grew by 3.6% in 2021 compared to 2020. This follows an increase of 1.5% in 2020 which came after a 3% drop in 2019. A substantial rise in filings by China, which made 88,504 more applications than it did in 2020, combined with robust contributions from the intellectual property (IP) office of the Republic of Korea (11,239 additional applications) and the European Patent Office (EPO) (8,432), was the main driver of growth in 2021. The IP offices of India (4,802) and South Africa (4,272) also made notable contributions to overall growth.

Patent applications filed worldwide grew by 3.6% in 2021

1.1. Patent applications worldwide, 2007–2021

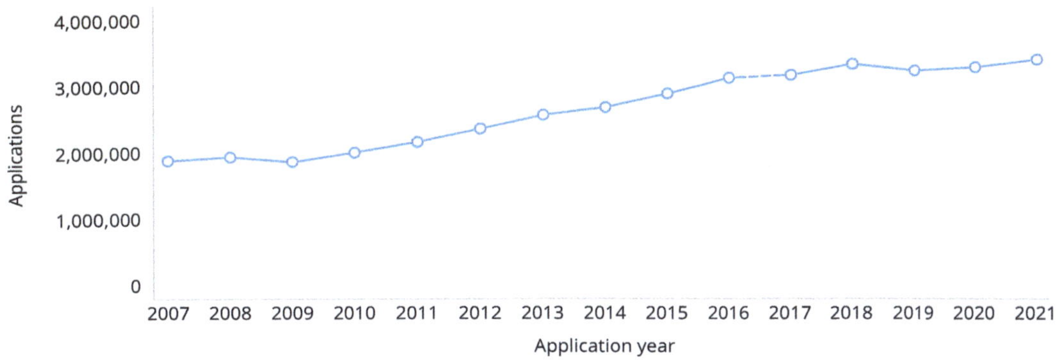

Source: Figure A1.

The 3.4 million applications filed worldwide comprised 2.4 million resident filings (70.1% of the total) and 1 million non-resident filings (29.9%). Following a 2.3% decrease at the height of the COVID-19 pandemic in 2020, non-resident filings grew by 4.7% in 2021. Resident filings increased by 3.2% in 2021 – the same rate of growth as in 2020. The long-term trend in patent applications worldwide is upwards, applications having doubled from approximately 1 million in 1995 to around 2 million by 2010, and reached the 3 million mark by 2016. A big increase in resident filings in China has also led to a substantial drop in the share of non-resident filings worldwide, declining from 38.1% in 2010 to 29.9% in 2021 (figure A2).

China received 1.59 million patent applications in 2021, more than double the number received by the United States of America

The National Intellectual Property Administration of the People's Republic of China (CNIPA) received 1.59 million patent applications in 2021, up 5.9% on 2020.[1] The volume of applications received by CNIPA is similar in magnitude to the combined total of the next 12 offices ranked from second to 13th in figure A7.

The United States Patent and Trademark Office (USPTO) – with 591,473 applications – ranked second, followed by the Japan Patent Office (JPO) (289,200), the Korean Intellectual Property Office (KIPO) (237,998) and the European Patent Office (EPO) (188,778). Together, the top five offices accounted for 85.1% of the world total in 2021, 6.6 percentage points higher than their combined share a decade earlier in 2011. This is entirely due to an unprecedented growth in

1 Patent applications data refer to invention patents and do not include utility model (UM) applications. UM applications data are reported separately (see figures A48–50). In the United States of America, invention patents are referred to as "utility patents," which are not be confused with utility models.

filings in China. China's share of the world total has almost doubled, from 24.4% in 2011 to 46.6% in 2021. By contrast, each of the other four offices in the top five experienced a decrease in their respective shares during the same period.

The composition and ranking of the top five IP offices globally has remained unchanged since 2011. The list of IP offices occupying sixth to 10th spots has likewise remained the same, but with slight changes in the respective rankings. India, Canada and Australia have moved up one spot to sixth, eighth and ninth, respectively, in 2021, while Germany dropped down a position to seventh and the Russian Federation fell two places to 10th (figure 1.2). Within the top 10 offices, there is a substantial variation in the source of applications (figure A7). For example, non-resident applicants accounted for nine out of 10 applications received by the IP office of Australia, but only one in 10 applications received by the IP office of China. Along with the IP office of Australia (90.8%), the offices of Canada (87.3%), the EPO (55.6%), India (57.3%) and the United States of America (US) (55.7%) received a majority of their applications from non-resident applicants. Beyond the top 10 offices, non-resident share is high at the offices of Brazil (80.7%), Indonesia (84.1%), Mexico (93.1%) and Singapore (86.1%).

Among the top 10 offices, non-resident applicants represent a large proportion of applications filed in Australia and Canada

1.2. Patent applications at the top 10 offices, 2021

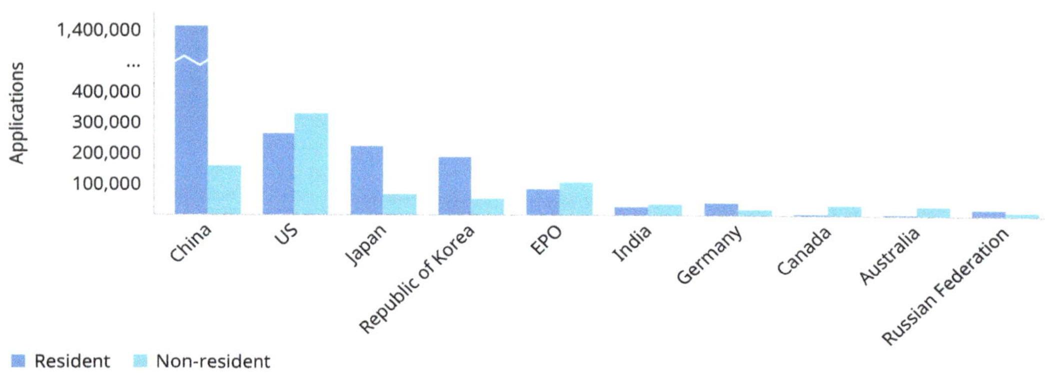

Source: Figure A7.

Among the top five offices, China and the Republic of Korea register a strong growth for a second consecutive year. Filings in China grew by 5.9% in 2021, following a 6.9% increase the previous year. The Republic of Korea received 5% more applications in 2021, compared to 3.6% growth in 2020. Filings in the US decreased by 1% in 2021, an improvement on the 3.9% decline in 2020. The EPO (+4.7%) and Japan (+0.3%) returned to growth in 2021 following a decline the previous year.

The majority of the top 20 offices - 15 out of 20 - received a greater number of patent applications in 2021 than in 2020 (figure A8). This is a considerable improvement on 2020, when only seven offices saw a growth in filings. Of these 15 offices, the largest increases were in South Africa (+63.9%), Israel (+18.3%), Mexico (+12.9%), Australia (+10.6%) and Singapore (+10%) - each reporting double-digit growth. In every one of these five offices, an increase in non-resident filings was the principal driver of overall growth.

Five offices among the top 20 received fewer applications in 2021 than in 2020, with the Russian Federation (-11.5%), the United Kingdom (UK) (-8.7%) and Germany (-5.7%) reporting the steepest declines. A fall in both resident and non-resident filings contributed to the overall decline in Germany and the UK, while a sharp drop in resident filings was the main driver of the total decrease in the Russian Federation.

Looking beyond the top 20 offices to selected offices of low- and middle-income countries shows the offices of Viet Nam (8,534), Türkiye (8,476) and Thailand (8,242) to have all received over 8,000 applications in 2021 (figure A9). For both Thailand and Viet Nam, a growth in non-resident filings was the main driver of overall growth, while an increase in resident filings was responsible for almost all the increase in Türkiye. A majority of the offices of selected low- and middle-income countries reported in figure A10 received more applications in 2021 compared to 2020. Non-resident filings were the primary contributor to the total growth in all these offices, except in the African Intellectual Property Organization (OAPI), Ecuador and Türkiye.

Among the four regional offices, OAPI (+27.8%) and the African Regional Intellectual Property Organization (ARIPO) (+10.5%) saw double digit-growth in 2021. The Eurasian Patent Organization (EAPO) (+7.9%) also reported a strong growth in filings. In contrast, the Patent Office of the Cooperation Council for the Arab States of the Gulf (GCC) received 86.4% fewer applications in 2021 compared to a year earlier.

Two-thirds of global patent filing activity took place in Asia

Of the top 20 offices, eight were located in Asia, six in Europe, two each in North America and Latin America and the Caribbean (LAC), and one each in Africa and Oceania.

Offices located in Asia received around 2.3 million applications in 2021, representing 67.6% of the world total (figure 1.3). Asia's share of all applications filed worldwide increased from 54.6% in 2011 to 67.6% a decade later in 2021. This has been primarily driven by a strong growth in filings in China, which accounted for 69% of all applications filed in the region in 2021. North America's share has declined from one-quarter (25%) in 2011 to 18.5% in 2021, while that of Europe has decreased by 5 percentage points to 10.5% over the same period. The combined share for Africa, LAC, and Oceania was 3.4% in 2021, down from 5% a decade ago.

Two-thirds of patent filings activity worldwide took place in Asia

1.3. Patent applications by region, 2011 and 2021

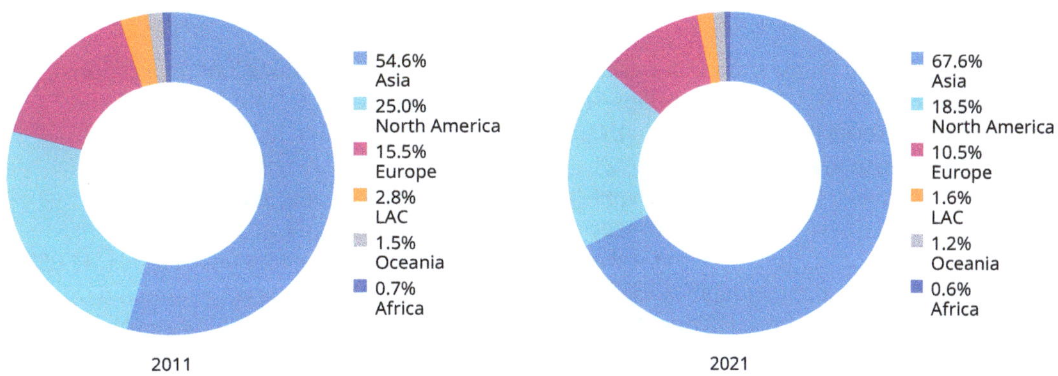

Source: Table A5.

Patent filings since 1883

From 1883 to 1963, the patent office of the US was the leading office for world filings. Application numbers in Japan and the US remained stable until the early 1970s, at which time Japan began to experience rapid growth – a pattern also observed for the US from the 1980s onward. Among the top five offices, Japan surpassed the US in 1968 and retained top position until 2005. Since the early 2000s, however, the number of applications filed in Japan has followed a downward trend. China surpassed the EPO and the Republic of Korea in 2005, Japan in 2010 and the US in 2011, and now receives the most applications worldwide. There has been a gradual upward trend in the combined share of the top five offices in the world total – from 78.5% in 2011 to 85.1% in 2021.

Trend in patent applications for the top five offices, 1883–2021

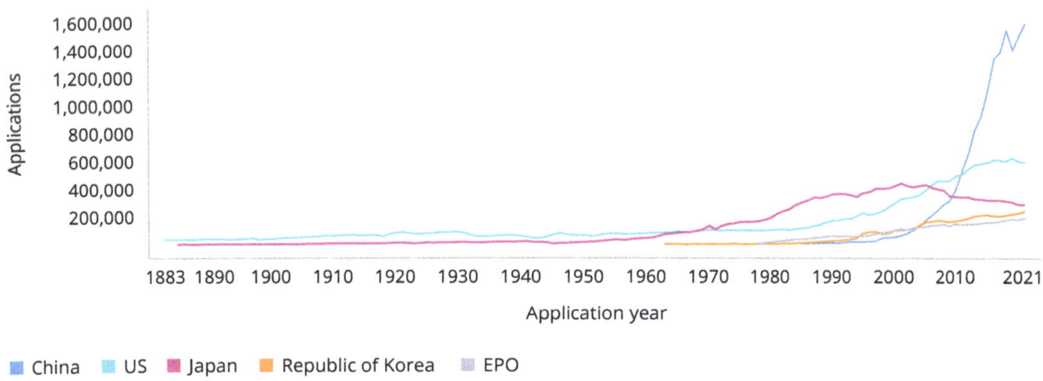

Source: Figure A6.

US applicants filed close to a quarter of a million patent applications aboard, more than double those filed by China applicants

Applications received by offices from resident and non-resident applicants are referred to as office data, whereas applications filed by applicants at a national or regional office (resident applications) or at a foreign office (applications abroad) are referred to as origin data. Here, patent statistics based on the origin of residence of the first named applicant are reported in order to complement the picture of patent activity worldwide.

Applicants from China filed around 1.54 million equivalent patent applications worldwide in 2021 (resident plus abroad filings). China was followed by the US (509,853), Japan (412,851), the Republic of Korea (267,517) and Germany (165,656) (figure A17). The composition of the top five origins has remained unchanged since 2003, when China surpassed France and the UK. However, the distribution of resident and abroad filings differs considerably between these five offices. China by far has the lowest share of applications filed abroad – only 7.3%. In contrast, filings abroad constituted a large proportion of total applications originating from Germany (60.3%), Japan (46.1%), the Republic of Korea (30.4%) and the US (48.6%). Among the top 20 origins, Canada (82.2%) and Israel (90.8%) have the highest proportions of total applications filed abroad. Every top 20 origin – presented in figure A17 – is a high-income country, with the exception of China, India and the Russian Federation, and the majority of origins are European countries. Brazil (6,900) – which has a similar level of filings as Ireland – is the highest ranked origin from the Latin America and the Caribbean region, while South Africa (2,751) is the top ranked origin for Africa.

Focusing on abroad filings shows US-based applicants filed the most equivalent applications abroad (247,609) in 2021, followed by Japan (190,399), China (111,905), Germany (99,899) and the Republic of Korea (81,272) (figure 1.4). China moved up one position to third, because of a 16.2% increase in abroad filings in 2021 compared to 2020. The US saw a 9.3% increase in aboard filings over the same period, while the Republic of Korea experienced modest growth of 1.4%. Japan – for a second consecutive year – filed fewer applications aboard, while Germany's 2021 applications aboard total is almost identical to the previous year. France (42,051), Switzerland (38,512), the UK (36,393), the Netherlands (24,122) and Canada (21,794) round out the top 10 rankings for abroad filings. Among the top 10 origins, along with China and the US, Canada (+12.3%) and Switzerland (+9.1%) also saw strong growth in 2021, while France (+2.8%) and the UK (+2.9%) each reported a similar size increase, whereas the Netherlands (–0.5%) saw a small decrease.

US residents filed close to a quarter of a million patent applications abroad in 2021

1.4. Patent applications filed abroad by the top 10 origins, 2021

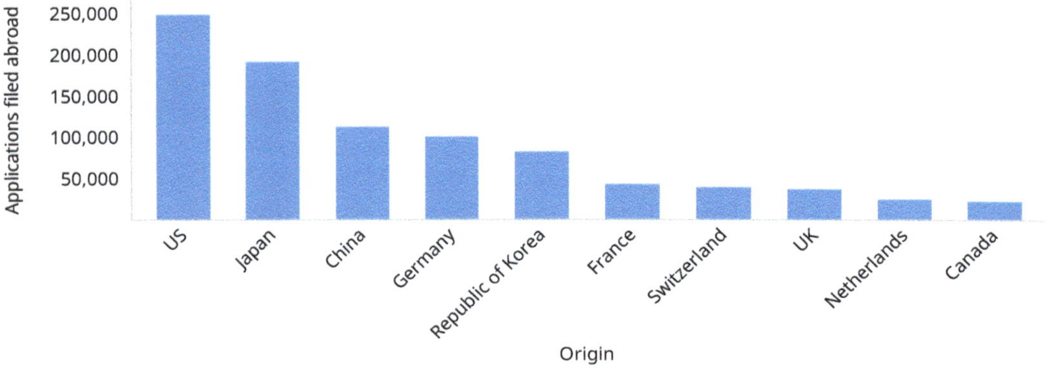

Source: Figure A17.

An analysis of the flow of non-resident applications between origins and offices shows that US applicants accounted for a large proportion of the non-resident filings at 12 of the 20 offices presented in table A18, ranging from 53.3% at the IP office of Israel to 22.7% at the Russian Federation. Applicants resident in Japan accounted for the largest non-resident share at four of the 20 offices – namely, China (29.6%), Germany (32.7%), Indonesia (28.4%) and the US (22.9%). German applicants accounted for 24.6% of all non-resident applications filed in France and 21% in Italy.

Equivalent application count

Applications at regional IP offices are equivalent to multiple applications in countries that are members of the organizations establishing those offices. More particularly, in order to calculate the number of equivalent applications for the African Intellectual Property Organization (OAPI), the Eurasian Patent Organization (EAPO) and the Patent Office of the Cooperation Council for the Arab States of the Gulf (GCC Patent Office), each application needs to be multiplied by the corresponding number of member states. For African Regional Intellectual Property Organization (ARIPO) and the European Patent Office (EPO) data, each application is counted as one application abroad, if the applicant does not reside in a member state, or as one resident application and one application abroad, if the applicant is resident in a member state. The equivalent application concept is used when reporting data by origin.

Republic of Korea residents filed the most patents per GDP and per population in 2021

Variations in the patenting activity across countries reflects differences in the size and structure of their economies. It is therefore informative to examine resident patent activity with regard to variables such as population, research and development spending, and gross domestic product (GDP).

With 8,159 resident patent applications per unit of USD 100 billion GDP, the Republic of Korea continued to be the country filing the most patent applications in 2021 (figure 1.5). Its patent-to-GDP ratio is almost twice that of third-place Japan.

China (5,738) scored the second highest ratio, followed by Japan (4,341), Switzerland (1,581) and Germany (1,494). These five have been the top ranking countries since 2018. Finland (1,351), the US (1,253), Sweden (1,216), Denmark (1,089) and the Netherlands (869) round out the top 10 origins. Among the top 10 origins, China has seen a considerable improvement in its resident patent applications-to-GDP ratio, which has increased from 3,194 in 2011 to 5,738 in 2021. In contrast, Japan's patent-to-GDP ratio declined from 5,897 to 4,341 over the same period.

Three Asian countries – China, Japan and the Republic of Korea – had the greatest number of resident patent applications per GDP in 2021

1.5. Resident patent applications per USD 100 billion GDP for the top 10 origins, 2011 and 2021

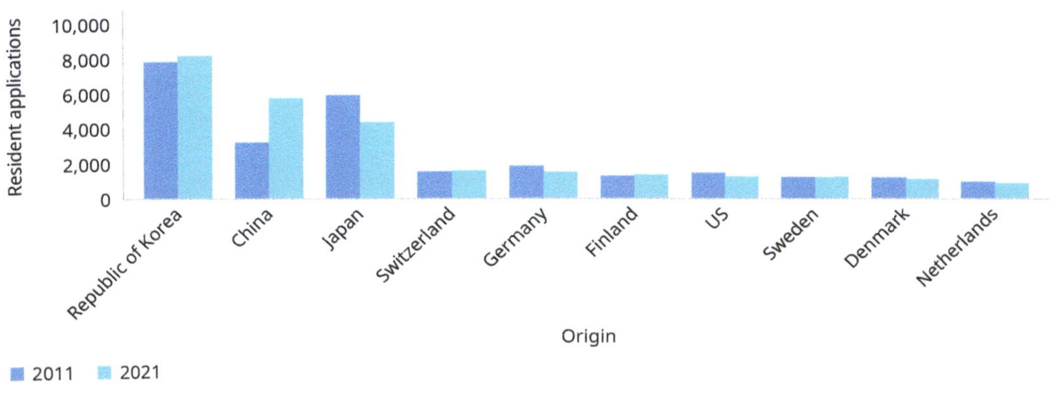

Source: Figure A35.

A number of countries with a low resident patent applications count, among them Denmark, Luxembourg, Norway and Singapore, rank among the top 20 origins, once resident patent applications are adjusted according to GDP (figure A35). The list of top 20 origins predominantly comprises high-income countries; however, three middle-income countries – China, the Russian Federation and Türkiye – also feature. Despite a considerable improvement in the patent-to-GDP ratio of India and South Africa, both remain outside the top 20. Brazil, with 149 resident patents per GDP, is the highest ranked origin in the LAC region.

The profile of resident applications per million population is similar to that adjusted for GDP, but there are subtle differences. The composition of the top 10 origins for resident applications according to GDP and by population is identical, except for a slight change in rank for a few origins. For example, China ranks fourth according to the patent-to-population measure, but occupies second position for patent-to-GDP ratio. The Republic of Korea (3,599) retains its lead when resident applications are expressed according to population, followed by Japan (1,770) and Switzerland (1,119), ahead of China (1,010) and Germany (791) (figure A36). Moving outside the top 10 origins finds Australia and Canada among the top 20 origins for resident patent application by population, which was not the case for patents according to GDP.

Patent filings for unique inventions dropped sharply in 2019

Patent rights are territorial in nature. In order to protect inventions in several countries, applicants often file patent applications for the same invention in multiple jurisdictions. This being the case, adding patent data from different jurisdictions would inflate the number of new inventions. Patent family data are therefore frequently used in order to eliminate (or at least minimize) double counting. The basic idea behind a patent family is to group together all applications – original and subsequent filings – related to each other via priority filing(s). WIPO has developed indicators for patent families with the aim of capturing the actual number of unique inventions by excluding double counting as far as possible. The drawback of such data is the consequent time lag which can be up to three years.

Patent families worldwide declined by 7.5% in 2019 (figure A21), the sharpest year-on-year drop since at least 1980. A 9.9% decline in patent applications in China in 2019 was the main factor in the overall decrease in patent families worldwide.

The total number of patent families worldwide amounted to 1.96 million in 2019, down from a peak of 2.12 million in 2018 (figure 1.6). Applicants from China accounted for more than three-fifths of all patent families (61.5%), followed by Japan (10.9%), the US (8.8%) and the Republic of Korea (7.5%). However, the US (206,947) and Japan (157,508) created by far the most foreign-oriented patent families for the period 2017–2018 (figure A24), and far more than China (69,435), Germany (61,452) or the Republic of Korea (54,880).

Patent filings for unique inventions amounted to 1.96 million in 2019

1.6. Patent applications and patent families worldwide, 2005–2021

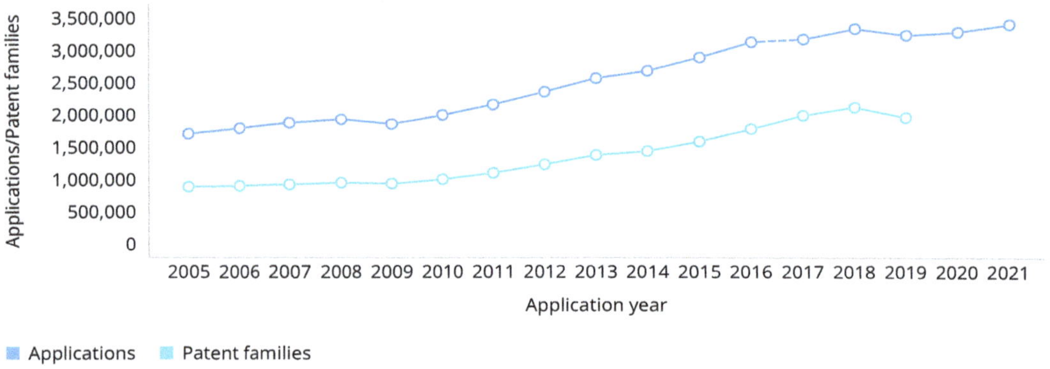

Sources: Figures A1 and A21.

The size of a patent family (i.e., the number of offices where a patent is filed) reflects its geographical coverage. Around 85% of the patent families created worldwide between 2017 and 2019 were filed at a single office (figure A22). This high share is mainly driven by the filing behavior of Chinese applicants who mostly tended to file applications at a single office. But there is considerable variation among top origins. For example, more than half of total patent families originating from France (55.7%), Italy (52.3%), the Netherlands (64%), Sweden (72.8%) and Switzerland (64.9%) covered two or more offices. In contrast, less than one-tenth of patent families originating from Brazil (9.8%), China (2.9%) and the Russian Federation (3.5%) filed at more than one office.

The origins whose patent families had the widest geographical coverage are Australia (10.9%), the Netherlands (11.2%), Sweden (11.8%) and Switzerland (17.7%), where more than 10% of patent families covered more than five offices.

Patent families

A patent family is a set of interrelated patent applications filed at one or more offices to protect the same invention. The patent applications in a family are interlinked by one or more of the following: priority claim, Patent Cooperation Treaty (PCT) national phase entry, continuation, continuation-in-part, internal priority, and addition or division. A special subset comprises foreign-oriented patent families – that is, those patent families that have at least one filing office different from the office of the applicant's country of origin. Some foreign-related patent families include only one filing office. This is because applicants may choose to file only at a foreign office. For example, if a Canadian applicant files a patent application directly with the United States Patent and Trademark Office (USPTO) without having previously filed with the patent office of Canada, that patent family will constitute a foreign-oriented patent family with just one office.

One-tenth of patent applications published worldwide in 2020 were in the field of computer technology

In 2020 – the latest year for which complete data are available due to the delay between application and publication – computer technology was the most frequently featured technology in published patent applications worldwide, accounting for one-tenth of all published applications (10.2% of world total) (table A27). It was followed by electrical machinery (6.5%), measurement (5.7%), digital communication (5.1%) and medical technology (5%). These five fields have occupied the top five spots in the ranking since 2012 – albeit in a varying order. Together, these five fields accounted for 32.6% of all published applications globally in 2020, which is five percentage points above its global share a decade earlier in 2010.

Each of the top 10 fields of technology recorded growth in published applications between 2010 and 2020. Computer technology (+9.6%) and machine tools (+9.1%) are the two to have witnessed the fastest average annual growth between 2010 and 2020, whereas electrical machinery apparatus (+5.8%) grew at the slowest rate. Published applications related to the pharmaceuticals field have experienced a year-on-year decline since a peak in 2016 – declining from 108,100 published applications in 2016 to 93,000 in 2020.

Among the top 10 origins during the period from 2018 to 2020, China (10% of all published applications), the Republic of Korea (8.4%), the UK (8.3%) and the US (12.2%) filed most heavily in computer technology (figure A28). Japan (9.9%) filed mostly in electrical machinery; France (11.5%) and Germany (11.4%) in transport; Switzerland (9.7%) in pharmaceuticals; the Netherlands (12.8%) and the Russian Federation (8.9%) in medical technology.

Among large middle-income countries during the same period, applicants residing in India (18.5% of total published applications) and Mexico (11.4%) filed most heavily in pharmaceuticals; Brazil (7.8%) in other special machines; South Africa in civil engineering (9.5%); and Türkiye (8.4%) in transport.

The number of energy-related – solar, fuel cell, wind, geothermal and hydro energy – published patent applications almost doubled from around 24,600 in 2006 to 47,400 in 2012, since when it has followed a downward trend (figure A29). The total number of energy-related published applications amounted to around 39,000 in 2020, 1,500 fewer than in 2019. Solar energy accounted for more than half (56.8%) of the total energy-related applications. The share of solar energy patents remained around 56% between 2017 and 2020.

Brazil's patent office granted 31.7% more patents in 2021 than in 2020 – representing a second successive year of double-digit growth

Offices carry out a formal and substantive examination before deciding whether to issue a patent. The procedure for granting a patent varies between offices, and differences in the numbers of patents granted among offices depend on factors such as examination capacity and procedural delays. For this reason, application data for a given year should not be compared with grant data from the same year.

In 2021, an estimated 1.76 million patents were granted worldwide, up 10% on 2020 (figure 1.7). China (695,946) issued the highest number of patents in 2021, followed by the US (327,307), Japan (184,372), the Republic of Korea (145,882) and the EPO (108,799) (figure A13). Among the top 10 offices, Brazil granted 31.7% more patents in 2021 than it did in 2020 (figure A14) – a second successive year of double-digit growth. China (+31.3%), Germany (+22%) and India (+16.5%) also recorded a double-digit growth in patents granted in 2021. A marked increase in patents granted to non-resident applicants drove overall growth in Brazil and India. In contrast, resident grants were responsible for the bulk of growth in China. As for Germany, both resident and non-resident grants contributed to total growth. The EPO (-18.6%), the Russian Federation (-17.8%) and the US (-7%) issued considerably fewer patents in 2021 than in 2020. Each issued fewer patents to both resident and non-residents applicants alike.

Looking beyond the top 10 offices to the top 20 list, Malaysia (6,876), Indonesia (6,850), Singapore (6,488) and South Africa (6,107) each issued between 6,000 and 7,000 patents - the bulk to non-resident applicants (figure A13). The offices of China, Hong Kong SAR (+91.5%) and South Africa (+76.2%) recorded substantial growth in 2021, primarily due to a strong growth in non-resident grants.

Patents granted worldwide grew by 10% in 2021 - the fastest rate of growth since 2012

1.7. Patent grants worldwide, 2007-2021

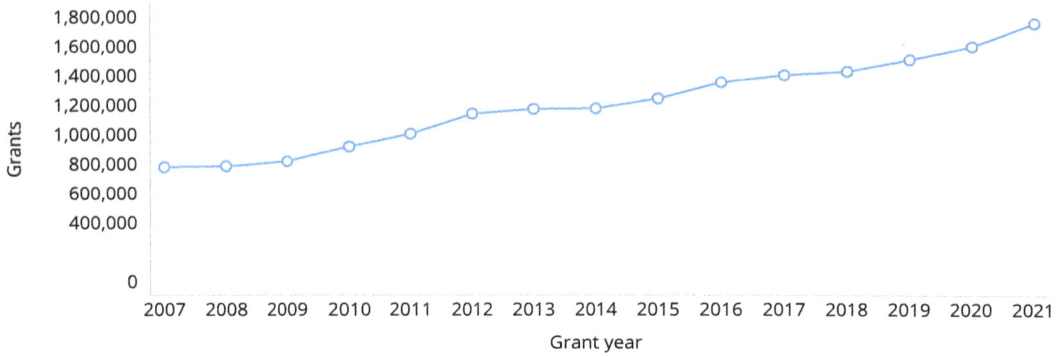

Source: Figure A3.

Asia's share of worldwide patent grants was 63.9% in 2021, 8.9 percentage points above its global share a decade earlier in 2011. This reflects the fact that three of the top five patent issuing authorities - China, Japan and the Republic of Korea - are located in the region, with China accounting for 39.6% of the world total. Offices located in North America accounted for a fifth (19.9%) of patent grants worldwide in 2021, while those in Europe accounted for 11.8% of the world total (table A11). The combined share for Africa, LAC, and Oceania was 4.3%.

China surpassed the US to become the top jurisdiction in terms of number of patents in force

Patent rights generally last for up to 20 years from the date an application is filed. An estimated 16.5 million patents were in force across 133 jurisdictions in 2021. This represents a 4.2% increase on 2020. In 2021, the highest number of patents in force was in China (3.6 million), followed by the US (3.33 million), Japan (2.02 million), the Republic of Korea (1.15 million) and Germany (877,763) (figure 1.8). Among the top five jurisdictions, China saw the fastest growth in patents in force in 2021 (+17.6%), resulting in it becoming the top jurisdiction for number of patents in force. Germany (+5.2%) and the Republic of Korea (+5.2%) also saw strong growth, whereas both Japan (-0.9%) and the US (-0.6%) reported a small decrease in 2021. Beyond the top five offices, India (+19.4%), Switzerland (+5.9%) and Canada (+5.7%) also recorded notable growth in 2021.

Patents in force in China grew by 17.6% in 2021

1.8. Patents in force at the top 10 offices, 2021

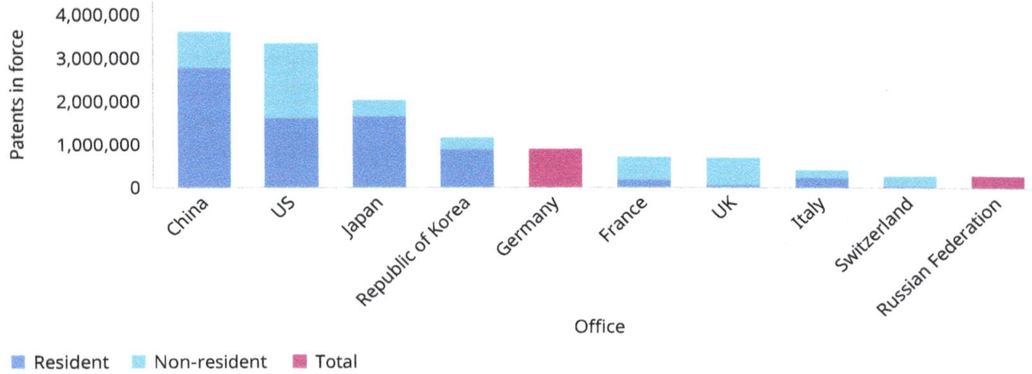

Source: Figure A38.

The source of the patents in force within the top five jurisdictions differs considerably (figure A38). More than half of all patents in force in the US (51.9%) originated from non-resident applicants, whereas non-resident applicants accounted for a smaller proportion of patents in force in China (23.1%), Japan (18.7%) and the Republic of Korea (23.5%). This is somewhat to be expected as resident patent grants have a high share of total grants at the latter three offices (figure A13). A resident versus non-resident breakdown is unavailable for Germany. Among the top 20 offices, non-resident patent holders accounted for a high share of all patents in force at the offices of Luxembourg (99.2%), Mexico (95.8%) and Australia (93.2%).

A holder must pay a maintenance/renewal fee in order for a patent to remain valid, and may opt to let a patent lapse before the end of its full term. For the 92 offices that reported in-force data broken down by year of filing, around 40.3% of patents granted remained in force for at least 8 years after the filing date, and about 18.1% lasted the full 20-year term (figure A39).

Although patents can be maintained for 20 years, the average age of patents varies across offices. Among the selected 20 offices reported in figure A40, the average age of all patents in force in 2020 ranged from 11.9 years in Brazil to 6.4 years in Morocco. Patents in force in Chile (11.2 years), India (11.5 years) and Spain (11.1 years) were of a similarly high average age to those in Brazil.

Germany, Türkiye and the US granted patents for under half of all applications processed in 2021

A patent office examines applications and decides whether to grant patent rights. Examination processes differ across offices, which makes cross-country comparisons difficult. Every effort has, however, been made to compile examination outcome data based on common definitions and concepts. In 2021, around 80 IP offices shared data on patent examination outcomes – granted, rejected or withdrawn – with WIPO.

Among 10 selected offices, Germany, Türkiye and the US granted patents for under half of all applications processed in 2021 (figure 1.9).[2] Rejected applications as a share of the total were highest in China (34.4%), Japan (24.2%), the Republic of Korea (24.9%) and the US (45.2%). In terms of absolute numbers, China rejected more than 443,000 applications, while the US rejected around 351,000 applications. The proportion of withdrawn or abandoned applications was greatest in Canada (35.8%), Germany (35.2%) and Türkiye (53.7%). In terms of absolute numbers, the IP office of Germany reported in excess of 17,000 applications as either withdrawn or abandoned. For Canada and Türkiye this was around 12,600 and 5,500 applications, respectively.

China rejected more than 443,000 patent applications in 2021

1.9. Distribution of patent examination outcomes for selected offices, 2021

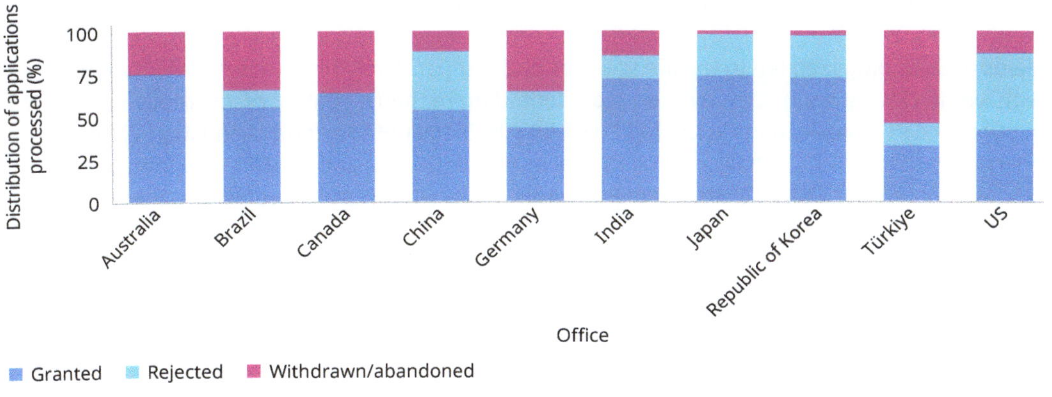

Source: Figure A41.

China recorded the highest stock of applications pending in 2021

Patent offices must assess whether the claims made in applications meet the standards of novelty, non-obviousness and industrial applicability defined in national laws. Processing patents

2 Patents granted out of total processed applications data presented here should not be interpreted as the "grant rate."

therefore consumes time and resources. The estimated total number of potential applications pending worldwide increased to 5.6 million in 2021, which is slightly higher than the 2020 total (5.2 million). This estimate is based on data from 110 offices. The rise in the stock of pending applications worldwide is due to a substantial increase at the offices of China, India and the US.

China had 1.3 million applications pending in 2021 – up from 1 million in 2020 (figure A42). The IP office of the US (1.1 million) is the only other office with more than 1 million applications pending. These two offices were followed by Japan (851,985), the EPO (576,351) and Germany (376,925).

Among the top 20 offices, Australia (+17.6%), China (+29.3%) and India (+91.5%) saw double-digit growth in the stock of applications pending between 2020 and 2021. While Brazil (-53.9%), France (-12%), Malaysia (-17%) and New Zealand (-23.3%) all managed to reduce considerably the stock of applications pending over the same period.

Australia (66.5%), Israel (68.5%), Japan (65.3%) and the Republic of Korea (77.4%) had a high share of their total stock of applications pending awaiting a request for examination. For such offices, scope to reduce the stock of applications pending is somewhat limited, as the office is unable to start the substantial examination process until an applicant files a request for examination.

Applications pending
Applications pending is defined as all patent applications, at any stage in the process, awaiting a final decision by a patent office, including those applications for which applicants have not filed a request for examination (where applicable).

Women inventors accounted for only 16.5% of all inventors listed in PCT applications in 2021

In 2021, women accounted for 16.5% of all inventors listed in PCT applications and men the remaining 83.5% (figure A31). The proportion of women inventors has increased from 10.6% in 2007 to 16.5% in 2021. Moreover, the proportion of women inventors has grown in every region of the world over the past decade. About 33.3% of PCT applications named at least one woman as inventor in 2021, and 95.9% named at least one man as inventor (figure A32). The share of PCT applications with at least one woman as inventor has risen from 20.5% in 2007 to 33.3% in 2021, whereas the share for those with at least one man as inventor has decreased within the same period, from 97.7% down to 95.9%.

The gender gap among PCT inventors varies considerably across countries. Within the top 20 origins, Spain (25.7%), Türkiye (24.2%) and China (23.7%) had the largest proportion of inventors who were women in 2021 (figure A33). Conversely, India (10.2%), Japan (9.8%) and Austria (8.6%) had the smallest. The share of PCT applications with at least one woman as inventor ranged from 47.1% in China to 15.9% in Austria.

Fields of technology related to the life sciences had comparatively high shares of PCT applications with women inventors in 2021. Women represented more than a quarter of inventors listed in published PCT applications in the fields of biotechnology (29.6%), food chemistry (29.1%), pharmaceuticals (28.7%), analysis of biological materials (25.6%) and organic fine chemistry (25.3%) (figure A34). The 2021 shares of PCT applications with women inventors in these five fields is similar to their 2020 share.

Utility model applications worldwide declined by 2.5% in 2021 – the first decline since 2014

A utility model (UM) is a special form of patent right granted by a state or jurisdiction to an inventor or the inventor's assignee for a fixed time period. The terms and conditions for granting a UM differ slightly from those for normal patents, including a shorter term of protection and less stringent eligibility requirements.

In 2021, the total number of UM applications worldwide declined by 2.5% in 2021 – the first decline since 2014. The 2.92 million applications in 2021 consisted of 2.90 million resident applications and only 21,830 non-resident applications (figure A48). The IP office of China received 97.5% of the world total – the other 81 offices together accounted for just 2.5%.

The IP office of China received 2.85 million applications in 2021, followed by Germany (10,576), the Russian Federation (9,079), Australia (7,844) and Japan (5,238) (figure A49). Among the top 10 offices, the office of Australia received 77.8% more applications in 2021, following on from 137.3% growth in 2020. The steep increase in applications recorded for two consecutive years could be explained by the fact that the Australian Government has begun phasing out innovation (i.e., UM) patents, prompting applicants to submit applications before the new legislation comes into force.[3] The offices of Indonesia (+40.6%) and Türkiye (+23.8%) are the two other offices among the top 10 to record double-digit growth in 2021.

In the long term, demand for UM patents appears to be uneven at the top 10 offices. Germany, Japan, the Republic of Korea, the Russian Federation and Ukraine experienced a decline in UM filings between 2011 and 2021. For example, applications at the office of Germany decreased from 16,024 in 2011 to 10,576 in 2021, while applications filed at the Russian Federation declined from 13,241 to 9,079 over the same period. In contrast, China has seen an enormous growth in UM patent filings over the same period – applications increasing from 585,467 in 2011 to 2.85 million by 2021. Australia, Indonesia, Thailand and Türkiye have also seen an upward trend in UM filings over the same period.

3 The last day for filing a new innovation patent in Australia was August 25, 2021. However, existing innovation patents filed on or before August 25, 2021 will continue in force until their expiry.

Patent statistics

Patent applications and grants worldwide

A1. Trend in patent applications worldwide, 2007–2021

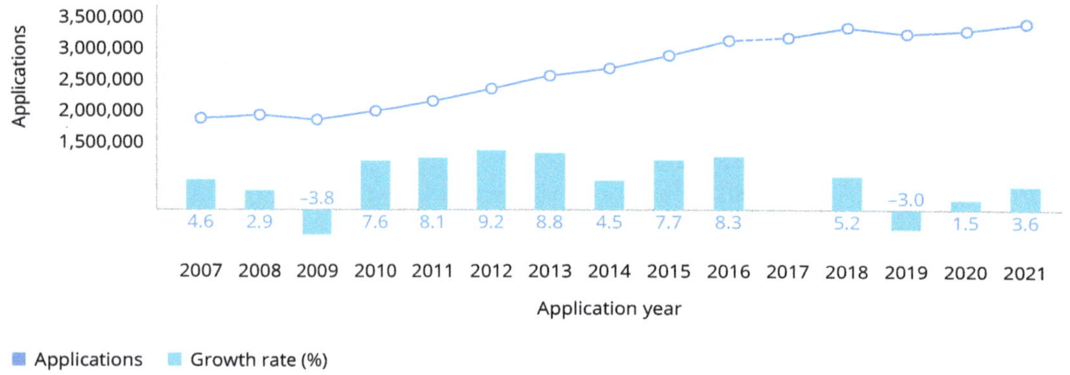

Note: World totals are WIPO estimates using data covering 160 patent offices. These totals include applications filed directly with national and regional offices and applications entering offices through the Patent Cooperation Treaty national phase (where applicable). China's pre-2017 data are not comparable due to a change in methodology. Due to this break in the data series, and to the large number of filings in China, it is not possible to report an accurate 2017 growth rate at world level (see the data description section in Additional information for details).

Source: WIPO Statistics Database, September 2022.

A2. Resident and non-resident patent applications worldwide, 2007–2021

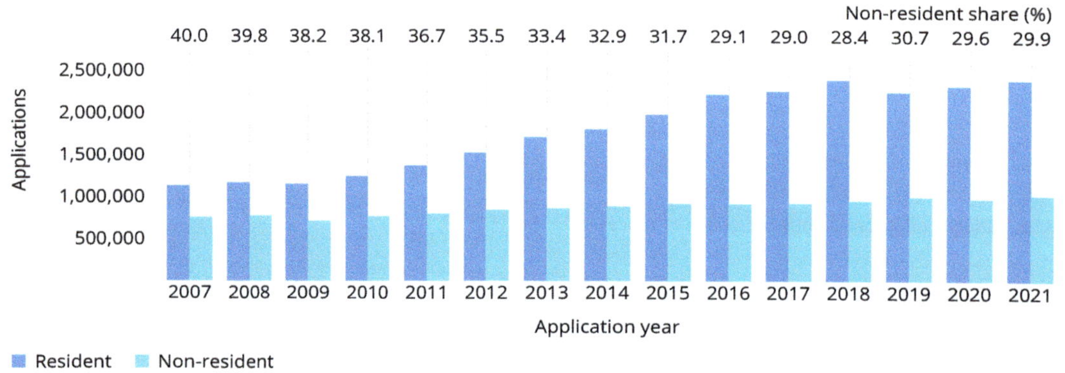

Note: World totals are WIPO estimates using data covering 160 patent offices. These totals include applications filed directly with national and regional offices and applications entering offices through the Patent Cooperation Treaty national phase (where applicable). See the glossary for definitions of resident and non-resident.

Source: WIPO Statistics Database, September 2022.

A3. Trend in patent grants worldwide, 2007–2021

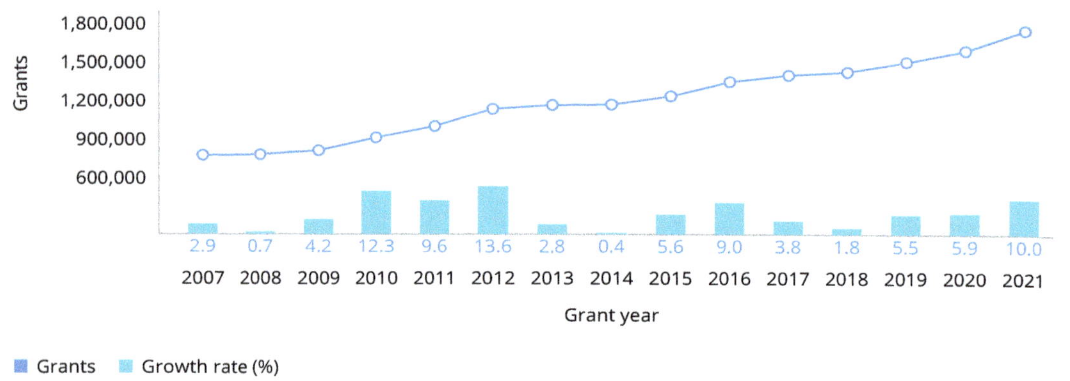

Note: World totals are WIPO estimates using data covering 153 patent offices. These totals include patent grants based on applications filed directly with national and regional offices and patents granted by offices on the basis of the Patent Cooperation Treaty national phase (where applicable).

Source: WIPO Statistics Database, September 2022.

A4. Resident and non-resident patent grants worldwide, 2007–2021

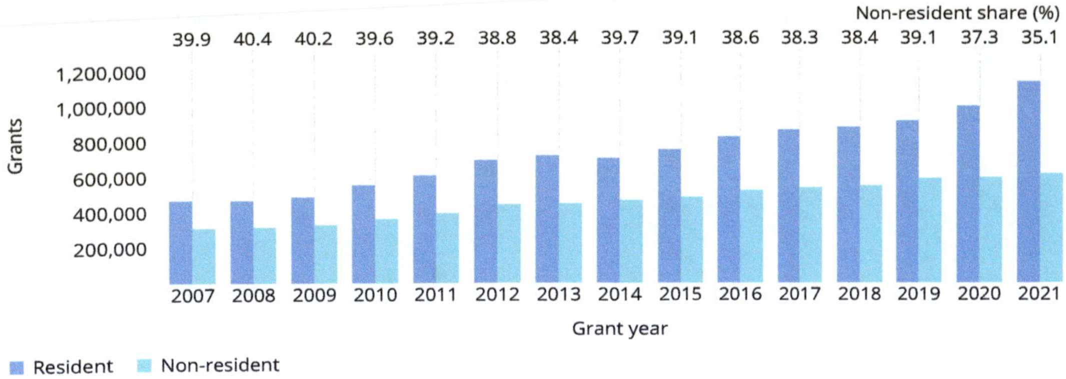

Note: World totals are WIPO estimates using data covering 153 patent offices. These totals include patent grants based on applications filed directly with national and regional offices and patents granted by offices on the basis of the Patent Cooperation Treaty national phase (where applicable). See the glossary for definitions of resident and non-resident.

Source: WIPO Statistics Database, September 2022.

Patent applications and grants by office

A5. Patent applications by region, 2011 and 2021

	Number of applications		Resident share (%)		Share of world total (%)		Average growth (%)
Region	**2011**	**2021**	**2011**	**2021**	**2011**	**2021**	**2011–2021**
Africa	14,700	20,900	15.0	22.0	0.7	0.6	3.6
Asia	1,178,800	2,299,600	74.9	82.7	54.6	67.6	6.9
Europe	334,100	357,900	64.8	56.2	15.5	10.5	0.7
Latin America and the Caribbean	60,100	54,800	12.1	13.7	2.8	1.6	-0.9
North America	538,700	628,600	46.9	42.5	25.0	18.5	1.6
Oceania	31,800	39,300	12.3	8.4	1.5	1.2	2.1
World	**2,158,200**	**3,401,100**	**63.3**	**70.1**	**100.0**	**100.0**	**4.7**

Note: Totals by geographical region are WIPO estimates using data covering 160 offices. Each region includes the following number of offices: Africa (31), Asia (45), Europe (45), Latin America and the Caribbean (32), North America (2) and Oceania (5).

Source: WIPO Statistics Database, September 2022.

A6. Trend in patent applications for the top five offices, 1883–2021

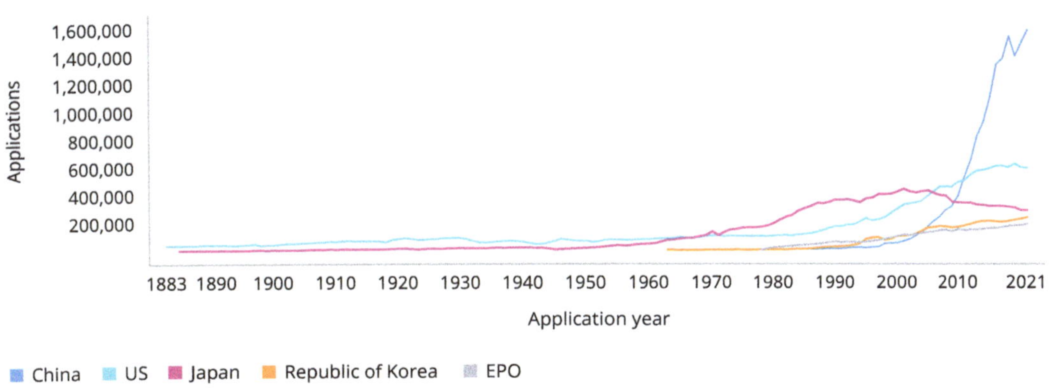

Note: EPO is the European Patent Office. The top five offices were selected based on their 2021 totals.

Source: WIPO Statistics Database, September 2022.

A7. Patent applications at the top 20 offices, 2021

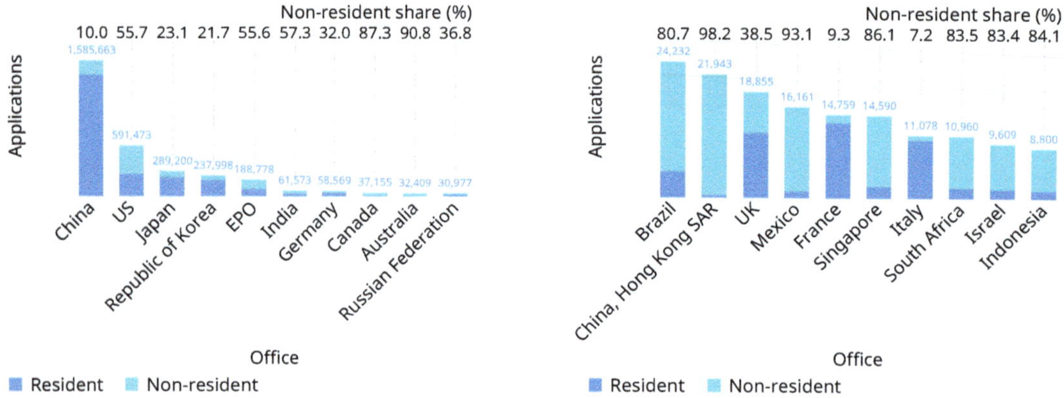

Note: EPO is the European Patent Office. In general, national offices of the EPO member states receive lower volumes of applications, because applicants may apply via the EPO to seek protection within any EPO member state.

Source: WIPO Statistics Database, September 2022.

A8. Contribution of resident and non-resident applications to total growth for the top 20 offices, 2020–2021

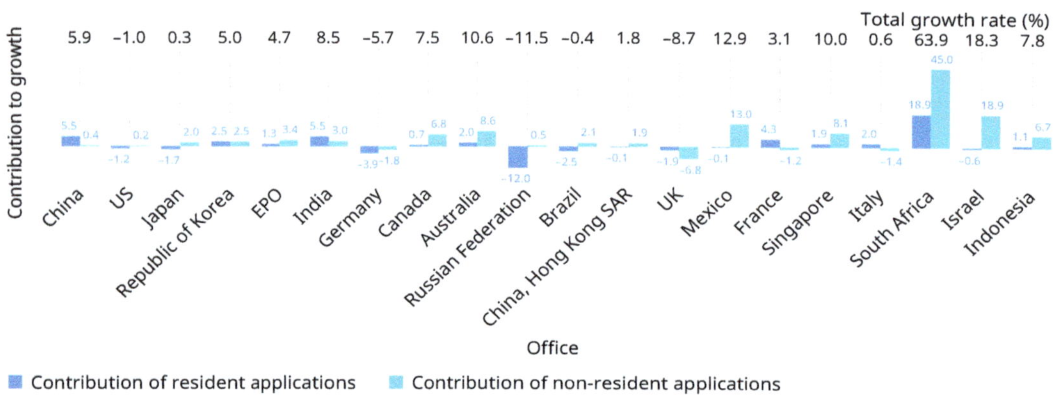

Note: EPO is the European Patent Office. This figure shows the total growth or decrease in applications at each office, broken down by the respective contributions of resident and non-resident applications. For example, applications filed at the IP office of China grew by 5.9%. Growth in resident applications accounted for 5.5 percentage points of this increase, while non-resident applications increased by 0.4 percentage points.

Source: WIPO Statistics Database, September 2022.

A9. Patent applications at offices of selected low- and middle-income countries, 2021

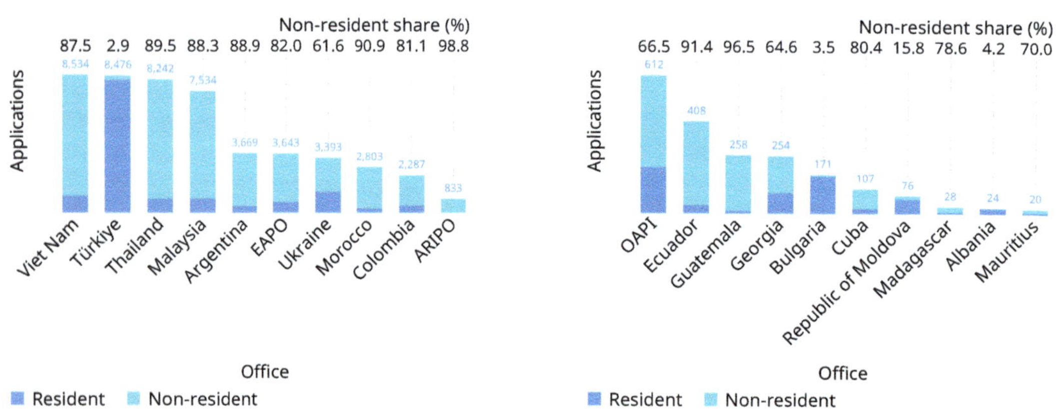

Note: ARIPO is the African Regional Intellectual Property Organization, EAPO is the Eurasian Patent Organization and OAPI is the African Intellectual Property Organization. The selected offices are from different world regions. Where available, data for all offices are presented in table A53.

Source: WIPO Statistics Database, September 2022.

A10. Contribution of resident and non-resident applications to total growth for offices of selected low- and middle-income countries, 2020–2021

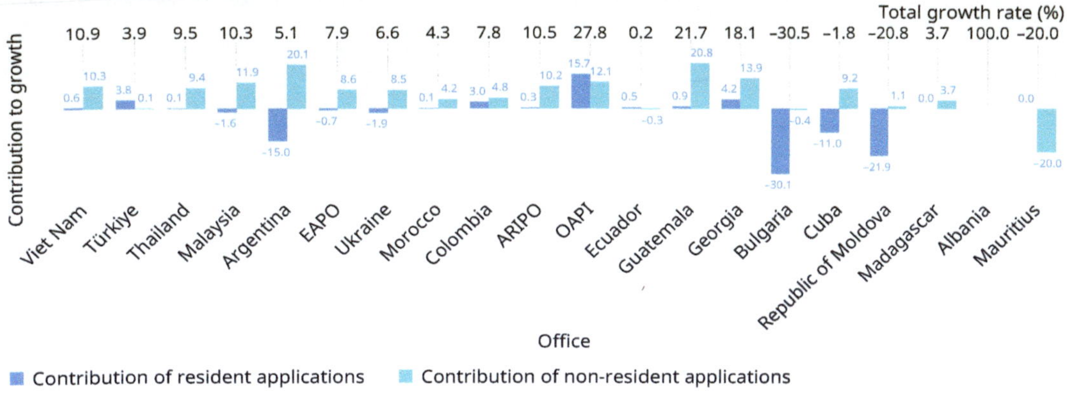

Note: ARIPO is the African Regional Intellectual Property Organization, EAPO is the Eurasian Patent Organization and OAPI is the African Intellectual Property Organization. The selected offices are from different world regions. This figure shows the total growth or decrease in applications at each office, broken down by the respective contributions of resident and non-resident applications. For example, applications filed at the IP office of Viet Nam grew by 10.9%. Growth in non-resident applications accounted for 10.3 percentage points of this increase, while resident applications increased by 0.6 percentage points. A resident versus non-resident breakdown is unavailable for Albania.

Source: WIPO Statistics Database, September 2022.

A11. Patent grants by region, 2011 and 2021

	Number of grants		Resident share (%)		Share of world total (%)		Average growth (%)
Region	2011	2021	2011	2021	2011	2021	2011-2021
Africa	10,500	10,800	11.9	12.8	1.0	0.6	0.3
Asia	550,900	1,122,400	72.4	76.6	55.0	63.9	7.4
Europe	153,100	208,100	61.9	54.9	15.3	11.8	3.1
Latin America and the Caribbean	19,300	45,900	5.8	10.3	1.9	2.6	9.0
North America	245,300	350,000	45.2	45.0	24.5	19.9	3.6
Oceania	22,600	19,300	7.0	5.9	2.3	1.1	-1.6
World	1,001,700	1,756,500	60.7	64.9	100.0	100.0	5.8

Note: Totals by geographical region are WIPO estimates using data covering 153 offices. Each region includes the following number of offices: Africa (30), Asia (43), Europe (45), Latin America and the Caribbean (28), North America (2) and Oceania (5).

Source: WIPO Statistics Database, September 2022.

A12. Trend in patent grants for the top five offices, 1883–2021

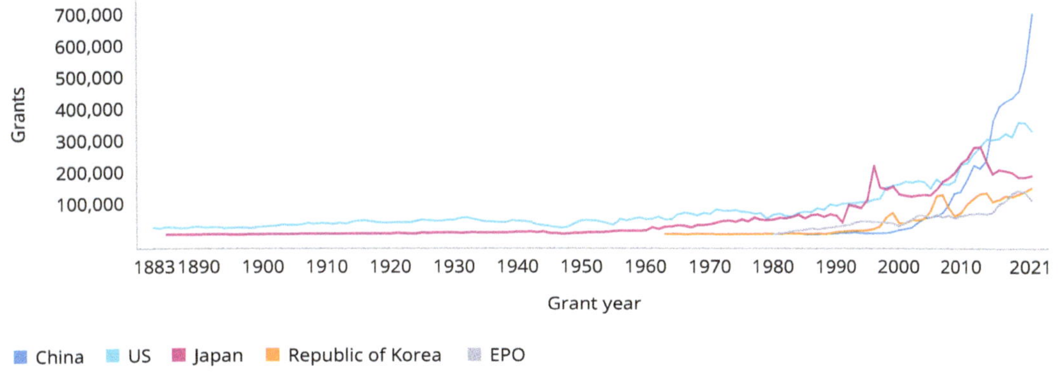

Note: EPO is the European Patent Office. The top five offices were selected based on their 2021 totals.

Source: WIPO Statistics Database, September 2022.

A13. Patent grants for the top 20 offices, 2021

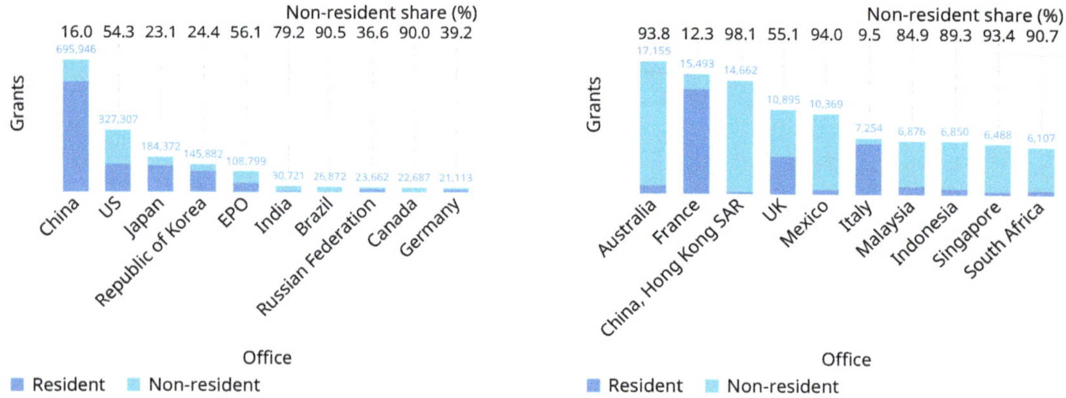

Note: EPO is the European Patent Office. The procedure for issuing patents varies between offices, and differences in the numbers of patents granted among offices depend on factors such as examination capacity and procedural delays. The examination process can take a long time therefore there is invariably a time lag between application and grant dates. For this reason, data on applications for a given year should not be compared with data on grants for the same year.

Source: WIPO Statistics Database, September 2022.

A14. Contribution of resident and non-resident grants to total growth for the top 20 offices, 2020–2021

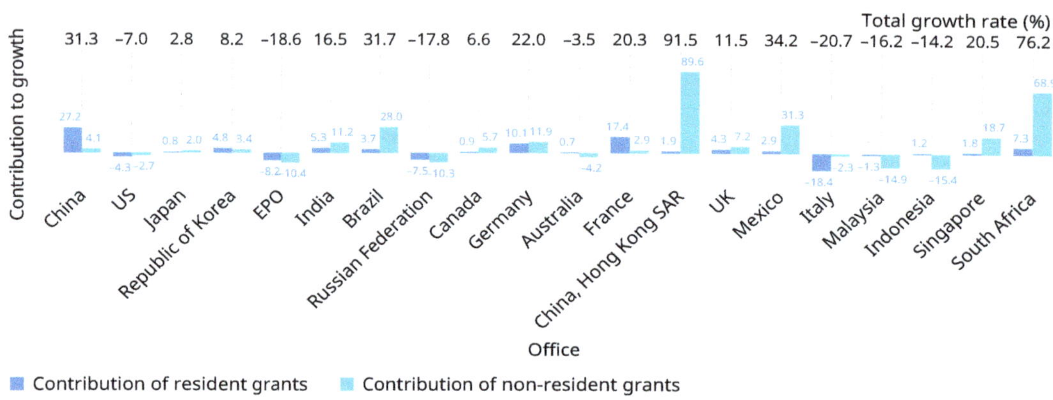

Note: EPO is the European Patent Office. This figure shows the total growth or decrease in grants at each office, broken down by the respective contributions of resident and non-resident grants. For example, the total number of patents granted by the IP office of China grew by 31.3%. Growth in resident grants accounted for 27.2 percentage points of this increase, while the remaining 4.1 percentage points came from growth in non-resident grants.

Source: WIPO Statistics Database, September 2022.

A15. Patent grants for offices of selected low- and middle-income countries, 2021

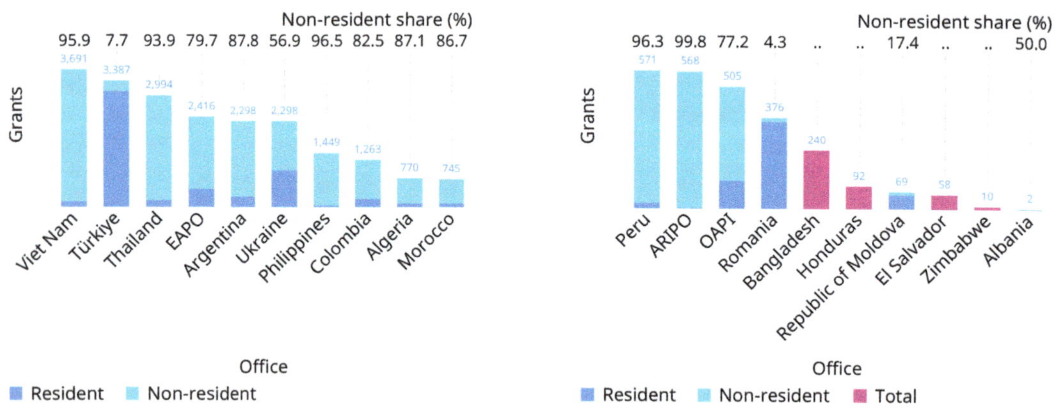

Note: ARIPO is the African Regional Intellectual Property Organization, EAPO is the Eurasian Patent Organization and OAPI is the African Intellectual Property Organization. The selected offices are from different world regions. Where available, data for all offices are presented in table A54.

.. indicates not available.

Source: WIPO Statistics Database, September 2022.

A16. Contribution of resident and non-resident grants to total growth for offices of selected low- and middle-income countries, 2020–2021

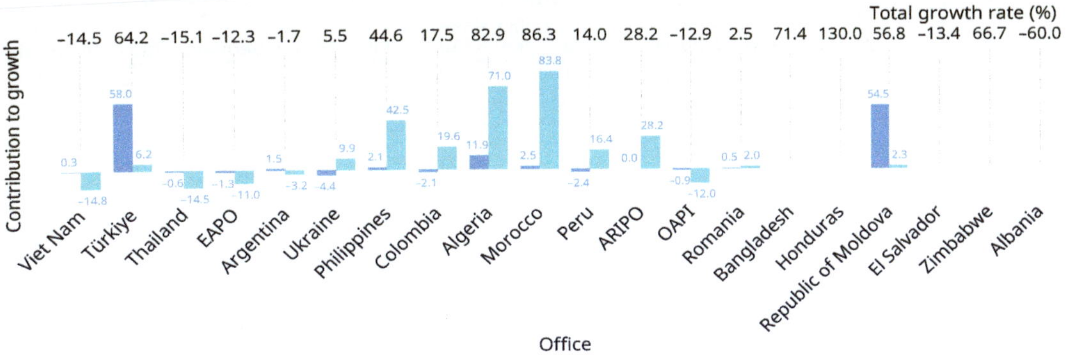

■ Contribution of resident grants ■ Contribution of non-resident grants

Note: ARIPO is the African Regional Intellectual Property Organization, EAPO is the Eurasian Patent Organization and OAPI is the African Intellectual Property Organization. This figure shows the total growth or decrease in grants at each office, broken down by the respective contributions of resident and non-resident grants. For example, the total number of patent granted by the IP office of Türkiye grew by 64.2%. Growth in resident grants accounted for 58.0 percentage point of this increase, while the remaining 6.2 percentage points came from growth in non-resident grants. A resident versus non-resident breakdown is unavailable for Albania, Bangladesh, El Salvador, Honduras and Zimbabwe.

Source: WIPO Statistics Database, September 2022.

Patent applications and grants by origin

A17. Equivalent patent applications for the top 20 origins, 2021

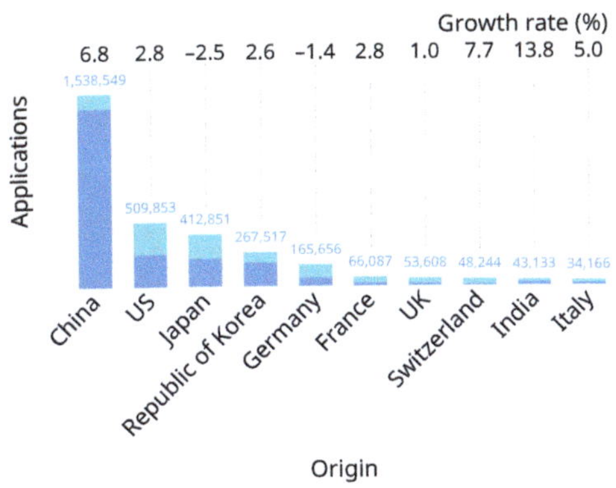

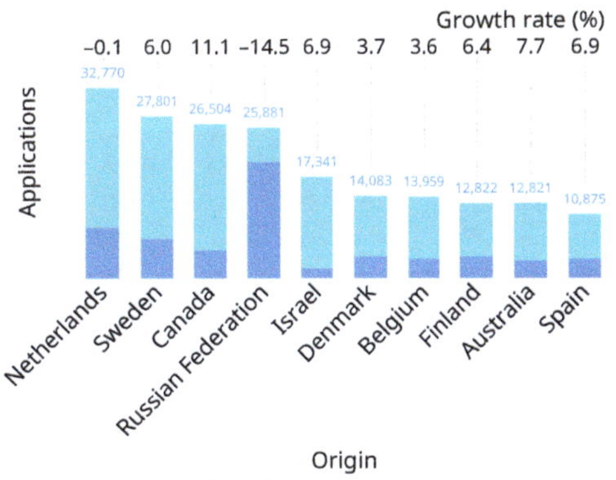

■ Resident ■ Abroad ■ Resident ■ Abroad

Note: Patent filing activity by origin includes resident applications and applications filed abroad. The origin of a patent application is determined by the residence of the first named applicant. Applications filed at regional offices are considered equivalent to multiple applications in the relevant member states. See the glossary for the definition of equivalent application.

Source: WIPO Statistics Database, September 2022.

A18. Patent applications for the top 20 offices and origins, 2021

	Office									
Origin	Australia	Brazil	Canada	China	China, Hong Kong SAR	EPO	France	Germany	India	Indonesia
Australia	2,966	198	516	740	187	1,026	6	6	313	68
Belgium	306	258	341	798	138	2,486	52	104	258	62
Canada	703	300	4,710	1,230	294	2,091	12	96	447	56
China	2,319	1,298	1,825	1,426,644	6,971	16,550	124	568	3,989	1,216
Denmark	326	271	324	1,154	126	2,620	2	28	367	72
Finland	178	209	318	1,073	168	2,108	12	46	475	111
France	756	1,064	1,510	4,964	375	10,650	13,386	397	1,093	176
Germany	1,352	1,757	1,949	16,481	763	25,935	338	39,822	2,705	329
India	205	188	164	337	44	815	4	29	26,267	210
Israel	390	246	408	1,204	194	1,724	8	55	357	19
Italy	398	552	584	1,938	203	4,924	90	85	565	64
Japan	1,528	1,257	1,392	47,010	1,195	21,591	94	6,128	4,617	2,101
Netherlands	505	565	560	3,133	156	6,568	15	146	1,007	263
Republic of Korea	763	542	430	17,691	376	9,386	20	1,558	2,639	376
Russian Federation	30	45	63	168	20	274	3	19	83	27
Sweden	496	456	499	2,489	237	4,950	54	320	803	81
Switzerland	1,183	1,278	1,205	4,365	908	8,444	90	866	1,254	290
Türkiye	10	17	17	112	8	737	7	27	31	1
UK	1,334	746	1,334	2,867	657	5,623	21	169	1,053	203
US	14,375	6,898	16,871	42,266	6,861	46,691	136	5,892	11,410	1,156
Others	2,286	6,087	2,135	8,999	2,062	13,585	285	2,208	1,840	1,919
Total	**32,409**	**24,232**	**37,155**	**1,585,663**	**21,943**	**188,778**	**14,759**	**58,569**	**61,573**	**8,800**

	Office									
Origin	Israel	Italy	Japan	Mexico	Republic of Korea	Russian Federation	Singapore	South Africa	UK	US
Australia	85	2	504	124	227	67	202	168	112	3,468
Belgium	111	18	517	166	294	105	90	128	86	2,476
Canada	198	5	825	324	528	89	171	153	155	12,580
China	224	85	9,369	740	6,300	1,242	1,578	2,987	604	45,842
Denmark	81		539	157	248	145	98	87	42	2,378
Finland	13		418	84	241	158	85	86	81	2,337
France	337	41	2,508	530	1,628	757	338	260	66	11,088
Germany	421	167	5,965	1,010	3,745	1,177	576	466	467	27,964
India	53	3	233	114	110	67	98	161	52	11,894
Israel	1,592	5	921	169	420	122	106	71	97	8,723
Italy	145	10,281	839	237	488	388	90	99	51	5,038
Japan	285	48	222,452	844	14,165	1,063	1,748	170	414	75,364
Netherlands	217	5	1,847	353	1,047	452	147	150	185	4,426
Republic of Korea	78		5,936	294	186,245	473	538	94	185	36,909
Russian Federation	36		82	25	65	19,569	28	34	15	1,123
Sweden	104	52	1,206	321	794	297	119	219	125	5,365
Switzerland	462	102	3,022	695	1,423	779	447	328	357	5,421
Türkiye	10	1	93	8	47	30	2	3	26	493
UK	457	28	2,179	431	1,322	460	383	532	11,592	12,745
US	4,274	64	24,999	7,473	15,508	2,585	4,780	2,367	2,586	262,244
Others	426	171	4,746	2,062	3,153	952	2,966	2,397	1,557	53,595
Total	**9,609**	**11,078**	**289,200**	**16,161**	**237,998**	**30,977**	**14,590**	**10,960**	**18,855**	**591,473**

Note: EPO is the European Patent Office. Origin data are based on absolute counts, not equivalent counts. The top 20 offices and origins are selected based on available 2021 data, broken down by country of origin.

Source: WIPO Statistics Database, September 2022.

A19. Flows of non-resident patent applications between the top five origins and the top 10 offices, 2021

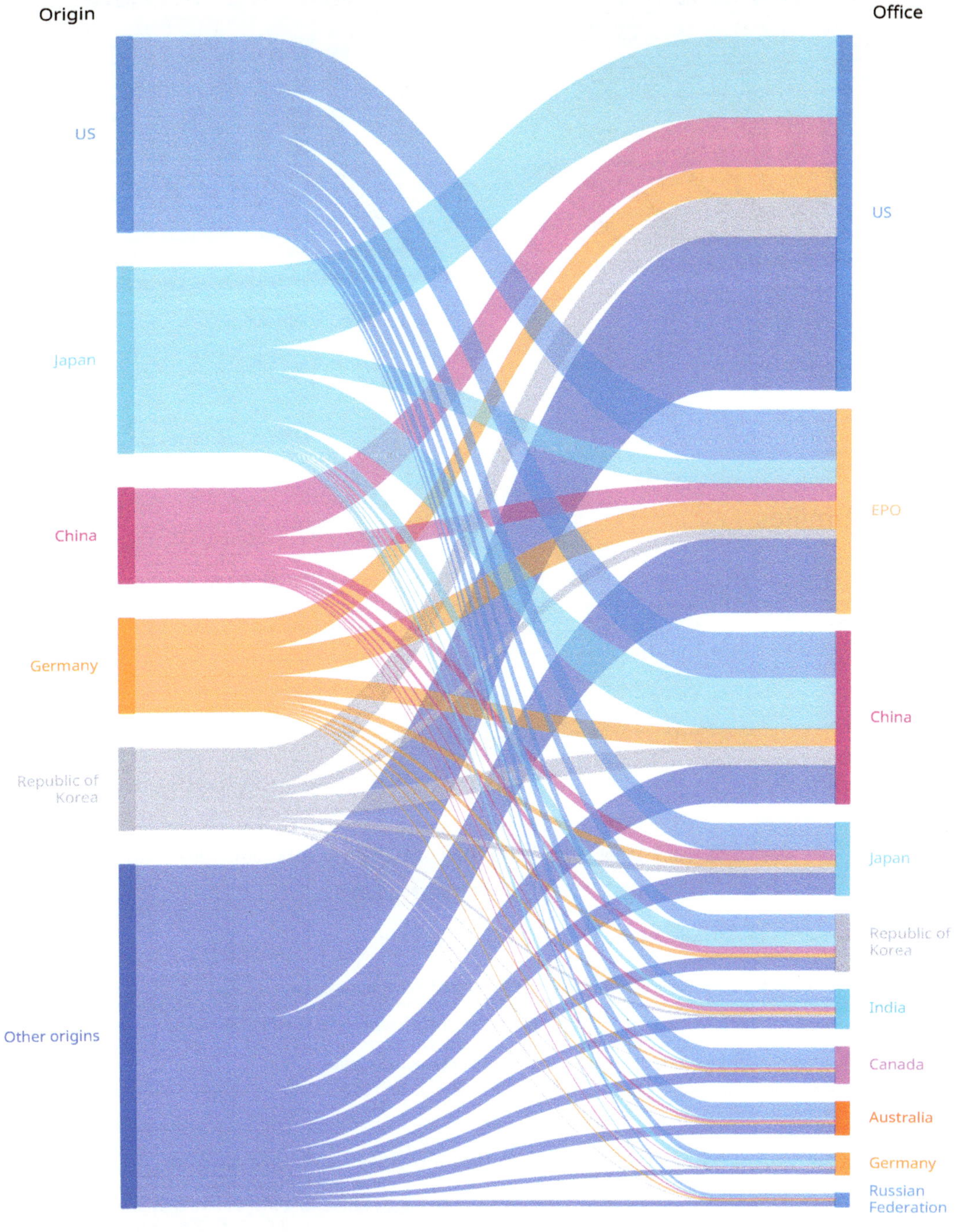

Note: EPO is the European Patent Office. Origin data are based on absolute rather than equivalent counts.
Source: WIPO Statistics Database, September 2022.

A20. Equivalent patent grants for the top 20 origins, 2021

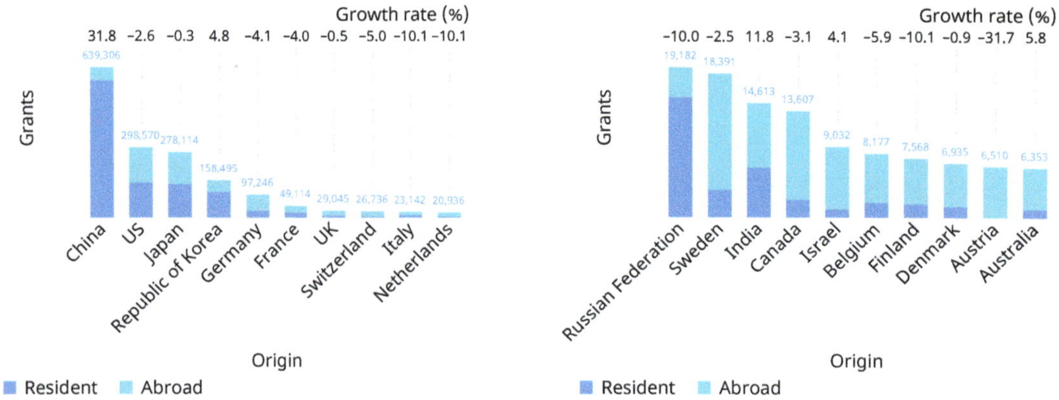

Note: See the glossary for the definition of equivalent grant.

Source: WIPO Statistics Database, September 2022.

Patent families

A21. Trend in patent families worldwide, 2005–2019

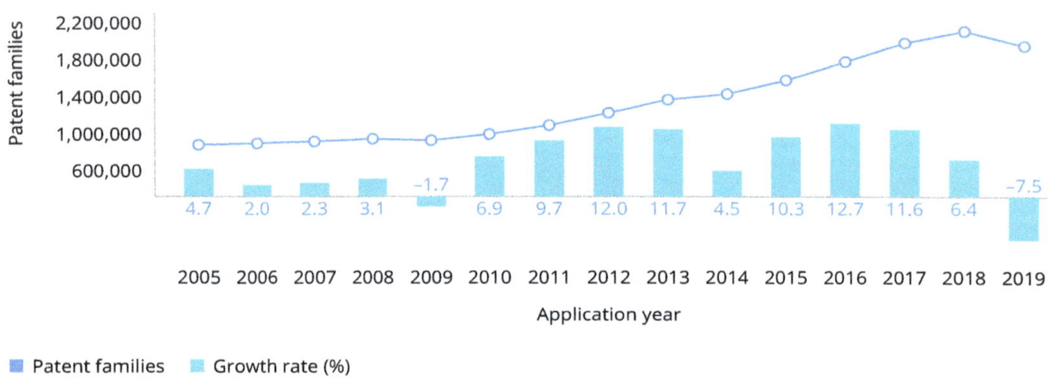

Note: Applicants often file patent applications in multiple jurisdictions therefore some inventions are recorded more than once. To take this into account, WIPO has indicators related to patent families, defined as patent applications interlinked by one or more of the following: priority claim, Patent Cooperation Treaty national phase entry, continuation, continuation-in-part, internal priority, and addition or division. Patent families here include only those families associated with patent applications for inventions and exclude those associated with utility model applications.

Sources: WIPO Statistics Database and EPO PATSTAT database, September 2022.

A22. Distribution of patent families by number of offices for the top origins, 2017–2019

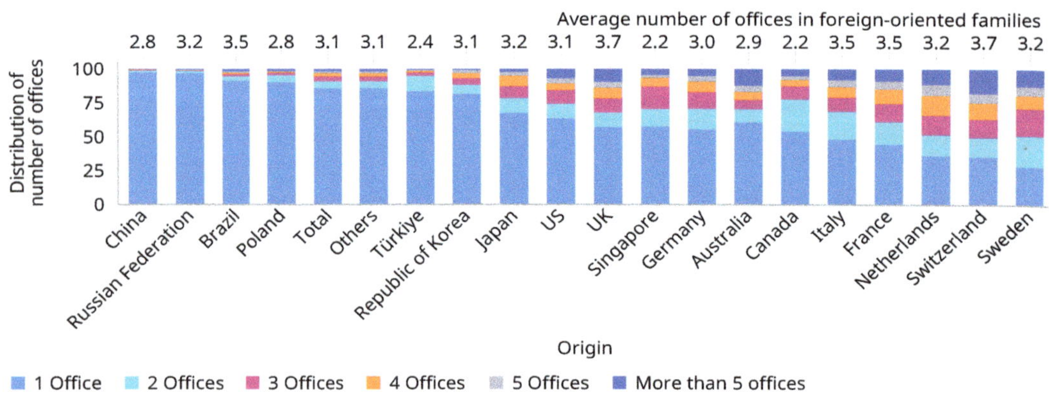

Note: A patent family is defined as patent applications interlinked by one or more of the following: priority claim, Patent Cooperation Treaty national phase entry, continuation, continuation-in-part, internal priority, and addition or division. Patent families here include only those families associated with patent applications for inventions and exclude those associated with utility model applications.

Sources: WIPO Statistics Database and EPO PATSTAT database, September 2022.

A23. Trend in foreign-oriented patent families worldwide, 2005–2018

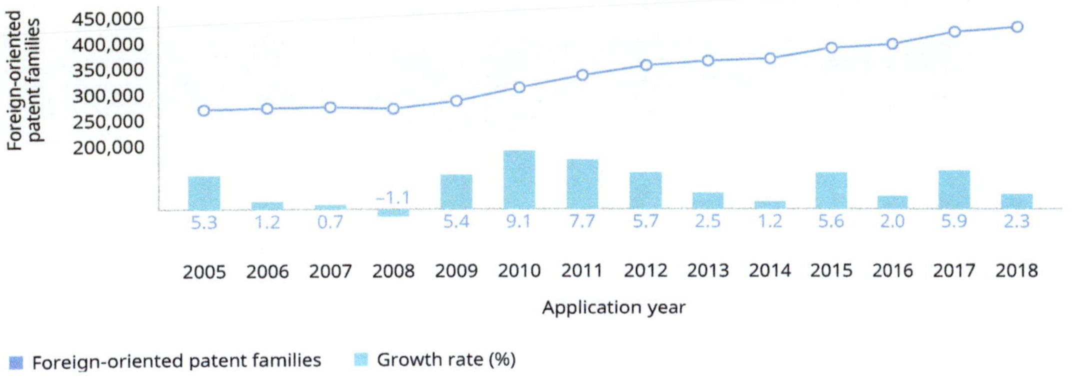

Note: A special subset of patent families comprises foreign-oriented patent families. This includes only patent families that have at least one filing office different from the office of the applicant's country of origin. Some foreign-oriented patent families include only one filing office, because applicants may choose to file directly with a foreign office. For example, if a Canadian applicant files a patent application directly with the United States Patent and Trademark Office (USPTO) without having previously filed with the patent office of Canada, that application and any applications filed subsequently with the USPTO will form a foreign-oriented patent family.

Sources: WIPO Statistics Database and EPO PATSTAT database, September 2022.

A24. Foreign-oriented patent families for the top 20 origins, 2017–2018

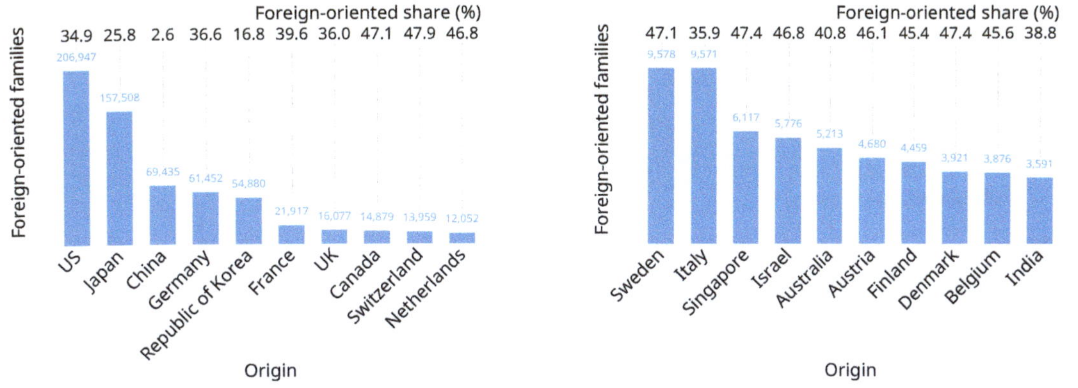

Note: A special subset of patent families comprises foreign-oriented patent families. This includes only patent families that have at least one filing office different from the office of the applicant's country of origin. Some foreign-oriented patent families include only one filing office, because applicants may choose to file directly with a foreign office. For example, if a Canadian applicant files a patent application directly with the United States Patent and Trademark Office (USPTO) without having previously filed with the patent office of Canada, that application and any applications filed subsequently with the USPTO will form a foreign-oriented patent family.

Sources: WIPO Statistics Database and EPO PATSTAT database, September 2022.

A25. Distribution of technology fields for selected applicants based on patent families, 2017–2019

Field of technology	Applicant									
	Canon Inc	Huawei Technologies	Toyota Motor Corp	IBM	Samsung Electronics	LG Electronics Inc	Mitsubishi Electric Corp	China Petroleum & Chemicals	Robert Bosch GmbH	Gree Electric
Electrical machinery, apparatus, energy	3.1	2.8	23.3	1.4	4.5	6.3	20.6	0.9	14.9	8.5
Audio-visual technology	16.4	7.0	1.2	3.1	9.1	7.6	4.3	0.1	1.9	2.0
Telecommunications	6.5	11.0	0.4	2.6	8.1	7.3	3.8	0.1	0.9	2.1
Digital communication	3.3	50.7	1.1	15.4	17.7	32.4	3.5	0.2	2.6	3.3
Basic communication processes	0.2	1.8	0.1	1.0	1.7	0.4	1.5	0.0	0.6	0.4
Computer technology	14.3	18.1	3.2	48.4	22.7	5.0	7.2	3.2	6.2	9.1
IT methods for management	0.5	0.7	2.1	5.3	1.0	0.6	1.7	1.8	0.5	1.4
Semiconductors	2.5	1.1	2.5	9.8	16.0	2.4	6.4	0.0	1.2	0.8
Optics	29.3	1.9	0.3	0.9	3.2	1.1	2.6	0.0	1.8	0.1
Measurement	2.1	1.8	4.2	2.5	3.2	1.5	6.6	11.7	12.6	2.6
Analysis of biological materials	0.1	0.0	0.0	0.2	0.1	0.0	0.0	0.7	0.4	0.1
Control	0.8	1.0	5.9	2.4	1.0	1.8	5.2	0.9	5.0	4.3
Medical technology	3.1	0.4	0.7	2.4	2.1	1.1	0.4	0.1	0.7	0.5
Organic fine chemistry	0.1	0.0	0.0	0.1	0.4	0.0	0.0	11.8	0.0	0.0
Biotechnology	0.1	0.0	0.1	0.1	0.1	0.0	0.0	0.7	0.2	0.0
Pharmaceuticals	0.0	0.0	0.0	0.1	0.0	0.0	0.0	0.0	0.0	0.0
Macromolecular chemistry, polymers	0.3	0.0	0.1	0.3	0.3	0.0	0.1	9.9	0.1	0.1
Food chemistry	0.0	0.0	0.0	0.0	0.0	0.3	0.0	0.0	0.0	0.1
Basic materials chemistry	0.6	0.0	0.2	0.2	0.7	0.2	0.1	16.9	0.1	0.3
Materials, metallurgy	0.2	0.1	1.6	0.1	0.4	0.3	0.2	4.3	0.9	0.1
Surface technology, coating	0.5	0.1	1.2	0.2	0.5	0.3	0.4	0.6	0.6	0.1
Micro-structural and nano-technology	0.1	0.0	0.0	0.3	0.2	0.0	0.0	0.3	1.2	0.0
Chemical engineering	0.2	0.0	0.7	0.3	0.3	0.9	0.5	14.5	1.0	1.3
Environmental technology	0.4	0.0	2.2	0.1	0.2	0.7	0.7	6.7	2.5	1.9
Handling	3.4	0.1	1.2	0.3	0.6	2.7	4.8	0.7	1.2	1.2
Machine tools	0.2	0.0	2.5	0.2	0.3	0.1	1.5	0.3	4.0	0.6
Engines, pumps, turbines	0.1	0.0	9.6	0.1	0.2	4.0	3.5	0.4	10.7	4.9
Textile and paper machines	9.4	0.0	0.1	0.0	0.0	0.0	0.4	1.1	0.1	0.0
Other special machines	1.3	0.0	1.3	0.3	0.3	0.6	0.6	1.5	1.9	0.4
Thermal processes and apparatus	0.0	0.1	0.5	0.1	1.2	7.5	13.8	0.5	1.3	38.8
Mechanical elements	0.5	0.1	7.9	0.1	0.3	0.9	1.0	1.1	5.6	1.9
Transport	0.1	0.7	24.7	0.6	0.5	2.0	4.4	0.2	18.4	1.6
Furniture, games	0.0	0.1	0.4	0.3	0.8	3.6	2.1	0.0	0.3	7.4
Other consumer goods	0.1	0.1	0.1	0.2	2.0	7.5	1.4	0.1	0.2	3.9
Civil engineering	0.0	0.0	0.5	0.1	0.2	0.6	0.5	8.8	0.5	0.4

Note: WIPO's International Patent Classification (IPC) technology concordance table was used to convert IPC symbols into 35 corresponding fields of technology. For an electronic version of the IPC technology concordance table, visit *www.wipo.int/ipstats*.

Sources: WIPO Statistics Database and EPO PATSTAT database, September 2022.

A26. Distribution of technology fields for selected universities and PROs based on patent families, 2017–2019

Field of technology	Applicant: Zhejiang University	Tianjin University	CEA	IFP Energies Nouvelles	Fraunhofer Ges Forschung	DLR	AIST	Tokyo University	Korea Electronics Telecomm	KAIST	University of California	MIT
Electrical machinery, apparatus, energy	6.9	7.1	13.5	5.1	5.5	6.8	8.9	7.2	2.6	5.8	3.4	5.0
Audio-visual technology	0.9	1.4	1.8	0.1	9.2	0.6	1.1	2.0	11.9	2.6	0.6	0.9
Telecommunications	1.4	1.8	1.8	0.0	7.3	3.2	0.6	0.9	7.3	4.2	1.3	2.4
Digital communication	1.8	1.8	2.3	0.0	10.0	1.9	0.4	1.2	27.6	6.6	1.3	1.6
Basic communication processes	0.4	2.2	2.4	0.1	1.8	2.1	0.3	0.4	1.3	1.9	1.1	0.9
Computer technology	14.3	16.6	8.1	1.4	7.0	3.4	2.9	7.3	22.9	18.9	5.8	7.1
IT methods for management	2.2	2.4	0.3	0.3	0.3	0.6	0.9	1.2	4.1	2.9	0.2	0.4
Semiconductors	1.4	1.4	19.0	0.1	4.8	1.0	9.7	2.7	3.3	6.9	3.8	4.0
Optics	1.8	1.1	4.4	0.0	3.8	1.1	3.0	1.5	3.7	3.6	2.7	2.7
Measurement	14.5	16.7	11.8	5.0	10.5	12.2	14.5	11.2	4.7	6.7	5.9	7.7
Analysis of biological materials	0.9	0.6	0.9	1.8	1.0	0.3	1.8	4.9	0.3	1.8	4.6	4.2
Control	3.7	2.3	1.0	0.6	1.3	4.0	0.7	1.6	3.3	1.4	0.6	1.0
Medical technology	3.7	3.0	2.2	0.6	2.4	1.9	3.7	6.0	2.5	5.6	11.5	6.7
Organic fine chemistry	2.9	2.6	0.7	10.8	0.5	0.0	6.3	2.9	0.0	0.9	5.6	2.6
Biotechnology	5.7	3.0	0.8	2.8	1.8	0.1	6.2	14.0	0.1	4.0	18.9	18.7
Pharmaceuticals	3.5	1.2	0.6	0.0	1.0	0.0	1.4	7.8	0.0	1.6	18.8	9.5
Macromolecular chemistry, polymers	2.1	2.3	0.8	1.2	1.7	0.4	2.7	4.8	0.1	1.3	1.1	1.8
Food chemistry	2.7	0.4	0.1	0.4	0.4	0.0	0.8	0.7	0.0	0.4	0.8	0.3
Basic materials chemistry	1.8	2.4	1.3	18.1	1.5	1.3	3.0	1.5	0.1	1.4	1.2	1.2
Materials, metallurgy	2.8	4.4	3.3	4.3	4.3	2.4	10.2	2.3	0.2	2.6	1.7	2.4
Surface technology, coating	1.1	1.9	3.2	0.6	3.6	2.7	4.0	1.8	0.1	2.1	1.0	2.2
Micro-structural and nano-technology	0.7	1.0	2.6	0.1	1.4	0.1	1.8	1.4	0.1	1.1	0.7	1.3
Chemical engineering	3.3	3.7	2.4	23.0	2.3	0.9	6.1	1.8	0.2	4.4	2.8	3.8
Environmental technology	2.8	3.3	1.7	5.7	0.8	0.7	1.7	0.2	0.0	1.4	0.8	1.7
Handling	1.5	1.2	1.4	0.3	1.1	6.6	0.6	1.5	0.5	1.0	0.4	1.2
Machine tools	0.9	1.8	1.1	0.2	3.7	0.8	1.0	1.7	0.1	0.2	0.2	0.6
Engines, pumps, turbines	1.8	1.8	1.6	8.6	1.0	5.9	0.4	1.2	0.1	1.4	0.2	0.9
Textile and paper machines	0.5	0.3	0.3	0.2	0.9	0.4	0.9	0.4	0.1	0.7	0.3	0.7
Other special machines	3.6	2.0	2.3	0.6	4.3	11.4	2.6	1.9	0.4	1.6	1.3	2.6
Thermal processes and apparatus	1.3	1.7	3.0	1.9	1.2	6.4	0.8	1.0	0.1	0.5	0.3	0.6
Mechanical elements	1.4	0.8	1.1	1.2	0.9	3.9	0.3	0.6	0.0	0.7	0.3	0.9
Transport	2.4	1.4	1.1	1.4	1.5	15.1	0.3	1.3	1.5	1.9	0.4	1.3
Furniture, games	0.4	0.3	0.2	0.1	0.2	0.4	0.1	0.4	0.4	0.5	0.2	0.0
Other consumer goods	0.3	0.3	0.4	0.0	0.5	0.6	0.2	0.2	0.1	0.5	0.2	0.2
Civil engineering	2.4	3.9	0.4	3.3	0.5	0.4	0.3	2.6	0.0	0.9	0.2	0.7

Note: PRO means public research organization. A patent family is defined as patent applications interlinked by one or more of the following: priority claim, Patent Cooperation Treaty national phase entry, continuation, continuation-in-part, internal priority, and addition or division. Patent families include only those families associated with patent applications for inventions and exclude those associated with utility model applications. Deutsches Zentrum für Luft- und Raumfahrt E.V. (DLR); Le Commissariat à l'énergie atomique et aux énergies alternatives (CEA); Korea Advanced Institute of Science and Technology (KAIST); National Institute of Advanced Industrial Science and Technology (AIST); and Massachusetts Institute of Technology (MIT).

Sources: WIPO Statistics Database and EPO PATSTAT database, September 2022.

Published patent applications by field of technology

A27. Published patent applications worldwide by field of technology, 2010, 2015 and 2020

		Number of published applications			Share of total (%)	Average growth (%)
Field of technology		**2010**	**2015**	**2020**	**2020**	**2010–2020**
Electrical engineering	Electrical machinery, apparatus, energy	116,573	181,185	205,816	6.5	5.8
	Audio-visual technology	77,858	78,662	92,903	2.9	1.8
	Telecommunications	56,416	52,637	55,537	1.8	-0.2
	Digital communication	77,892	124,354	162,501	5.1	7.6
	Basic communication processes	16,592	16,578	18,518	0.6	1.1
	Computer technology	128,882	194,563	323,595	10.2	9.6
	IT methods for management	23,203	42,644	78,952	2.5	13.0
	Semiconductors	76,546	84,614	96,823	3.1	2.4
Instruments	Optics	63,953	66,595	73,401	2.3	1.4
	Measurement	77,745	125,143	180,737	5.7	8.8
	Analysis of biological materials	11,598	15,448	19,387	0.6	5.3
	Control	29,136	50,585	76,421	2.4	10.1
	Medical technology	79,154	111,908	159,456	5.0	7.3
Chemistry	Organic fine chemistry	54,937	63,720	61,710	2.0	1.2
	Biotechnology	39,559	55,240	70,099	2.2	5.9
	Pharmaceuticals	71,285	102,590	92,990	2.9	2.7
	Macromolecular chemistry, polymers	28,771	45,864	47,974	1.5	5.2
	Food chemistry	28,243	63,863	44,436	1.4	4.6
	Basic materials chemistry	44,921	82,569	69,304	2.2	4.4
	Materials, metallurgy	38,068	64,570	69,154	2.2	6.2
	Surface technology, coating	33,023	43,393	47,410	1.5	3.7
	Micro-structural and nano-technology	3,553	5,112	5,429	0.2	4.3
	Chemical engineering	37,391	61,215	96,626	3.1	10.0
	Environmental technology	25,950	43,171	62,258	2.0	9.1
Mechanical engineering	Handling	43,106	69,045	99,511	3.1	8.7
	Machine tools	43,597	77,605	104,275	3.3	9.1
	Engines, pumps, turbines	48,868	65,946	58,732	1.9	1.9
	Textile and paper machines	31,114	39,146	44,581	1.4	3.7
	Other special machines	50,275	91,141	118,031	3.7	8.9
	Thermal processes and apparatus	29,955	43,610	53,451	1.7	6.0
	Mechanical elements	46,697	70,522	75,684	2.4	4.9
	Transport	67,788	106,873	139,785	4.4	7.5
Other fields	Furniture, games	43,112	63,090	74,505	2.4	5.6
	Other consumer goods	32,552	51,570	59,255	1.9	6.2
	Civil engineering	57,131	90,940	123,035	3.9	8.0
	Unknown	5,810	4,967	932	0.0	-16.7
Total		**1,741,254**	**2,550,678**	**3,163,214**	**100.0**	**6.2**

Note: Data refer to published patent applications. There is a minimum delay of 18 months between the application date and the publication date. WIPO's International Patent Classification (IPC) technology concordance table was used to convert IPC symbols into 35 corresponding fields of technology. For an electronic version of the IPC technology concordance table, visit *www.wipo.int/ipstats*.

Sources: WIPO Statistics Database and EPO PATSTAT database, September 2022.

A28. Distribution of published patent applications by technology field for the top 10 origins, 2018–2020

Field of technology	China	US	Japan	Republic of Korea	Germany	France	UK	Switzerland	Netherlands	Russian Federation
Electrical machinery, apparatus, energy	6.4	4.2	9.9	8.4	9.1	6.4	5.3	6.3	6.6	3.8
Audio-visual technology	2.4	2.7	4.3	4.8	1.5	1.9	1.9	0.9	1.8	0.6
Telecommunications	1.6	2.2	2.2	2.4	1.0	1.6	1.5	0.6	1.3	1.4
Digital communication	4.8	7.6	2.9	5.8	2.0	3.5	2.7	1.4	2.4	0.9
Basic communication processes	0.3	0.8	0.7	0.6	0.6	0.6	0.7	0.3	0.8	0.9
Computer technology	10.0	12.2	5.9	8.4	3.6	4.9	8.3	2.5	5.9	3.2
IT methods for management	2.5	2.8	1.7	3.4	0.6	0.9	1.4	0.8	0.5	0.7
Semiconductors	1.7	2.7	5.3	6.4	2.0	2.3	1.4	0.8	3.0	0.8
Optics	1.4	1.9	5.7	3.0	1.8	2.1	1.8	0.9	5.8	0.8
Measurement	6.7	3.9	4.8	3.7	6.4	4.8	4.7	8.1	5.6	8.3
Analysis of biological materials	0.5	0.9	0.4	0.5	0.6	0.8	1.1	1.1	0.7	2.1
Control	2.7	2.3	2.6	1.9	2.4	1.5	1.6	1.7	1.2	1.8
Medical technology	3.2	9.0	3.6	4.1	4.4	5.0	7.3	9.3	12.8	8.9
Organic fine chemistry	1.7	2.7	1.4	2.0	2.8	4.5	4.0	5.3	4.0	1.7
Biotechnology	1.6	4.2	1.1	1.7	2.0	3.1	5.0	5.9	3.7	2.1
Pharmaceuticals	2.1	6.1	1.3	2.1	2.4	4.3	7.5	9.7	3.7	4.3
Macromolecular chemistry, polymers	1.6	1.3	2.4	1.5	1.9	2.0	0.8	1.7	2.7	0.9
Food chemistry	2.4	1.0	0.8	2.1	0.4	1.0	0.8	3.3	3.4	5.9
Basic materials chemistry	2.9	2.3	2.2	1.8	2.8	2.3	2.3	3.0	3.8	2.8
Materials, metallurgy	3.0	1.2	2.4	1.9	1.9	2.4	1.4	1.4	0.9	4.2
Surface technology, coating	1.4	1.2	2.5	1.5	1.6	1.7	1.0	1.5	1.6	1.4
Micro-structural and nano-technology	0.2	0.2	0.1	0.1	0.2	0.2	0.2	0.1	0.1	0.8
Chemical engineering	4.2	2.2	1.5	2.3	2.6	2.8	3.0	2.4	2.4	4.0
Environmental technology	2.9	1.1	1.1	1.6	1.5	1.3	1.7	0.8	1.4	2.7
Handling	3.6	2.2	3.2	2.3	3.3	2.5	2.5	6.0	3.1	1.2
Machine tools	4.9	1.6	2.4	1.9	3.6	1.3	1.3	1.9	1.2	2.4
Engines, pumps, turbines	1.3	1.9	2.6	1.7	5.0	4.5	3.6	1.4	0.9	4.4
Textile and paper machines	1.5	0.9	2.5	0.8	1.5	0.7	1.0	2.0	1.4	0.5
Other special machines	4.7	3.3	2.9	3.1	4.1	4.3	2.9	2.7	5.1	5.9
Thermal processes and apparatus	2.1	0.9	1.8	1.9	1.5	1.6	0.9	0.9	0.9	1.8
Mechanical elements	2.0	1.9	3.1	2.3	6.8	4.3	3.1	1.9	1.4	4.1
Transport	3.2	3.9	6.2	4.8	11.4	11.5	5.2	2.0	2.4	5.5
Furniture, games	2.2	2.2	4.5	2.6	1.8	1.5	2.6	2.4	2.2	1.3
Other consumer goods	1.7	1.8	1.5	3.0	1.8	2.6	5.1	6.4	2.2	1.1
Civil engineering	4.6	2.9	2.3	3.9	3.2	3.0	4.5	2.2	3.0	6.9

Origin (column group heading)

Note: Data refer to published patent applications. There is a minimum delay of 18 months between the application date and the publication date. WIPO's International Patent Classification (IPC) technology concordance table was used to convert IPC symbols into 35 corresponding fields of technology. For an electronic version of the IPC technology concordance table, visit *www.wipo.int/ipstats*. The top 10 origins were selected based on their 2018–2020 total published applications.

Sources: WIPO Statistics Database and EPO PATSTAT database, September 2022.

A29. Trend in patent applications in energy-related technologies, 2005–2020

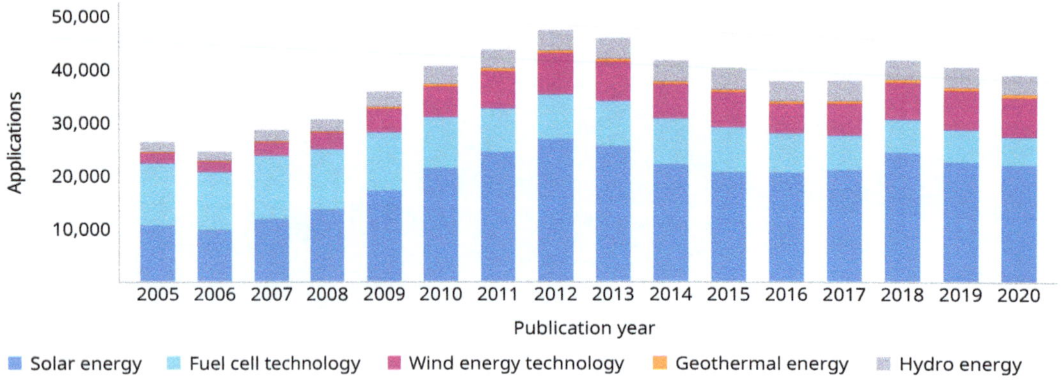

Note: For definitions of the technologies – fuel cell, geothermal, solar, wind and hydro energy – see annex A. The correspondence between International Patent Classification (IPC) symbols and technology fields is not always apparent (there is no one-to-one correspondence). It is therefore difficult to capture all patents in a specific technology field. Even so, the IPC-based definitions are likely to capture the vast majority of patent applications in these areas. Data refer to published patent applications.

Sources: WIPO Statistics Database and EPO PATSTAT database, September 2022.

A30. Share of patent applications in energy-related technologies for the top five origins, 2018–2020

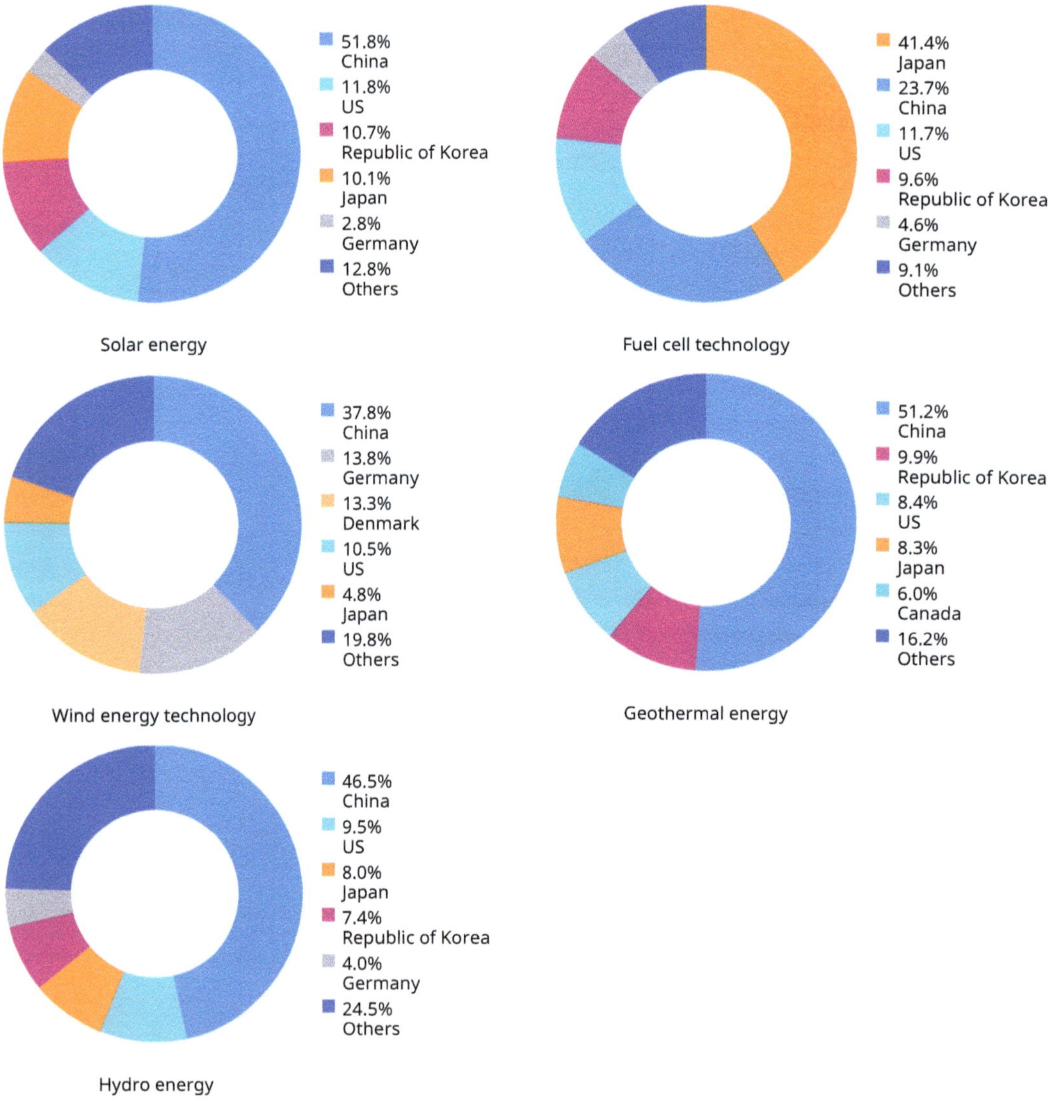

Note: For definitions of the technologies – fuel cells, geothermal, solar, wind and hydro energy – see annex A. The correspondence between International Patent Classification (IPC) symbols and technology fields is not always apparent (there is no one-to-one correspondence). It is therefore difficult to capture all patents in a specific technology field. Even so, the IPC-based definitions are likely to capture the vast majority of patent applications in these areas. Data refer to published patent applications.

Sources: WIPO Statistics Database and EPO PATSTAT database, September 2022.

Participation of women inventors in PCT applications

A31. Share of women among listed inventors in PCT applications, 2007–2021

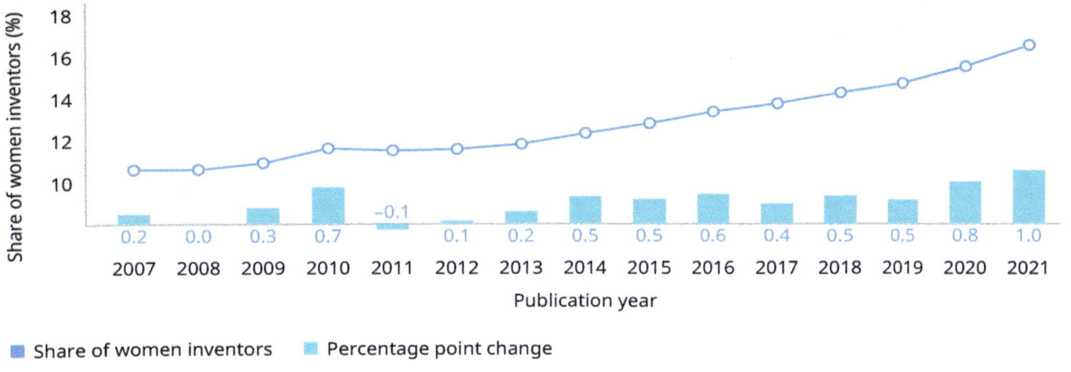

Note: In order to attribute gender to inventors' names recorded in PCT applications, WIPO produced a world gender-name dictionary based on information from 13 different public sources. Gender is attributed to a given name on a country-by-country basis, because certain names may be considered male in one country but female in another.

Source: WIPO Statistics Database, September 2022.

A32. Share of PCT applications with at least one woman as inventor and with at least one man as inventor, 2007–2021

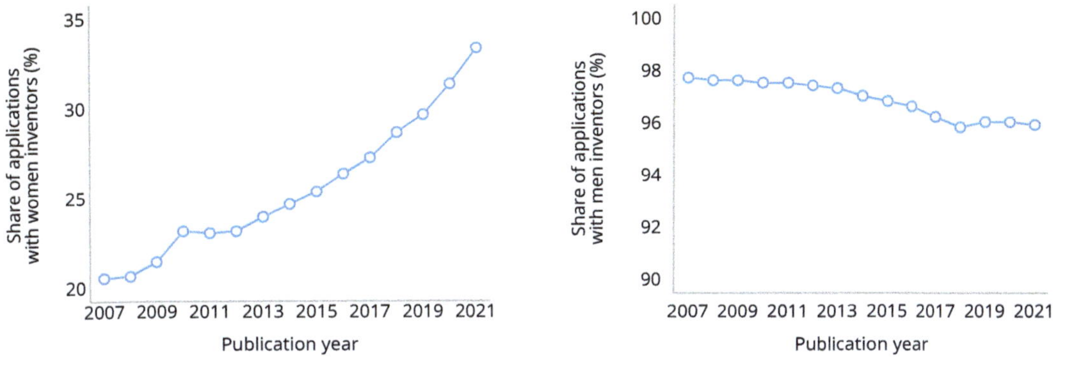

Note: In order to attribute gender to inventors' names recorded in PCT applications, WIPO produced a gender-name dictionary based on information from 13 different public sources. Gender is attributed to a given name on a country-by-country basis, because certain names may be considered male in one country but female in another.

Source: WIPO Statistics Database, September 2022.

A33. Share of women among listed inventors and share of PCT applications with at least one woman as inventor for the top 20 origins, 2021

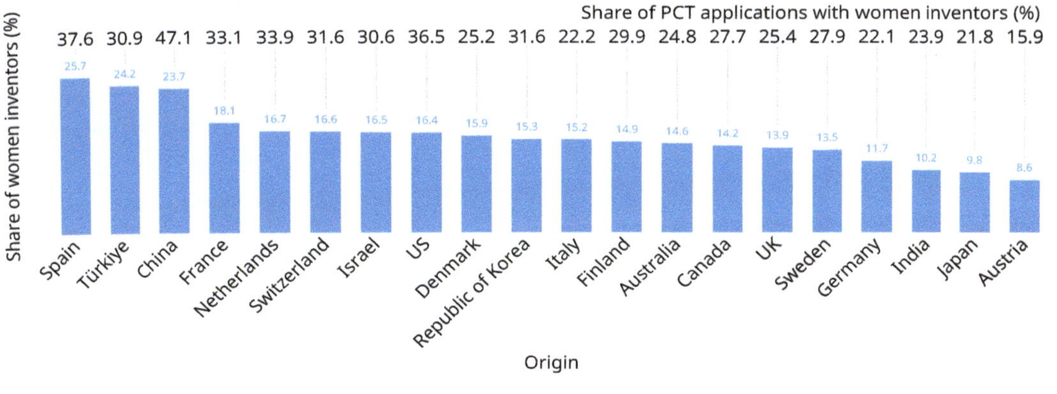

Note: In order to attribute gender to inventors' names recorded in PCT applications, WIPO produced a gender-name dictionary based on information from 13 different public sources. Gender is attributed to a given name on a country-by-country basis, because certain names may be considered male in one country but female in another.

Source: WIPO Statistics Database, September 2022.

A34. Share of PCT patent applications with women inventors by field of technology, 2021

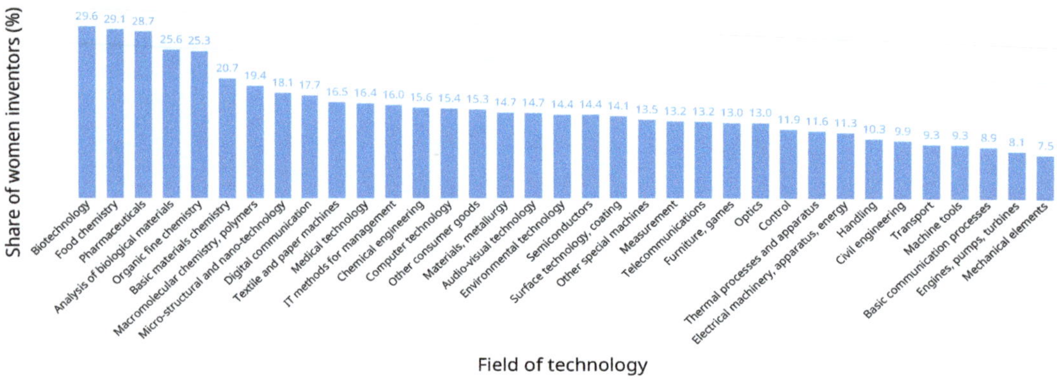

Note: In order to attribute gender to inventors' names recorded in PCT applications, WIPO produced a gender-name dictionary based on information from 13 different public sources. Gender is attributed to a given name on a country-by-country basis, because certain names may be considered male in one country but female in another.

Source: WIPO Statistics Database, September 2022.

Patent applications in relation to GDP and population

A35. Resident patent applications per USD 100 billion GDP for the top 20 origins, 2011 and 2021

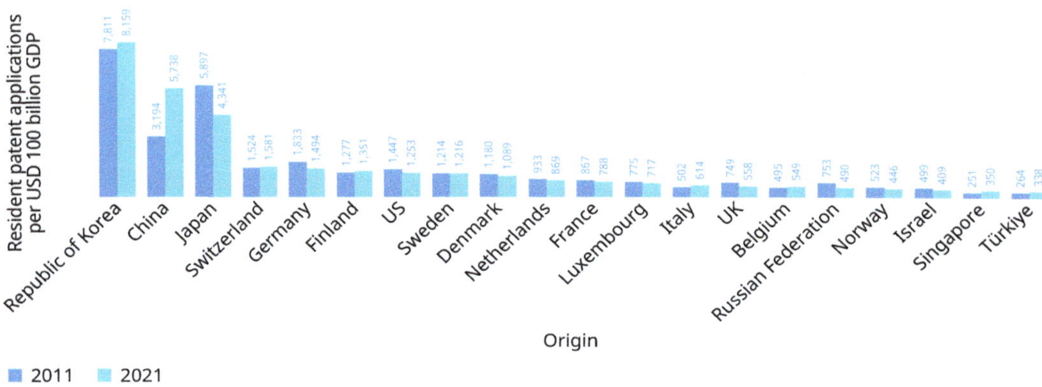

Note: GDP data are in 2017 US purchasing power parity (PPP) dollars. The top 20 origins were included if they had a GDP greater than USD 25 billion PPP and more than 100 resident patent applications. Due to space constraints, only the top 20 origins to fulfil these criteria are presented.

Sources: WIPO Statistics Database and World Bank, September 2022.

A36. Resident patent applications per million population for the top 20 origins, 2011 and 2021

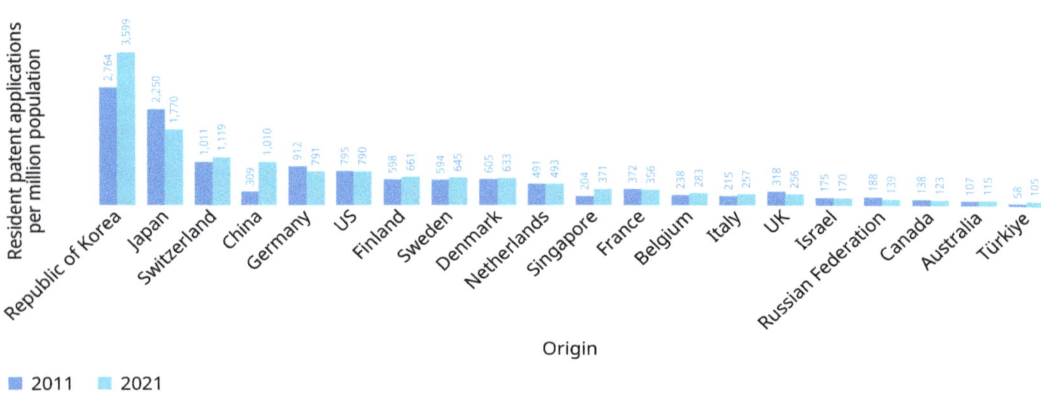

Note: The top 20 origins were included if they had a population greater than 5 million and if they had more than 100 resident patent applications. Due to space constraints, only the top 20 origins to fulfil these criteria are presented.

Sources: WIPO Statistics Database and World Bank, September 2022.

Patents in force

A37. Trend in patents in force worldwide, 2008–2021

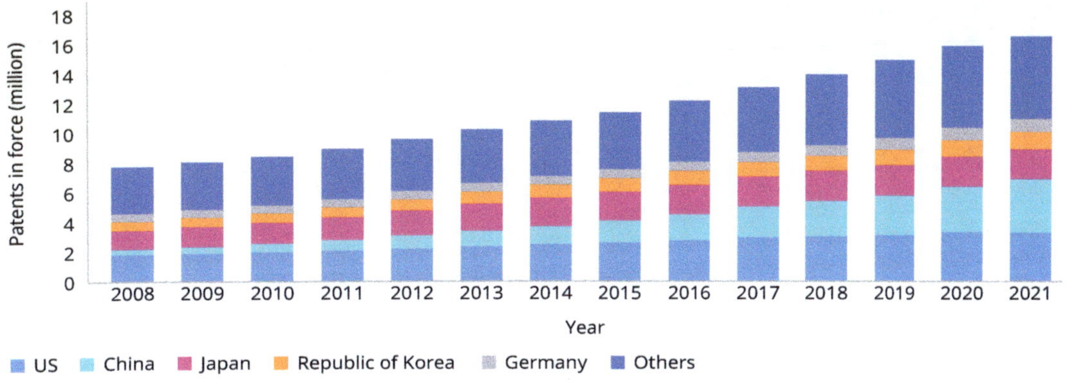

Note: World totals are WIPO estimates using data covering 133 offices.

Source: WIPO Statistics Database, September 2022.

A38. Patents in force at the top 20 offices, 2021

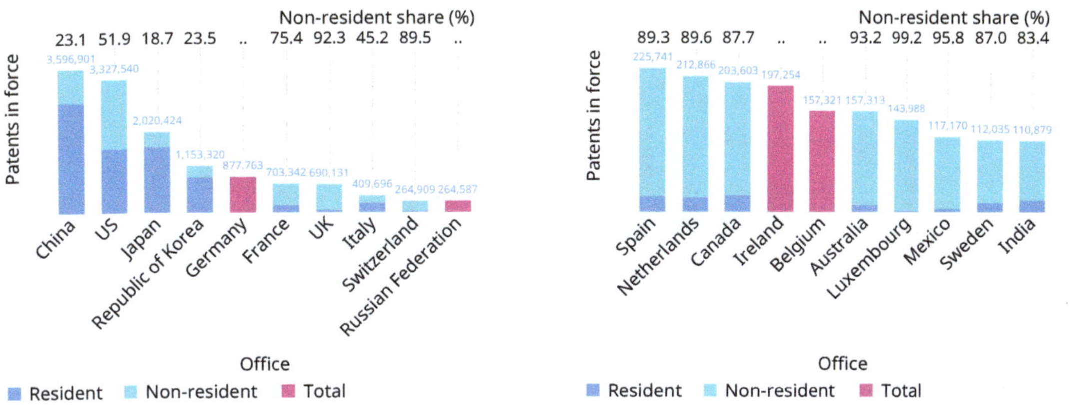

.. indicates not available.

Source: WIPO Statistics Database, September 2022.

A39. Patents in force in 2021 as a percentage of total applications

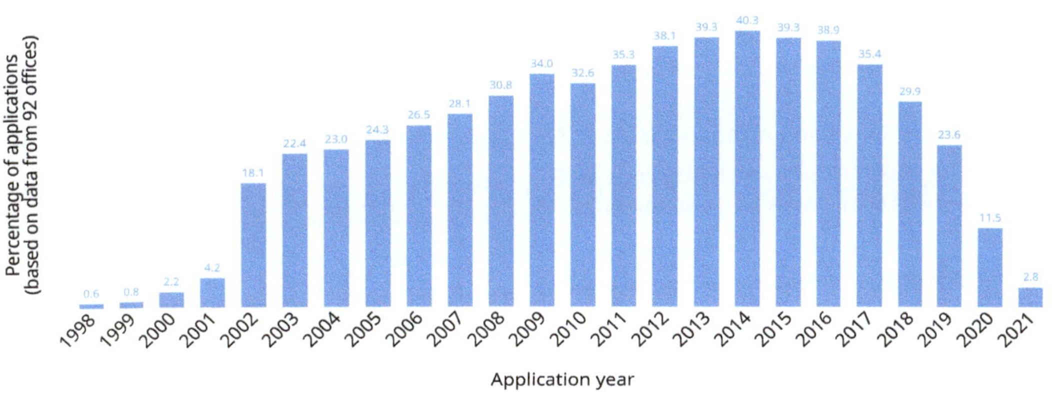

Note: Percentages are calculated as the number of patent applications filed in year *t* and in force in 2020, divided by the total number of patent applications filed in year *t*. Patent holders must pay maintenance fees to maintain the validity of their patents. Depending on technological and commercial considerations, patent holders may opt to let a patent lapse before the end of the full protection term. This figure shows the distribution of patents in force in 2021 as a percentage of total applications in the year of filing. However, not all offices provide these data. Data for 92 offices show that 40.3% of the applications for which patents were eventually granted remained in force for at least 8 years after the application date, and about 18.1% lasted the full 20-year term.

Source: WIPO Statistics Database, September 2022.

A40. Average age of patents in force at selected offices, 2016 and 2021

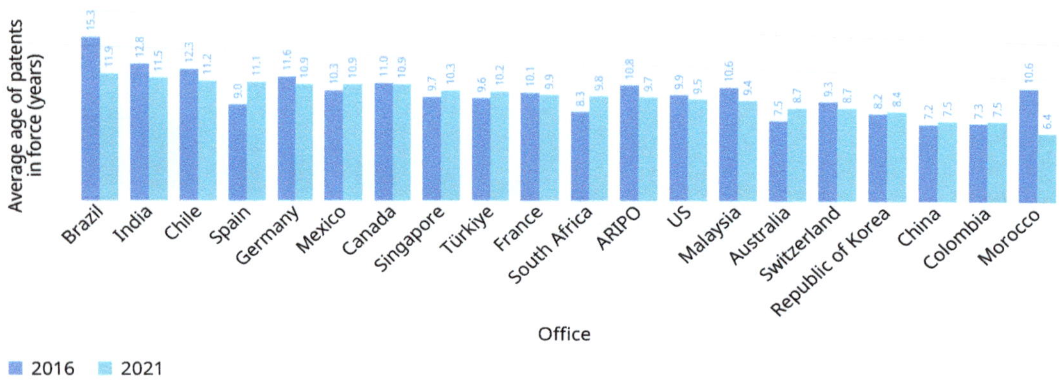

Note: ARIPO is the African Regional Intellectual Property Organization. The average age of patents in force is calculated using the following formula: $\Sigma(p*y)/\Sigma p$, where p is the number of patents in force and y the number of years between filing and reporting year.

Source: WIPO Statistics Database, September 2022.

Patent office procedural data

A41. Distribution of patent examination outcomes for selected offices, 2021

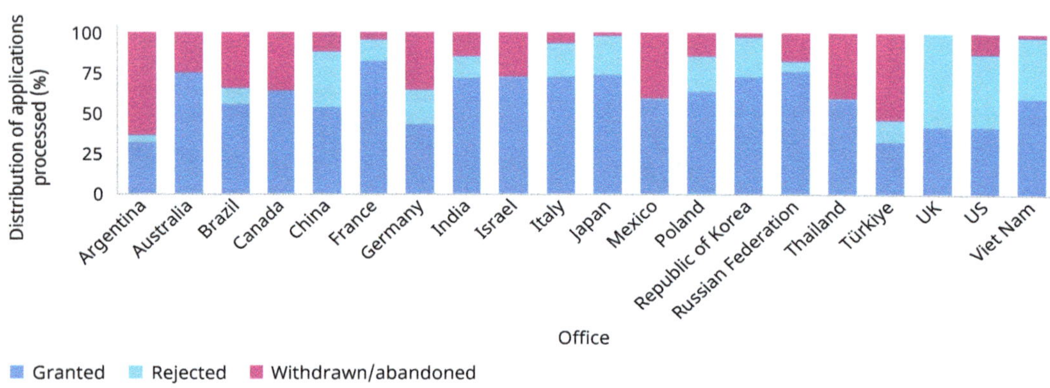

Note: The share of applications granted should not be interpreted as grant rates, as they are based on the examination date rather than the date when the application was filed. The number of grants in a given year relates to applications filed in previous years. WIPO collects data from IP offices using a common questionnaire and methodology. However, due to differences in patent procedures between offices, data cannot be fully harmonized. Therefore, caution should be exercised when making comparisons across offices.

Source: WIPO Statistics Database, September 2022.

A42. Potentially pending applications at the top 20 offices, 2021

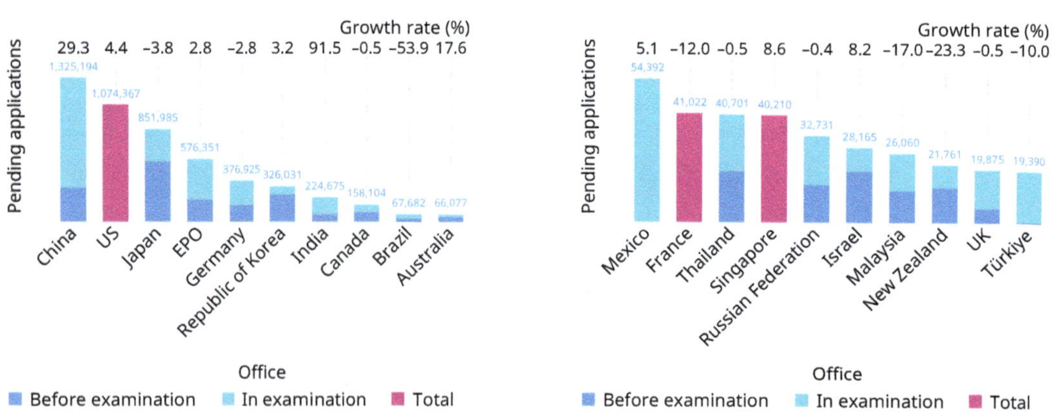

Note: EPO is the European Patent Office. Application processing varies between offices, making it difficult to measure pending applications. In some offices, patent applications automatically proceed to the examination stage, unless applicants withdraw them; in others, applications do not proceed to examination, unless applicants file a separate request for examination. To take account of procedural differences, pending application data are separated between (a) all patent applications, at any stage in the process, that are awaiting a final decision by a patent office, including those for which applicants have not filed a request for examination (where applicable), and (b) patent applications undergoing examination for which the applicant has requested examination (where such separate requests are necessary).

Source: WIPO Statistics Database, September 2022.

A43. Average pendency times for first office action and final decision at selected offices, 2021

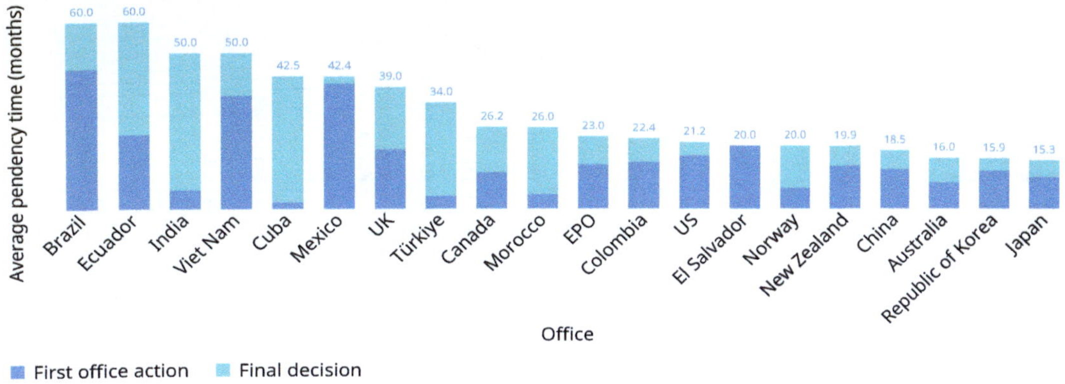

Note: EPO is the European Patent Office. WIPO collects data from IP offices using a common questionnaire and methodology. However, due to differences in patent procedures between offices, data cannot be fully harmonized. Therefore, caution should be exercised when making comparisons across offices.

Source: WIPO Statistics Database, September 2022.

A44. Number of patent examiners for selected offices, 2021

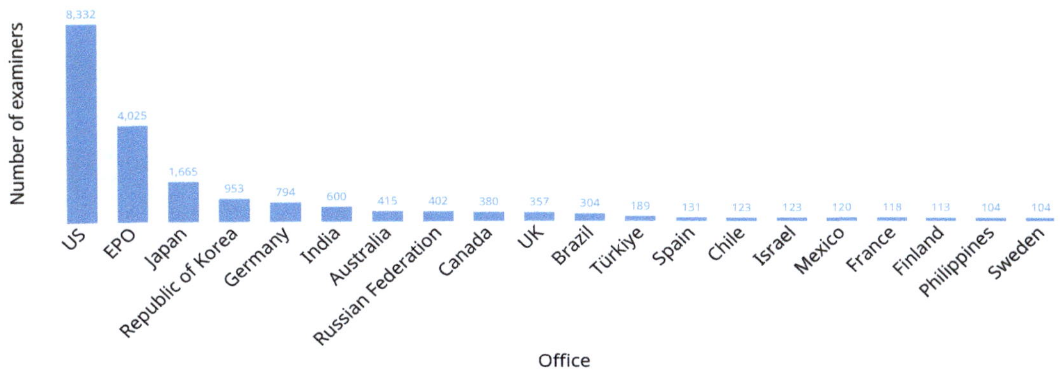

Note: EPO is the European Patent Office

Source: WIPO Statistics Database, September 2022

A45. Average years of experience of patent examiners for selected offices, 2021

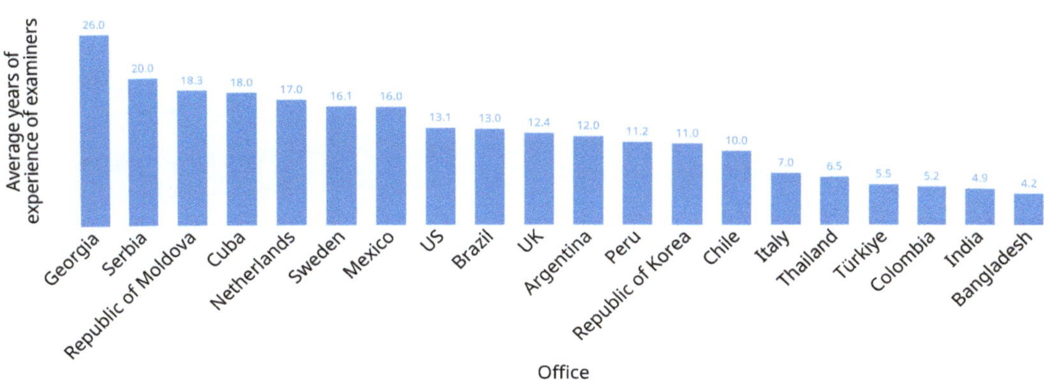

Source: WIPO Statistics Database, September 2022.

Patent prosecution highway (PPH)

A46. PPH requests by office of first filing and offices of later examination, 2021

	Office of first filing															
Office of later examination	**Australia**	**Canada**	**China**	**EPO**	**Finland**	**Germany**	**Israel**	**Japan**	**Netherlands**	**Republic of Korea**	**Russian Federation**	**Singapore**	**UK**	**US**	**Others**	**Total**
Australia	31	15	17	76	6	11	4	43	5	5	4	5	34	820	66	**1,142**
Brazil			90	71		2		63		28		1	15	305	23	**598**
Canada	66	120	61	543	6	2	9	96		28	15	8	12	2,124	16	**3,106**
China		19		1,086	36	57	9	1,366		260	17	39	55	2,757	53	**5,754**
EPO	20	51	179				13	305		72	15	2		730	3	**1,390**
Germany		2	15		3		2	222		8		1	38	402	7	**700**
Israel	25	9		135		3	40	26		9	3	3	2	310	11	**576**
Japan*		19	185	765	12	12	10	1,219		110	4	8	15	1,519	72	**3,950**
Mexico	1	3	35	83		18	2	63	2	4	1		11	362	70	**655**
Philippines								77		29				88		**194**
Republic of Korea	35	15	153	469	6	18	14	812		36	16	17	15	1,806	47	**3,459**
Russian Federation	1	5	46		6	28	2	49	102	5	1	13	9	151	76	**494**
Singapore	11		80	33	2		2	51		16		5	2	111		**313**
Thailand								346								**346**
US	103	163	1,324	1,780	56	77	96	1,106		493	62	18	86	983	138	**6,485**
Viet Nam								186		27						**213**
Others	51	6	57	31	4	6		125		6	1	1	10	255	56	**609**
Total	**344**	**427**	**2,242**	**5,072**	**137**	**234**	**203**	**6,155**	**109**	**1,136**	**139**	**121**	**304**	**12,723**	**638**	**29,984**

Note: EPO is the European Patent Office. A patent prosecution highway is a bilateral agreement between two offices that enables applicants to request a fast-track examination whereby patent examiners can use the work already undertaken by the other office.

* indicates data based on office of earlier examination rather than office of first filing.

Source: WIPO Statistics Database, September 2022.

A47. **Flows of PPH requests between offices of first filing and offices of later examination, 2021**

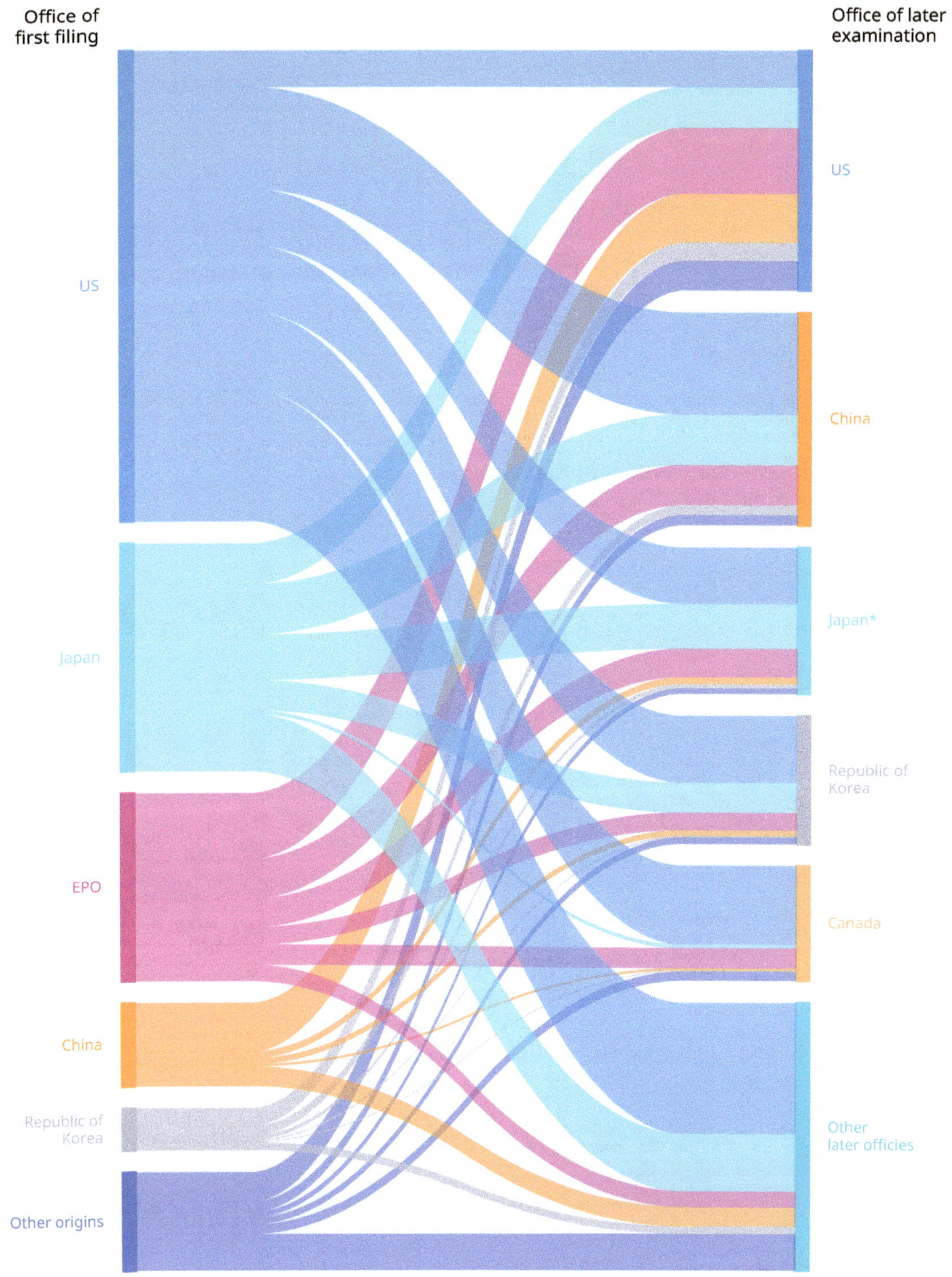

Note: EPO is the European Patent Office. Japan data refers to the office of earlier examination rather than the office of first filing. A patent prosecution highway (PPH) is a bilateral agreement between two offices that enables applicants to request a fast-track examination whereby patent examiners can use the work already undertaken by the other office. This graph shows the flows of PPH requests between offices of first filing and offices of later examination.

* indicates data based on office of earlier examination rather than office of first filing.

Source: WIPO Statistics Database, September 2022.

Utility model applications

A48. Trend in utility model applications worldwide, 2007–2021

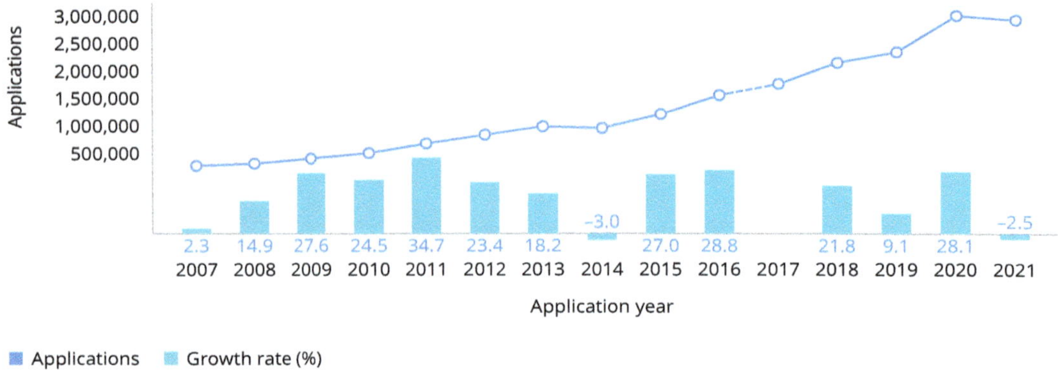

Note: World totals are WIPO estimates using data covering 82 patent offices. These totals include applications filed directly with national and regional offices and applications entering offices through the Patent Cooperation Treaty national phase (where applicable). China's pre-2017 data are not comparable due a change in methodology. Due to this break in the data series and to the large number of filings in China, it is not possible to report accurately the 2017 growth rate at world level (see the data description section in Additional information for details).

Source: WIPO Statistics Database, September 2022.

A49. Utility model applications for the top 20 offices, 2021

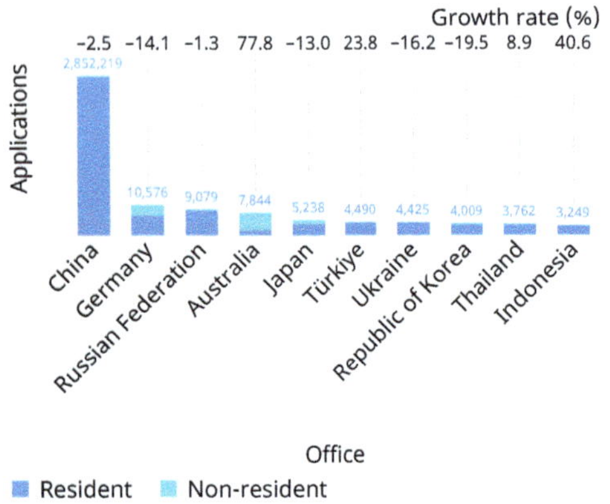

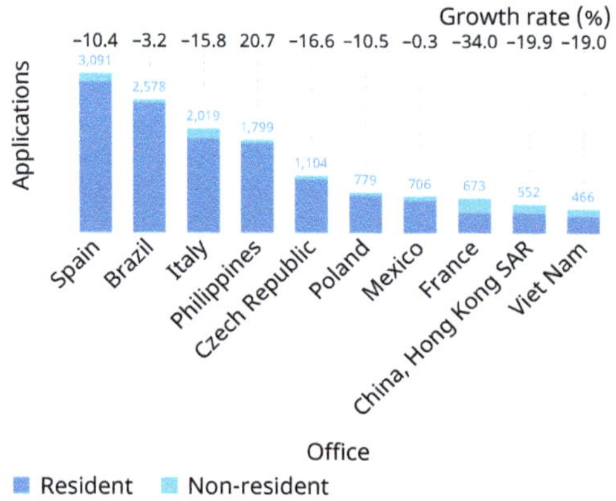

Source: WIPO Statistics Database, September 2022.

A50. Utility model applications for offices of selected low- and middle-income countries, 2021

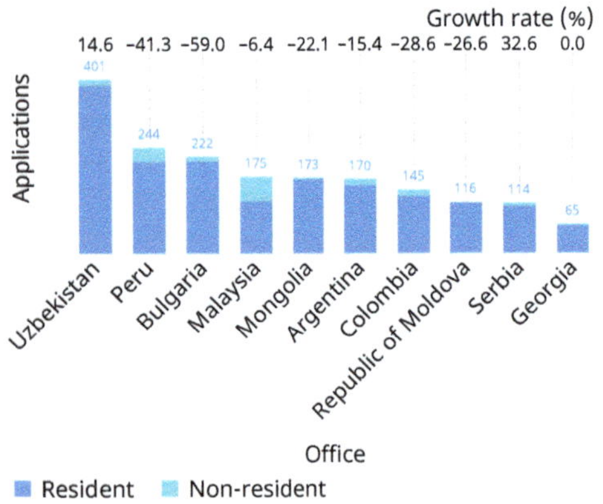

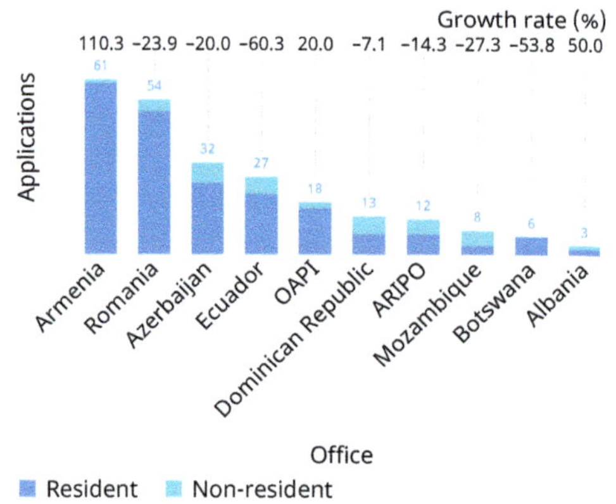

Note: ARIPO is the African Regional Intellectual Property Organization and OAPI is the African Intellectual Property Organization.

Source: WIPO Statistics Database, September 2022.

Microorganisms

A51. Trend in microorganism deposits worldwide, 2007–2021

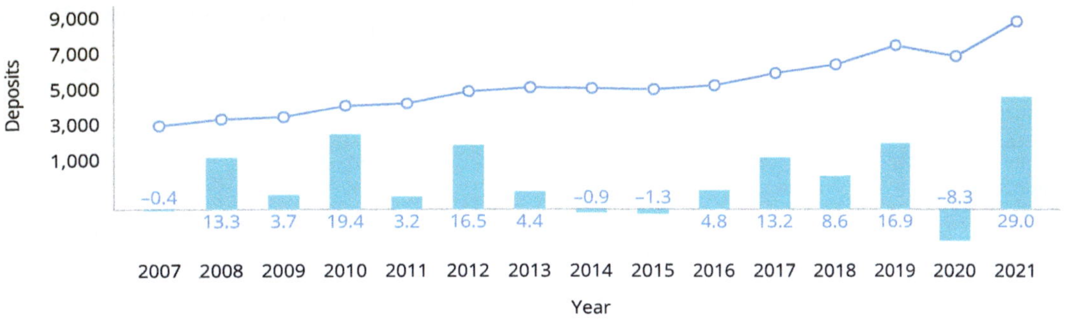

Note: Deposits of microorganisms for patent procedures are important for biotechnological inventions. Disclosing an invention is a requirement for receiving a patent.

Source: WIPO Statistics Database, September 2022.

A52. Deposits at the top international depositary authorities, 2021

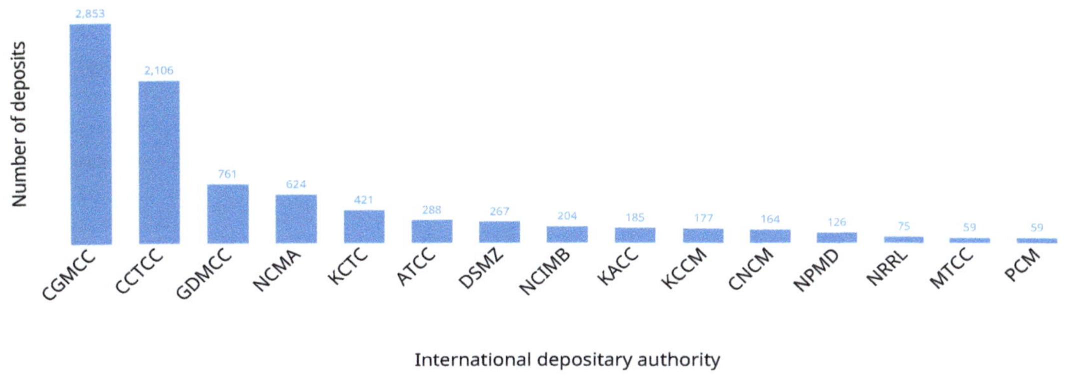

Note: ATCC is the American Type Culture Collection (US), CCTCC is the China Center for Type Culture Collection (China), CGMCC is the China General Microbiological Culture Collection Center (China), CNCM is the Collection Nationale de Cultures de Microorganisms (France), DSMZ is the Leibniz-Institut DSMZ (Deutsche Sammlung von Mikroorganismen und Zellkulturen GmbH; Germany), GDMCC is the Guangdong Microbial Culture Collection Center (China), KACC is the Korean Agricultural Culture Collection (Republic of Korea), KCCM is the Korean Culture Center of Microorganisms (Republic of Korea), KCTC is the Korean Collection for Type Cultures (Republic of Korea), MTCC is the Microbial Type Culture Collection and Gene Bank (India), NCIMB is the National Collection of Industrial, Food and Marine Bacteria (UK), NCMA is the Provasoli-Guillard National Center for Marine Algae and Microbiota (US), NPMD is the National Institute of Technology and Evaluation, Patent Microorganisms Depositary (Japan), NRRL is the Agriculture Research Service Culture Collection (US) and PCM is the Polish Collection of Microorganisms (Poland).

Source: WIPO Statistics Database, September 2022.

A53. Patent applications by office and origin, 2021

	Applications by office				Equivalent applications by origin		PCT national phase entry	
Name	Total	Resident	Non-resident	Change over previous year	Total (a)	Change over previous year	Office	Origin
Afghanistan (b)	..	..	..	..	1	..	..	1
African Intellectual Property Organization	612	205	407	133	n.a.	n.a.	397	n.a.
African Regional Intellectual Property Organization	833	10	823	79	n.a.	n.a.	791	n.a.
Albania	24	23	1	12	39	+36	1	3
Algeria	849	268	581	139	281	+108	569	8
Andorra	11	3	8	3	27	–18	..	16
Angola	86	86	0	1	87	+87	86	86
Antigua and Barbuda	8	0	8	5	408	–124	..	310
Argentina	3,669	406	3,263	177	716	–523	..	133
Armenia	48	40	8	–22	105	–30	1	22
Australia	32,409	2,966	29,443	3,115	12,821	+914	23,381	8,489
Austria (b)	..	..	..	..	11,595	..	..	6,448
Azerbaijan	135	119	16	27	338	+94	15	8
Bahamas (b)	..	..	..	..	55	..	..	32
Bahrain	329	3	326	65	17	–20	306	2
Bangladesh	447	74	373	45	90	+34	..	2
Barbados	73	73	0	44	767	+100	73	176
Belarus	386	276	110	–8	1,118	–160	70	63
Belgium	1,214	799	415	64	13,959	+481	..	8,246
Belize	27	0	27	4	21	+2	27	3
Benin (b,c)	n.a.	n.a.	n.a.	n.a.	171	+120	n.a.	..
Bhutan	7	0	7	1	..	..	..	..
Bolivia (Plurinational State of) (b)	..	..	..	..	1	..	..	1
Bosnia and Herzegovina	61	53	8	6	64	+3	8	2
Botswana	3	3	0	–1	4	–2	..	..
Brazil	24,232	4,666	19,566	–106	6,900	–371	18,496	1,558
Brunei Darussalam	139	2	137	19	5	–5	131	2
Bulgaria	171	165	6	–75	466	–136	5	110
Burkina Faso (b,c)	n.a.	n.a.	n.a.	n.a.	85	–68	n.a.	..
Cabo Verde	2	1	1	–3	1	0	..	..
Cambodia (b)	..	..	..	..	5	..	..	1
Cameroon (b,c)	n.a.	n.a.	n.a.	n.a.	1,074	+360	n.a.	1
Canada	37,155	4,710	32,445	2,590	26,504	+2,649	30,383	12,105
Central African Republic (b,c)	n.a.	n.a.	n.a.	n.a.	17	–51	n.a.	..
Chad (b,c)	n.a.	n.a.	n.a.	n.a.	51	0	n.a.	..
Chile	3,082	402	2,680	277	930	68	2,676	482
China	1,585,663	1,426,644	159,019	88,504	1,538,549	97,463	93,608	63,022
China, Hong Kong SAR	21,943	401	21,542	387	3,261	1,130	..	612
China, Macao SAR	37	2	35	–29	163	128	..	1
Colombia	2,287	432	1,855	166	692	95	1,822	203
Congo (b,c)	n.a.	n.a.	n.a.	n.a.	71	–133	n.a.	1
Cook Islands (b)	..	..	..	..	2	..	..	..
Costa Rica	581	15	566	45	129	42	562	46
Côte d'Ivoire (b,c)	n.a.	n.a.	n.a.	n.a.	697	419	n.a.	..
Croatia	88	77	11	–41	303	55	3	168
Cuba	107	21	86	–2	111	–59	79	82
Curaçao (b)	..	..	..	..	14	..	..	4
Cyprus	3	1	2	0	414	54	..	275
Czech Republic	600	541	59	–129	1,920	–33	29	738
Democratic People's Republic of Korea (b)	..	..	..	..	27	..	..	12
Democratic Republic of the Congo (b)	..	..	..	..	1	..	..	..
Denmark	1,276	1,090	186	–202	14,083	497	58	8,386
Dominica	11	0	11	9	5	2	..	1

			Applications by office		Equivalent applications by origin		PCT national phase entry	
Name	Total	Resident	Non-resident	Change over previous year	Total (a)	Change over previous year	Office	Origin
Dominican Republic	227	7	220	10	46	11	221	29
Ecuador	408	35	373	1	51	3	..	5
Egypt	2,224	881	1,343	17	997	-190	1,313	42
El Salvador	146	2	144	-1	2	-4	130	..
Estonia	26	25	1	3	350	53	1	162
Eswatini (b)	..	..	..	..	4	..	..	2
Ethiopia (b)	..	..	..	..	12	..	..	2
Eurasian Patent Organization	3,643	657	2,986	266	n.a.	n.a.	2,764	n.a.
European Patent Office	188,778	83,825	104,953	8,432	n.a.	n.a.	115,103	n.a.
Finland	1,662	1,557	105	-23	12,822	769	37	7,308
France	14,759	13,386	1,373	446	66,087	1,800	..	35,124
Gabon (b,c)	n.a.	n.a.	n.a.	n.a.	359	291	n.a.	2
Georgia	254	90	164	39	132	12	159	25
Germany	58,569	39,822	18,747	-3,536	165,656	-2,436	6,900	70,988
Ghana (b)	..	..	..	..	1	..	..	..
Greece	926	394	532	163	1,387	258	..	492
Grenada (b)	..	..	..	..	1	..	..	..
Guatemala	258	9	249	46	15	-3	242	1
Guinea (b,c)	n.a.	n.a.	n.a.	n.a.	52	-17	n.a.	1
Guyana	40	40	0	..	40	..	16	16
Honduras	188	0	188	27	2	2	182	..
Hungary	446	433	13	-10	1,463	164	6	829
Iceland	36	34	2	-11	371	85	2	246
India	61,573	26,267	35,306	4,802	43,133	5,238	28,852	5,480
Indonesia	8,800	1,397	7,403	640	1,445	87	6,494	44
Iran (Islamic Republic of) (b)	..	..	..	..	140	..	..	32
Iraq (b)	..	..	..	..	12	..	..	1
Ireland	117	75	42	-12	7,058	-7	..	3,516
Israel	9,609	1,592	8,017	1,486	17,341	1,118	8,549	8,370
Italy	11,078	10,281	797	70	34,166	1,615	15	15,237
Jamaica	76	16	60	19	23	12	..	1
Japan	289,200	222,452	66,748	728	412,851	-10,413	72,782	137,319
Jordan	347	25	322	10	53	-22	299	10
Kazakhstan (b)	..	..	..	..	753	..	..	47
Kenya (b)	..	..	..	..	39	..	..	3
Kuwait (b)	..	..	..	..	71	..	..	24
Kyrgyzstan	87	83	4	23	120	-7	1	7
Latvia	108	104	4	14	281	50	..	104
Lebanon (b)	..	..	..	..	42	..	..	16
Lesotho (b)	..	..	..	..	1	..	..	1
Liberia (b)	..	..	..	..	1	..	..	..
Liechtenstein (b)	..	..	..	..	1,472	..	..	815
Lithuania	90	81	9	-23	477	152	..	103
Luxembourg	1,553	112	1,441	745	2,695	9	194	1,829
Madagascar	28	6	22	1	6	-3	22	..
Malawi (b)	..	..	..	..	2	..	..	2
Malaysia	7,534	883	6,651	706	1,862	-61	5,610	422
Mali (b,c)	n.a.	n.a.	n.a.	n.a.	194	121	n.a.	1
Malta	10	5	5	-1	407	-21	..	155
Marshall Islands (b)	..	..	..	..	3	..	..	..
Mauritania (b,c)	n.a.	n.a.	n.a.	n.a.	36	16	n.a.	1
Mauritius	20	6	14	-5	165	49	..	65
Mexico	16,161	1,117	15,044	1,849	1,993	-109	13,003	512
Micronesia (Federated States of) (b)	..	..	..	..	1	..	..	..
Monaco	8	5	3	-5	137	-18	..	79
Mongolia	186	109	77	38	113	43	70	1
Montenegro (b)	..	..	..	..	7	..	..	6
Morocco	2,803	254	2,549	115	399	59	2,199	134

	Applications by office				Equivalent applications by origin		PCT national phase entry	
Name	Total	Resident	Non-resident	Change over previous year	Total (a)	Change over previous year	Office	Origin
Mozambique	46	30	16	6	30	4	16	..
Myanmar (b)	..	..	..	..	2	..	..	..
Namibia (b)	..	..	..	..	16	..	..	..
Nepal (b)	..	..	..	..	2	..	..	1
Netherlands	3,470	2,080	1,390	447	32,770	-42	..	19,275
New Zealand	6,852	330	6,522	1,087	2,679	302	5,209	1,532
Niger (b,c)	n.a.	n.a.	n.a.	n.a.	68	-68	n.a.	..
Nigeria (b)	..	..	..	..	23	..	..	3
North Macedonia	42	42	0	-5	73	-18	1	28
Norway	1,580	946	634	136	5,841	-141	559	3,585
Oman	546	546	0	17	582	541	96	116
Pakistan	993	426	567	93	490	114	..	6
Panama	436	35	401	117	70	-12	310	28
Papua New Guinea (b)	..	..	..	..	4	..	..	..
Paraguay (b)	..	..	..	..	4	..	..	2
Patent Office of the Cooperation Council for the Arab States of the Gulf	318	81	237	-2,025	n.a.	n.a.	..	n.a.
Peru	1,235	94	1,141	-32	160	-58	1,101	52
Philippines	4,393	490	3,903	400	695	65	3,663	68
Poland	3,488	3,377	111	-610	5,916	-418	58	1,202
Portugal	753	711	42	-205	1,985	111	16	824
Qatar	769	47	722	84	121	-89	81	52
Republic of Korea	237,998	186,245	51,753	11,239	267,517	6,903	43,419	36,925
Republic of Moldova	76	64	12	-20	75	-57	6	8
Romania	817	772	45	-47	1,114	-43	11	128
Russian Federation	30,977	19,569	11,408	-4,007	25,881	-4,402	9,621	2,849
Rwanda (b)	..	..	..	..	2	..	..	..
Saint Kitts and Nevis (b)	..	..	..	..	28	..	..	22
Saint Lucia (b)	..	..	..	..	15	..	..	15
Saint Vincent and the Grenadines	11	0	11	6	..	..	11	..
Samoa	1	1	0	-1	17	-17	..	4
San Marino	729	7	722	11	58	21	..	19
Saudi Arabia	3,979	1,398	2,581	411	4,865	-4,917	2,875	1,626
Senegal (b,c)	n.a.	n.a.	n.a.	n.a.	606	367	n.a.	8
Serbia	156	138	18	10	270	34	6	78
Seychelles (b)	..	..	..	..	51	..	..	23
Singapore	14,590	2,024	12,566	1,325	9,764	1,818	10,458	4,254
Sint Maarten (Dutch Part) (b)	..	..	..	..	3	..	..	1
Slovakia	159	146	13	-62	410	-159	9	135
Slovenia (b)	..	..	..	..	522	..	..	284
Somalia (b)	..	..	..	..	1	..	..	..
South Africa	10,960	1,804	9,156	4,272	2,751	1,294	6,311	883
Spain	1,434	1,308	126	-121	10,875	705	73	5,568
Sri Lanka	539	266	273	-65	328	-84	257	29
Sudan (b)	..	..	..	..	3	..	..	2
Sweden	2,196	1,771	425	0	27,801	1,580	49	18,672
Switzerland	1,555	1,288	267	-130	48,244	3,438	84	28,639
Syrian Arab Republic	125	..	..	33	4	-78	..	3
Tajikistan (b)	..	..	..	..	97	..	..	..
Thailand	8,242	867	7,375	717	1,547	35	6,647	431
Timor-Leste (b)	..	..	..	..	10	..	..	10
Togo (b,c)	n.a.	n.a.	n.a.	n.a.	81	-4	n.a.	47
Trinidad and Tobago	151	2	149	39	15	11	149	10
Tunisia (b)	..	..	..	..	24	..	..	11
Türkiye	8,476	8,234	242	318	10,868	758	320	2,150
Turkmenistan (b)	..	..	..	..	3	..	..	3
Uganda (b)	..	..	..	..	6	..	..	3
Ukraine	3,393	1,302	2,091	210	1,703	-7	1,816	180

			Applications by office		Equivalent applications by origin		PCT national phase entry	
Name	**Total**	**Resident**	**Non-resident**	**Change over previous year**	**Total (a)**	**Change over previous year**	**Office**	**Origin**
United Arab Emirates	2,423	69	2,354	515	655	-182	2,240	313
United Kingdom	18,855	11,592	7,263	-1,794	53,608	529	2,355	29,454
United Republic of Tanzania	44	..	..	-17	18	13	..	12
United States of America	591,473	262,244	329,229	-5,699	509,853	13,730	169,483	210,953
Uruguay (b)	..	..	..	..	104	..	..	82
Uzbekistan	665	413	252	77	428	49	225	1
Vanuatu (b)	..	..	..	..	3	..	..	3
Venezuela (Bolivarian Republic of)	291	..	..	84	8	-1	..	5
Viet Nam	8,534	1,066	7,468	839	1,205	72	6,663	47
Yemen	42	20	22	-26	22	-41	..	..
Zambia (b)	..	..	..	..	2	..	..	..
Zimbabwe	51	..	..	40	10	3	..	1
Others/Unknown	..	..	..	..	45,136	-9,190	..	7,772
Total (2021 estimates)	**3,401,100**	**2,385,200**	**1,015,900**				**715,200**	

(a) Equivalent applications by origin data are incomplete, because some offices do not report by origin.
(b) The office did not report resident applications therefore the equivalent applications by origin data may be incomplete.
(c) The African Intellectual Property Organization (OAPI) acts as the national office for patent applications.

.. indicates not available.

n.a. indicates not applicable.

Source: WIPO Statistics Database, September 2022.

A54. Patent grants by office and origin, and patents in force, 2021

			Grants by office		Equivalent grants by origin		In force by office	
Name	**Total**	**Resident**	**Non-resident**	**Change over previous year**	**Total (a)**	**Change over previous year**	**Total**	**Change over previous year**
African Intellectual Property Organization	505	115	390	-75	n.a.	n.a.	..	..
African Regional Intellectual Property Organization	568	1	567	125	n.a.	n.a.	2,358	272
Albania	2	1	1	-3	7	3	6,519	686
Algeria	770	99	671	349	104	55	4,646	327
Andorra	12	4	8	-1	18	4	39	6
Angola	49	49	0	16	49	49	86	1
Antigua and Barbuda	..	..	..	..	62	..	..	..
Argentina	2,298	281	2,017	-39	501	62	13,411	-1,139
Armenia	27	24	3	-45	66	-40	12	-177
Australia	17,155	1,070	16,085	-623	6,353	350	157,313	-1,991
Austria	..	..	..	..	7,837	..	..	..
Azerbaijan	119	102	17	9	322	-14	272	20
Bahamas	..	..	..	..	21	..	..	..
Bahrain	67	0	67	33	11	2	114	-17
Bangladesh	240	..	..	100	23	14	2,114	382
Barbados	..	..	..	..	466	..	..	..
Belarus	316	263	53	-131	951	-252	1,555	-197
Belgium	1,005	727	278	11	8,177	-510	157,321	-7,314
Belize	12	0	12	9	13	8	57	12
Benin (b)	n.a.	n.a.	n.a.	n.a.	68	17	..	..
Bhutan	..	..	..	..	..	..	1	0
Bolivia (Plurinational State of)	..	..	..	..	2	..	..	..
Bosnia and Herzegovina	4	0	4	-14	5	2	152	-8
Brazil	26,872	2,552	24,320	6,465	3,607	748	75,529	17,587
Brunei Darussalam	31	0	31	4	8	-2	1,521	869
Bulgaria	182	169	13	-33	435	66	15,291	501
Burkina Faso (b)	n.a.	n.a.	n.a.	n.a.	85	17	..	..
Burundi	..	..	..	..	1	..	..	..
Cabo Verde	2	0	2	..	..	..	..	..
Cambodia	..	..	..	..	3	..	..	..

	Grants by office				Equivalent grants by origin		In force by office	
Name	Total	Resident	Non-resident	Change over previous year	Total (a)	Change over previous year	Total	Change over previous year
Cameroon (b)	n.a.	n.a.	n.a.	n.a.	514	-132	..	..
Canada	22,687	2,272	20,415	1,403	13,607	-439	203,603	10,935
Central African Republic (b)	n.a.	n.a.	n.a.	n.a.	17	-17	..	..
Chile	2,379	253	2,126	-525	560	28	14,359	-2,761
China	695,946	584,891	111,055	165,819	639,306	154,147	3,596,901	539,057
China, Hong Kong SAR	14,662	283	14,379	7,004	2,030	838	61,446	7,720
China, Macao SAR	15	0	15	-3	137	68	348	-5
Colombia	1,263	221	1,042	188	360	3	8,457	92
Congo (b)	n.a.	n.a.	n.a.	n.a.	170	102	..	..
Cook Islands	..	..	..	..	1	..	..	..
Costa Rica	130	0	130	-40	60	16	1,188	13
Côte d'Ivoire (b)	n.a.	n.a.	n.a.	n.a.	425	50	..	..
Croatia	7	3	4	-3	67	1	11,876	835
Cuba	81	13	68	43	81	24	494	-87
Curaçao	..	..	..	..	35	..	..	..
Cyprus	..	..	..	..	259	..	14	-7
Czech Republic	444	404	40	-55	1,247	-99	51,153	960
Democratic People's Republic of Korea	..	..	..	..	19	..	..	..
Denmark	368	267	101	15	6,935	-63	69,784	823
Dominica	11	0	11	9	..	..	..	..
Dominican Republic	227	8	219	89	13	3	938	77
Ecuador	17	0	17	8	7	-2	80	0
Egypt	508	63	445	13	128	13	5,386	-269
El Salvador	58	0	58	-9	2	-1	..	..
Estonia	8	8	0	-4	122	19	11,768	324
Eswatini	..	..	..	..	6	..	..	..
Ethiopia	..	..	..	..	1	..	..	..
Eurasian Patent Organization	2,416	490	1,926	-338	n.a.	n.a.	n.a.	n.a.
European Patent Office	108,799	47,714	61,085	-24,907	n.a.	n.a.	n.a.	n.a.
Fiji	..	..	..	..	1	..	..	..
Finland	545	511	34	-57	7,568	-849	56,847	949
France	15,493	13,584	1,909	2,619	49,114	-2,055	703,342	29,008
Gabon (b)	n.a.	n.a.	n.a.	n.a.	119	68	..	..
Georgia	128	42	86	-24	60	10	898	-12
Germany	21,113	12,840	8,273	3,808	97,246	-4,207	877,763	43,029
Ghana	..	..	..	..	1	..	..	..
Greece	252	240	12	29	652	-2	29,228	736
Guatemala	38	0	38	-2	6	-2	854	15
Guinea (b)	n.a.	n.a.	n.a.	n.a.	51	33	..	..
Guinea-Bissau (b)	n.a.	n.a.	n.a.	n.a.	17	17	..	..
Guyana	21	21	0	..	21	..	24	..
Honduras	92	0	92	52	1	1	349	97
Hungary	107	94	13	13	625	-101	34,797	1,231
Iceland	7	4	3	-2	163	11	9,330	329
India	30,721	6,384	24,337	4,360	14,613	1,544	110,879	17,982
Indonesia	6,850	736	6,114	-1,131	756	91	..	..
Iran (Islamic Republic of)	..	..	..	..	84	..	..	..
Iraq	..	..	..	..	4	..	..	..
Ireland	43	26	17	1	3,968	-38	197,254	-20,132
Israel	5,488	1,006	4,482	820	9,032	358	35,539	443
Italy	7,254	6,564	690	-1,898	23,142	-2,613	409,696	7,075
Jamaica	5	2	3	0	6	-6	319	2
Japan	184,372	141,853	42,519	4,989	278,114	-821	2,020,424	-18,616
Jordan	166	10	156	-168	34	-8	821	127
Kazakhstan	651	521	130	-58	898	-214	3,137	-15
Kenya	..	..	..	..	47	..	..	..
Kuwait	..	..	..	..	26	..	..	..

	Grants by office				Equivalent grants by origin		In force by office	
Name	Total	Resident	Non-resident	Change over previous year	Total (a)	Change over previous year	Total	Change over previous year
Kyrgyzstan	39	39	0	−10	50	−19	173	−21
Lao People's Democratic Republic	..	..	..	..	2	..	..	..
Latvia	76	71	5	16	144	38	10,726	1,477
Lebanon	..	..	..	..	46	..	..	..
Liberia	..	..	..	..	1	..	..	..
Libya	..	..	..	..	1	..	..	..
Liechtenstein	..	..	..	..	771	..	..	..
Lithuania	83	73	10	−23	203	44	12,718	364
Luxembourg	1,036	106	930	598	2,219	−54	143,988	−21,261
Madagascar	48	0	48	44	..	..	223	14
Malaysia	6,876	1,040	5,836	−1,330	1,583	−134	34,141	2,166
Mali (b)	n.a.	n.a.	n.a.	n.a.	157	2	..	..
Malta	11	2	9	1	264	26	233	−15
Marshall Islands	..	..	..	..	3	..	..	..
Mauritania (b)	n.a.	n.a.	n.a.	n.a.	17	17	..	..
Mauritius	4	0	4	−13	53	−26	20	..
Mexico	10,369	618	9,751	2,643	1,307	204	117,170	3,840
Monaco	9	4	5	−7	92	0	108,388	−825
Mongolia	186	69	117	62	72	21	1,445	128
Montenegro	..	..	..	..	6	..	..	..
Morocco	745	99	646	345	203	60	10,215	23
Mozambique	..	..	..	..	..	..	4,259	468
Myanmar	..	..	..	..	2	..	..	..
Namibia	..	..	..	..	3	..	..	..
Nepal	..	..	..	..	2	..	..	..
Netherlands	2,264	1,608	656	353	20,936	−2,342	212,866	11
New Zealand	2,149	69	2,080	308	1,333	22	25,749	−2,299
Nicaragua	..	..	..	..	1	..	..	..
Niger (b)	n.a.	n.a.	n.a.	n.a.	121	70	..	..
Nigeria	..	..	..	..	2	..	..	..
North Macedonia	51	43	8	29	45	21	4,903	293
Norway	650	381	269	−257	4,024	112	48,407	2,001
Oman	..	..	..	..	5	..	..	..
Pakistan	234	46	188	33	63	22	2,054	81
Panama	476	4	472	192	22	−9	2,430	940
Papua New Guinea	..	..	..	..	1	..	..	..
Paraguay	..	..	..	..	1	..	..	..
Patent Office of the Cooperation Council for the Arab States of the Gulf	..	..	..	..	n.a.	n.a.	6,646	−1,125
Peru	571	21	550	70	48	−6	3,740	83
Philippines	1,449	50	1,399	447	167	36	26,973	1,258
Poland	3,319	3,244	75	1,011	4,538	929	93,364	−9,167
Portugal	191	179	12	81	836	59	41,927	553
Qatar	83	4	79	79	35	−12	83	−122
Republic of Korea	145,882	110,351	35,531	11,116	158,495	7,308	1,153,320	56,599
Republic of Moldova	69	57	12	25	82	−4	293	4
Romania	376	360	16	9	537	−4	27,264	−211
Russian Federation	23,662	15,012	8,650	−5,126	19,182	−2,129	264,587	−1,602
Saint Kitts and Nevis	..	..	..	..	9	..	..	..
Saint Lucia	..	..	..	..	2	..	..	..
Saint Vincent and the Grenadines	..	..	..	..	2	..	20	1
Samoa	3	0	3	..	33	..	51	..
San Marino	729	7	722	14	32	−2	..	..
Saudi Arabia	1,746	373	1,373	1,041	2,316	−503	6,017	1,842
Senegal (b)	n.a.	n.a.	n.a.	n.a.	119	−239	..	..
Serbia	45	44	1	−20	109	−34	8,198	670
Seychelles	..	..	..	..	24	..	..	..

Name	Total	Resident	Non-resident	Grants by office: Change over previous year	Equivalent grants by origin: Total (a)	Equivalent grants by origin: Change over previous year	In force by office: Total	In force by office: Change over previous year
Singapore	6,488	431	6,057	1,102	4,032	-56	47,801	1,161
Sint Maarten (Dutch Part)	..	..	..	..	2	..	..	..
Slovakia	106	92	14	17	305	66	21,940	28
Slovenia	..	..	..	..	368	..	..	..
South Africa	6,107	565	5,542	2,641	1,312	289	85,431	6,644
Spain	716	648	68	75	5,380	36	225,741	1,286
Sri Lanka	194	66	128	-79	98	29	995	56
Sudan	..	..	..	..	4	..	..	..
Sweden	717	575	142	-817	18,391	-464	112,035	246
Switzerland	724	510	214	-21	26,736	-1,404	264,909	14,766
Syrian Arab Republic	..	..	..	..	1	..	125	60
Tajikistan	..	..	..	..	56	..	..	..
Thailand	2,994	182	2,812	-531	625	57	18,817	1,511
Togo (b)	n.a.	n.a.	n.a.	n.a.	85	0	..	..
Trinidad and Tobago	40	0	40	-27	3	-19	1,075	..
Tunisia	..	..	..	..	14	..	..	..
Türkiye	3,387	3,125	262	1,324	4,148	904	82,425	-6,328
Ukraine	2,298	990	1,308	119	1,239	-92	18,478	-2,712
United Arab Emirates	655	3	652	149	375	80	2,705	289
United Kingdom	10,895	4,894	6,001	1,123	29,045	-133	690,131	7,886
United Republic of Tanzania	13	..	..	6	6	5	..	..
United States of America	327,307	149,538	177,769	-24,686	298,570	-7,954	3,327,540	-20,991
Uruguay	..	..	..	..	41	..	..	..
Uzbekistan	298	203	95	20	233	52	1,217	58
Venezuela (Bolivarian Republic of)	..	..	..	..	9	..	212	..
Viet Nam	3,691	153	3,538	-628	227	33	14,444	1,819
Yemen	4	1	3	-15	1	-5	..	..
Zimbabwe	10	..	..	4	2	-3	4	0
Others/Unknown	..	..	..	..	22,824	-436	..	..
Total (2021 estimates)	**1,756,500**	**1,139,200**	**617,300**				**16,545,000**	

(a) Equivalent grants by origin data are incomplete, because some offices do not report by origin.
(b) The African Intellectual Property Organization (OAPI) acts as the national office for patent grants.

.. indicates not available.

n.a. indicates not applicable.

Source: WIPO Statistics Database, September 2022.

A55. Patent office procedural data, 2021

Office	Total applications processed	Granted	Rejected	Withdrawn or abandoned	Number of examiners (FTE)	First office action (months)	Final office decision (months)
African Intellectual Property Organization	..	..	..	..	5.0	..	..
Albania	4	2	1	1	3.0	..	..
Algeria	..	285	330	..	3.0	..	12.0
Argentina	7,321	2,361	334	4,626	61.0	33.0	46.8
Armenia	..	21	..	19	6.0	1.5	4.1
Australia	22,801	17,153	22	5,626	415.1	8.3	16.1
Azerbaijan	129	85	1	43	11.0	4.0	12.0
Bahrain	73	65	1	7	5.0	4.0	12.0
Bangladesh	..	240	..	189	6.0	10.0	18.0
Belarus	382	309	72	1	10.0	11.0	..
Bhutan	..	..	..	..	2.0	24.0	60.0
Bosnia and Herzegovina	..	4	4	..	5.0	2.0	30.0
Botswana	..	..	..	..	..	1.0	24.0
Brazil	48,085	26,872	4,883	16,330	304.0	45.0	60.0
Brunei Darussalam	..	67	..	6	..	5.0	39.0
Cabo Verde	..	..	..	..	1.0	..	..
Canada	..	22,685	..	12,627	380.0	11.6	26.2

Office	Total applications processed	Granted	Rejected	Withdrawn or abandoned	Number of examiners (FTE)	First office action (months)	Final office decision (months)
Chile	4,535	2,765	700	1,070	123.0	..	..
China	1,287,953	695,946	443,071	148,936	..	12.5	18.5
China, Hong Kong SAR	..	7	..	41	5.8	8.6	10.7
China, Macao SAR	..	15	26	..	..	4.7	10.8
Colombia	1,910	1,263	503	144	46.0	14.9	22.4
Costa Rica	..	130	651	..	..	..	..
Croatia	..	7	9	..	6.0	19.0	33.0
Cuba	180	81	7	92	10.0	2.0	42.5
Czech Republic	825	444	151	230	32.0	..	..
Denmark	1,301	368	4	929	57.2	5.5	20.0
Dominica	..	..	..	..	1.0	..	..
Dominican Republic	..	227	193	..	..	..	..
Ecuador	..	..	..	..	5.0	24.0	60.0
Egypt	1,925	509	441	975	100.0	18.0	..
El Salvador	..	..	..	..	4.0	20.0	20.0
Estonia	20	10	2	8	10.0	0.2	37.0
European Patent Office	..	108,799	..	..	4,025.5	14.1	23.0
Finland	1,397	545	6	846	113.0	6.1	26.4
France	18,358	15,169	2,416	773	118.0	..	..
Georgia	215	128	13	74	18.0	15.0	21.0
Germany	48,494	21,113	10,324	17,057	794.7	..	..
Guatemala	215	38	18	159	4.0	6.0	48.0
Guyana	..	21	..	..	1.0	1.0	2.0
Honduras	..	92	45	..	..	..	..
Hungary	500	107	23	370	38.0	4.1	21.6
Iceland	..	..	..	15	..	0.3	4.0
India	42,525	30,721	5,720	6,084	600.0	6.0	50.0
Israel	7,547	5,490	30	2,027	123.0	27.0	42.8
Italy	9,948	7,254	2,092	602	20.0	..	24.0
Japan	233,333	172,996	56,552	3,785	1,665.0	10.1	15.3
Jordan	..	166	600	..	4.0	12.0	24.0
Kazakhstan	222	198	10	14	3.0	7.0	7.0
Kyrgyzstan	..	..	..	..	7.0	4.0	18.0
Latvia	97	76	11	10	5.0	..	..
Lithuania	90	76	8	6	4.0	0.4	3.0
Madagascar	62	48	6	8	3.0	3.0	3.0
Mauritius	..	..	..	..	1.0	..	..
Mexico	18,041	10,662	101	7,278	120.0	40.3	42.4
Monaco	..	9	..	..	1.5	6.0	8.0
Mongolia	229	186	37	6	6.0	7.0	7.0
Morocco	882	705	153	24	15.0	4.5	26.0
Mozambique	..	..	..	..	2.0	..	..
Netherlands	2,914	2,264	351	299	26.0	6.0	9.0
New Zealand	..	2,149	..	2,269	67.0	13.7	19.9
North Macedonia	1,273	1,242	29	2	4.0	12.0	18.0
Norway	1,655	650	4	1,001	79.0	6.6	20.0
Pakistan	..	234	..	133	7.0	18.0	36.0
Panama	..	476	..	..	6.0	12.0	24.0
Patent Office of the Cooperation Council for the Arab States of the Gulf	..	..	200	5	31.0	12.6	20.7
Peru	..	566	176	..	26.0	35.8	40.3
Philippines	1,818	1,311	10	497	104.0	..	36.8
Poland	4,663	2,974	1,021	668	..	..	..
Portugal	356	183	155	18	12.0	..	43.5
Qatar	..	83	..	52	10.0	12.0	18.0
Republic of Korea	184,710	134,338	46,074	4,298	953.0	12.1	15.9
Republic of Moldova	107	49	20	38	10.0	3.0	14.0
Romania	1,026	376	329	321	39.0	32.0	50.0
Russian Federation	30,100	22,962	1,926	5,212	402.0	3.6	3.6
Saint Vincent and the Grenadines	..	..	..	..	2.0	0.2	6.0

Office	Total applications processed	Granted	Rejected	Withdrawn or abandoned	Number of examiners (FTE)	First office action (months)	Final office decision (months)
Saudi Arabia	3,781	2,080	883	818	66.0	5.2	11.7
Serbia	171	45	53	73	12.0	12.0	18.0
Singapore	..	..	..	..	100.0	..	..
Slovakia	260	106	67	87	24.0	32.3	37.4
Spain	2,833	2,241	298	294	131.0	0.6	5.8
Sri Lanka	995	194	790	11	8.0	41.2	48.2
Sweden	1,948	717	13	1,218	105.0	7.6	24.9
Switzerland	842	724	110	8	15.0	2.5	12.0
Thailand	5,076	2,994	30	2,052	104.0	37.2	37.9
Trinidad and Tobago	..	..	..	..	6.0	..	..
Türkiye	10,367	3,387	1,410	5,570	189.0	4.0	34.0
Ukraine	3,481	2,319	127	1,035	104.0	15.8	19.1
United Arab Emirates	..	655	..	1	24.0	39.9	..
United Kingdom	..	10,895	15,069	..	357.0	19.0	39.0
United States of America	777,667	327,320	351,760	98,587	8,332.0	16.9	21.2
Uzbekistan	623	380	83	160	10.0	2.0	38.0
Venezuela (Bolivarian Republic of)	..	428	..	36	6.0	12.0	12.0
Viet Nam	6,163	3,689	2,348	126	74.0	36.4	50.0
Zimbabwe	..	..	..	..	1.0	..	..

Note: FTE is full time equivalent. Grant data differ slightly from grant data reported elsewhere in this report due to different dates of extraction. Every effort has been made to compile procedural data based on common definitions and concepts, but procedural differences make it extremely difficult to fully harmonize such data. For instance, "rejection" is not recorded as a final decision in Canada, where applicants are informed of the action they must take or questions that they must answer in order for their application to be considered; and if an applicant cannot provide the required information, they are regarded as having abandoned the application. A similar situation exists in Australia.

.. indicates not available.

Source: WIPO Statistics Database, September 2022.

A56. Utility model applications and grants by office and origin, 2021

	Applications by office			Equivalent applications by origin	Grants by office		
Name	Total	Resident	Non-resident	Total (a)	Total	Resident	Non-resident
African Intellectual Property Organization	18	16	2	n.a.	17	17	0
African Regional Intellectual Property Organization	12	7	5	n.a.	9	4	5
Albania	3	2	1	2	1	1	0
Andorra	..	..	..	1	..	..	..
Argentina	170	156	14	175	105	77	28
Armenia	61	60	1	64	46	45	1
Australia	7,844	1,696	6,148	1,807	8,067	1,757	6,310
Austria	..	..	..	267	..	..	..
Azerbaijan	32	25	7	25	27	20	7
Bahrain	..	..	..	1	..	..	..
Bangladesh	..	..	..	1	..	..	..
Barbados	..	..	..	20	..	..	..
Belarus	339	300	39	363	294	259	35
Belgium	..	..	..	92	..	..	..
Belize	..	..	..	1	..	..	..
Bhutan	..	..	..	2	..	..	..
Botswana	6	6	0	7	..	..	..
Brazil	2,578	2,522	56	2,547	701	654	47
Bulgaria	222	212	10	217	196	190	6
Burkina Faso	..	..	..	1	..	..	..
Cabo Verde	1	0	1	..	..	..	..
Cambodia	..	..	..	7	..	..	..
Canada	..	..	..	85	..	..	..
Chile	113	82	31	110	51	34	17
China	2,852,219	2,844,555	7,664	2,850,363	3,119,990	3,111,943	8,047
China, Hong Kong SAR	552	394	158	1,180	684	460	224
China, Macao SAR	31	16	15	85	10	2	8

		Applications by office		Equivalent applications by origin		Grants by office	
Name	Total	Resident	Non-resident	Total (a)	Total	Resident	Non-resident
Colombia	145	131	14	137	123	104	19
Comoros	..	..	..	67	..	..	..
Cook Islands	..	..	..	1	..	..	..
Costa Rica	11	6	5	6	5	3	2
Côte d'Ivoire	..	..	..	1	..	..	..
Croatia	72	0	72	4	78	68	10
Cuba	1	1	0	1	1	0	1
Cyprus	..	..	..	26	..	..	..
Czech Republic	1,104	1,044	60	1,187	951	909	42
Democratic People's Republic of Korea	..	..	..	2	..	..	..
Democratic Republic of the Congo	..	..	..	2	..	..	..
Denmark	118	76	42	144	85	52	33
Dominican Republic	13	7	6	7	10	9	1
Ecuador	27	21	6	26	4	2	2
Egypt	8	7	1	12	8	5	3
Estonia	51	36	15	44	31	24	7
Ethiopia	..	..	..	10	..	..	..
Finland	259	240	19	387	219	204	15
France	673	397	276	849	324	105	219
Georgia	65	63	2	65	41	30	11
Germany	10,576	7,025	3,551	7,919	9,972	6,497	3,475
Ghana	..	..	..	1	..	..	..
Greece	21	13	8	21	24	18	6
Guatemala	5	3	2	3	2	1	1
Honduras	1	0	1	..	2	0	2
Hungary	211	189	22	214	147	137	10
Iceland	..	..	..	3	..	..	..
India	..	..	..	2,371	..	..	..
Indonesia	3,249	3,186	63	3,190	1,385	1,314	71
Iran (Islamic Republic of)	..	..	..	8	..	..	..
Iraq	..	..	..	8	..	..	..
Ireland	112	90	22	132	48	30	18
Israel	..	..	..	93	..	..	..
Italy	2,019	1,829	190	2,286	1,768	1,576	192
Japan	5,238	3,761	1,477	5,884	5,499	3,911	1,588
Jordan	..	..	..	2	..	..	..
Kazakhstan	..	..	..	10	1,122	1,038	84
Kenya	..	..	..	2	..	..	..
Kuwait	..	..	..	5	..	..	..
Kyrgyzstan	17	15	2	16	22	17	5
Lao People's Democratic Republic	..	..	..	4	..	..	..
Latvia	..	..	..	4	..	..	..
Lebanon	..	..	..	1	..	..	..
Liechtenstein	..	..	..	18	..	..	..
Lithuania	..	..	..	5	..	..	..
Luxembourg	..	..	..	29	..	..	..
Malaysia	175	120	55	177	186	128	58
Malta	..	..	..	3	..	..	..
Marshall Islands	..	..	..	4	..	..	..
Mauritius	..	..	..	1	..	..	..
Mexico	706	627	79	642	357	299	58
Monaco	..	..	..	5	..	..	..
Mongolia	173	170	3	171	107	104	3
Morocco	..	..	..	1	..	..	..
Mozambique	8	3	5	3	7	3	4
Netherlands	..	..	..	277	..	..	..
New Zealand	..	..	..	78	..	..	..
Nigeria	..	..	..	2	..	..	..

		Applications by office		Equivalent applications by origin		Grants by office	
Name	Total	Resident	Non-resident	Total (a)	Total	Resident	Non-resident
Norway	..	..	..	30	..	..	..
Oman	..	..	..	18	..	..	..
Pakistan	..	..	..	1	..	..	..
Panama	4	3	1	6	3	0	3
Papua New Guinea	..	..	..	3	..	..	..
Peru	244	211	33	220	265	249	16
Philippines	1,799	1,744	55	1,751	1,053	993	60
Poland	779	722	57	797	571	544	27
Portugal	102	59	43	81	61	33	28
Qatar	..	..	..	1	..	..	..
Republic of Korea	4,009	3,642	367	4,709	1,817	1,618	199
Republic of Moldova	116	115	1	115	109	104	5
Romania	54	50	4	55	39	26	13
Russian Federation	9,079	8,873	206	8,999	6,955	6,733	222
Rwanda	..	..	..	4	..	..	..
Samoa	..	..	..	1	..	..	..
San Marino	..	..	..	3	..	..	..
Saudi Arabia	..	..	..	38	..	..	..
Serbia	114	108	6	109	53	49	4
Seychelles	..	..	..	4	..	..	..
Singapore	..	..	..	227	..	..	..
Slovakia	297	253	44	296	409	355	54
Slovenia	..	..	..	11	..	..	..
South Africa	..	..	..	15	..	..	..
Spain	3,091	2,933	158	3,182	3,320	3,167	153
Sri Lanka	..	..	..	1	..	..	..
Sweden	..	..	..	151	..	..	..
Switzerland	..	..	..	455	..	..	..
Tajikistan	..	..	..	2	..	..	..
Thailand	3,762	3,612	150	3,654	1,869	1,778	91
Trinidad and Tobago	1	1	0	2	..	..	..
Türkiye	4,490	4,418	72	4,473	2,591	2,513	78
Ukraine	4,425	4,333	92	4,432	4,363	4,214	149
United Arab Emirates	5	0	5	25	1	0	1
United Kingdom	..	..	..	247	..	..	..
United States of America	..	..	..	2,244	..	..	..
Uruguay	..	..	..	2	..	..	..
Uzbekistan	401	389	12	391	199	190	9
Viet Nam	466	337	129	344	250	187	63
Yemen	..	..	..	..	3	3	0
Zambia	..	..	..	2	..	..	..
Zimbabwe	..	..	..	8	..	..	..
Others/Unknown	..	..	..	1,433	..	..	..
Total (2021 estimates)	**2,924,490**	**2,902,660**	**21,830**				

(a) Equivalent applications by origin data are incomplete, because some offices do not report by origin.
.. indicates not available.
n.a. indicates not applicable.
Source: WIPO Statistics Database, September 2022.

Trademarks

Highlights

Applications increased by 4% in 2021

An estimated 13.9 million trademark applications were filed worldwide in 2021. This is 541,400 more than filed in 2020 and represents an increase of 4% on the year (figure 2.1). This was the twelfth consecutive year of growth following the end of the global financial crisis in 2009. However, the increase is much lower than the 16.4% recorded in 2020, despite the onset of the COVID-19 pandemic and the ensuing global economic slowdown. Trademark applications in 2021 were four times the number filed in 2007, due in large part to the double-digit increases recorded in seven out of the last 15 years, and despite the small declines seen in both 2008 and 2009.

An estimated 13.9 million trademark applications were filed worldwide in 2021

2.1. Trademark applications worldwide, 2007–2021

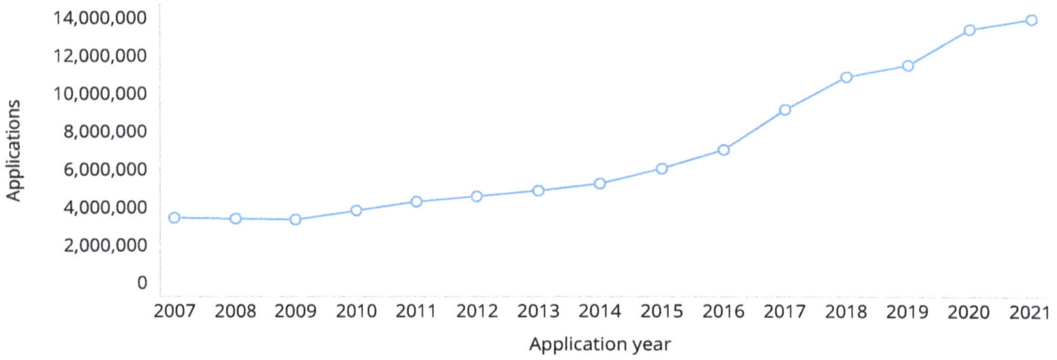

Source: Figure B1.

When differences in filing systems across national and regional offices are harmonized using the application class count, trademark filing in 2021 grew by 5.5% on the previous year. The total number of classes specified in applications – known as the application class count – reached an estimated 18.1 million (figure 2.2).

The total number of classes specified in trademark applications increased by 5.5% from 2020 to 2021

2.2. Trademark application class counts worldwide, 2007–2021

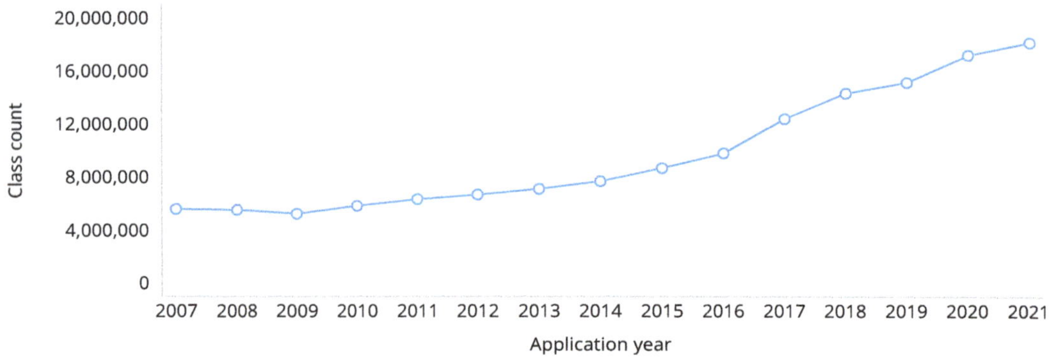

Source: Figure B2.

Class count

A trademark application may refer to different classes of goods or services. Many offices use the Nice Classification, an international classification of goods and services for registering trademarks and service marks. Applications received at these offices are classified according to one or more of the 45 Nice classes (see *www.wipo.int/classifications/nice*). Some offices only allow single-class filing, which means applicants have to file a separate application for each class. Others permit multi-class filings, enabling applicants to file a single application in which a number of classes can be specified. To improve international comparisons of the numbers of applications received, it helps to compare class counts across offices. Class counts are also used to make trademark registration internationally comparable. This method for comparing offices began in 2004, the first year for which complete class count data are available.

Offices with the most trademark filing

As is the case with other forms of intellectual property (IP), the increase in total trademark filing worldwide over time (measured in application class counts) has been largely due to the sheer volume of trademark applications filed in China. For example, in 2021, the IP office of China alone accounted for 11.5% of the annual increase in global trademark filing using this measure. However, the IP office of the United Kingdom (UK) had an exceptionally high share in 2021, accounting for 18.1% of the overall annual increase. These two offices were followed by those of Brazil (10.1%), Türkiye (7.4%), India (6.7%) and the European Union Intellectual Property Office (EUIPO) (6.2%), each constituting a considerable portion of the total increase. For comparison, the office of the United States of America (US) accounted for 3.1% of the annual increase.

China's class count of about 9.5 million was followed by a count of 899,678 at the office of the US (figure 2.3). These have been the top two offices since the early 2000s; however, China's class count has grown during that time from just under twice that of the US in 2007 to almost 11 times as much by 2021. This is mainly due to the high number of trademark applications filed domestically by residents in China. These two top-ranked offices were followed by the EUIPO (497,542), the office of India (488,526) and the office of the UK (450,815). About 65% of worldwide trademark filing was concentrated at these five offices, up from almost 42% held by the top five offices a decade earlier in 2011, comprising China, France, the Russian Federation and the US, as well as the EUIPO.

Of the top 20 offices, 18 had higher levels of trademark filing in 2021 than in 2020. Ten recorded a high growth rate of between 12% and 32% – and one even surpassed 60%. The largest increases seen were in the UK (+61.8%), Brazil (+32.3%), Mexico (+22.7%) and Canada (+19.5%), followed by Türkiye (+19.4%), Italy (+18.5%) and Australia (+16.4%). The UK's incredibly fast growth in filing was driven mainly by high demand from abroad. Before 2021, foreign trademark holders could extend protection for their marks to the UK via the EUIPO. As the UK is no longer a member of the European Union (EU), holders seeking trademark protection in the UK are now required to file applications either directly at the office of the UK or via the WIPO-administered Madrid System by designating the UK. Unlike the 18 top offices that received more trademark filing in 2021 than the previous year, Japan (–13.5%) and the Russian Federation (–0.6%) saw a decrease over the same period (figure B10).

In 2021, nine of the top 20 offices were in either low- or middle-income countries. Other offices located in selected low- and middle-income countries, namely, Ukraine (71,234), Thailand (68,103), the Philippines (64,946) and Colombia (55,606), saw comparatively high volumes of trademark filing (figure B11). Among 20 selected offices located in countries from both these income groups, annual growth exceeded 20% in the Dominican Republic (+20.5%), Mongolia (+30.2%), Mozambique (+27.7%), Pakistan (+26.5%) and Uzbekistan (+20.9%) (figure B12).

At most offices, trademark applications are filed mainly by residents seeking protection within their domestic jurisdiction. In 2021, residents filing at their home or regional office accounted for 84% of global filing, with the remaining 16% associated with non-resident filings (figure B3). Over the last decade, the growth in domestic filings has generally outpaced that of non-resident filings. In 2021, however, filings by non-residents grew faster than those by residents. This amounted to an annual increase of 21.8% in the world non-resident application class count in 2021. Among the top 20 offices, 15 had a higher annual growth in non-resident as opposed to resident filing. Standing at only 2.9%, the increase in the resident application class count worldwide was much lower in comparison. Contributors to this low rate of increase, the top two offices, China (+0.8%) and the US (+0.4%), saw almost zero growth in resident filing from 2020 to 2021.

Due primarily to the large volume of resident trademark applications filed in China, non-resident filing as a proportion of the global total has shrunk by about 16 percentage points, from 31.9% in 2007 down to the 16% for 2021 previously mentioned. However, when China is excluded from the overall count, the non-resident share is seen to have fallen by only four percentage points over this period.

Recording filings in excess of the global non-resident share, six of the top 20 offices received a third or more of their total filing from non-residents, with Australia (44.2%), Canada (62.2%), the EUIPO (37.5%), Switzerland (60.2%), the UK (50.4%) and the US (38.7%) reporting the highest shares (figure B9). The lowest non-resident shares were recorded at the offices of China (2.8%), France (5.4%) and Türkiye (9%). The low non-resident shares for France and several other EU member state offices, such as those of Germany (9.6%) and Italy (9.5%), can be explained by the fact that many non-resident applicants file for protection in EU countries via the EUIPO.

Resident filing overwhelmingly drove the 15% or higher annual growth rate in Brazil, India, Italy, Mexico and Türkiye in 2021, whereas non-resident filing accounted for the greater share of the 15% or higher overall growth in Australia, Canada, Switzerland and the UK (figure B10). In Japan and the Russian Federation, the decline in total filing can be attributed wholly to a drop in resident applications. For Germany and Indonesia, an increase in filing by residents was sufficient to offset a drop in filing by non-residents on the previous year and result in a net annual increase.

Non-resident applicants only accounted for between about 3–9% of total trademark filing in China and Türkiye

2.3. Trademark application class counts for the top 10 offices, 2021

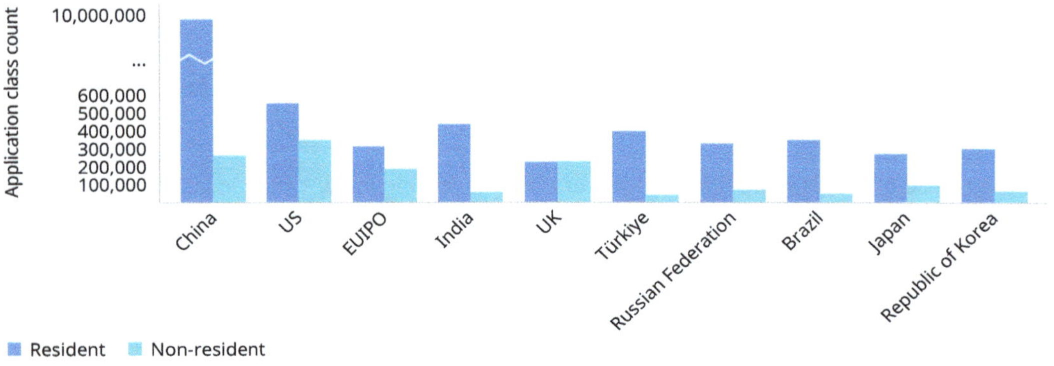

Note: EUIPO is the European Union Intellectual Property Office.
Source: Figure B9.

The list of top 20 offices in 2021 is largely the same as it was in 2020, but with a few notable differences. For the reason given earlier, a big increase in non-resident trademark filing at the office of the UK propelled it up from 12th in the ranking in 2020 to fifth spot in 2021. The office of Türkiye moved up two places in the ranking, from eighth in 2020 to sixth in 2021. Brazil moved from 10th position to eighth in 2021, ahead of Japan and the Republic of Korea. The biggest decline in ranking was for the office of Japan, which dropped down from sixth spot in 2020 to ninth in 2021.

In 2021, 11 of the top 20 offices were in high-income economies. Six were in upper middle-income (Argentina, Brazil, China, Mexico, the Russian Federation and Türkiye) and three in lower middle-income countries (India, Indonesia and Viet Nam).

Offices in Asia accounted for 69.7% of all trademark filing in 2021

2.4. Trademark application class counts by region, 2011 and 2021

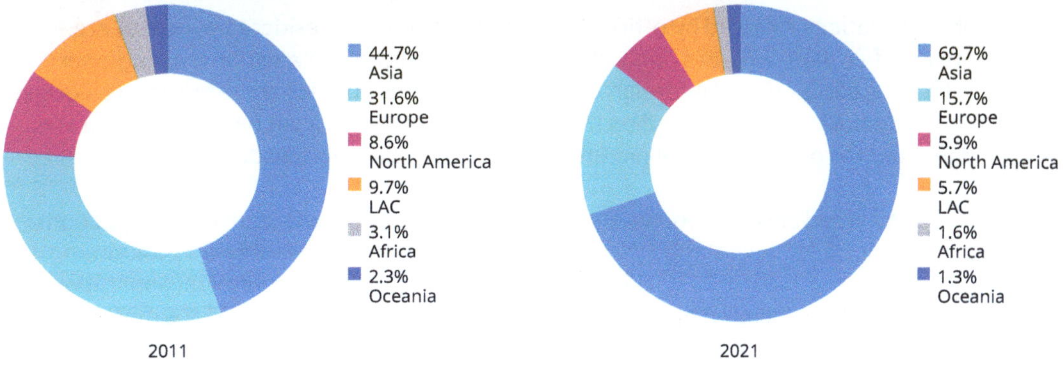

Note: LAC is Latin America and the Caribbean.
Source: Table B7.

Of the top 20 ranking offices in 2021, Asia and Europe each had seven, Latin America and the Caribbean (LAC) three, North America two and Oceania one. Offices in Asia accounted for 69.7% of all trademark filing globally, up from a combined share of 44.7% in 2011. This partly explains the decline in overall shares for the five other geographical regions over the same period (figure 2.4). Offices in Europe accounted for 15.7% of the world total in 2021, followed by North America (5.9%), LAC (5.7%), Africa (1.6%) and Oceania (1.3%).

Trademark applications filed since 1883

Trademark applications remained fairly low and stable up until the mid-1980s. Applications filed at the China office took off in the 1990s, and in 2001 exceeded those received by the US office, making it the largest office in terms of applications received. Even so, applications at the US office have more than tripled since the mid-1990s, despite declines in 2001 and 2002 at the end of the dot-com era and again during the global financial crisis in 2008 and 2009. Having remained below 100,000 until 2006, India's annual trademark applications were almost 465,000 in 2021. At the office of Brazil, applications were about 375,000, while in the Republic of Korea they were approximately 285,000.

Trend in trademark applications for the top five offices, 1883–2021

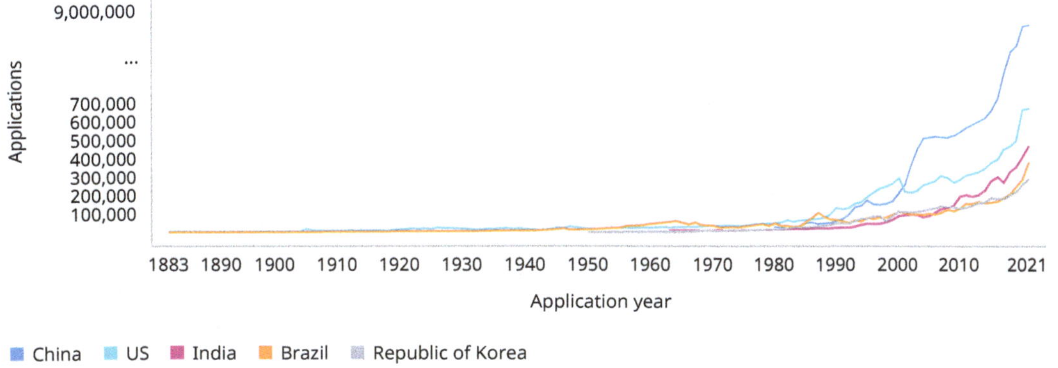

Source: Figure B8.

Equivalent application class count

An application filed at a regional IP office is equivalent to filing an application in every member country of the organization that established that particular regional office. For example, to calculate the number of equivalent applications for the EUIPO, each application is multiplied by the corresponding number of EU member states. So, an application filed with the EUIPO in 2021 by an applicant residing outside the EU is counted as 27 applications abroad – equivalent to the 27 member countries of the EU. An application filed by an applicant residing in an EU country is counted as 1 resident application and 26 applications abroad for 2021. The same multiplier is applied to the classes specified in such an application. The equivalent application class count concept is used for reporting data by origin.

German applicants continue to file the greatest number of applications abroad

Trademark applications received by offices from resident and non-resident applicants are referred to as office data, whereas applications filed by applicants at a national or regional office (resident applications) or at foreign offices (applications abroad) are referred to as origin data. Here, trademark statistics based on the origin where the applicant has residence are reported in order to complement the picture of trademark filing worldwide.

In terms of filing abroad based on equivalent class count, more applicants from Germany sought protection for their trademarks abroad than did applicants from any other origin, a position Germany has held since 2006. In 2021, German filing abroad recorded an equivalent application class count of 2.6 million, followed by applicants from China (2 million) and the US (1.6 million). These top three countries of origin were followed by Italy (1.1 million), which surpassed the UK (974,206) to become the fourth most active origin in terms of filing abroad (figure B19).[1] The high equivalent class counts for applications abroad from these origins can be explained not only by the high application class counts at numerous offices abroad, but also by the frequent use of the EUIPO – with its multiplier effect – to seek protection within the EU as a whole.

Looking at absolute counts – thereby removing the EUIPO's multiplier effect – 94.8% of all filing (application class counts) undertaken by China-based applicants in 2021 was in China alone, with only 5.2% attributable to seeking protection abroad. In fact, every year for the last two decades, at least 93% of all filing made by China-based applicants has been domestic. Similarly, applicants residing in many of the middle-income countries with high trademark filing volumes, such as Argentina, Brazil, India, Indonesia, Mexico, the Russian Federation, Türkiye and Viet Nam, directed less than 13% of trademark filing toward seeking protection abroad. With regard to applicants based in Brazil, only 2% of their total filing was directed abroad.

Among the top 20 origins, 74.7% of filing by Switzerland-based applicants occurred outside the country, the highest share of application class counts abroad as a proportion of total filing globally. Switzerland was followed by top origins the UK (49.6%), the US (46.4%), Canada (44.1%) and the Netherlands (42.2%).

Between about 10% and 18% of all trademark filing by applicants from the middle-income countries of Colombia (13%), Costa Rica (9.6%), Georgia (17.7%), Kazakhstan (18%) Thailand (14.3%) and Ukraine (14.9%) took place abroad. However, applicants based in Bulgaria (42.9%), Mauritius (46.3%) and Serbia (54.3%) had a far higher proportion of total filing abroad. For the low- and lower middle-income countries of Algeria, Madagascar and Pakistan, the share was no more than about 1–3%.

When deciding where to seek trademark protection, applicants consider such factors as the relative appeal of the various foreign markets for selling their goods and services, geographical proximity to those markets and the existence of well-established historical ties between the trademark holder's country of residence and the destination country. In 2021, over a quarter (25.5%) of all non-resident filing in China came from US applicants, followed by 11.5% from Japan and 9.5% from the UK. Together, applicants from these three countries accounted for 46.5% of all non-resident trademark filing in China for the year (figure 2.5). Applicants from China alone accounted for over half (53.2%) of non-resident trademark filing in the US in 2021. They were followed by the much smaller volumes held by applicants from the UK (6.6%) and Canada (5.9%) for a combined share of almost two-thirds (65.7%) of all filing received by the office of the US from abroad. In India, the three origins contributing the largest shares of total non-resident filing were the US (23.5%), China (9.6%) and Germany (9.3%), together accounting for 42.4% of total non-resident filing in that country. For the EUIPO, 67.8% of its non-resident filing originated from applicants based in just three countries: China (29.6%), the US (23%) and the UK (15.2%).

In addition to being the most active foreign filers in both the US and at the EUIPO, applicants from China were the most active at five other top 20 offices ranked in terms of filing. They accounted for between about 16% and 29% of application class counts in filings received

1 Equivalent application class counts differ from the absolute class counts presented in figure B17, which do not take account of the multiplying effect of regional offices.

from abroad by the offices of Germany, Indonesia, Italy, Japan and Viet Nam. Likewise, US-based applicants were the principal source of non-resident filing at 10 of the top 20 offices, accounting for between 16% of the total at the office of the Russian Federation and 39% at the office of Canada. Germany-based applicants filed the largest volume of non-resident trademarks received by the offices of Switzerland (33.4%) and Türkiye (16.1%). In addition to claiming a large proportion of foreign filing in China, applicants located in Japan were the third largest origin of foreign filing at the offices of regional neighbors Indonesia, the Republic of Korea and Viet Nam.

Applicants from China were the most active foreign filers in the US and at the EUIPO

2.5. Share of total non-resident filing by origin at selected offices, 2021

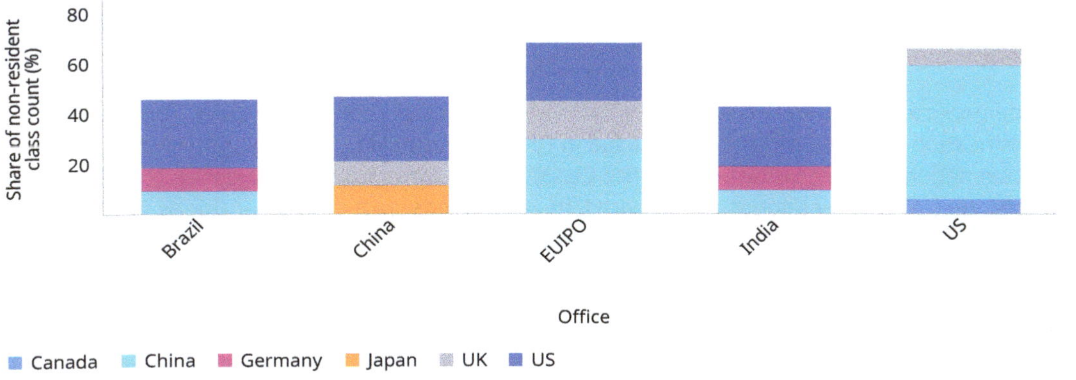

Note: EUIPO is the European Union Intellectual Property Office.
Source: Figure B22.

Adjusting for GDP and population

Variations in trademark filing across countries reflect differences in the size and structure of their economies. It is therefore informative to examine resident application class counts with regard to gross domestic product (GDP) and population size.

When resident trademark applications are viewed as class counts and adjusted according to GDP, countries with a relatively lower number of classes specified in resident applications, such as New Zealand and Viet Nam, may rank above countries like the UK and the US that have higher class counts. Of selected origins, China (36,976), the Republic of Korea (13,125), Brazil (11,087), New Zealand (10,859) and the Russian Federation (8,024) had among the highest ratios of resident application class count to GDP in 2021 (figure 2.6). China (+27,192), Brazil (+7,034), the Republic of Korea (+5,607), the Russian Federation (+3,873) and the UK (+3,390) all saw particularly large increases in the resident application class count per unit of GDP between 2011 and 2021.

Brazil, China, the Republic of Korea, the Russian Federation and the UK all saw a large increase in resident application class count per unit of GDP between 2011 and 2021

2.6. Resident trademark application class count per USD 100 billion GDP for selected origins, 2011 and 2021

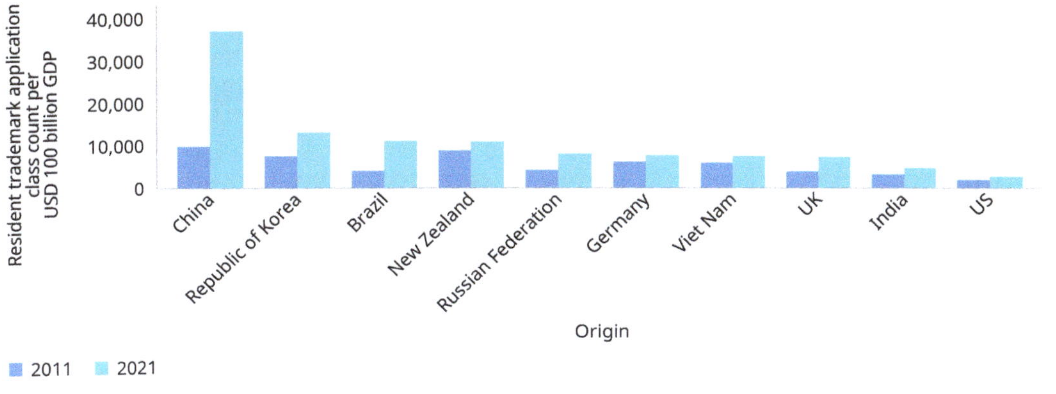

Source: Figure B30.

Data reflecting application class count per million population show that China, with a population of about 1.4 billion, had a resident application class count of 6,509 per million population – one of the most intensive among all countries of origin in 2021. The Republic of Korea, with a population of around 51.7 million, recorded a resident application class count of 5,790 per million population. Switzerland, whose population is far smaller, at approximately 8.7 million in 2021, had a relatively high resident application class count per million population ratio of 5,336. Among other selected origins, this ratio ranged from almost 2,300 to about 4,650 for the following: Australia (3,776), Chile (2,786), Germany (4,064), Italy (2,491), the Russian Federation (2,282), Singapore (2,766), Türkiye (4,647) and the UK (3,319). It was between 1,000 and about 1,750 for Argentina (1,531), Brazil (1,620), Canada (1,737), Mexico (1,090), Ukraine (1,009) and the US (1,662). India, South Africa and Thailand had ratios of between about 315 and 480 (figure B31).

Which classes and industries attracted the most filing from applicants filing abroad?

Trademarks are registered in relation to particular classes of goods or services. The Nice Classification of goods and services is used in the international trademark system and at certain national and regional offices. Nice Classification statistics offer insights into the relative importance of different goods and services. In 2021, goods class 9, which includes scientific, photographic, measuring instruments, recording equipment, computers and software, was represented in 11.0% of all reported non-resident trademark filing by class. Nice class 9 is followed by services class 35 (7.3%), which covers advertising, business management, business administration and office functions, and by services class 42 (6.0%) and goods class 5, which accounted for 5.3% of the total. Services class 42 includes scientific and technological services, design and development of computer hardware and software, and goods class 5 relates to pharmaceutical preparations, baby food, dietary supplements for humans and animals, disinfectants, fungicides and herbicides (figure B23).

The 11 service-related classes accounted for 29.5% of all Nice classes specified in applications filed abroad in 2021, up from 27.2% in 2020 (figure B24). Services classes accounted for between about 29% and 35% of all filing in China, India, Indonesia and the US, and 48% or more at the offices of Argentina, Brazil, France, Mexico and Türkiye, with Brazil (62.9%) recording the highest share among top offices (figure B27).

It is useful to group the 45 Nice classes into 10 industry sectors. Research and technology was the top sector in which applicants sought trademark protection abroad in 2021, accounting for 20% of the global non-resident trademark filing reported. It was followed by the health (13.8%), clothing and accessories (12.8%) and leisure and education (10.5%) sectors. Trademarks relating to household equipment (9.7%), agriculture (9.6%) and business services (9.5%) accounted for the next largest shares of the total. In contrast, industries relating to chemicals (2.8%), construction (5.2%) and transportation (6%) accounted for the smallest shares of filing abroad (figure B25).

Research and technology was the sector to attract the biggest proportion of total filing at the EUIPO (21.3%) and at the offices of Japan (18.7%), the UK (20.4%) and the US (17.7%) (figure B26). Agriculture was the top sector in China (25.2%), the Republic of Korea (18.4%) and the Russian Federation (14.2%), and was the second largest sector in India (15.1%) and Türkiye (14.8%). Filing for marks related to the health sector attracted the largest proportion of applications filed in India (23.1%), the second largest in Japan (13.9%) and the third largest in China (11.3%). Business services topped the list of industry sectors in Brazil (26.3%) and Türkiye (23.3%), accounting for the largest share of total trademark filing. Business services, clothing and accessories, and research and technology all ranked among the top three sectors at six of the top 10 offices. Filing related to leisure and education featured as either the second or third top sector at four offices, namely, Brazil, Japan, the UK and the US.

11 million trademark registrations were recorded worldwide in 2021

After concluding the examination process, an office may decide to register a trademark. The number of registrations issued can fluctuate greatly from year to year, due in part to the varying amount of resources offices are able to dedicate to examining trademark applications. For this reason, it is not possible to accurately compare the number of applications filed at a particular office in any given year with the number of registrations issued by that office in the same year.

The estimated 11 million trademark registrations recorded worldwide in 2021 represents a considerable increase of 28.4%, or 2.4 million more registrations, compared to the previous year (figure B4). This is a reversal of the 7.1% decrease seen in 2020.

Just as class counts make application filing activity internationally comparable, they also permit a more meaningful comparison of registrations. In 2021, an estimated 14 million classes were specified in trademark registrations, 26% more than the previous year's total (figure B5). Like for registrations, this represents a return to strong growth. Registrations measured in class counts at the office of China saw a large increase of almost 2 million from 2020 to 2021, resulting in a growth rate of 34.4% and contributing most to an overall increase in worldwide registration activity. Considerable increases in registration class counts of between about 70,700 and 177,400 at the EUIPO (+70,721) and the offices of France (+82,625), India (+96,452), Türkiye (+73,024), the UK (+177,384) and the US (+90,783) also contributed to the overall growth in trademark registration worldwide.

China's office registered trademarks in which about 7.8 million classes were specified, with that office accounting for over half (55.6%) of all trademark registration recorded in 2021. China was followed by the office of the US (490,998), the EUIPO (455,675), and the offices of the UK (383,041) and India (354,963) (figure B15). Combined, these four offices accounted for 12% of total registration activity.

In addition to China, 13 other top 20 offices in terms of registration activity saw double-digit growth in 2021, which was highest at the offices of the UK (+86.3%), Argentina (+67.7%), India (37.3%) and France (+35%). In contrast, China, Hong Kong SAR (-5.4%) and Indonesia (-19.2%) were the only two top offices to record a decrease on the previous year.

Active trademarks grew by 14.3%

Unlike most forms of IP, trademarks can be maintained indefinitely through the payment of renewal fees at defined time intervals. In 2021, there were an estimated 73.7 million active trademark registrations at 149 IP offices worldwide, representing an increase of 14.3% on 2020 figures (figure B34).

Once again, the office of China had by far the greatest number of trademark registrations in force in 2021, with 37.2 million. It was followed by the offices of the US, with 2.8 million registrations in force, India (2.6 million) and Japan (2.1 million). Each reporting between 1.3 and 1.6 million trademark registrations in force, the EUIPO and the offices of Brazil, France, Mexico, the Republic of Korea and Türkiye also recorded high numbers of active trademarks. The offices of Argentina (956,081) and Germany (984,350) had a comparable number of trademark registrations in force, while Italy (517,611) and Switzerland (534,960) also each had a similar amount (figure B35).

About 18.5 million trademark registrations in force at 74 offices in 2021 can be distributed according to the year in which they were initially registered. This represents about 60% of a total of approximately 31.1 million trademark registrations recorded at these offices between 1997 and 2021.

One-fifth (20%) of those trademarks registered in 1997 remained in force in 2021, a testimony to the enduring value of marks (figure B36). For the trademarks registered in 2012 or later, the percentage rises above 70%. Over half (52.2%) of the 18.5 million registrations in force have a recent registration date, dating back a decade to 2011.

Trademark statistics

Trademark applications and registrations worldwide

B1. Trend in trademark applications worldwide, 2007–2021

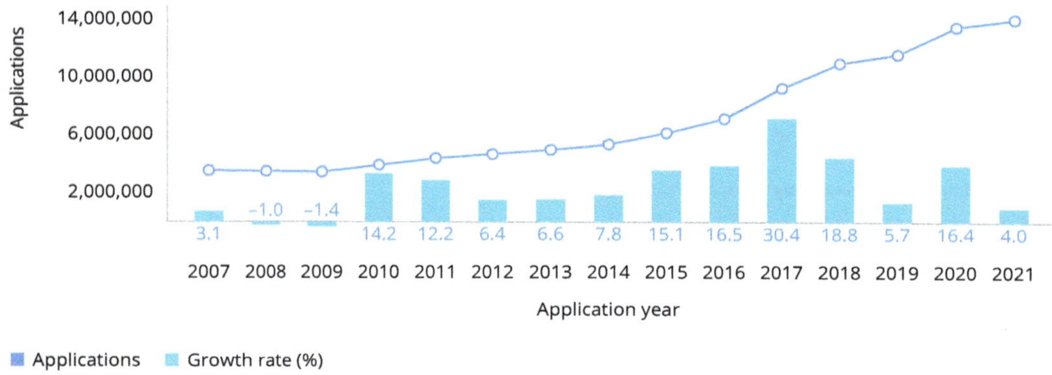

Note: World totals are WIPO estimates using data covering 169 IP offices. Each total includes the number of applications filed directly with national or regional offices (the Paris route), as well as the number of designations received by offices via the Madrid System (where applicable).

Source: WIPO Statistics Database, September 2022.

B2. Trend in trademark application class counts worldwide, 2007–2021

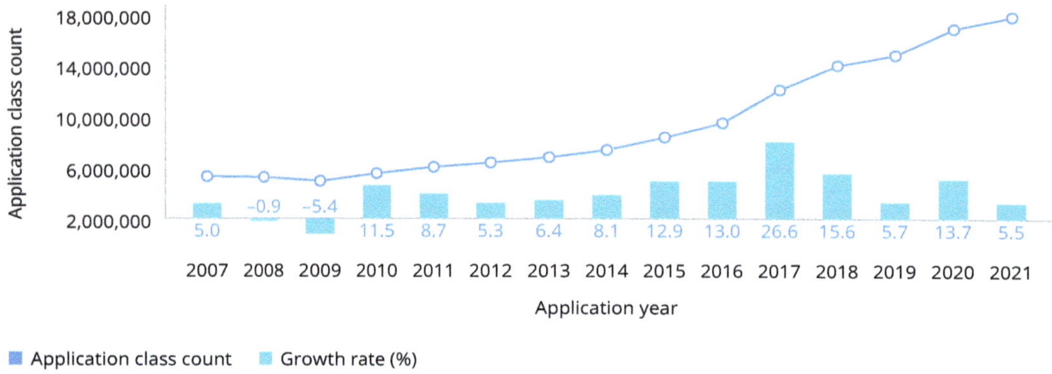

Note: World totals are WIPO estimates using data covering 169 IP offices. These totals include class counts in applications filed directly with national and regional offices (the Paris route), as well as class counts in designations received by offices via the Madrid System (where applicable). See the glossary for the definition of class count.

Source: WIPO Statistics Database, September 2022.

B3. Resident and non-resident trademark application class counts worldwide, 2007–2021

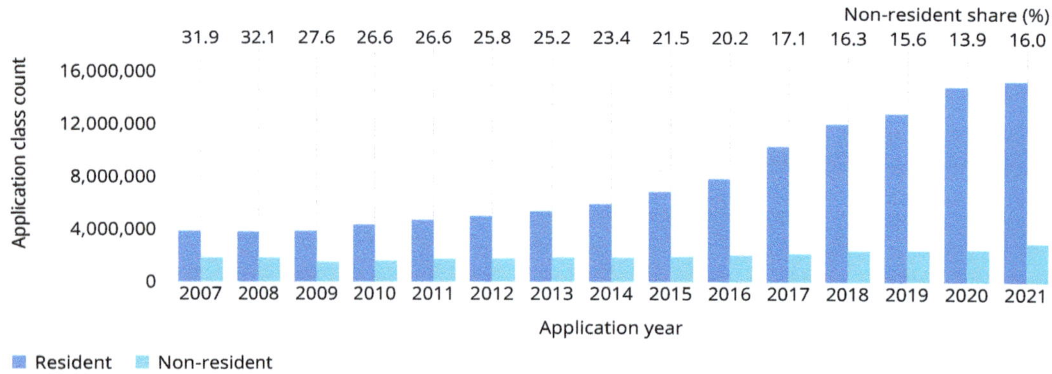

Note: World totals are WIPO estimates using data covering 169 IP offices. These totals include class counts in applications filed directly with national and regional offices (the Paris route), as well as class counts in designations received by offices via the Madrid System (where applicable). See the glossary for definitions of class count, resident and non-resident.

Source: WIPO Statistics Database, September 2022.

B4. Trend in trademark registrations worldwide, 2007–2021

Note: World totals are WIPO estimates using data covering 169 IP offices. Each total includes the number of registrations issued by national and regional offices for applications filed directly with offices (the Paris route), as well as the number of designations received by offices via the Madrid System (where applicable).

Source: WIPO Statistics Database, September 2022.

B5. Trend in trademark registration class counts worldwide, 2007–2021

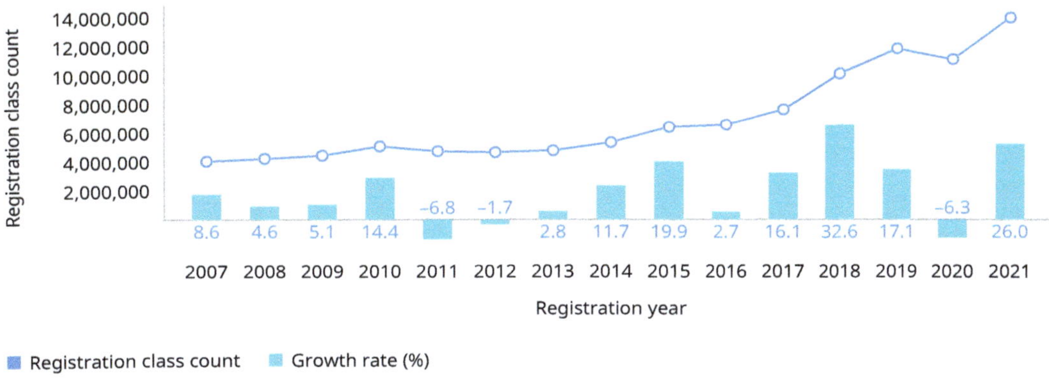

Note: World totals are WIPO estimates using data covering 169 IP offices. These totals include class counts in registrations issued by national and regional offices for applications filed directly with offices (the Paris route), as well as designations received by offices via the Madrid System (where applicable). See the glossary for the definition of class count.

Source: WIPO Statistics Database, September 2022.

B6. Resident and non-resident trademark registration class counts worldwide, 2007–2021

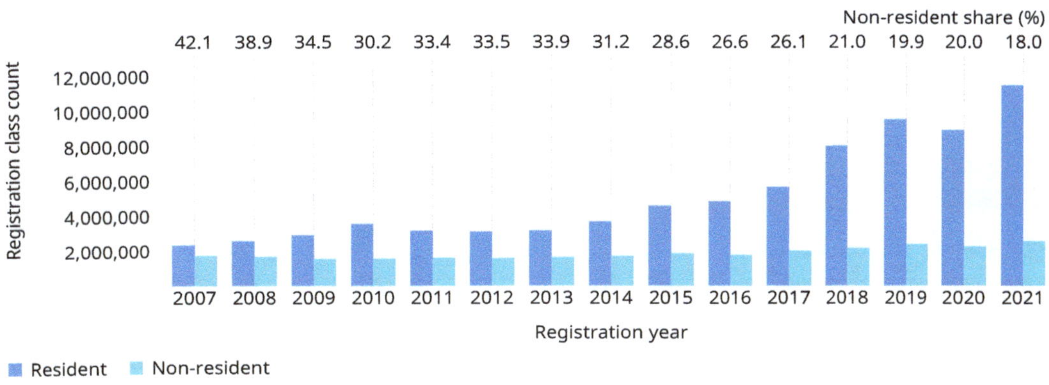

Note: World totals are WIPO estimates using data covering 169 IP offices. These totals include class counts in registrations issued by national and regional offices for applications filed directly with offices (the Paris route), as well as for designations received by offices via the Madrid System (where applicable). See the glossary for definitions of class count, resident and non-resident.

Source: WIPO Statistics Database, September 2022.

Trademark applications and registrations by office

B7. Trademark application class counts by region, 2011 and 2021

Region	Application class count 2011	Application class count 2021	Resident share (%) 2011	Resident share (%) 2021	Share of world total (%) 2011	Share of world total (%) 2021	Average growth (%) 2011–2021
Africa	194,800	292,800	46.4	44.3	3.1	1.6	4.2
Asia	2,825,600	12,648,000	78.9	91.7	44.7	69.7	16.2
Europe	1,999,000	2,850,300	72.2	70.1	31.6	15.7	3.6
Latin America and the Caribbean	611,800	1,034,000	64.9	74.1	9.7	5.7	5.4
North America	544,700	1,075,700	72.1	57.5	8.6	5.9	7.0
Oceania	144,600	244,300	58.0	49.7	2.3	1.3	5.4
World	**6,320,500**	**18,145,100**	**73.4**	**84.0**	**100.0**	**100.0**	**11.1**

Note: Totals by geographical region are WIPO estimates using data covering 169 IP offices. Each region includes the following number of offices: Africa (34), Asia (47), Europe (43), Latin America and the Caribbean (37), North America (2) and Oceania (6).

Source: WIPO Statistics Database, September 2022.

B8. Trend in trademark applications for the top five offices, 1883–2021

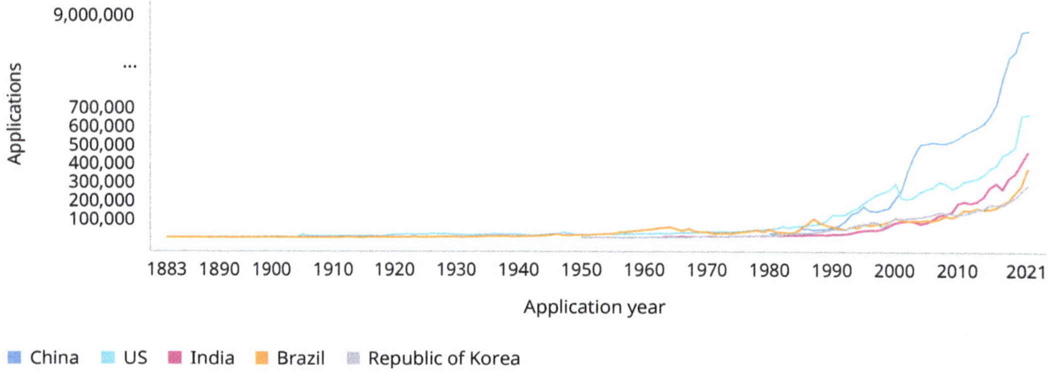

Note: Data are based on the numbers of applications filed; that is, differences between single-class and multi-class filing systems across IP offices are not taken into account. The top five offices were selected based on 2021 application totals.

Source: WIPO Statistics Database, September 2022.

B9. Trademark application class counts for the top 20 offices, 2021

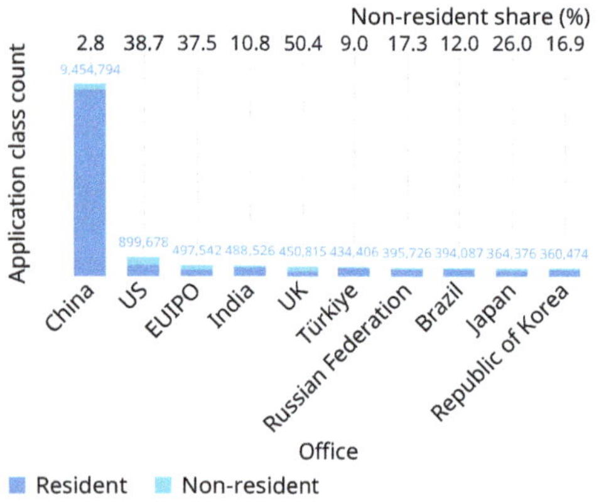

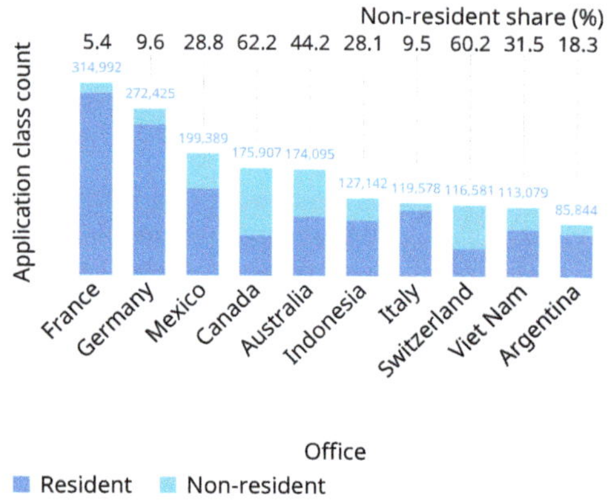

Note: EUIPO is the European Union Intellectual Property Office.

Source: WIPO Statistics Database, September 2022.

B10. **Contribution of resident and non-resident application class counts to total growth for the top 20 offices, 2020–2021**

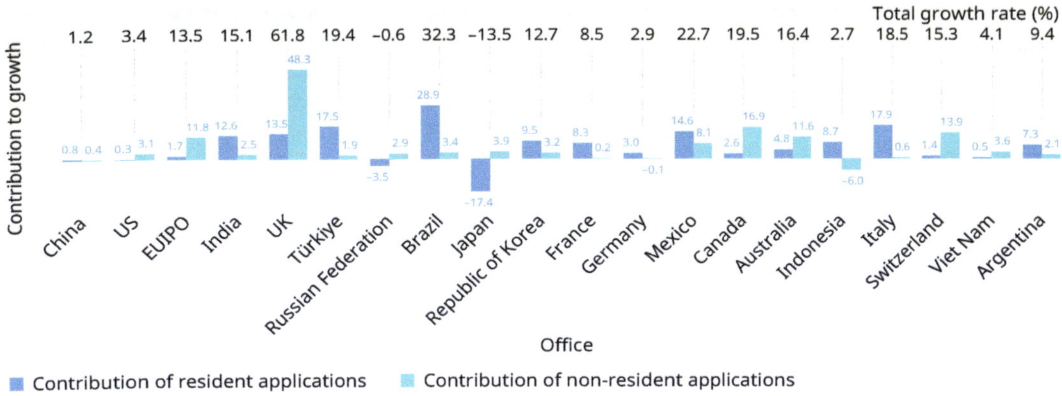

Note: EUIPO is the European Union Intellectual Property Office. This figure shows the total growth or decrease in application class counts for each office, broken down by the respective contributions made by resident and non-resident filing activity.

Source: WIPO Statistics Database, September 2022.

B11. **Trademark application class counts for offices of selected low- and middle-income countries, 2021**

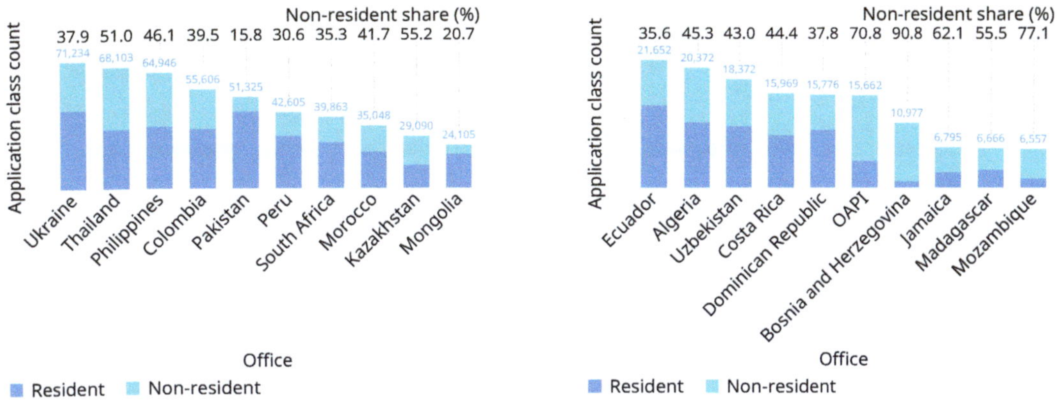

Note: The selected offices are from different world regions and income groups (low-income, lower middle-income and upper middle-income). OAPI is the African Intellectual Property Organization, which receives applications on behalf of its 17 member states. Where available, data for all offices are presented in statistical table B44 toward the end of this section.

Source: WIPO Statistics Database, September 2022.

B12. **Contribution of resident and non-resident application class counts to total growth for offices of selected low- and middle-income countries, 2020–2021**

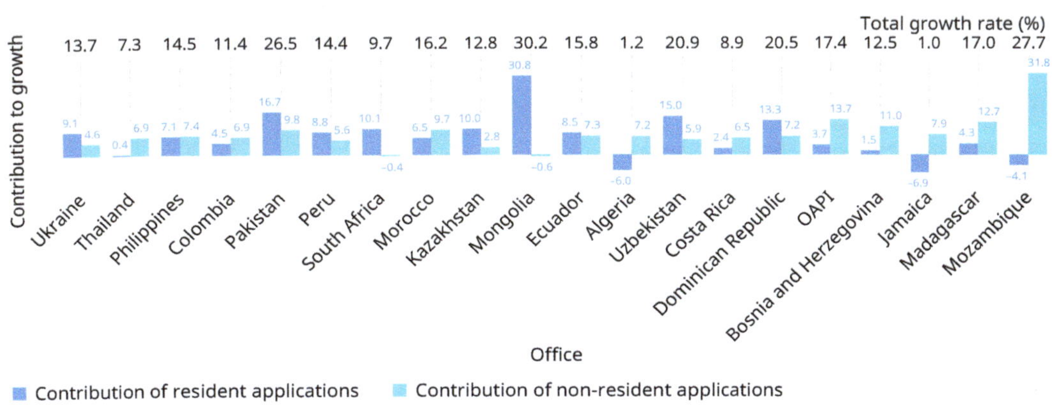

Note: The selected offices are from different world regions and income groups (low-income, lower middle-income and upper middle-income). OAPI is the African Intellectual Property Organization, which receives applications on behalf of its 17 member states. Where available, data for all offices are presented in statistical table B44 toward the end of this section. This figure shows the total growth or decrease in application class counts for each office, broken down by the respective contributions of resident and non-resident applications.

Source: WIPO Statistics Database, September 2022.

B13. Trademark registration class counts by region, 2011 and 2021

Region	Registration class count 2011	Registration class count 2021	Resident share (%) 2011	Resident share (%) 2021	Share of world total (%) 2011	Share of world total (%) 2021	Average growth (%) 2011–2021
Africa	160,200	196,900	34.3	39.4	3.4	1.4	2.1
Asia	2,029,700	9,900,300	71.9	90.4	43.0	70.8	17.2
Europe	1,687,800	2,385,300	66.9	68.5	35.7	17.1	3.5
Latin America and the Caribbean	400,800	676,400	59.1	66.2	8.5	4.8	5.4
North America	350,900	613,200	61.9	41.9	7.4	4.4	5.7
Oceania	93,600	202,100	51.4	46.5	2.0	1.4	8.0
World	**4,723,000**	**13,974,200**	**66.6**	**82.0**	**100.0**	**100.0**	**11.5**

Note: Totals by geographical region are WIPO estimates based on data covering 169 offices. Each region includes the following number of offices: Africa (34), Asia (47), Europe (43), Latin America and the Caribbean (37), North America (2) and Oceania (6).

Source: WIPO Statistics Database, September 2022.

B14. Trend in trademark registrations for the top five offices, 1883–2021

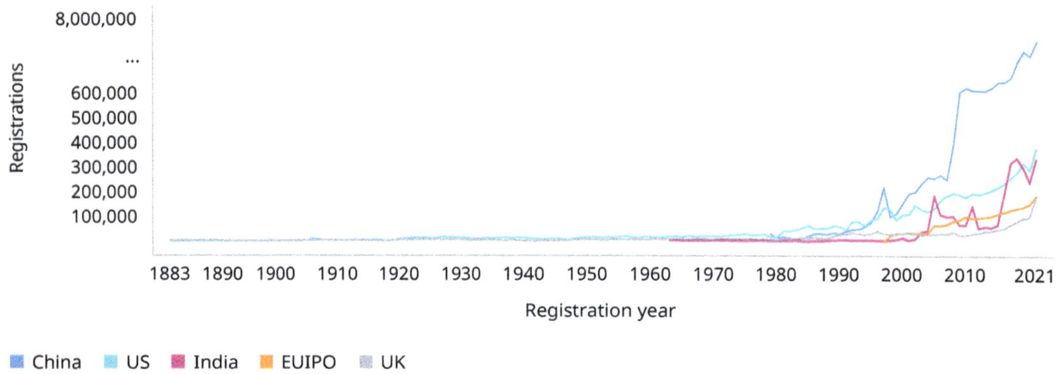

Note: EUIPO is the European Union Intellectual Property Office. Data are based on the numbers of registrations recorded; that is, differences between single-class and multi-class registration systems across IP offices are not taken into account. The top five offices were selected based on 2021 registration totals.

Source: WIPO Statistics Database, September 2022.

B15. Trademark registration class counts for the top 20 offices, 2021

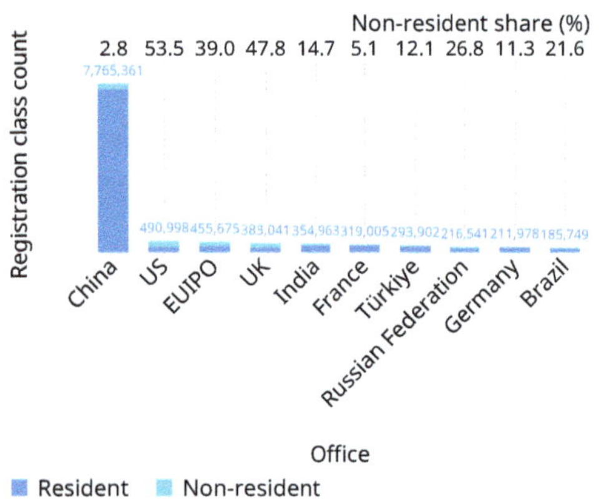

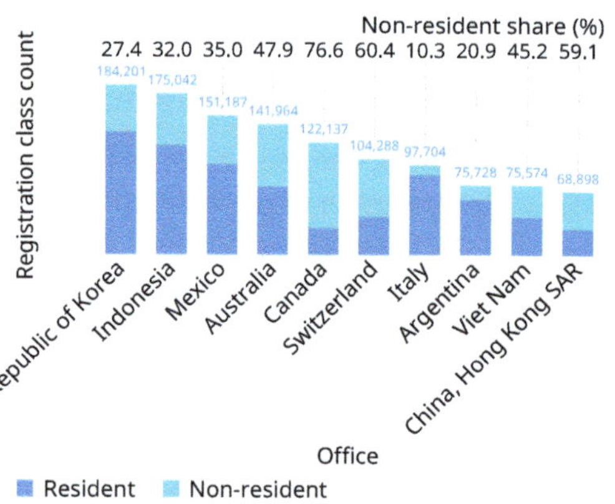

Note: EUIPO is the European Union Intellectual Property Office. On the basis of an examination, a registration may be issued for a trademark application. The number of registrations issued may fluctuate greatly from one year to the next, in part reflecting the amount of resources that IP offices dedicate to examining trademark applications.

Source: WIPO Statistics Database, September 2022.

B16. Trademark registration class counts for offices of selected low- and middle-income countries, 2021

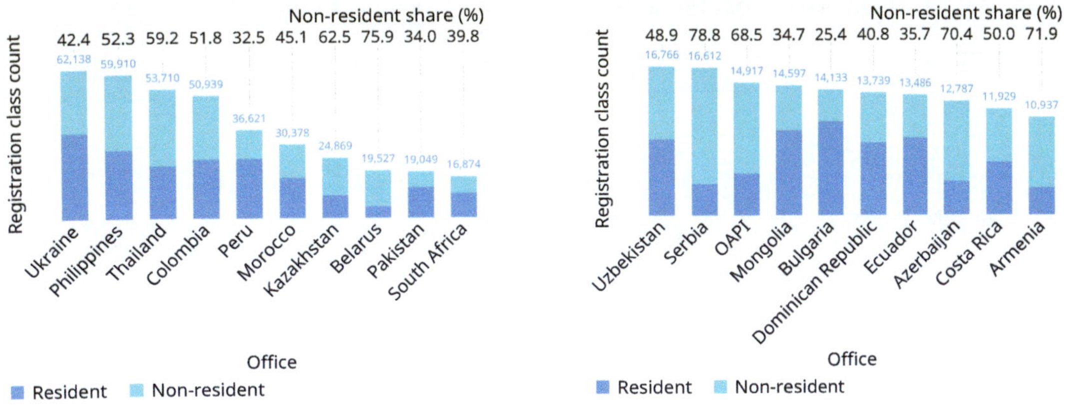

Note: The offices selected are from different world regions and income groups (low-income, lower middle-income and upper middle-income). OAPI is the African Intellectual Property Organization, which receives applications on behalf of its 17 member states. Where available, data for every office is presented in statistical table B45 toward the end of this section.

Source: WIPO Statistics Database, September 2022.

Trademark applications by origin

B17. Trademark application class counts for the top 20 origins, 2021

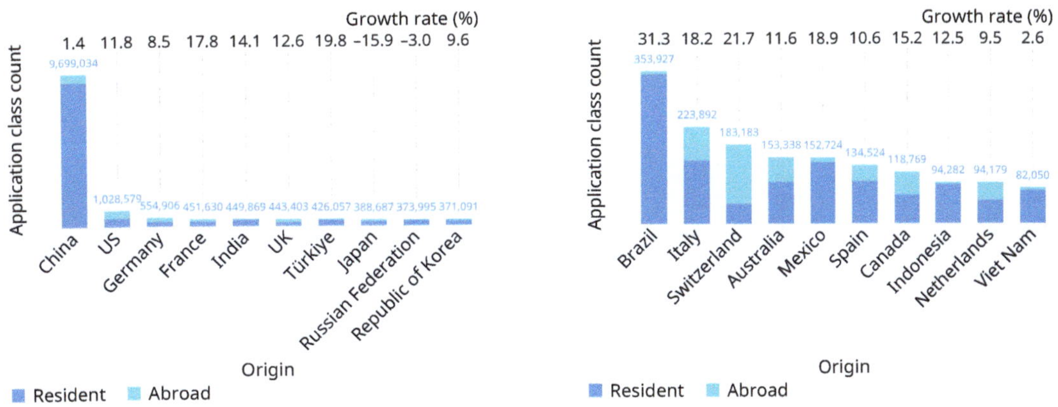

Note: In this figure, trademark application filing activity by origin includes the number of classes specified in resident applications and in applications filed abroad and is based on an absolute not equivalent count. The origin of a trademark application is determined by the residence of the applicant. An application filed at a regional office is considered a resident filing, if the applicant is a resident of one of the relevant member states.

Source: WIPO Statistics Database, September 2022.

B18. Trademark application class counts for selected low- and middle-income origins, 2021

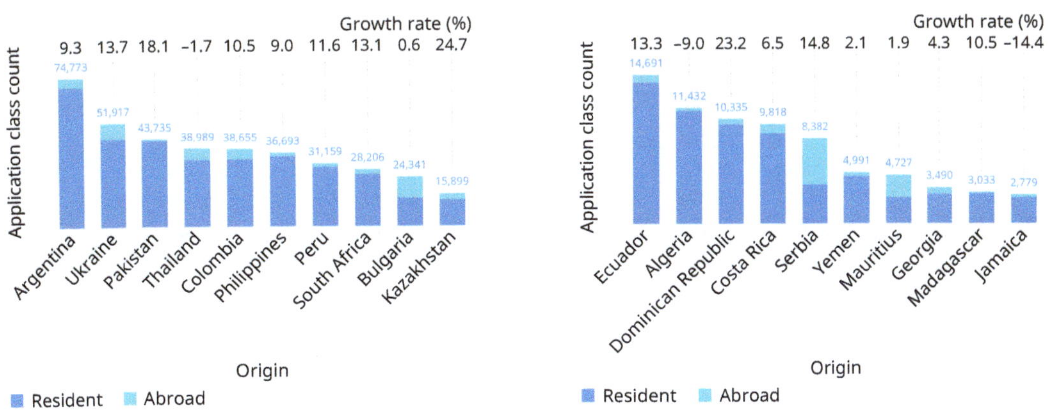

Note: In this figure, trademark application filing activity by origin includes the number of classes specified in resident applications and in applications filed abroad and is based on an absolute not equivalent count. The origin of a trademark application is determined by the residence of the applicant. The origins selected are from different world regions and income groups (low-income, lower middle-income and upper middle-income). Where available, data for all origins are presented in statistical table B44 toward the end of this section.

Source: WIPO Statistics Database, September 2022.

B19. Trademark application class counts abroad for the top 20 origins, 2021

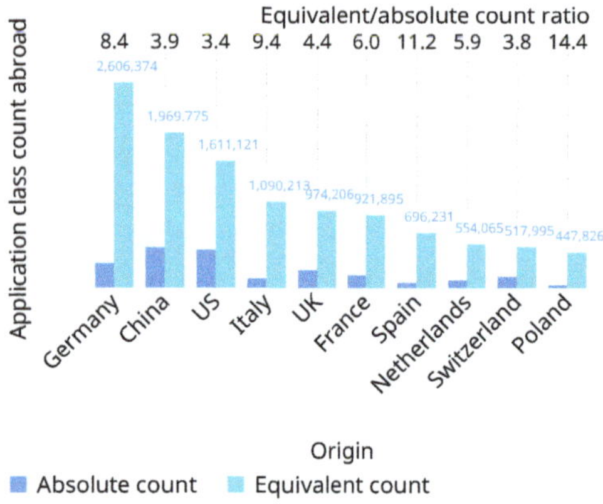

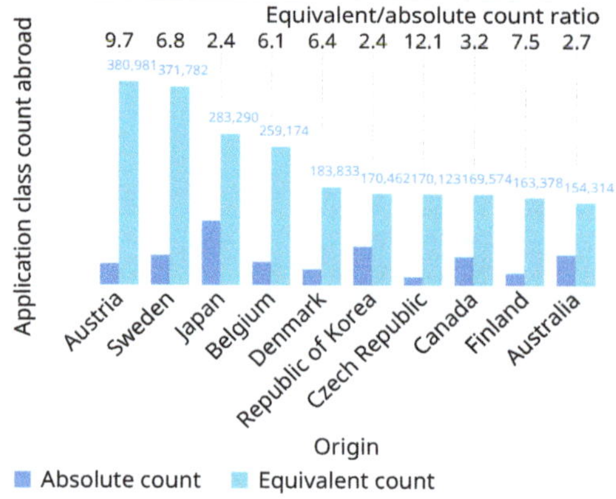

Note: This figure distinguishes between absolute and equivalent counts for filing activity abroad; that is, resident applications are excluded.

Source: WIPO Statistics Database, September 2022.

B20. Trademark application class counts for the top 20 offices and origins, 2021

	Office									
Origin	**Argentina**	**Australia**	**Brazil**	**Canada**	**China**	**EUIPO**	**France**	**Germany**	**India**	**Indonesia**
Australia	111	97,204	669	2,840	7,345	3,685	174	238	1,160	992
Brazil	453	69	346,748	166	528	611	39	32	45	67
Canada	166	2,109	686	66,435	4,897	4,458	235	267	817	260
China	1,402	7,740	4,420	13,853	9,192,749	55,119	2,186	7,589	5,097	6,222
France	860	2,424	2,409	4,761	10,918	29,616	298,103	1,158	2,086	1,179
Germany	1,033	5,763	4,285	6,792	17,549	91,555	1,017	246,291	4,925	1,908
India	56	491	255	561	741	840	59	58	435,580	279
Indonesia		73	8	21	742	82	9	19	104	91,362
Italy	545	1,746	2,071	2,457	8,379	38,864	419	349	1,692	743
Japan	479	2,664	1,510	2,963	30,194	6,163	417	361	2,683	3,485
Mexico	425	84	320	314	469	483	14	18	109	43
Netherlands	314	1,183	829	1,546	3,979	16,795	355	799	851	637
Republic of Korea	223	1,349	853	1,569	18,214	3,727	256	262	799	2,085
Russian Federation	22	235	453	496	2,403	1,647	576	798	565	287
Spain	741	722	1,176	1,029	2,965	25,261	400	179	607	220
Switzerland	898	3,144	2,853	3,335	8,656	14,285	2,354	3,537	3,047	1,763
Türkiye	39	334	296	558	1,039	2,827	440	822	380	225
UK	592	8,326	3,160	7,683	24,964	28,332	1,291	1,652	4,542	2,326
US	4,809	22,297	12,777	42,997	66,782	42,907	1,862	2,271	12,437	4,959
Viet Nam		106	14	97	337	146	42	47	81	113
Others	72,676	16,032	8,295	15,434	50,944	130,139	4,744	5,678	10,919	7,987
Total	**85,844**	**174,095**	**394,087**	**175,907**	**9,454,794**	**497,542**	**314,992**	**272,425**	**488,526**	**127,142**

	Office									
Origin	**Italy**	**Japan**	**Mexico**	**Republic of Korea**	**Russian Federation**	**Switzerland**	**Türkiye**	**UK**	**US**	**Viet Nam**
Australia	141	1,637	526	1,140	612	406	230	5,556	8,051	800
Brazil	26	126	433	69	48	35	28	341	994	20
Canada	59	1,238	1,254	906	588	562	279	4,563	20,554	332
China	1,758	25,190	5,653	10,719	6,493	3,153	3,425	40,927	185,096	6,406
France	1,147	3,768	2,168	2,813	3,780	7,381	1,938	13,817	7,898	1,296
Germany	901	6,445	3,599	4,751	7,914	23,406	6,302	28,093	15,976	2,012
India	76	322	241	157	343	129	199	1,046	1,702	353
Indonesia	4	78	6	66	14	6	12	44	111	158
Italy	108,257	2,505	1,414	1,848	3,341	3,163	1,771	9,909	6,112	833
Japan	257	269,515	1,619	5,659	1,822	1,313	1,009	5,914	8,353	3,246
Mexico	20	86	142,012	46	114	57	33	213	2,856	36
Netherlands	188	1,128	816	769	1,108	1,735	842	6,214	3,439	323
Republic of Korea	92	5,864	965	299,621	1,421	362	674	2,572	8,355	3,044
Russian Federation	539	480	267	489	327,407	549	1,014	1,143	1,462	502

	Office									
Origin	**Italy**	**Japan**	**Mexico**	**Republic of Korea**	**Russian Federation**	**Switzerland**	**Türkiye**	**UK**	**US**	**Viet Nam**
Spain	209	768	1,955	633	965	701	522	5,224	3,108	259
Switzerland	1,347	3,999	2,985	2,950	4,161	46,410	2,672	9,629	7,298	1,562
Türkiye	373	337	263	252	1,326	405	395,159	2,302	1,881	151
UK	964	5,349	2,985	3,920	4,007	4,467	2,834	223,471	23,063	1,865
US	1,075	20,283	21,539	14,019	10,945	7,918	6,297	45,022	551,748	4,865
Viet Nam	21	152	21	149	93	14	56	164	979	77,404
Others	2,124	15,106	8,668	9,498	19,224	14,409	9,110	44,651	40,642	7,612
Total	**119,578**	**364,376**	**199,389**	**360,474**	**395,726**	**116,581**	**434,406**	**450,815**	**899,678**	**113,079**

Note: EUIPO is the European Union Intellectual Property Office. The office and origin data shown consist of absolute rather than equivalent application class counts.

Source: WIPO Statistics Database, September 2022.

B21. Flows of non-resident trademark application class counts between selected top origins and offices, 2021

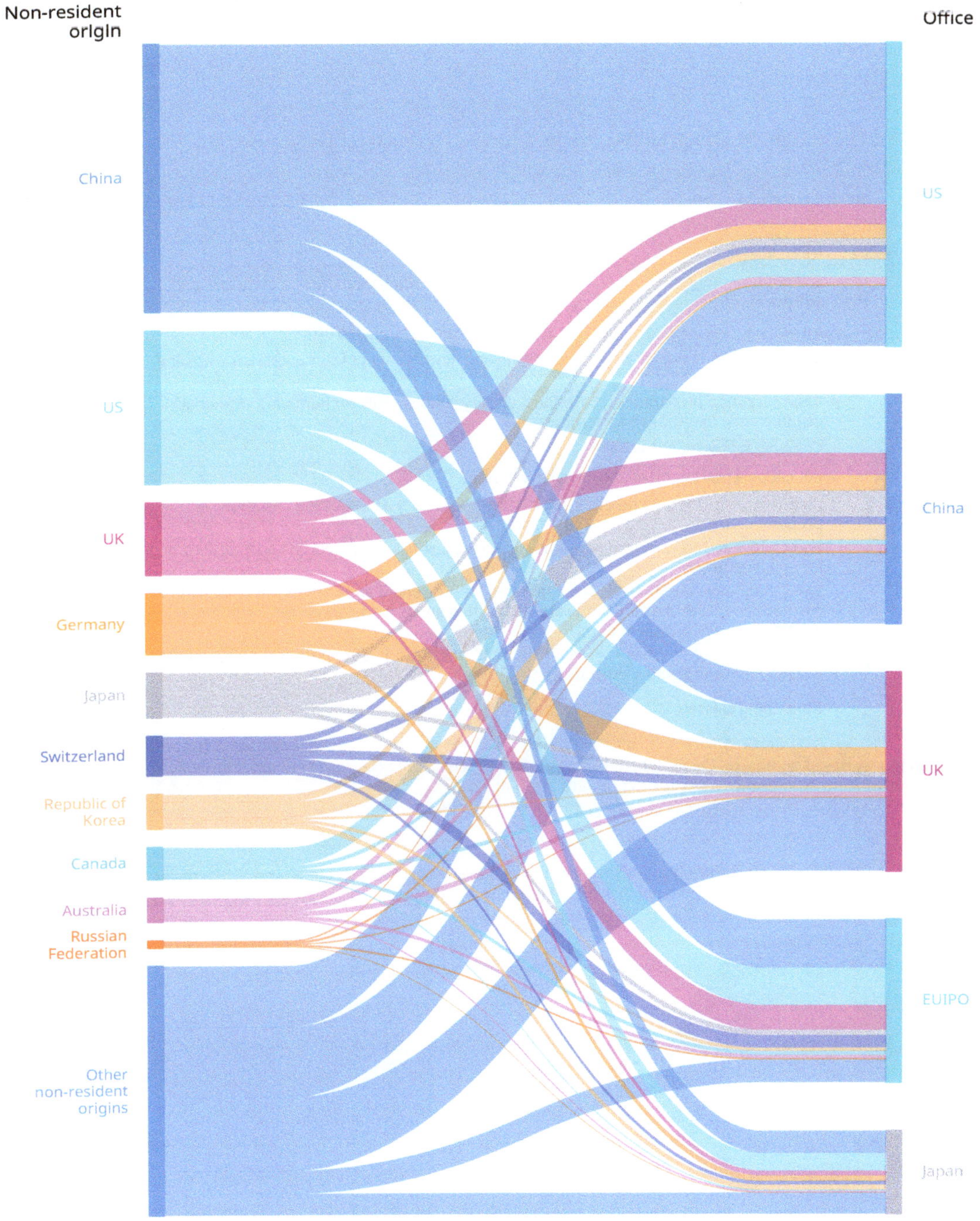

Note: EUIPO is the European Union Intellectual Property Office. The office and non-resident origin data shown consist of absolute rather than equivalent application class counts.

Source: WIPO Statistics Database, September 2022.

B22. **Distribution of trademark application class counts for the top 15 offices and selected non-resident origins, 2021**

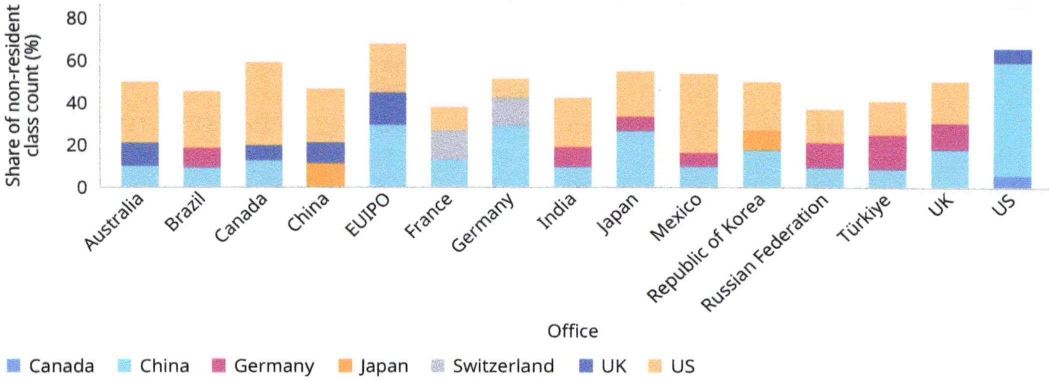

Note: EUIPO is the European Union Intellectual Property Office. The office and origin data shown consist of absolute rather than equivalent application class counts.

Source: WIPO Statistics Database, September 2022.

Trademark applications by Nice class and industry sector

B23. **Distribution of non-resident trademark applications by top Nice classes, 2021**

Rank	Class	Description	Share (%)
1	9	Scientific, photographic, measuring instruments; recording equipment; computers and software	11.0
2	35	Advertising, business management, business administration and office functions	7.3
3	42	Scientific and technological services, design and development of computer hardware and software	6.0
4	5	Pharmaceutical preparations, baby food, dietary supplements for humans and animals, disinfectants, fungicides and herbicides	5.3
5	25	Clothing, footwear, headwear	5.0
6	41	Education, entertainment and sporting activities	4.3
7	3	Bleaching preparations and other substances for laundry use; cleaning and abrasive preparations; soaps, perfumery and cosmetics	4.3
8	28	Games, toys and playthings; video game apparatus; gymnastic and sporting articles; decorations for Christmas trees.	3.3
9	21	Small, hand-operated utensils and apparatus for household and kitchen use, as well as cosmetic and toilet utensils, glassware and certain goods made of porcelain, ceramic, earthenware, terra-cotta or glass	3.3
10	11	Apparatus for lighting, heating, steam generating, cooking, refrigerating, drying, ventilating, water supply and sanitary purposes	3.1
		Remaining classes	**47**

Note: Figures based on non-resident filing data from 137 IP offices. Some classes listed are abbreviated. See *www.wipo.int/classifications/nice* for a complete list of all classes.

Source: WIPO Statistics Database, September 2022.

B24. **Non-resident trademark applications by goods and services classes, 2021**

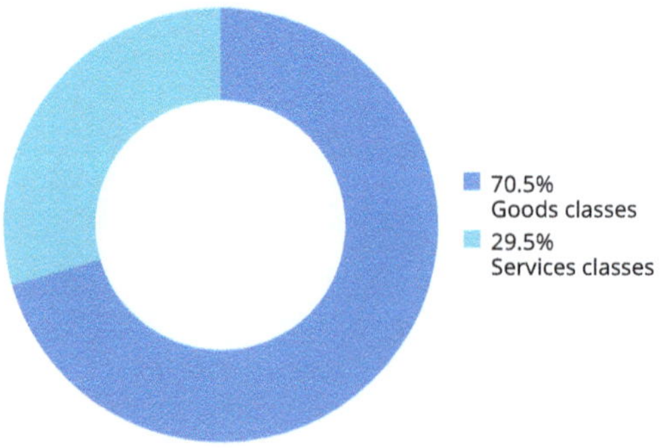

Note: In the 45-class Nice Classification, the first 34 classes indicate goods and the remaining 11 refer to services. See *www.wipo.int/classifications/nice* for a complete list of classes. These figures are based on non-resident filing data from 137 IP offices.

Source: WIPO Statistics Database, September 2022.

B25. Non-resident trademark applications by industry sector, 2021

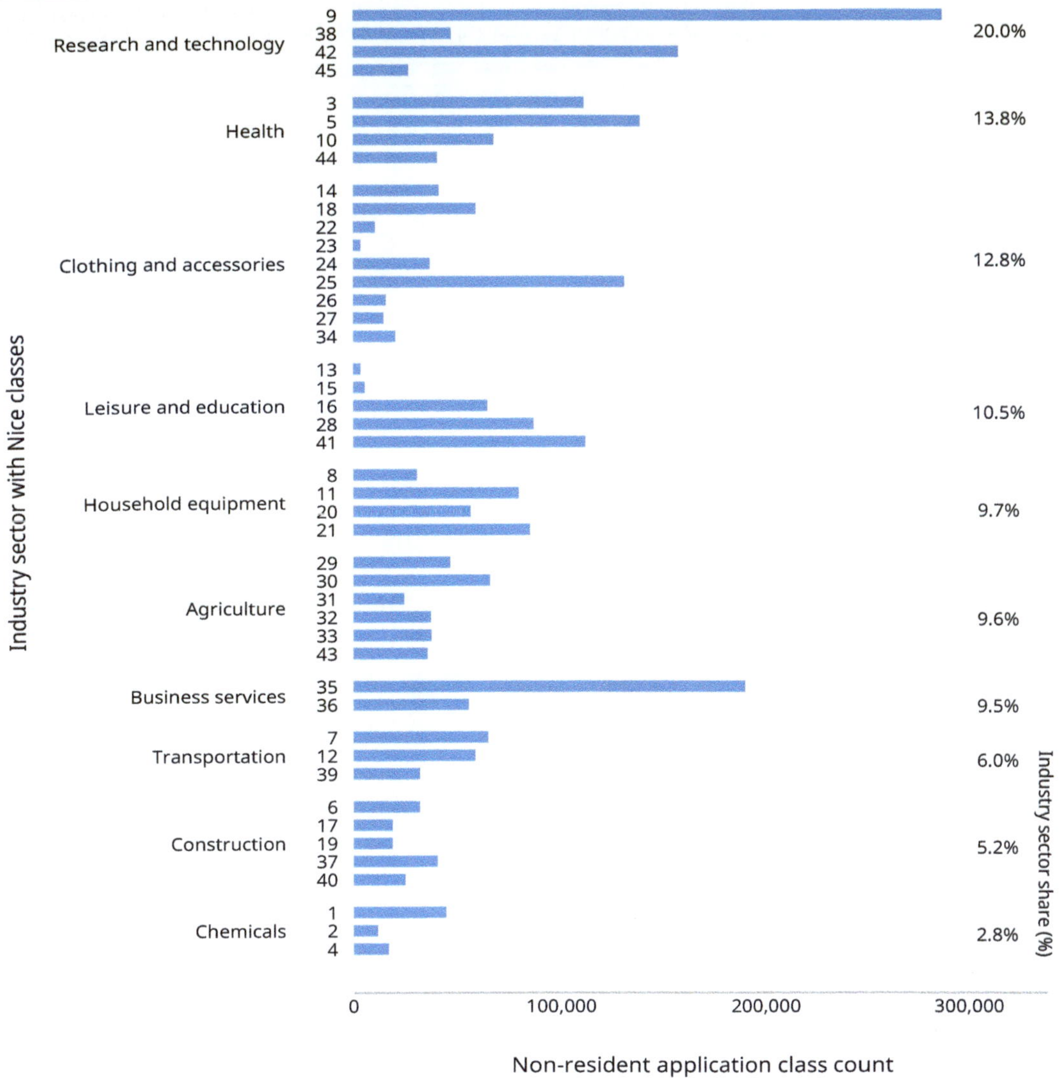

Note: Industry sectors based on class groups are those defined by Edital. Some industry sectors are abbreviated. See annex B for full definitions and the composition of Nice goods and services classes. Figures based on non-resident filing data from 137 IP offices.

Source: WIPO Statistics Database, September 2022.

B26. Trademark applications by top three sectors at the top offices, 2021

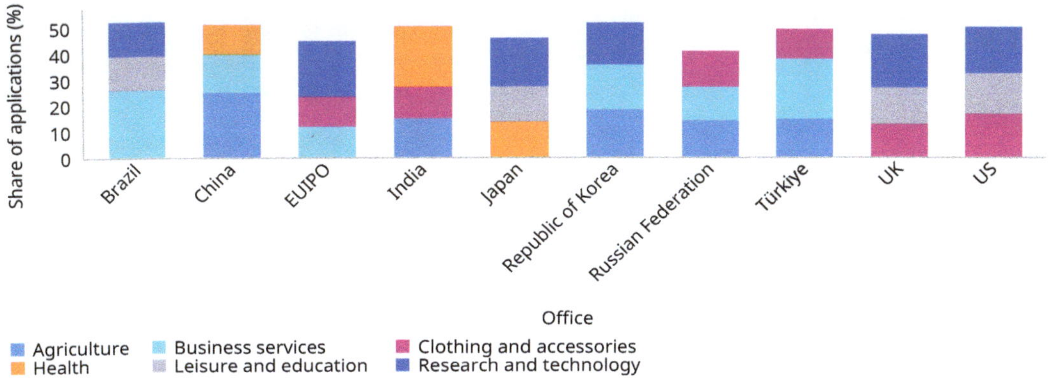

Note: EUIPO is the European Union Intellectual Property Office. Industry sectors based on class groups are those defined by Edital. Some industry sectors are abbreviated. See *www.wipo.int/classifications/nice* for a complete list of classes. The top three sectors and top offices were selected based on 2021 totals.

Source: WIPO Statistics Database, September 2022.

B27. Distribution of trademark applications by goods and services at the top offices, 2021

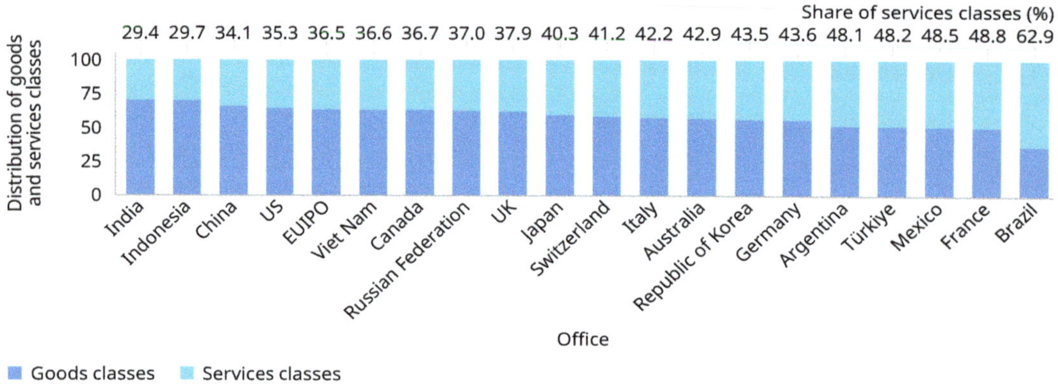

Note: EUIPO is the European Union Intellectual Property Office.
Source: WIPO Statistics Database, September 2022.

B28. Trademark applications by top three sectors for the top origins, 2021

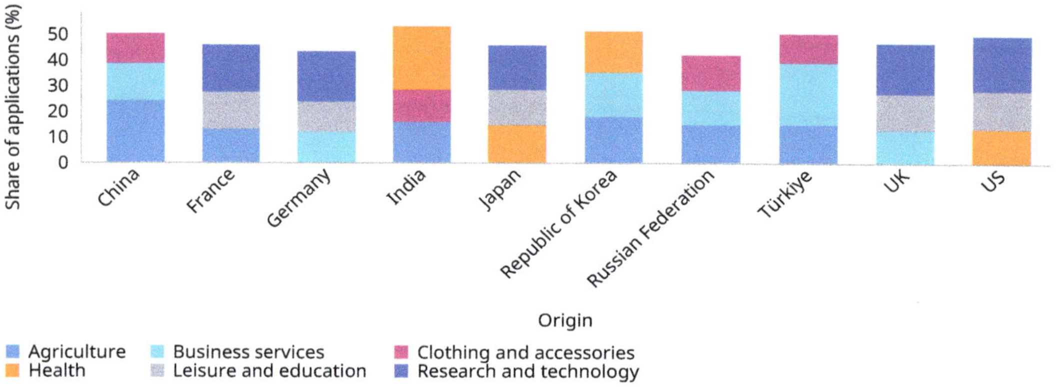

Note: Industry sectors based on class groups are those defined by Edital. Some industry sectors are abbreviated. See annex B for full definitions. The top three sectors and top origins were selected based on 2021 totals.
Source: WIPO Statistics Database, September 2022.

B29. Distribution of trademark applications by goods and services for the top origins, 2021

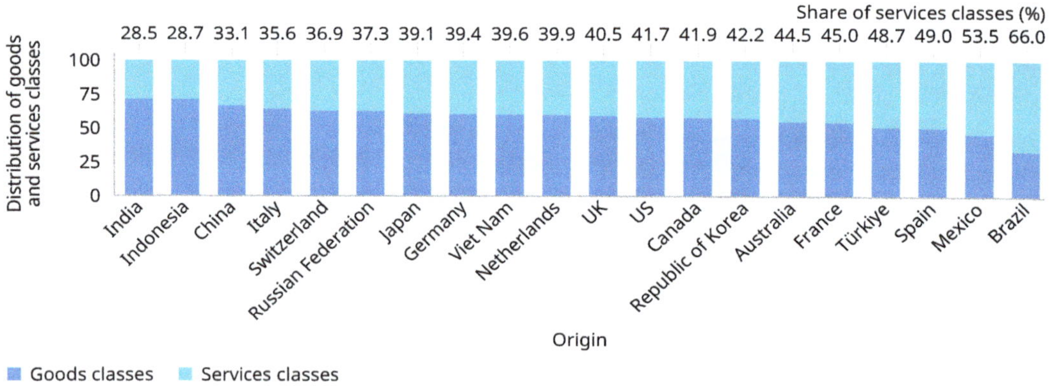

Source: WIPO Statistics Database, September 2022.

Trademark application class count in relation to GDP and population

B30. Resident trademark application class count per USD 100 billion GDP for selected origins, 2011 and 2021

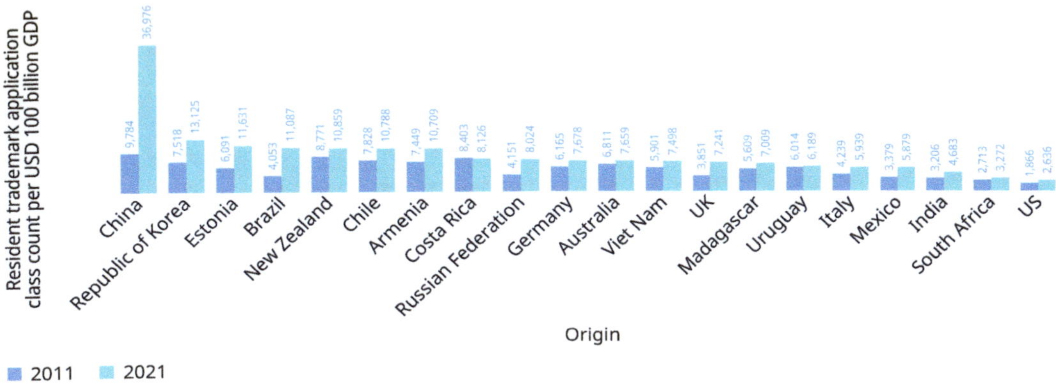

Note: GDP data are in 2017 US purchasing power parity (PPP) dollars. The selected 20 origins were included if they had a GDP greater than USD 25 billion PPP and a resident trademark application class count of at least 100. This figure does not provide an overall ranking of all origins; rather, it shows a selection across geographical regions and income groups.

Sources: WIPO Statistics Database and World Bank, September 2022.

B31. Resident trademark application class count per million population for selected origins, 2011 and 2021

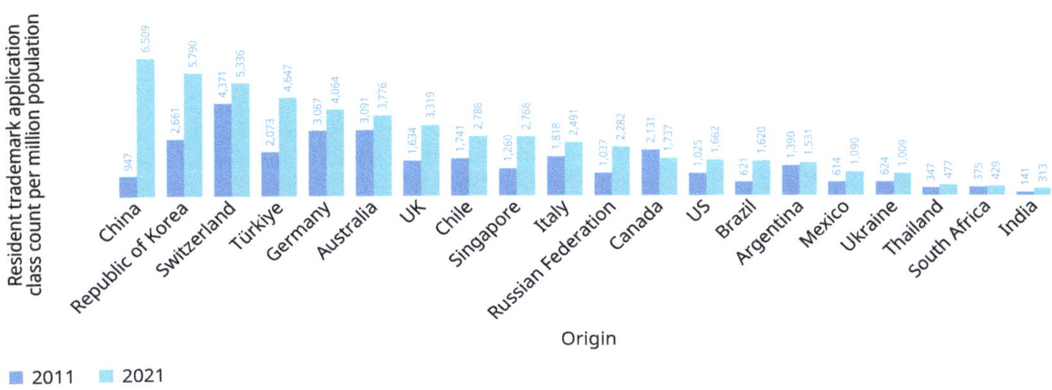

Note: The selected 20 origins were included if they had a population greater than 5 million and a resident trademark application class count of at least 100. This figure does not provide an overall ranking of all origins; rather, it shows a selection across geographical regions and income groups.

Sources: WIPO Statistics Database and World Bank, September 2022.

Collective and certification trademark applications by office

B32. Collective trademark applications for the top 20 offices, 2021

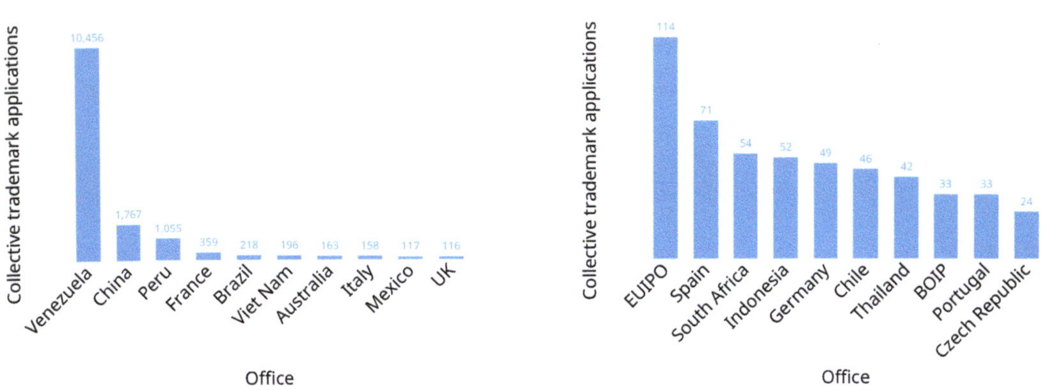

Note: EUIPO is the European Union Intellectual Property Office and BOIP is the Benelux Office for Intellectual Property.

Source: WIPO Statistics Database, September 2022.

B33. Certification trademark applications for the top 20 offices, 2021

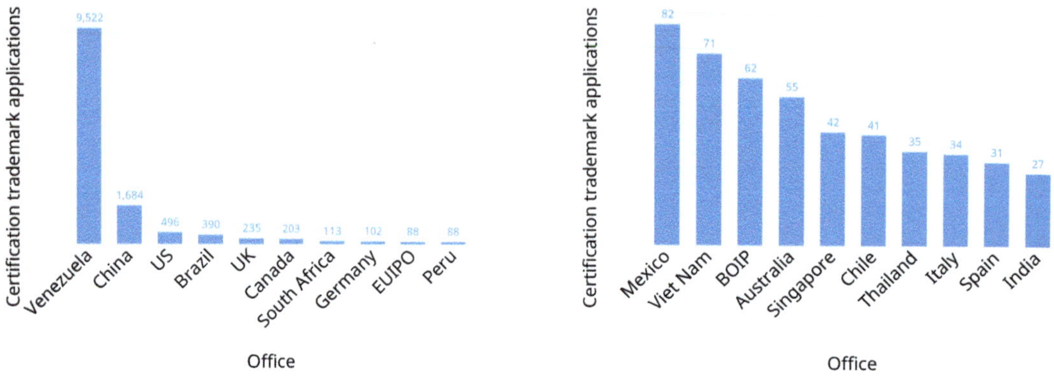

Note: EUIPO is the European Union Intellectual Property Office and BOIP is the Benelux Office for Intellectual Property.
Source: WIPO Statistics Database, September 2022.

Trademark registrations in force

B34. Trend in trademark registrations in force worldwide, 2010–2021

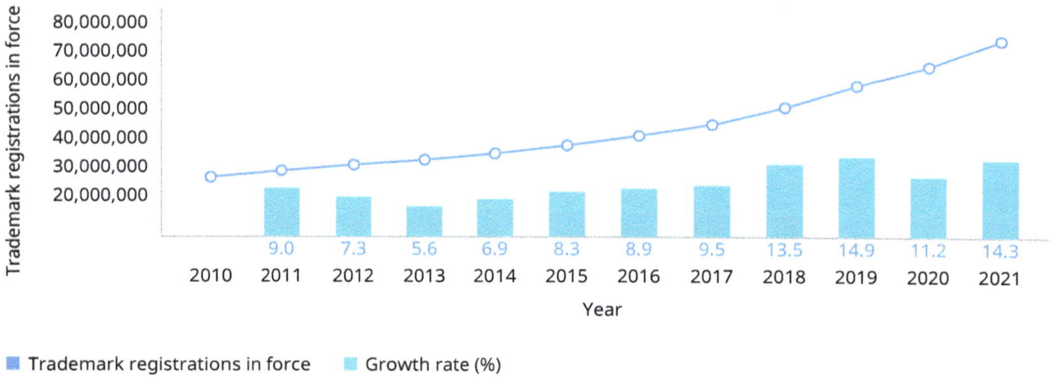

Note: World totals are WIPO estimates using data covering 149 IP offices. Data refer to the number of trademark registrations in force, not the number of classes specified in those registrations. Trademark rights can be maintained indefinitely by paying renewal fees at defined intervals. Trademarks in force provides information on the volume of trademark registrations currently active, as well as the historical trademark life cycle.
Source: WIPO Statistics Database, September 2022.

B35. Trademark registrations in force for the top 20 offices, 2021

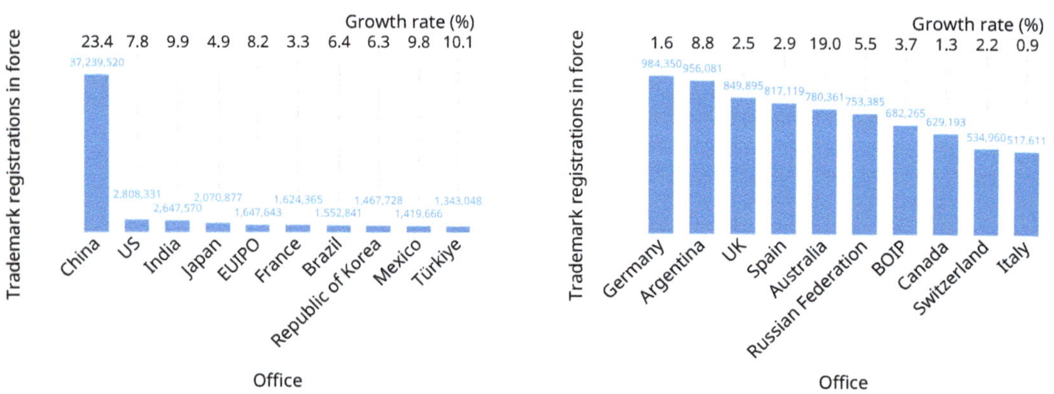

Note: EUIPO is the European Union Intellectual Property Office and BOIP is the Benelux Office for Intellectual Property. Data refer to the number of trademark registrations in force, not the number of classes specified in those registrations.
Source: WIPO Statistics Database, September 2022.

B36. Trademark registrations in force in 2021 as a percentage of total registrations recorded between 1997 and 2021

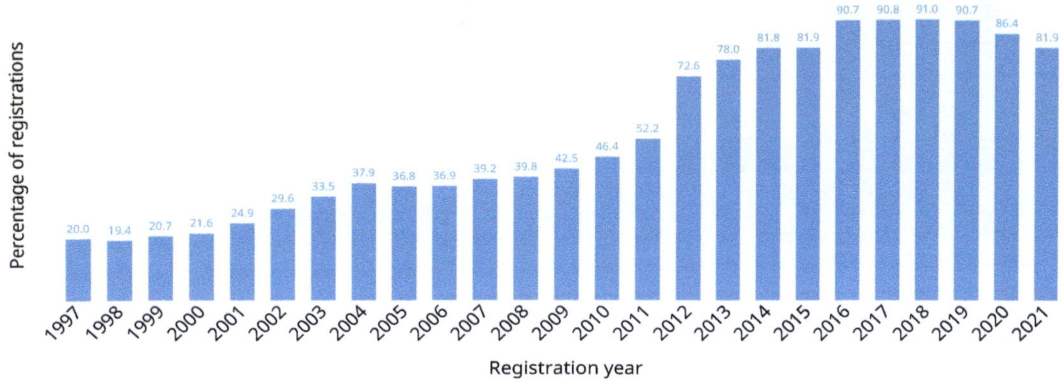

Note: Percentages are calculated as follows: the number of trademark registrations issued in year *t* and in force in 2021 divided by the total number of trademark registrations issued in year *t*. Trademark holders must pay renewal fees to v the validity of their marks, which in most cases can be maintained indefinitely. This figure is based on about 18.5 million active trademark registrations reported by the 74 offices that provided a breakdown by year of registration. Detailed data for several of the larger offices, such as those of China, Japan and Switzerland, are not available.

Source: WIPO Statistics Database, September 2022.

B37. Average age of trademarks in force at selected offices, 2016 and 2021

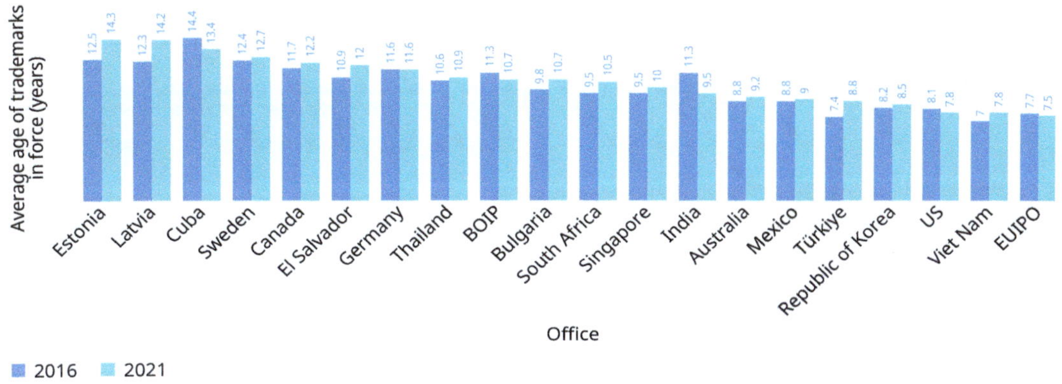

Note: BOIP is the Benelux Office for Intellectual Property and EUIPO is the European Union Intellectual Property Office.

Source: WIPO Statistics Database, September 2022.

Trademark office procedural data

B38. Distribution of trademark examination outcomes for selected offices, 2021

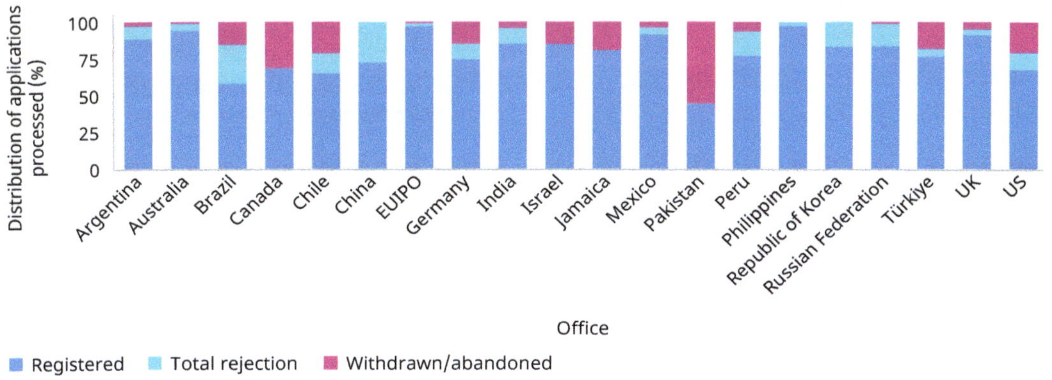

Note: EUIPO is the European Union Intellectual Property Office. WIPO collects data from IP offices using a common questionnaire and methodology. However, due to differences in the application processing procedures between offices, data cannot be fully harmonized. Therefore caution should be exercised when making comparisons across offices.

Source: WIPO Statistics Database, September 2022.

B39. Potentially pending trademark applications for selected offices, 2021

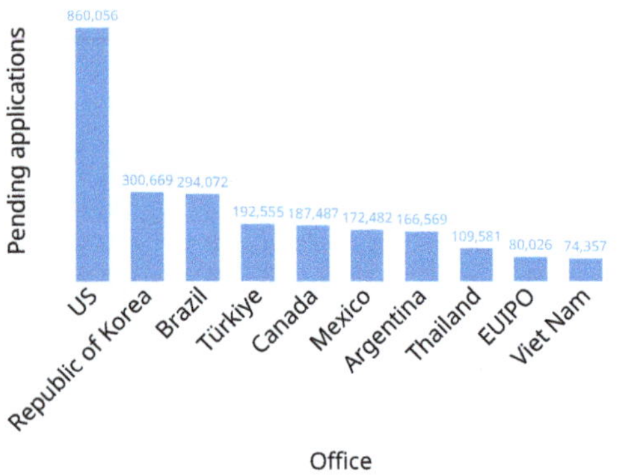

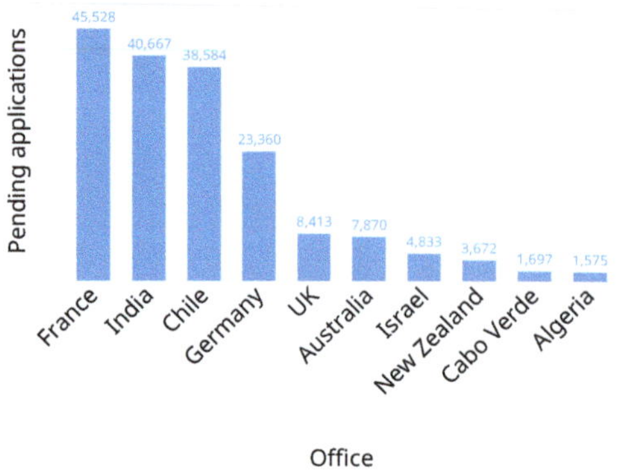

Note: EUIPO is the European Union Intellectual Property Office. WIPO collects data from IP offices using a common questionnaire and methodology. However, due to differences in the application processing procedures between offices, data cannot be fully harmonized. Therefore caution should be exercised when making comparisons across offices. Detailed data for several larger offices, such as those of China and Japan, are not available.

Source: WIPO Statistics Database, September 2022.

B40. Number of trademark examiners for selected offices, 2021

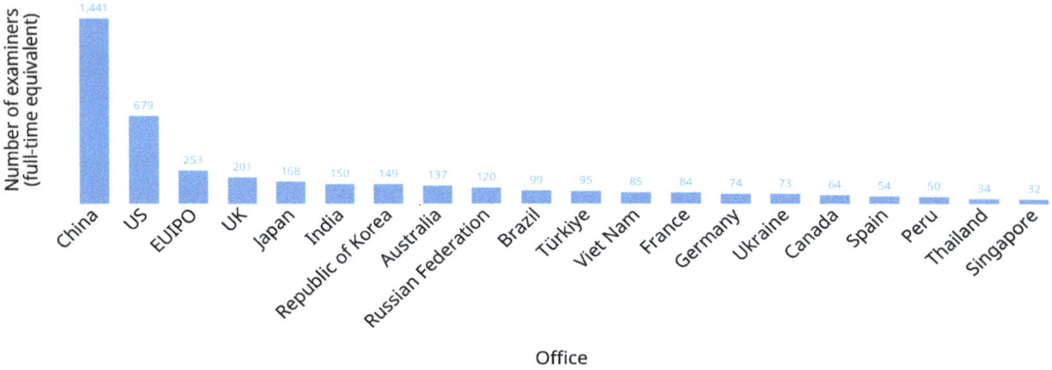

Note: EUIPO is the European Union Intellectual Property Office.

Source: WIPO Statistics Database, September 2022.

B41. Duration of trademark examination for selected offices, 2021

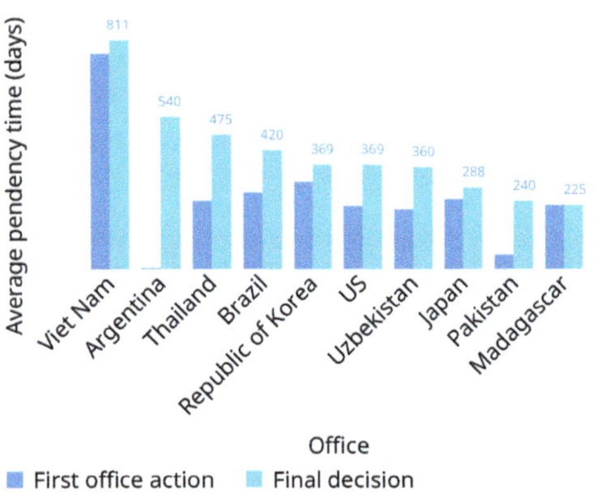

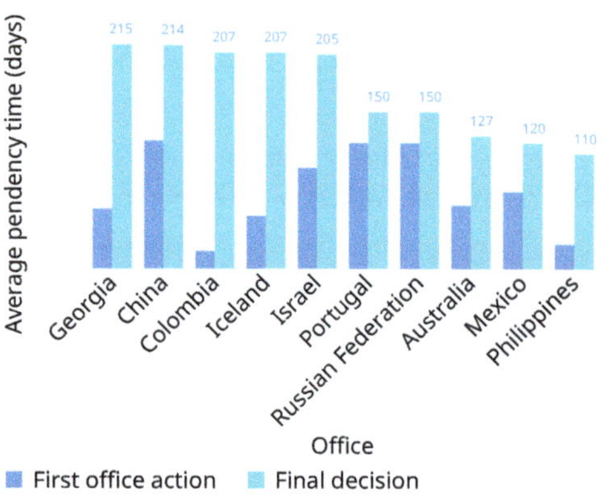

Note: WIPO collects data from IP offices using a common questionnaire and methodology. However, due to differences in application processing procedures between offices, data cannot be fully harmonized. Therefore caution should be exercised when making comparisons across offices.

Source: WIPO Statistics Database, September 2022.

B42. Third-party oppositions for selected offices, 2021

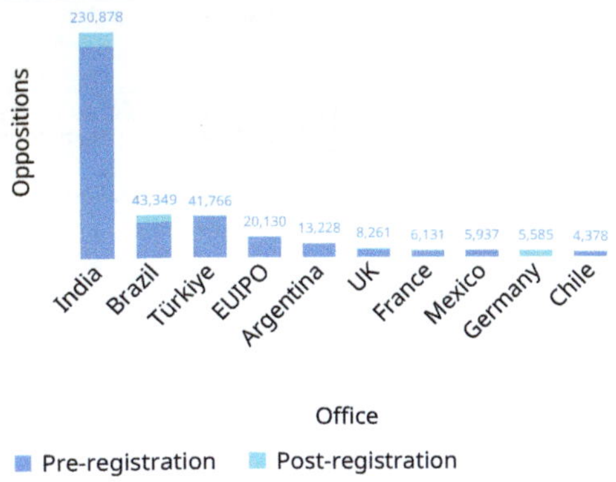

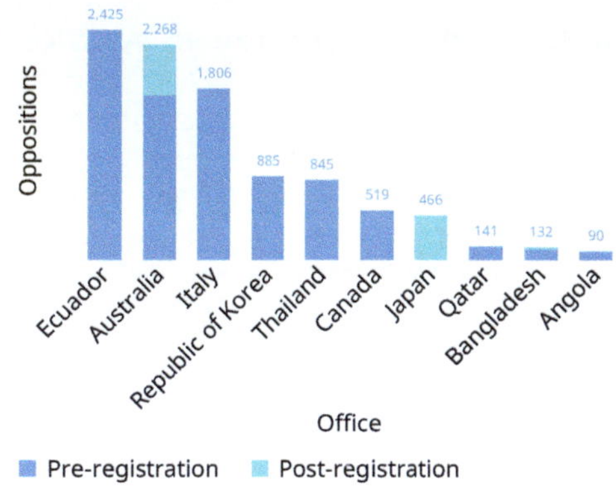

Note: EUIPO is the European Union Intellectual Property Office.
Source: WIPO Statistics Database, September 2022.

B43. Appeals against decisions for selected offices, 2021

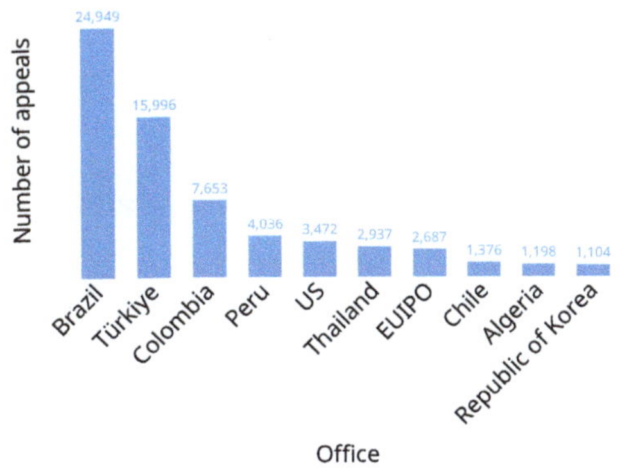

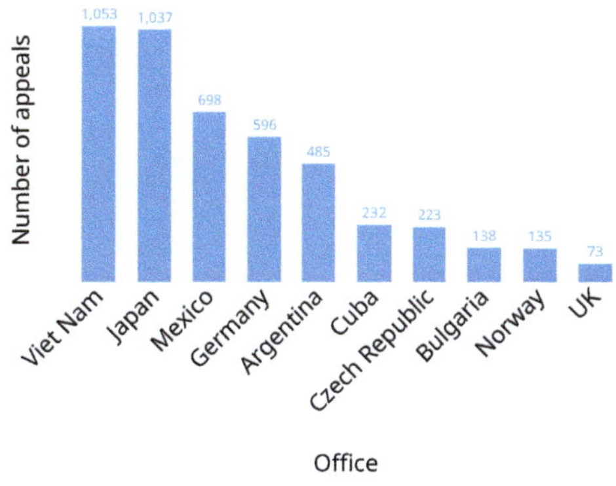

Note: EUIPO is the European Union Intellectual Property Office.
Source: WIPO Statistics Database, September 2022.

B44. Trademark applications by office and origin, 2021

	Application class count by office				Application class count by origin	Equivalent application class count by origin	
Name	Total	Resident	Non-resident	Change over previous year	Total (a)	Total (a)	Change over previous year
Afghanistan (b)	..	..	..	..	175	175	..
African Intellectual Property Organization	15,662	4,577	11,085	+2,325	n.a.	n.a.	n.a.
African Regional Intellectual Property Organization	1,050	320	730	+375	n.a.	n.a.	n.a.
Albania	9,439	1,823	7,616	+1,139	2,131	2,765	+280
Algeria	20,372	11,147	9,225	+251	11,432	11,844	-1,673
Andorra	3,213	919	2,294	+1,075	1,637	7,539	+1,390
Angola (g)	4,224	..	..	+304	43	201	-2,531
Antigua and Barbuda	2,201	371	1,830	+328	942	1,922	+1,226
Argentina	85,844	70,131	15,713	+7,344	74,773	82,437	+8,445
Armenia	11,878	4,233	7,645	+731	4,910	5,494	+269
Australia	174,095	97,204	76,891	+24,590	153,338	251,518	+26,658
Austria (b)	..	..	..	..	39,391	394,603	..
Azerbaijan	14,714	5,657	9,057	+2,398	5,993	6,135	+1,085
Bahamas (b)	..	..	..	..	529	1,439	..
Bahrain	14,132	405	13,727	+4,249	626	1,224	-19
Bangladesh	15,527	10,831	4,696	+1,836	10,942	10,994	+1,003
Barbados	987	194	793	+88	2,925	17,043	+13,692
Belarus	19,553	4,610	14,943	+224	8,692	12,260	+632
Belgium (c)	n.a.	n.a.	n.a.	n.a.	42,276	281,784	+10,150
Belize (b)	..	..	..	..	361	647	..
Benelux Office for Intellectual Property (d)	63,753	53,891	9,862	+2,006	n.a.	n.a.	n.a.
Benin (b,h)	n.a.	n.a.	n.a.	n.a.	212	3,596	+909
Bhutan	2,211	155	2,056	-166	157	157	-101
Bolivia (Plurinational State of) (b)	..	..	..	..	97	97	..
Bonaire, Sint Eustatius and Saba (b,i)	..	..	..	..	6	110	..
Bosnia and Herzegovina	10,977	1,013	9,964	+1,216	1,523	1,873	-843
Botswana (g)	6,003	..	..	+2,826	66	75	-722
Brazil	394,087	346,748	47,339	+96,155	353,927	370,087	+88,594
Brunei Darussalam	4,369	177	4,192	+426	209	729	+445
Bulgaria	14,987	10,906	4,081	+664	24,341	105,261	+9,245
Burkina Faso (b,h)	n.a.	n.a.	n.a.	n.a.	363	6,147	+851
Burundi (b)	..	..	..	..	16	16	..
Cabo Verde	271	65	206	+57	69	147	-37
Cambodia (g)	12,827	..	..	-103	78	156	-67
Cameroon (b,h)	n.a.	n.a.	n.a.	n.a.	881	13,245	+2,307
Canada	175,907	66,435	109,472	+28,682	118,769	236,009	+42,452
Central African Republic (b,h)	n.a.	n.a.	n.a.	n.a.	4	68	+68
Chad (b,h)	n.a.	n.a.	n.a.	n.a.	19	163	-366
Chile	69,115	53,520	15,595	+9,182	60,022	66,128	+10,356
China	9,454,794	9,192,749	262,045	+109,084	9,699,034	11,162,524	+272,478
China, Hong Kong SAR	76,700	31,154	45,546	+6,727	54,928	138,552	+79
China, Macao SAR	14,743	2,504	12,239	+1,276	2,932	3,660	+372
Colombia	55,606	33,616	21,990	+5,704	38,655	42,665	+5,060
Comoros (b)	..	..	..	..	10	138	..
Congo (b,h)	n.a.	n.a.	n.a.	n.a.	51	707	-303
Cook Islands (b)	..	..	..	..	210	912	..
Costa Rica	15,969	8,878	7,091	+1,306	9,818	10,910	+1,397
Côte d'Ivoire (b,h)	n.a.	n.a.	n.a.	n.a.	1,215	19,631	-2,203
Croatia	7,334	3,351	3,983	-858	7,304	30,778	+3,763
Cuba	5,675	1,840	3,835	-630	2,023	2,517	-880
Curaçao (i)	2,793	157	2,636	+800	465	2,397	+1,919
Cyprus	3,918	1,595	2,323	+485	15,696	90,848	+11,636
Czech Republic	27,875	22,855	5,020	+1,664	36,886	199,208	+47,649

		Application class count by office			Application class count by origin	Equivalent application class count by origin	
Name	Total	Resident	Non-resident	Change over previous year	Total (a)	Total (a)	Change over previous year
Democratic People's Republic of Korea (b)	..	..	..	..	226	382	..
Democratic Republic of the Congo (b)	..	..	..	..	5	63	..
Denmark	9,814	5,517	4,297	+618	34,094	195,528	+17,776
Djibouti (b)	..	..	..	..	5	5	..
Dominica	190	8	182	+12	29	29	-145
Dominican Republic	15,776	9,806	5,970	+2,681	10,335	11,063	+2,270
Ecuador	21,652	13,951	7,701	+2,960	14,691	15,497	+1,995
Egypt (b)	..	..	..	..	1,102	3,396	..
El Salvador	12,778	4,883	7,895	+3,476	5,400	5,608	+1,999
Equatorial Guinea (b,h)	n.a.	n.a.	n.a.	n.a.	11	187	+49
Eritrea (b)	..	..	..	..	4	4	..
Estonia	6,436	3,390	3,046	+902	8,793	74,407	+19,880
Eswatini (b)	..	..	..	..	29	29	..
Ethiopia (b)	..	..	..	..	15	15	..
European Union Intellectual Property Office (e)	497,542	311,073	186,469	+59,073	n.a.	n.a.	n.a.
Fiji (b)	..	..	..	..	19	19	..
Finland	9,323	5,747	3,576	+70	27,669	174,767	-2,223
France	314,992	298,103	16,889	+24,793	451,630	1,249,614	+176,243
Gabon (b,h)	n.a.	n.a.	n.a.	n.a.	76	1,228	+183
Gambia (b)	..	..	..	..	..	..	..
Georgia	10,775	2,874	7,901	+984	3,490	4,510	+488
Germany	272,425	246,291	26,134	+7,753	554,906	2,944,220	+238,564
Ghana (b)	..	..	..	..	69	607	..
Greece (b)	..	..	..	..	6,185	110,617	..
Grenada (b)	..	..	..	..	12	12	..
Guatemala (g)	13,650	..	..	+3,241	2,146	2,434	+174
Guinea (b,h)	n.a.	n.a.	n.a.	n.a.	309	5,045	-690
Guinea-Bissau (b,h)	n.a.	n.a.	n.a.	n.a.	26	426	-237
Guyana (g)	1,215	..	..	..	30	30	..
Haiti (b)	..	..	..	..	27	27	..
Holy See (b)	..	..	..	..	5	5	..
Honduras	7,368	2,293	5,075	+1,987	2,664	2,950	+965
Hungary	12,080	7,979	4,101	+1,015	14,785	69,897	+4,067
Iceland	10,713	1,419	9,294	+1,290	2,311	6,133	+36
India	488,526	435,580	52,946	+63,978	449,869	475,599	+56,938
Indonesia	127,142	91,362	35,780	+3,362	94,282	96,990	+10,836
Iran (Islamic Republic of) (b)	..	..	..	..	2,220	4,632	..
Iraq (b)	..	..	..	..	724	1,302	..
Ireland (g)	8,373	..	..	+1,162	17,531	123,593	+23,299
Israel	26,102	5,076	21,026	+4,302	15,290	44,042	-1
Italy	119,578	108,257	11,321	+18,708	223,892	1,237,334	+63,942
Jamaica	6,795	2,576	4,219	+69	2,779	2,935	-366
Japan	364,376	269,515	94,861	-56,782	388,687	552,805	-80,157
Jordan (b)	..	..	..	..	1,105	2,867	..
Kazakhstan	29,090	13,043	16,047	+3,305	15,899	17,123	+3,280
Kenya (b)	..	..	..	..	148	848	..
Kuwait (b)	..	..	..	..	1,299	3,677	..
Kyrgyzstan	8,125	495	7,630	+816	755	833	+39
Lao People's Democratic Republic (b)	..	..	..	..	8	8	..
Latvia	5,630	2,321	3,309	+810	7,132	27,778	+6,902
Lebanon (b)	..	..	..	..	856	6,918	..
Lesotho (b)	..	..	..	..	5	5	..
Liberia (b)	..	..	..	..	76	648	..
Libya (b)	..	..	..	..	98	904	..
Liechtenstein	9,223	396	8,827	+509	3,675	15,283	-2,183
Lithuania	6,620	3,377	3,243	+116	7,914	62,976	+18,494
Luxembourg (c)	n.a.	n.a.	n.a.	n.a.	16,200	97,752	-10,121

	Application class count by office				Application class count by origin	Equivalent application class count by origin	
Name	Total	Resident	Non-resident	Change over previous year	Total (a)	Total (a)	Change over previous year
Madagascar	6,666	2,966	3,700	+969	3,033	3,267	+410
Malawi (b)	..	..	..	..	2	4	..
Malaysia (b)	..	..	..	..	8,336	13,476	..
Maldives (b)	..	..	..	..	5	5	..
Mali (b,h)	n.a.	n.a.	n.a.	n.a.	384	5,760	+2,193
Malta	1,572	1,245	327	+110	9,964	78,936	+21,401
Marshall Islands (b)	..	..	..	..	505	2,299	..
Mauritania (b,h)	n.a.	n.a.	n.a.	n.a.	210	2,466	+653
Mauritius	5,023	2,540	2,483	+589	4,727	8,423	-853
Mexico	199,389	142,012	57,377	+36,856	152,724	165,502	+25,115
Micronesia (Federated States of) (b)	..	..	..	..	1	1	..
Monaco	10,059	1,525	8,534	+1,490	3,983	15,351	-3,633
Mongolia	24,105	19,104	5,001	+5,596	19,249	19,487	+5,826
Montenegro (b)	..	..	..	..	156	234	..
Morocco	35,048	20,432	14,616	+4,878	63,123	106,387	+79,546
Mozambique	6,557	1,499	5,058	+1,424	1,587	1,587	-246
Myanmar (b)	..	..	..	..	151	151	..
Namibia (b)	..	..	..	..	343	795	..
Nauru (b)	..	..	..	..	207	207	..
Nepal (b)	..	..	..	..	142	142	..
Netherlands (c)	n.a.	n.a.	n.a.	n.a.	94,179	608,471	+28,403
New Zealand	66,714	24,087	42,627	+11,072	35,386	55,212	+4,395
Nicaragua (b)	..	..	..	..	57	57	..
Niger (b,h)	n.a.	n.a.	n.a.	n.a.	63	815	-766
Nigeria (b)	..	..	..	..	332	2,212	..
Niue (b)	..	..	..	..	23	23	..
North Macedonia	10,608	2,137	8,471	..	3,212	4,618	..
Norway	52,580	11,791	40,789	+10,385	24,740	93,994	+30,742
Oman (g)	15,905	..	..	+3,313	147	485	-8,803
Pakistan	51,325	43,233	8,092	+10,747	43,735	44,355	+5,435
Panama	11,735	4,782	6,953	+753	8,280	12,368	-1,932
Papua New Guinea (b)	..	..	..	..	29	29	..
Paraguay (b)	..	..	..	..	296	504	..
Peru	42,605	29,557	13,048	+5,355	31,159	32,311	+3,098
Philippines	64,946	34,976	29,970	+8,243	36,693	37,579	+3,089
Poland	42,755	35,855	6,900	+5,116	67,029	500,323	+114,554
Portugal	37,764	32,344	5,420	+3,022	42,523	168,579	+24,173
Qatar	9,587	1,545	8,042	+2,434	3,711	10,497	+4,671
Republic of Korea	360,474	299,621	60,853	+40,529	371,091	470,083	+39,672
Republic of Moldova	12,430	3,971	8,459	+368	5,006	6,216	+164
Romania	25,583	20,988	4,595	-45	27,602	130,830	+21,625
Russian Federation	395,726	327,407	68,319	-2,476	373,995	419,031	-6,610
Rwanda (b)	..	..	..	..	13	39	..
Saint Kitts and Nevis (b)	..	..	..	..	228	604	..
Saint Lucia (b)	..	..	..	..	153	205	..
Saint Vincent and the Grenadines	558	17	541	+240	84	386	-248
Samoa	1,620	47	1,573	-55	240	864	+126
San Marino (b)	..	..	..	..	472	2,948	..
Sao Tome and Principe	2,685	4	2,681	+1,277	24,415	24,415	+24,208
Saudi Arabia	38,130	0	38,130	+7,946	2,225	7,153	-17,973
Senegal (b,h)	n.a.	n.a.	n.a.	n.a.	802	12,556	+3,309
Serbia	17,621	3,833	13,788	+605	8,382	16,632	+3,698
Seychelles (b)	..	..	..	..	2,238	5,420	..
Sierra Leone (g)	3,493	..	..	+1,203	5	21	-195
Singapore	62,491	15,086	47,405	+10,256	54,408	103,736	+25,687
Sint Maarten (Dutch Part) (b,i)	..	..	..	..	14	14	..
Slovakia	14,888	10,112	4,776	+1,860	14,494	62,086	+12,631
Slovenia (b)	..	..	..	..	5,817	44,675	..
Solomon Islands (b)	..	..	..	..	4	4	..

Name	Application class count by office Total	Resident	Non-resident	Change over previous year	Application class count by origin Total (a)	Equivalent application class count by origin Total (a)	Change over previous year
Somalia (b)	..	..	..	..	3	3	..
South Africa	39,863	25,786	14,077	+3,540	28,206	36,750	+1,427
South Sudan (b)	..	..	..	..	4	4	..
Spain	82,163	72,612	9,551	+1,712	134,524	794,104	+55,369
Sri Lanka	9,947	6,321	3,626	..	6,745	7,677	..
Sudan (b)	..	..	..	..	21	21	..
Suriname	1,122	340	782	+120	494	528	+151
Sweden	19,982	15,190	4,792	+232	69,820	399,594	+50,554
Switzerland	116,581	46,410	70,171	+15,494	183,183	564,405	+67,133
Syrian Arab Republic	22,900	12,120	10,780	+9,128	12,884	14,198	+2,876
Tajikistan (b)	..	..	..	..	24	24	..
Thailand	68,103	33,401	34,702	+4,626	38,989	43,349	-1,231
Timor-Leste (b)	..	..	..	..	2	2	..
Togo (b,h)	n.a.	n.a.	n.a.	n.a.	458	6,982	+2,907
Tonga (b)	..	..	..	..	4	4	..
Trinidad and Tobago	4,505	662	3,843	+1,952	864	954	-182
Tunisia (b)	..	..	..	..	307	1,515	..
Türkiye	434,406	395,159	39,247	+70,714	426,057	504,769	+79,941
Turkmenistan (b)	..	..	..	..	67	67	..
Uganda (b)	..	..	..	..	22	74	..
Ukraine	71,234	44,202	27,032	+8,580	51,917	64,793	+4,870
United Arab Emirates (b)	..	..	..	..	10,848	35,970	..
United Kingdom	450,815	223,471	227,344	+172,157	443,403	1,197,677	-107,068
United Republic of Tanzania (g)	4,703	..	..	+1,078	47	52	-2,049
United States of America	899,678	551,748	347,930	+29,402	1,028,579	2,162,869	+287,506
Uruguay	11,075	4,835	6,240	+1,739	6,787	9,049	+2,265
Uzbekistan	18,372	10,476	7,896	+3,177	10,920	10,946	+2,452
Vanuatu (b)	..	..	..	..	29	185	..
Venezuela (Bolivarian Republic of)	9,522	9,522	0	+1,749	9,856	10,194	+1,969
Viet Nam	113,079	77,404	35,675	+4,436	82,050	86,100	+2,818
Yemen	6,568	4,662	1,906	+474	4,991	5,541	+486
Zambia (b)	..	..	..	..	87	113	..
Zimbabwe (g)	4,627	..	..	+1,340	354	658	+343
Others/Unknown	44	0	44	+32	46,684	129,356	-27,938
Total (2021 estimates)	**18,145,100**	**15,233,500**	**2,911,600**		**18,145,100**		

(a) Data on application class count by origin are incomplete, because some offices do not report detailed statistics containing the origin of application class counts.

(b) Only Madrid designation data are available therefore application class count by office and origin data may be incomplete.

(c) This country does not have a national trademark office. All applications for trademark protection are filed at the Benelux Office for Intellectual Property or the European Union Intellectual Property Office.

(d) Resident applications include those filed by residents of Belgium, Luxembourg and the Netherlands.

(e) Resident applications include those filed by residents of EU member states.

(f) Origin is defined as the country/territory of the stated residence of the applicant in an international application.

(g) Total includes an aggregate direct application class count that cannot be broken down into direct and non-resident components.

(h) The African Intellectual Property Office (OAPI) is the competent office for processing applications.

(i) This country or municipality is not a Madrid member. The Netherlands has extended the application of the Madrid Protocol to the territories of Curaçao and Sint Maarten, Bonaire, Sint Eustatius and Saba.

n.a. indicates not applicable.

.. indicates not available.

Source: WIPO Statistics Database, September 2022.

B45. Trademark registrations by office and origin, and trademarks in force, 2021

Name	Registration class count by office			Registration class count by origin	Equivalent registration class count by origin	In force by office	
	Total	Resident	Non-resident	Total (a)	Total (a)	Total	Change over previous year
Afghanistan (b)	..	..	..	107	107	..	..
African Intellectual Property Organization	14,917	4,700	10,217	n.a.	n.a.	76,452	+4,755
African Regional Intellectual Property Organization	590	93	497	n.a.	n.a.	2,813	+303
Albania	9,108	1,367	7,741	1,688	2,286	10,521	-1,457
Algeria (b)	..	..	..	163	281	44,539	+8,054
Andorra	3,237	943	2,294	1,473	7,141	20,999	+621
Angola (b)	..	..	..	20	250	64,423	+38,326
Antigua and Barbuda	1,455	64	1,391	271	583	..	..
Argentina	75,728	59,915	15,813	62,821	69,123	956,081	+77,368
Armenia	10,937	3,074	7,863	3,810	4,582	23,103	+1,151
Australia	141,964	73,909	68,055	124,753	223,235	780,361	+124,766
Austria (b)	..	..	..	35,314	350,720	..	..
Azerbaijan	12,787	3,787	9,000	3,931	4,095	77,852	+3,443
Bahamas (b)	..	..	..	626	1,510	..	..
Bahrain	11,544	297	11,247	477	1,179	77,428	+1,889
Bangladesh	3,945	660	3,285	720	788	67,502	+6,187
Barbados (b)	..	..	..	2,288	14,014	..	..
Belarus	19,527	4,700	14,827	8,343	11,281	129,325	-1,277
Belgium (c)	n.a.	n.a.	n.a.	43,139	280,729	n.a.	n.a.
Belize (b)	..	..	..	352	742	..	..
Benelux Office for Intellectual Property (d)	63,116	53,877	9,239	n.a.	n.a.	682,265	+24,501
Benin (b,h)	n.a.	n.a.	n.a.	227	3,759	..	..
Bhutan	1,932	129	1,803	132	132	..	..
Bolivia (Plurinational State of) (b)	..	..	..	63	167	..	..
Bonaire, Sint Eustatius and Saba (b,i)	..	..	..	18	200	..	..
Bosnia and Herzegovina	10,519	959	9,560	1,687	2,527	82,253	+2,041
Botswana (g)	4,535	..	..	36	121	33,179	+12,783
Brazil	185,749	145,668	40,081	151,265	164,007	1,552,841	+93,051
Brunei Darussalam	3,670	54	3,616	96	616	19,579	-3,461
Bulgaria	14,133	10,546	3,587	19,523	85,119	56,639	+1,260
Burkina Faso (b,h)	n.a.	n.a.	n.a.	364	6,112	..	..
Burundi (b)	..	..	..	10	10	..	..
Cabo Verde	360	55	305	59	59	2,768	+376
Cambodia (g)	13,745	..	..	97	97	..	..
Cameroon (b,h)	n.a.	n.a.	n.a.	760	11,988	..	..
Canada	122,137	28,612	93,525	65,597	173,959	629,193	+8,333
Central African Republic (b,h)	n.a.	n.a.	n.a.	5	69	..	..
Chad (b,h)	n.a.	n.a.	n.a.	27	411	..	..
Chile	34,886	26,094	8,792	30,016	35,146	390,621	+7,609
China	7,765,361	7,545,435	219,926	7,971,361	9,484,489	37,239,520	+7,066,435
China, Hong Kong SAR	68,898	28,205	40,693	46,726	128,688	476,443	+15,638
China, Macao SAR	13,136	2,162	10,974	2,469	2,989	144,895	+6,577
Colombia	50,939	24,540	26,399	27,734	30,738	364,321	+18,391
Comoros (b)	..	..	..	3	51	..	..
Congo (b,h)	n.a.	n.a.	n.a.	50	786	..	..
Cook Islands (b)	..	..	..	47	541	..	..
Costa Rica	11,929	5,968	5,961	6,533	6,975	125,389	+1,492
Côte d'Ivoire (b,h)	n.a.	n.a.	n.a.	1,281	21,313	..	..
Croatia	5,969	2,788	3,181	6,208	23,828	99,143	-4,169
Cuba	5,652	1,721	3,931	1,905	2,249	46,898	+5,828
Curaçao (i)	2,173	176	1,997	548	2,356	22,613	-98
Cyprus	3,586	1,623	1,963	14,112	77,586	52,338	+7,482
Czech Republic	25,818	21,546	4,272	33,666	152,722	127,272	+576

	Registration class count by office			Registration class count by origin	Equivalent registration class count by origin	In force by office	
Name	Total	Resident	Non-resident	Total (a)	Total (a)	Total	Change over previous year
Democratic People's Republic of Korea (b)	..	..	..	161	317	..	..
Democratic Republic of the Congo (b)	..	..	..	8	50	..	..
Denmark	8,499	4,899	3,600	33,780	187,282	112,787	-4,038
Djibouti (b)	..	..	..	5	5	..	..
Dominica	144	8	136	15	15	..	..
Dominican Republic	13,739	8,137	5,602	8,360	8,646	134,128	+3,843
Ecuador	13,486	8,667	4,819	9,222	9,820	148,467	..
Egypt (b)	..	..	..	880	2,720	..	..
El Salvador	7,060	3,965	3,095	4,351	4,455	94,898	+2,922
Equatorial Guinea (b,h)	n.a.	n.a.	n.a.	4	52	..	..
Estonia	5,023	2,726	2,297	6,784	57,086	53,101	-1,378
Eswatini (b)	..	..	..	36	36	..	..
Ethiopia (b)	..	..	..	2	2	..	..
European Union Intellectual Property Office (e)	455,675	277,921	177,754	n.a.	n.a.	1,647,643	+124,178
Fiji (b)	..	..	..	16	16	..	..
Finland	7,780	4,964	2,816	27,120	172,154	93,557	-3,031
France	319,005	302,840	16,165	449,819	1,188,689	1,624,365	+51,639
Gabon (b,h)	n.a.	n.a.	n.a.	89	1,401	..	..
Gambia (b)	..	..	..	..	..	..	..
Georgia	9,010	1,505	7,505	2,167	2,787	66,063	+55
Germany	211,978	187,931	24,047	485,670	2,634,388	984,350	+15,506
Ghana (b)	..	..	..	51	409	..	..
Greece (b)	..	..	..	5,195	85,735	..	..
Grenada (b)	..	..	..	7	7	..	..
Guatemala (g)	9,331	..	..	1,611	1,795	..	..
Guernsey (b)	..	..	..	n.a.	n.a.	..	..
Guinea (b,h)	n.a.	n.a.	n.a.	376	6,264	..	..
Guinea-Bissau (b,h)	n.a.	n.a.	n.a.	37	629	..	..
Guyana (g)	640	..	..	4	4	..	..
Haiti (b)	..	..	..	30	30	..	..
Holy See (b)	..	..	..	11	141	..	..
Honduras	5,360	1,581	3,779	1,801	1,827	91,694	+1,233
Hungary	9,459	6,154	3,305	13,165	60,929	54,124	-127
Iceland	9,795	986	8,809	2,250	6,748	61,119	-310
India	354,963	302,633	52,330	313,785	336,359	2,647,570	+238,565
Indonesia	175,042	118,944	56,098	121,589	124,317	..	..
Iran (Islamic Republic of) (b)	..	..	..	1,721	3,139	..	..
Iraq (b)	..	..	..	424	1,022	..	..
Ireland (g)	6,136	..	..	16,023	108,317	71,223	-1,247
Israel	24,639	4,185	20,454	12,849	39,387	146,263	+2,568
Italy	97,704	87,646	10,058	202,915	1,134,165	517,611	+4,525
Jamaica	3,161	1,466	1,695	1,561	1,665	..	..
Japan (b)	..	..	..	119,814	285,150	2,070,877	+97,237
Jordan (b)	..	..	..	637	2,093	..	..
Kazakhstan	24,869	9,331	15,538	11,525	12,535	84,230	+34,979
Kenya (b)	..	..	..	162	848	..	..
Kuwait (b)	..	..	..	795	1,915	..	..
Kyrgyzstan	7,761	391	7,370	490	568	11,487	+291
Lao People's Democratic Republic (b)	..	..	..	18	18	..	..
Latvia	4,354	1,674	2,680	4,369	20,937	25,820	-121
Lebanon (b)	..	..	..	767	6,509	..	..
Lesotho (b)	..	..	..	14	18	..	..
Liberia (b)	..	..	..	31	369	..	..
Libya (b)	..	..	..	38	142	..	..
Liechtenstein (b)	..	..	..	4,429	15,093	..	..
Lithuania	6,125	3,372	2,753	7,175	50,689	37,025	-580

	Registration class count by office			Registration class count by origin	Equivalent registration class count by origin	In force by office	
Name	Total	Resident	Non-resident	Total (a)	Total (a)	Total	Change over previous year
Luxembourg (c)	n.a.	n.a.	n.a.	16,078	108,314	n.a.	n.a.
Madagascar	6,460	3,355	3,105	3,396	3,630	25,267	-3,350
Malawi (b)	..	..	..	4	7	..	..
Malaysia (b)	..	..	..	6,063	11,131	..	..
Maldives (b)	..	..	..	21	21	..	..
Mali (b,h)	n.a.	n.a.	n.a.	336	5,312	..	..
Malta	420	281	139	5,961	61,713	23,733	+420
Marshall Islands (b)	..	..	..	576	2,930	..	..
Mauritania (b,h)	n.a.	n.a.	n.a.	132	2,084	..	..
Mauritius	4,186	2,114	2,072	3,791	8,289	..	..
Mexico	151,187	98,333	52,854	105,505	116,097	1,419,666	+127,128
Monaco	8,030	1,255	6,775	3,404	13,330	10,489	+135
Mongolia	14,597	9,536	5,061	9,598	9,780	17,807	+104
Montenegro (b)	..	..	..	34	190	..	..
Morocco	30,378	16,687	13,691	18,446	26,308	..	..
Mozambique	4,469	1,190	3,279	1,276	1,328	32,692	+2,277
Myanmar (b)	..	..	..	176	176	..	..
Namibia (b)	..	..	..	245	620	..	..
Nauru (b)	..	..	..	2	6	..	..
Nepal (b)	..	..	..	29	29	..	..
Netherlands (c)	n.a.	n.a.	n.a.	90,537	570,583	n.a.	n.a.
New Zealand	58,265	20,063	38,202	30,698	50,566	301,919	+16,500
Nicaragua (b)	..	..	..	65	169	..	..
Niger (b,h)	n.a.	n.a.	n.a.	81	1,329	..	..
Nigeria (b)	..	..	..	203	1,401	..	..
North Macedonia	10,065	1,735	8,330	2,501	3,709	18,364	..
Norway	47,543	10,365	37,178	21,610	83,138	236,401	+3,185
Oman (g)	10,677	..	..	361	1,069	..	..
Pakistan	19,049	12,564	6,485	12,909	13,859	220,520	+16,429
Panama	9,531	4,297	5,234	6,474	9,688	188,704	-4,037
Papua New Guinea (b)	..	..	..	6	58	..	..
Paraguay (b)	..	..	..	255	543	..	..
Peru	36,621	24,732	11,889	26,069	27,095	403,280	+22,955
Philippines	59,910	28,594	31,316	30,654	31,610	172,325	+10,941
Poland	38,601	32,422	6,179	57,609	381,077	248,303	+11,349
Portugal	34,506	29,920	4,586	37,208	138,120	233,667	-68,841
Qatar	8,821	1,021	7,800	1,892	3,532	130,590	..
Republic of Korea	184,201	133,793	50,408	199,557	301,741	1,467,728	+87,103
Republic of Moldova	10,465	2,388	8,077	3,509	4,627	75,260	+1,272
Romania	19,795	16,106	3,689	20,966	102,134	87,662	+3,579
Russian Federation	216,541	158,445	58,096	209,713	253,059	753,385	+39,552
Rwanda (b)	..	..	..	..	..	..	..
Saint Kitts and Nevis (b)	..	..	..	131	695	..	..
Saint Lucia (b)	..	..	..	248	248	..	..
Saint Vincent and the Grenadines	53	2	51	94	354	..	..
Samoa (b)	..	..	..	212	654	5,509	+782
San Marino (b)	..	..	..	521	2,919	..	..
Sao Tome and Principe (b)	..	..	..	1	1	..	..
Saudi Arabia	26,144	14,174	11,970	15,837	19,973	..	..
Senegal (b,h)	n.a.	n.a.	n.a.	803	12,821	..	..
Serbia	16,612	3,518	13,094	8,873	18,521	32,265	+957
Seychelles (b)	..	..	..	1,676	5,776	..	..
Sierra Leone (g)	2,015	..	..	8	72	..	..
Singapore	55,722	12,096	43,626	44,224	87,996	357,402	+12,805
Sint Maarten (Dutch Part) (b,i)	..	..	..	39	39	..	..
Slovakia	11,819	8,062	3,757	11,831	50,203	47,542	+84
Slovenia (b)	..	..	..	4,037	39,073	..	..
Solomon Islands (b)	..	..	..	9	9	..	..

Name	Registration class count by office: Total	Resident	Non-resident	Registration class count by origin: Total (a)	Equivalent registration class count by origin: Total (a)	In force by office: Total	Change over previous year
Somalia (b)	..	..	..	1	1	..	..
South Africa	16,874	10,162	6,712	12,039	20,009	383,595	+2,501
South Sudan (b)	..	..	..	44	44	..	..
Spain	65,596	57,261	8,335	114,329	727,253	817,119	+23,185
Sri Lanka	5,459	2,734	2,725	3,137	4,033	54,654	..
Sudan (b)	..	..	..	28	28	..	..
Suriname	4,105	3,455	650	3,469	3,507	12,400	+370
Sweden	16,721	12,906	3,815	63,815	376,857	125,430	–134
Switzerland	104,288	41,287	63,001	164,756	504,750	534,960	+11,260
Syrian Arab Republic	8,517	6,309	2,208	6,814	8,374	..	..
Tajikistan (b)	..	..	..	31	31	..	..
Thailand	53,710	21,932	31,778	27,488	31,674	434,178	+11,117
Togo (b,h)	n.a.	n.a.	n.a.	368	6,206	..	..
Tonga (b)	..	..	..	1	1	..	..
Trinidad and Tobago	3,139	668	2,471	769	879	24,724	+1,624
Tunisia (b)	..	..	..	335	1,825	..	..
Türkiye	293,902	258,481	35,421	283,725	347,569	1,343,048	+122,998
Turkmenistan (b)	..	..	..	48	48	..	..
Uganda (b)	..	..	..	11	16	..	..
Ukraine	62,138	35,790	26,348	42,660	54,776	211,732	+10,679
United Arab Emirates (b)	..	..	..	7,673	32,075	..	..
United Kingdom	383,041	199,963	183,078	341,823	1,068,763	849,895	+20,966
United Republic of Tanzania (g)	3,005	..	..	33	35	..	..
United States of America	490,998	228,246	262,752	625,900	1,641,022	2,808,331	+202,415
Uruguay	8,939	3,456	5,483	4,940	6,812	83,603	+615
Uzbekistan	16,766	8,566	8,200	8,932	9,052	28,141	+3,659
Vanuatu (b)	..	..	..	11	11	..	..
Venezuela (Bolivarian Republic of)	8,185	8,185	0	8,494	8,754	..	..
Viet Nam	75,574	41,423	34,151	45,167	48,731	292,578	+20,289
Yemen	4,388	3,137	1,251	3,401	3,777	..	..
Zambia (b)	..	..	..	67	93	..	..
Zimbabwe (g)	2,183	..	..	83	172	69,190	+964
Others/Unknown	..	..	..	36,545	113,973	..	..
Total (2021 estimates)	**13,974,200**	**11,454,300**	**2,519,900**	**13,974,200**		**73,736,300**	

(a) Data on registration class count by origin are incomplete, because some offices do not report detailed statistics containing the origin of registration class counts.

(b) Only Madrid designation data are available therefore registration class count by office and origin data may be incomplete.

(c) This country does not have a national trademark office. All trademark registrations for this country are issued by the Benelux Office for Intellectual Property or the European Union Intellectual Property Office.

(d) Resident registrations include those issued to residents of Belgium, Luxembourg and the Netherlands.

(e) Resident registrations include those issued to residents of EU member states.

(f) Origin is defined as the country/territory of the stated residence of the holder of an international registration.

(g) Total includes an aggregate direct registration class count that cannot be broken down into direct and non-resident components.

(h) The African Intellectual Property Office (OAPI) is the competent office for issuing registrations.

(i) This country or municipality is not a Madrid member. The Netherlands has extended the application of the Madrid Protocol to the territories of Curaçao and Sint Maarten, Bonaire, Sint Eustatius and Saba.

n.a. indicates not applicable.

.. indicates not available.

Source: WIPO Statistics Database, September 2022.

B46. Trademark office procedural data, 2021

Office	Total applications processed	Registered	Total rejections	Withdrawn or abandoned	Applications pending	Number of examiners (FTE)	First office action (days)	Final office decision (days)
African Intellectual Property Organization	..	..	..	..	250	8.0	..	..
Albania	508	465	24	19	896	4.0	45.0	180.0
Algeria	2,782	748	2,027	7	1,575	16.0	240.0	185.0
Angola	2,856	2,719	89	48	1,368	8.0	90.0	120.0
Argentina	85,314	75,637	7,487	2,190	166,569	15.0	4.0	540.0
Armenia	1,248	850	341	57	632	8.0	10.0	100.0
Australia	56,187	53,050	2,635	502	7,870	137.3	60.0	127.0
Azerbaijan	2,632	1,227	889	516	..	9.0	30.0	150.0
Bangladesh	15,527	3,945	226	11,356	46,385	10.0	30.0	50.0
Belarus	3,374	3,120	..	254	..	23.0	60.0	300.0
Bhutan	776	742	31	3	12	2.0	30.0	90.0
Bosnia and Herzegovina	1,239	1,027	48	164	849	5.0	220.0	410.0
Botswana	664	556	108	..	480	4.0	5.0	3.0
Brazil	270,589	158,653	71,517	40,419	294,072	99.0	270.0	420.0
Brunei Darussalam	197	56	..	141	215	3.0	7.0	30.0
Bulgaria	4,290	3,633	122	535	2,236	10.0	7.0	173.0
Cabo Verde	..	..	..	..	1,697	3.0	..	..
Cambodia	5,087	1,221	..	3,866	..	11.0	5.0	2.0
Canada	31,725	21,769	66	9,890	187,487	64.0	875.0	1,028.0
Chile	43,246	28,289	5,898	9,059	38,584	20.0	..	..
China	10,664,193	7,738,947	2,925,246	..	..	1,441.0	122.0	214.0
China, Hong Kong SAR	36,679	32,719	3,203	757	21,164	40.0	42.0	127.0
China, Macao SAR	14,058	13,136	836	86	5,115	7.0	173.0	173.0
Colombia	39,714	27,986	10,944	784	17,591	70.0	16.4	207.0
Croatia	879	685	77	117	439	3.0	22.0	44.0
Cuba	1,431	1,068	229	134	2,082	7.0	60.0	855.0
Curaçao	464	462	2	..	13	4.0	60.0	60.0
Cyprus	781	745	31	5	69	7.0	..	30.0
Czech Republic	6,675	6,049	537	89	4,228	20.0	..	264.0
Denmark	2,712	2,409	154	149	720	17.0	1.0	22.8
Dominica	..	..	..	..	..	1.0	..	..
Ecuador	13,941	13,486	403	52	6,830	5.0	20.0	120.0
El Salvador	..	..	..	..	..	19.0	5.0	5.0
Estonia	1,662	1,404	4	254	813	9.0	3.0	105.0
European Union Intellectual Property Office	158,707	154,075	3,560	1,072	80,026	253.0	16.0	11.1
France	127,581	115,520	8,311	3,750	45,528	84.0	..	..
Georgia	2,989	1,486	197	1,306	848	11.0	57.0	215.0
Germany	91,618	68,602	9,634	13,382	23,360	73.8	52.1	84.1
Greece	..	..	..	..	..	4.0	..	30.0
Guyana	596	586	..	10	166	2.0	1.0	4.0
Hungary	4,329	3,404	141	784	2,406	12.0	15.0	178.0
Iceland	1,195	952	191	52	72	6.0	50.0	207.0
India	374,243	319,764	39,422	15,057	40,667	150.0	30.0	45.0
Israel	5,464	4,653	..	811	4,833	17.0	96.0	205.0
Italy	42,366	39,102	2,307	957	..	10.0	..	180.0
Jamaica	1,816	1,471	..	345	1,993	4.0	14.0	180.0
Japan	189,342	167,561	21,781	..	..	168.0	247.0	288.0
Kazakhstan	6,026	5,353	392	281	2,909	37.0	10.0	285.0
Kyrgyzstan	799	742	42	15	104	5.0	15.0	240.0
Latvia	677	602	50	25	233	4.5	1.0	59.0
Lithuania	2,563	2,280	253	30	285	5.0	4.0	33.0
Madagascar	1,369	1,329	38	2	63	3.0	225.0	225.0
Malta	671	420	30	221	..	3.0	1.0	60.0
Mauritius	2,373	2,188	185	..	..	7.0	2.0	20.0
Mexico	134,765	123,466	6,529	4,770	172,482	45.0	73.0	120.0
Monaco	649	607	32	10	..	2.0	5.0	36.0
Mongolia	3,161	2,730	415	16	1,579	3.0	90.0	180.0

Office	Total applications processed	Registered	Total rejections	Withdrawn or abandoned	Applications pending	Number of examiners (FTE)	First office action (days)	Final office decision (days)
Mozambique	..	..	..	..	189	11.0	..	..
New Zealand	9,769	9,342	..	427	3,672	39.0	22.1	24.3
North Macedonia	1,153	1,127	21	5	114	5.0	30.0	14.0
Norway	7,514	6,265	101	1,148	3,031	20.0	72.0	..
Oman	9,338	5,117	98	4,123	..	7.0	10.0	90.0
Pakistan	38,467	17,206	133	21,128	4,199	6.0	50.0	240.0
Panama	6,540	5,783	319	438	85	8.0	45.0	60.0
Peru	45,363	35,131	7,449	2,783	11,417	50.0	4.0	58.0
Philippines	27,247	26,611	636	..	16,648	31.0	22.7	109.8
Poland	15,552	12,959	1,283	1,310	..	..	..	..
Portugal	24,975	19,789	4,756	430	1,380	22.0	120.0	150.0
Qatar	4,564	4,193	242	129	4,564	10.0	30.0	30.0
Republic of Korea	241,343	201,381	39,962	..	300,669	149.0	308.0	369.0
Republic of Moldova	2,251	1,630	218	403	2,579	8.0	11.0	241.0
Romania	9,292	8,269	812	211	2,398	44.0	7.0	180.0
Russian Federation	71,868	60,363	10,948	557	21,330	120.0	120.0	150.0
Saint Vincent and the Grenadines	50	34	16	..	216	4.0	7.0	14.0
Samoa	135	135	..	..	..	3.0	7.0	30.0
San Marino	..	..	..	..	80	1.0	..	..
Saudi Arabia	40,218	26,144	6,389	7,685	333	10.0	73.0	81.0
Serbia	2,610	2,255	197	158	545	7.0	30.0	180.0
Sierra Leone	497	495	2	..	..	3.0	1.0	3.0
Singapore	..	..	..	..	7,421	32.0	..	..
Slovakia	3,192	2,741	147	304	206	8.0	..	150.0
Spain	12,118	11,220	476	422	39,467	54.0	26.0	186.0
Sri Lanka	57,732	54,654	8	3,070	8,404	17.0	90.0	120.0
Suriname	..	..	..	..	592	3.0	..	..
Sweden	9,368	7,366	254	1,748	1,277	23.0	42.0	95.0
Thailand	87,989	..	52,180	35,809	109,581	34.0	240.0	475.0
Trinidad and Tobago	..	..	..	..	2,538	7.0	..	..
Türkiye	168,194	129,423	8,810	29,961	192,555	95.0	11.0	78.0
Ukraine	33,551	25,326	2,636	5,589	46,250	73.0	354.0	663.0
United Kingdom	159,524	146,237	6,161	7,126	8,413	201.0	34.0	43.0
United States of America	250,354	170,619	28,684	51,051	860,056	679.0	222.0	369.0
Uruguay	451	..	410	41	11,632	..	259.0	..
Uzbekistan	7,421	5,648	223	1,550	1,557	10.0	210.0	360.0
Venezuela (Bolivarian Republic of)	10,366	8,185	2,044	137	10,456	6.0	30.0	180.0
Viet Nam	54,212	46,313	7,684	215	74,357	85.0	763.8	811.0
Zimbabwe	..	..	..	..	934	6.0	..	..

Note: FTE is full time equivalent. WIPO collects data from IP offices using a common questionnaire and methodology. Every effort has been made to compile procedural data based on common definitions and concepts, but procedural differences make it extremely difficult to fully harmonize such data. Therefore caution should be exercised when making comparisons across offices. The total number of applications processed for a given office may be incomplete due to the omission of one or several elements by the office.

.. indicates not available.

Source: WIPO Statistics Database, September 2022.

Industrial designs

Highlights

Designs in industrial design applications saw a sharp increase of 9.2% in 2021

In 2021, about 1.2 million industrial design applications were filed worldwide. This represents an increase of 6.8% on 2020 (figure 3.1). Since 2007, industrial design applications have increased every year, except for 2014. Applications during this period have more than doubled, due in large part to a rapid growth in applications filed in China.

Statistics based on the number of designs contained in industrial design applications - known as application design counts - improve comparability worldwide by harmonizing data from those offices that allow several designs to be contained in a single application with those that allow only one. An estimated 1.5 million designs were contained in applications filed worldwide in 2021 (figure 3.2). This corresponds to an increase of 9.2% on 2020 - the sharpest growth rate since 2013.

Overall, designs contained in resident applications grew by 5.6%. Resident activity in China, India, Türkiye and the United Kingdom (UK) contributed the most to the global increase. Designs contained in non-resident applications grew by 29.4% in 2021. This is the sharpest growth since 2005. Two main reasons may explain such an exceptional increase. First, filing activity abroad rebounded sharply after a year of rapid contraction (-5.5% in 2020) likely due to global containment measures consequent on the COVID-19 pandemic; and second, 2021 was the first year since the UK left the European Union Intellectual Property Office (EUIPO) on its withdrawal from the European Union.

Filings at the UK office more than doubled compared to 2020

The office of China received 805,710 designs in applications in 2021, representing more than half (53.2%) of activity worldwide. It was followed by the EUIPO (117,049), the UK (74,781), the Republic of Korea (69,248) and Türkiye (65,924) (figure 3.3). The office of the UK received 2.3 times more designs in applications than in 2020, taking it up four positions in the world ranking within a year, making it the third most active office in terms of application design count in 2021.

Combined, the top 20 offices accounted for 93.7% of all the designs contained in applications. Of these, 16 saw rises in application design count, nine of which were double-digit or triple-digit increases (figure C10). The three offices where growth was strongest were the UK (+128.5%), India (+67.6%) and Mexico (+38.4%). In contrast, the three offices with the sharpest decreases were Germany (-9%), Thailand (-2.3%) and the Republic of Korea (-2.2%).

In 2021, a majority (11) of the top 20 offices recorded a rise in the number of designs contained in resident and in non-resident applications. In contrast, Germany and Spain saw a decrease in both resident and non-resident filing activity. Growth in resident designs was particularly strong at the offices of India, the Russian Federation, Türkiye and the UK. In regard to non-resident design counts, the sharpest increases were at the offices of Canada, Mexico and the UK.

About 1.2 million industrial design applications were filed worldwide in 2021

3.1. Industrial design applications worldwide, 2007–2021

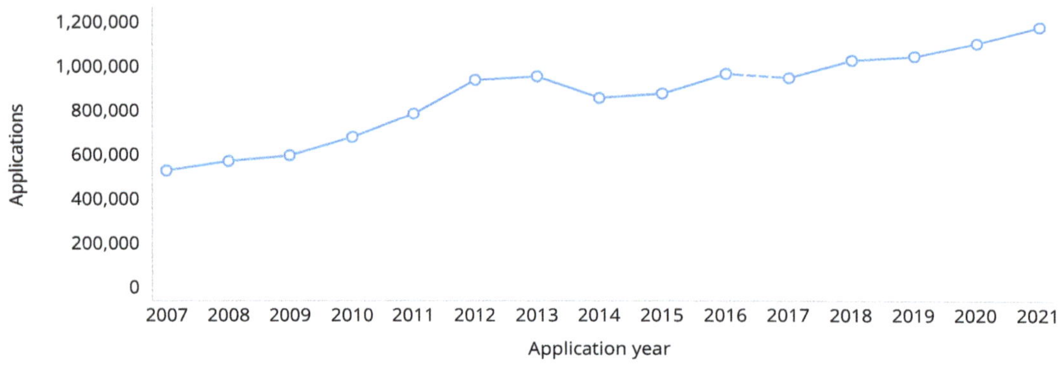

Source: Figure C1.

Designs contained in applications totaled 1.5 million

3.2. Number of designs in industrial design applications worldwide, 2007–2021

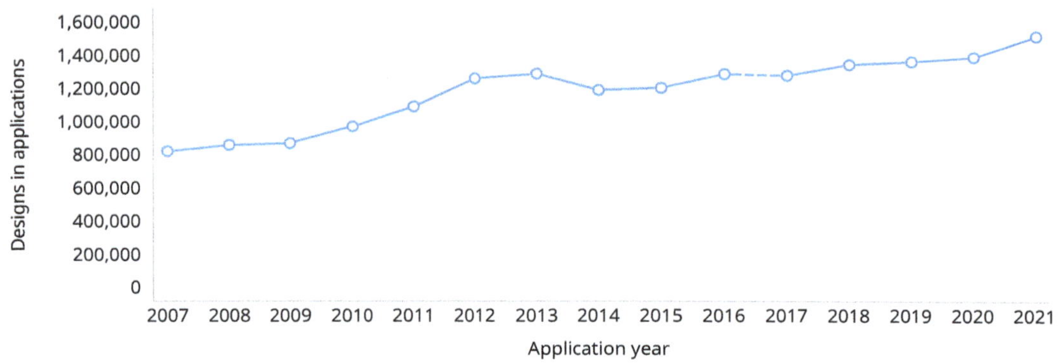

Source: Figure C2.

China received 53.2% of all designs contained in applications filed worldwide

3.3. Application design counts for the top 10 offices, 2021

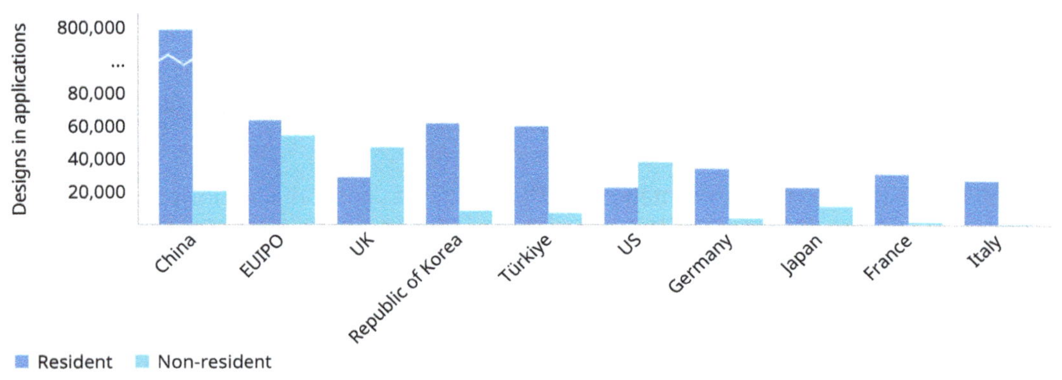

Source: Figure C9.

Among offices located in low- and middle-income countries, the annual growth rate in 2021 was especially high for Mongolia (+72%), Jordan (+44.9%) and Peru (+40.9%). Albeit from a low base, the Syrian Arab Republic (–54.9%), Serbia (–16%) and the African Intellectual Property Organization (OAPI) (–10.1%) all saw a sharp decline in both resident and non-resident design counts (figure C12).

Designs contained in resident applications amounted to 82% of the world total design count in 2021. The particularly high resident design share of China (97.5%) mostly explains a correspondingly large proportion of resident designs at world level. Resident design counts also accounted for a majority of filing activity at 13 of the top 20 offices (figure C9). Principal exceptions were Canada (7.5%), Mexico (22.9%) and Switzerland (28.8%), for whom non-resident activity accounted for the bulk of total.

Asia accounted for 69.3% of all designs in applications filed worldwide in 2021 (figure 3.4). Asia was followed by Europe (23.3%) and North America (4.6%). Between 2011 and 2021, North America (+6.8%) and Asia (+4.2%) saw the largest average increases in designs in applications filed.

Design count
Some offices allow industrial design applications to contain more than one design for the same good or in the same class; others allow only one design per application. In order to capture the differences in application filing systems across offices, the respective application and registration design counts needed to be compared.

Equivalent design count
Designs in applications filed at regional offices are equivalent to multiple designs in applications filed in the respective member states of those offices. To calculate the number of equivalent designs for the OAPI, which has 17 member states, the Benelux Office for Intellectual Property (BOIP), which has three, and EUIPO (27), each design is multiplied by the corresponding number of member states. However, the African Regional Intellectual Property Organization (ARIPO) and the Eurasian Patent Organization (EAPO) do not register industrial designs with an automatic region-wide applicability. Therefore, for these offices, each application is counted as one application abroad, if the applicant does not reside in a member state, or as one resident application and one application abroad, if the applicant resides in a member state.

Offices located in Asia accounted for 69.3% of total filing activity

3.4. Application design counts by region, 2011 and 2021

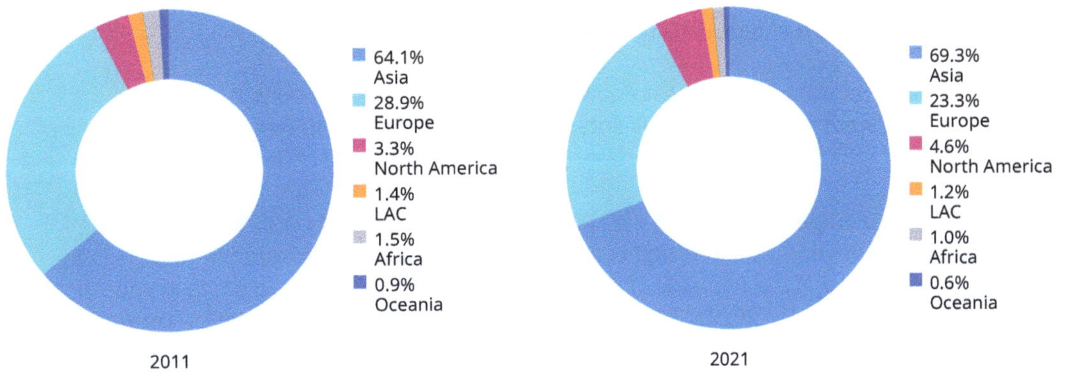

Note: LAC is Latin America and the Caribbean.
Source: Table C7.

Industrial design applications filed since 1883
Between 1883 and the early 1950s, the offices of Japan and the United States of America (US) averaged a similar number of applications, rarely exceeding 10,000. The office of Japan received the highest number of applications per year from the 1950s thru to the late 1990s, reaching approximately 50,000 annual filings at its peak. The office of China, which received 640 applications when it first began receiving applications in 1985, saw unprecedented growth until 2013, with 660,000 applications filed that year. The office of the Republic of Korea surpassed the office of Japan in 2004 and has remained in second position ever since. In 2012, the office of the US moved ahead of Japan to become the third largest globally. The EUIPO began receiving applications in 2003 and moved-up to fourth position in 2019. Among these top five offices, the EUIPO is the only one to have a multiple design system. Applications filed at the EUIPO contained 117,049 designs in 2021.

Trend in industrial design applications for the top five offices, 1883–2021

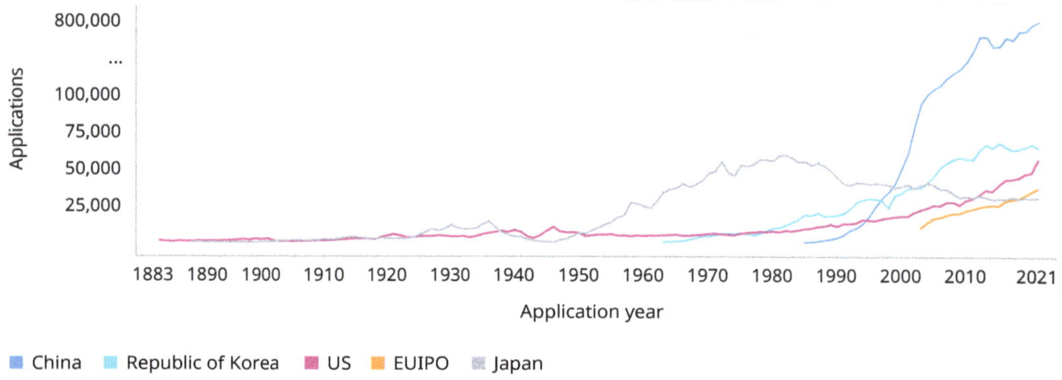

Source: Figure C8.

Applicants from China had far the most equivalent designs in applications filed abroad

Applications received by offices from resident and non-resident applicants are referred to as office data, whereas applications filed by applicants at their home office (resident applications) or at foreign offices (applications abroad) are referred to as origin data. When the equivalent count concept is applied, applications filed by applicants at some regional offices are considered equivalent to multiple applications in the member states of those offices. Here, industrial design statistics based on the origin of residence of the first named applicant are reported in order to complement the picture of industrial design activity worldwide.

Applicants from China had the highest equivalent application design count in 2021, with 1.5 million. They were followed by applicants residing in Germany (540,644), the United States of America (US) (392,236), Italy (350,434) and France (227,866).

Among the top 10 origins, France (+16.3%), Poland (+16.1%) and China (+13.2%) recorded the sharpest increases in equivalent design counts. In contrast, applicants from the UK (-31.1%), Switzerland (-17.6%) and the Republic of Korea (-13%) saw the steepest decreases in equivalent design counts compared to 2020 (figure C16). The sharp drop in equivalent design count from applicants within the UK contrasts with the exceptional increase in filings at the office of the UK. Brexit may again explain this trend, as applicants from the UK had never before filed so few applications at the EUIPO as they did in 2021.

A total of 14 European countries dominates the top 20 origins, followed by five located in Asia and one in North America. In terms of income categories, 18 of the top 20 origins belong to the high-income group, while China and Türkiye are the only two upper middle-income countries to feature.

Equivalent designs in applications filed abroad accounted for over three-quarters of total filing activity from the top 20 origins, except for China (48.1%), the Republic of Korea (47.5%) and Türkiye (24.7%).

In 2021, applicants from China had by far the highest number of equivalent designs in applications filed abroad, with 726,985 such designs, representing an annual growth rate of 24.5%. Over the past decade, the number of equivalent designs in applications filed abroad from China has grown almost tenfold. China was followed by Germany (489,249), the US (370,323) and Italy (312,486).

The Republic of Korea and Türkiye top the ranking when adjusting for population

Adjusting resident filing according to gross domestic product (GDP) and population helps when comparing the intensity of industrial design filing by residents across origins.

China (3,161) had the highest resident design count per USD 100 billion of GDP in 2021 (figure 3.5). China was followed by the Republic of Korea (2,682) and Türkiye (2,233). In contrast, Japan (430), India (188) and the US (105) had far lower ratios. Compared to a decade earlier, in 2011, the 2021 ratios have increased markedly for the UK (+556) and decreased steeply for China (-737).

The Republic of Korea (1,183) had by far the highest resident design count per million population in 2021 (figure C27). It was followed by Türkiye (698), Italy (642) and Germany (618) which shared similar counts. Compared to the ratios for 2011, those for 2021 increased sharply for the UK (+267), Türkiye (+215) and China (+179). In contrast, the ratios for Switzerland (-166), Spain (-158) and Germany (-155) decreased markedly during this 10-year period.

The top four sectors accounted for a majority of filings worldwide

Grouping the 32 Locarno classes into 12 industry sectors serves to highlight the most important industry sectors for designs contained in industrial design applications filed. In 2021, the sectors with the biggest shares of the world total were furniture and household goods (17.8%), textiles and accessories (14.7%), tools and machines (11.8%) and electricity and lighting (9.9%). Combined, these four sectors accounted for a majority (54.2%) of all recorded classes (figure C23).

For all the top 10 offices for which data were available, between 35% and 61% of total classes was concentrated in just three sectors, although the top three sectors varied between offices (figure 3.6). Furniture and household goods accounted for a large proportion of the total at the offices of Türkiye (26.9%), China (19.2%), Australia (13.1%) and Canada (12.5%). Textiles and accessories was the top sector at the offices of Germany (24.7%), India (23.2%), the UK (16.9%), the EUIPO (16.1%) and the Russian Federation (14.1%). Tools and machines was the main sector for the Republic of Korea (22%) (figure C24).

All top 10 origins filed more than 42% of applications across their top three sectors (figure C25). Textiles and accessories was a top three sector for four of the top 10 origins, followed by furniture and household goods for three, ICT and audiovisual for two and tools and machines for one.

The top 20 offices accounted for 95% of all applications registered worldwide in 2021

An estimated 1.1 million industrial design applications were registered worldwide in 2021. This represents an increase of 5.8% on 2020 (figure C4). The number of applications registered worldwide doubled between 2010 and 2021, mainly due to a considerable rise in registrations issued by the office of China.

Nearly 1.4 million designs were contained in applications registered in 2021, up 6.9% on the preceding year (figure C5). The office of China accounted for 58% of all designs in applications registered worldwide, and the top 20 offices combined accounted for 94.9%. Of these, 14 offices recorded an annual growth, including sharp increases at the offices of the UK (+117.2%), Mexico (+82%) and India (+49.2%). In contrast, the offices of France (-21.1%), Germany (-17.1%) and the US (-12.4%) were the ones to see the steepest declines in designs registered among the top 20 offices (figure C13).

For a third consecutive year, active registrations worldwide saw double-digit growth

Industrial design rights generally last for up to 15 years from the date an application is filed. In 2021, there were an estimated 5.3 million active industrial design registrations at 130 offices worldwide. This represents an increase of 10.9% on 2020, almost identical to the preceding year (11%) but slightly below that recorded in 2019 (13%) (figure C28). Registrations in force in China grew by 18% to reach 2.6 million, representing nearly half (48.9%) the world total in 2021 (figure C29). China was followed by the Republic of Korea (388,500), the US (381,549), the EUIPO (268,150) and Japan (263,274). Combined, the top 20 offices accounted for 94.3% of active industrial design registrations globally.

China had the most designs per unit of GDP in 2021

3.5. Resident application design count per USD 100 billion GDP for selected origins, 2011 and 2021

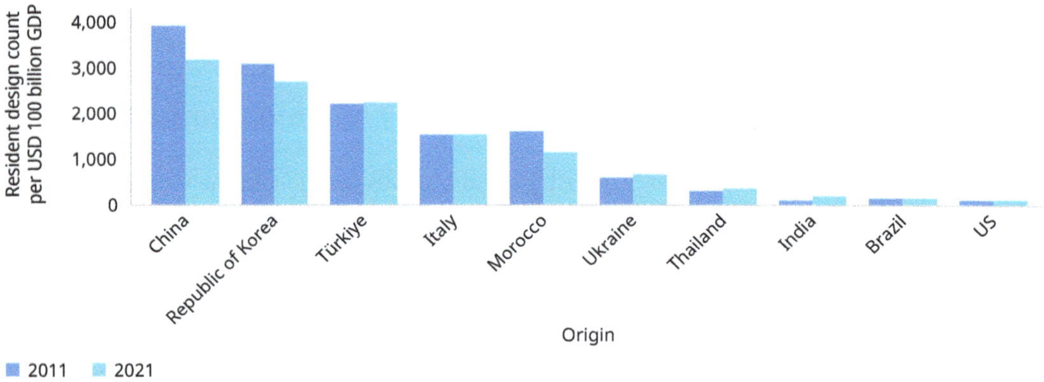

Source: Figure C26.

The top three sectors accounted for almost half of application design counts in India

3.6. Distribution of application design counts by the top three sectors for selected offices, 2021

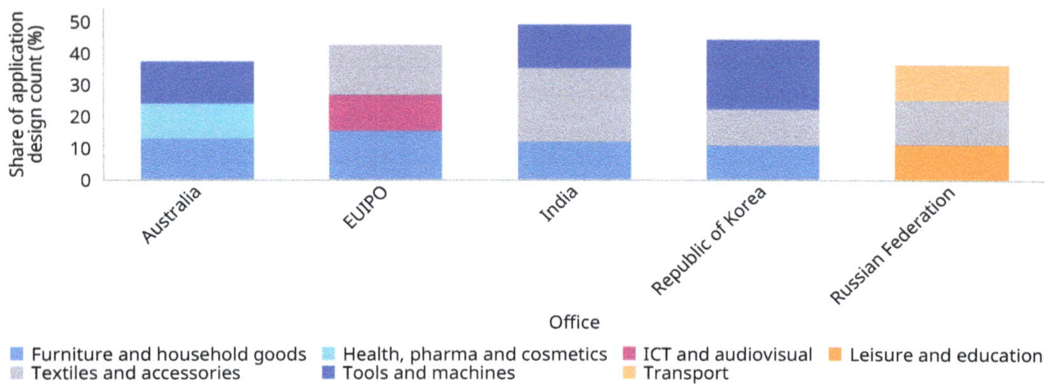

Source: Figure C24.

About 4.8 million of the active industrial design registrations at 90 offices in 2021 can be distributed according to the year in which they were first registered (figure C30). Almost a quarter of the industrial design applications registered in 2007 remained in force in 2021. A majority of those registered in 2012 remained active in 2021, along with over two-thirds of those registered in 2016.

The average age of active industrial design registrations varied across offices. For example, in 2021, the average age of all the industrial design registrations in force in Israel was 10.1 years, and in China 2.9 years (figure C31).

China, the EUIPO and the UK registered over 90% of applications processed in 2021

An industrial design office examines applications and decides whether to register them. Examination processes differ across offices, which makes cross-office comparisons difficult. Every effort has been made to compile examination outcome data based on common definitions and concepts. In 2021, 76 offices shared data on industrial design examination outcomes – registered, rejected or withdrawn/abandoned – with WIPO.

The distribution of examination outcomes differs widely across offices. Among the top five offices in application design count, the EUIPO (97.7%) had the largest proportion of processed applications registered in 2021. It was followed by the UK (94.9%), China (91.2%), Türkiye (87.6%) and the Republic of Korea (86%) (figure C32). The offices of Italy (98.3%) and India (97.8%) also registered a large proportion of processed applications. The share of applications rejected was particularly high at the offices of Israel (35.1%), Saudi Arabia (26.4%), Viet Nam (24.2%) and the US (22%). Applications withdrawn or abandoned accounted for a large share of total applications processed in Mexico (35.8%), Thailand (31.8%) and Bangladesh (23.4%).

About 471,300 applications were potentially pending worldwide in 2021

In general, to qualify for protection an industrial design must be new, original and have individual character. At some offices, no search is made and no examination as to substance is carried out prior to registration. At other offices, a substantive examination is conducted, whereby the design is checked against designs on the register for novelty and/or originality. Potentially pending applications are all industrial design applications, at any stage in the process, awaiting a final decision by an office. Based on data from 70 offices, the total number of pending applications worldwide stood at 471,300 in 2021, 17.8% lower than the 2020 total. This drop is mainly due to a 30.9% decrease in pending applications in China.

In 2021, China had 291,609 applications pending (figure C33). It was followed by the offices of the US (76,749) and the Republic of Korea (28,296). The EUIPO (2,908) and the UK (4,689), which feature as the second and third largest offices in terms of application design count in 2021, had far lower volumes of applications pending. Among middle-income countries, India (15,058) and Thailand (11,988) had a considerable number of applications pending in 2021.

On average, an industrial design application was processed the day following its filing at the office of Switzerland, as compared with the office of Mexico, where it was within 480 days (figure C34). The average time between filing and a final office decision was under three days both in Argentina and at the EUIPO. On average, first action and final decision were on the same day at the office of Türkiye. However, in Thailand, final office decisions were not made until 583 days after the first office action.

Industrial design statistics

Industrial design applications and registrations worldwide

C1. Trend in industrial design applications worldwide, 2007–2021

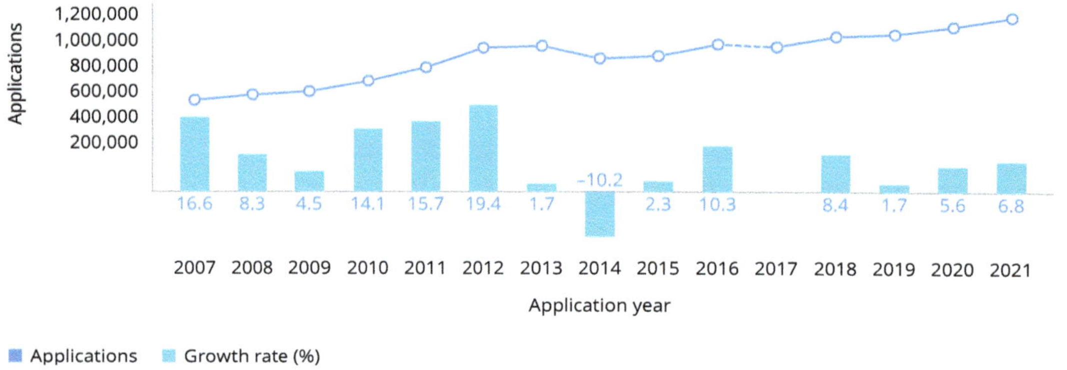

Note: From 2017 onwards, industrial design application data provided by the IP office of China include only those applications for which the necessary application fees has been paid. Because China accounts for the bulk of the global total, this means it is not possible to report the 2017 worldwide application growth rate. World totals are WIPO estimates using data covering 151 IP offices. These totals include applications filed directly with national and regional offices (known as the Paris route), as well as the designations received via the Hague System (where applicable).

Source: WIPO Statistics Database, September 2022.

C2. Trend in application design counts worldwide, 2007–2021

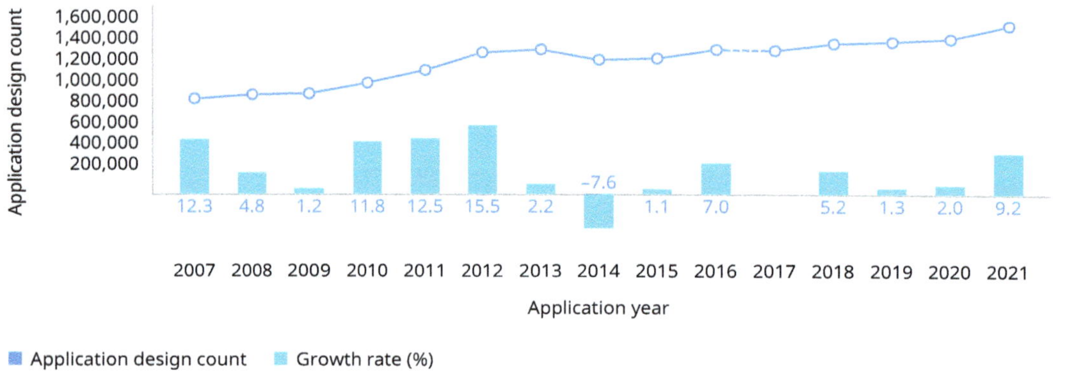

Note: From 2017 onwards, industrial design application data provided by the IP office of China include only those applications for which the necessary application fees have been paid. Because China accounts for the bulk of the global total, this means it is not possible to report the 2017 worldwide application growth rate. World totals are WIPO estimates using data covering 151 IP offices. These totals include designs contained in applications filed directly with national and regional offices (known as the Paris route), as well as designs contained in designations received via the Hague System (where applicable). See the glossary for the definition of design count.

Source: WIPO Statistics Database, September 2022.

C3. Resident and non-resident application design counts worldwide, 2007–2021

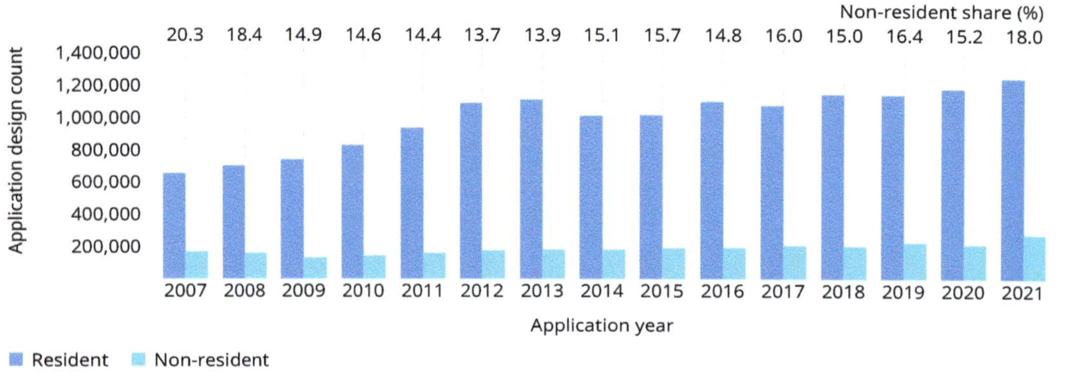

Note: World totals are WIPO estimates using data covering 151 IP offices. These totals include designs contained in applications filed directly with national and regional offices (known as the Paris route), as well as designs contained in designations received via the Hague System (where applicable). See the glossary for the definition of design count.

Source: WIPO Statistics Database, September 2022.

C4. **Trend in industrial design registrations worldwide, 2007–2021**

Note: World totals are WIPO estimates using data covering 151 IP offices. These totals include the registrations issued by national and regional offices for applications filed directly with offices (known as the Paris route), as well as for designations received via the Hague System (where applicable).

Source: WIPO Statistics Database, September 2022.

C5. **Trend in registration design counts worldwide, 2007–2021**

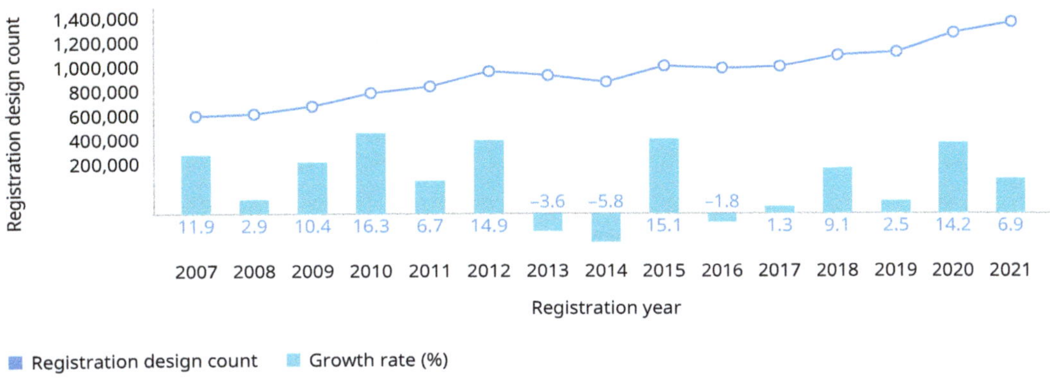

Note: World totals are WIPO estimates using data covering 151 IP offices. These totals include designs contained in registrations issued by national and regional offices for applications filed directly with offices (known as the Paris route), as well as for designations received via the Hague System (where applicable). See the glossary for the definition of design count.

Source: WIPO Statistics Database, September 2022.

C6. **Resident and non-resident registration design counts worldwide, 2007–2021**

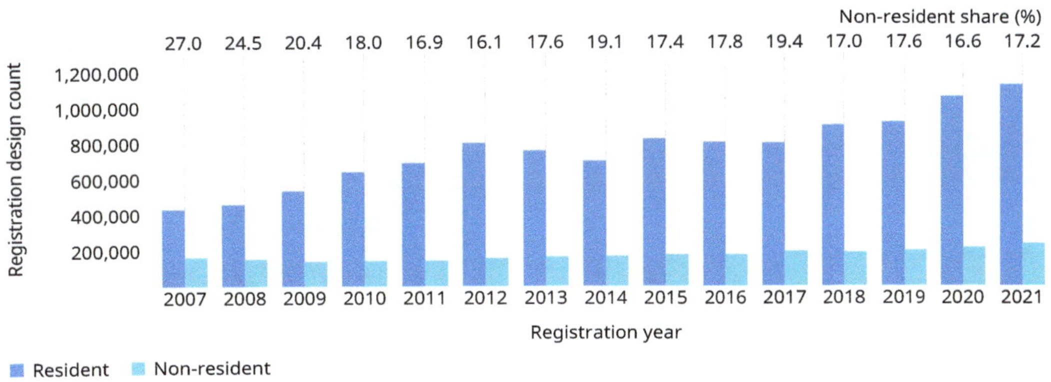

Note: World totals are WIPO estimates using data covering 151 IP offices. These totals include designs contained in registrations issued by national and regional offices for applications filed directly with offices (known as the Paris route), as well as for designations received via the Hague System (where applicable). See the glossary for the definition of design count.

Source: WIPO Statistics Database, September 2022.

Industrial design applications and registrations by office

C7. Application design counts by region, 2011 and 2021

	Application design count		Resident share (%)		Share of world total (%)		Average growth (%)
Region	**2011**	**2021**	**2011**	**2021**	**2011**	**2021**	**2011–2021**
Africa	16,000	15,500	58.1	64.9	1.5	1.0	-0.3
Asia	698,400	1,049,700	92.7	93.3	64.1	69.3	4.2
Europe	314,400	353,700	55.1	61.7	28.9	23.3	1.2
Latin America and the Caribbean	15,600	17,700	51.9	46.9	1.4	1.2	1.3
North America	35,700	69,000	51.1	32.8	3.3	4.6	6.8
Oceania	9,500	9,600	38.8	30.4	0.9	0.6	0.1
World	**1,089,600**	**1,515,200**	**77.7**	**85.0**	**100.0**	**100.0**	**3.4**

Note: Totals by geographical region are WIPO estimates using data covering 151 IP offices. Each region includes the following number of offices: Africa (33), Asia (43), Europe (42), Latin America and the Caribbean (27), North America (2) and Oceania (4). For information on geographical region classification, see the Data description section.

Source: WIPO Statistics Database, September 2022.

C8. Trend in industrial design applications for the top five offices, 1883–2021

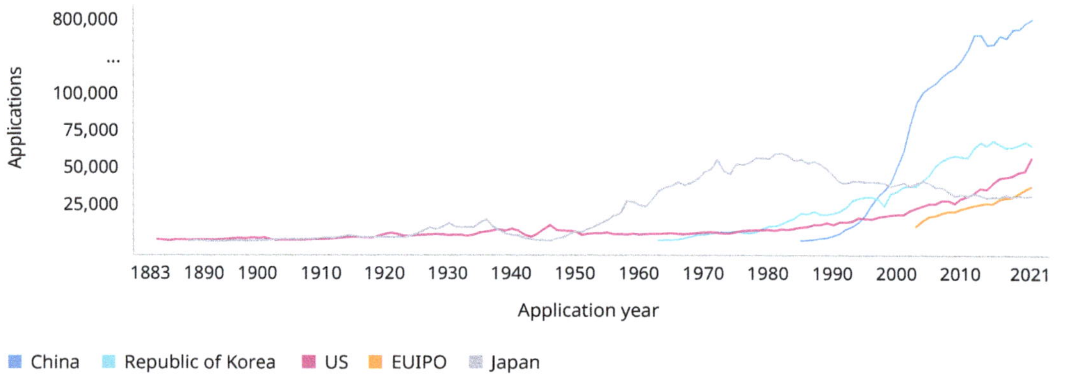

Note: The decrease in applications at the IP office of China in 2017 is most likely explained by the new way in which that office counts applications data. Starting from 2017, China's application count data include only those applications for which the necessary application fees have been paid. EUIPO is the European Union Intellectual Property Office. Data are based on the numbers of applications filed; differences between single-design and multiple-design filing systems across IP offices are not taken into account. The top five offices are selected based on 2021 totals.

Source: WIPO Statistics Database, September 2022.

C9. Application design counts for the top 20 offices, 2021

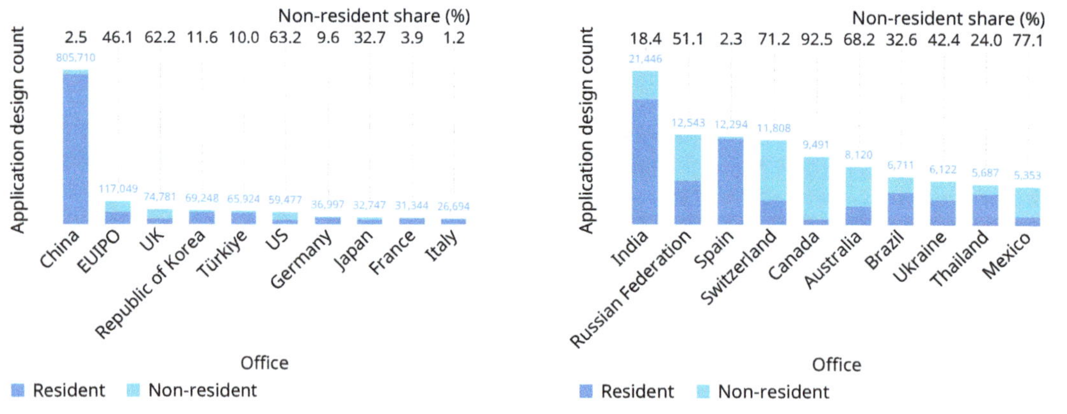

Note: EUIPO is the European Union Intellectual Property Office.

Source: WIPO Statistics Database, September 2022.

C10. Contribution of resident and non-resident application design counts to total growth for the top 20 offices, 2020–2021

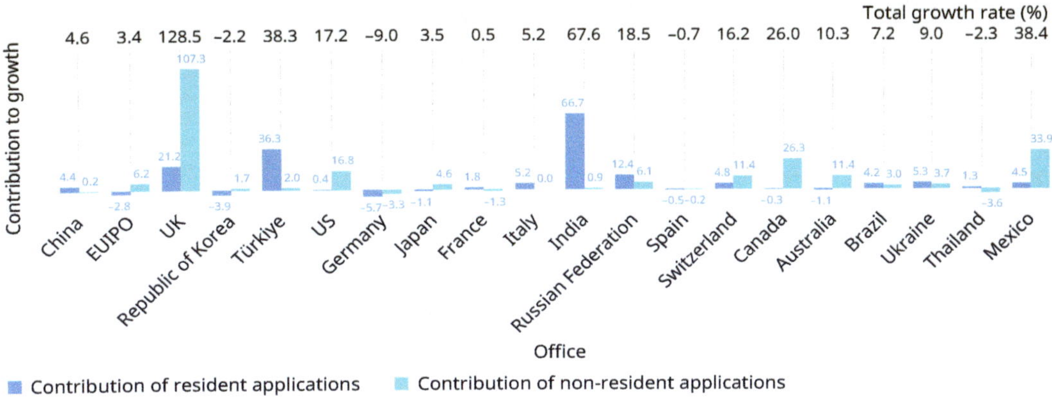

Note: EUIPO is the European Union Intellectual Property Office. This figure shows total growth in application design counts, broken down by the respective contributions of resident and non-resident filings. For example, total design counts in Germany decreased by 9%, with resident applicants contributing 5.7 percentage points to the overall decline and non-resident applicants 3.3 percentage points.

Source: WIPO Statistics Database, September 2022.

C11. Application design counts for offices of selected low- and middle-income countries, 2021

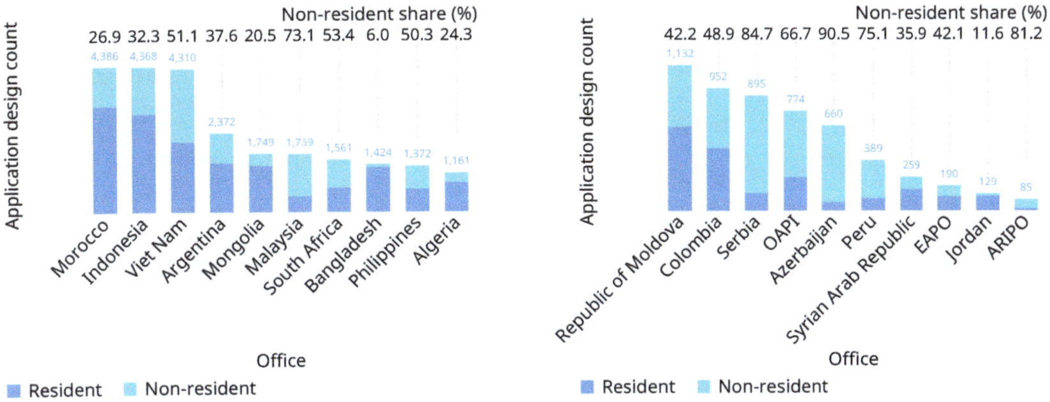

Note: ARIPO is the African Regional Intellectual Property Organization, EAPO is the Eurasian Patent Organization and OAPI is the African Intellectual Property Organization. The selected offices are from different world regions and income groups (low-income, lower middle-income and upper middle-income). Where available, data for all offices are presented in statistical table C36 at the end of this section.

Source: WIPO Statistics Database, September 2022.

C12. Contribution of resident and non-resident application design counts to total growth for offices of selected low- and middle-income countries, 2020–2021

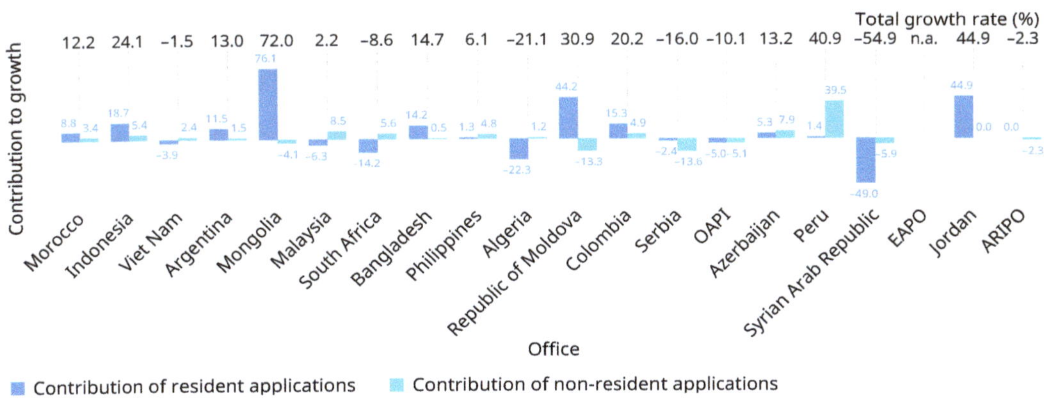

Note: ARIPO is the African Regional Intellectual Property Organization, EAPO is the Eurasian Patent Organization and OAPI is the African Intellectual Property Organization. The selected offices are from different world regions and income groups (low-income, lower middle-income and upper middle-income). Where available, data for all offices are in the statistical table C37 at the end of this section. This figure shows total growth in design counts, broken down by the respective contributions made by resident and non-resident filings. For example, the total design count in Indonesia grew by 24.1%, with resident applicants contributing 18.7 percentage points to overall growth and non-resident applicants 5.4 percentage points.

n.a. indicates not applicable.

Source: WIPO Statistics Database, September 2022.

C13. Registration design counts for the top 20 offices, 2021

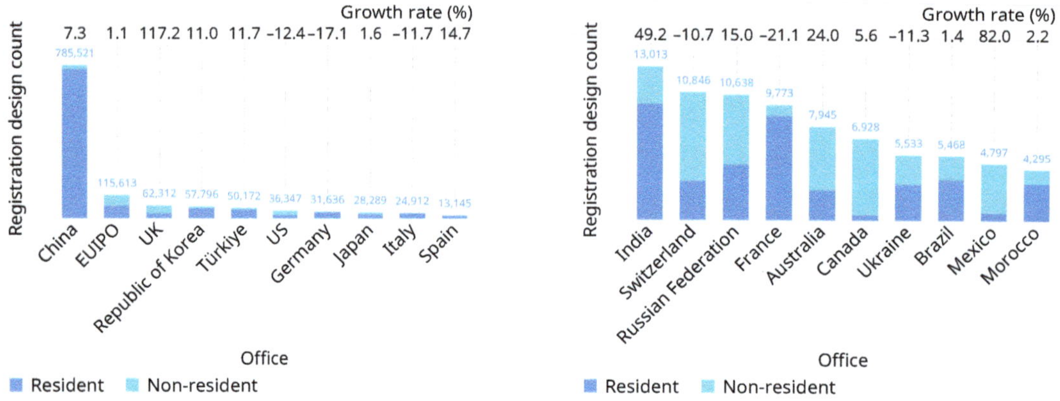

Note: EUIPO is the European Union Intellectual Property Office.

Source: WIPO Statistics Database, September 2022.

C14. Registration design counts for offices of selected low- and middle-income countries, 2021

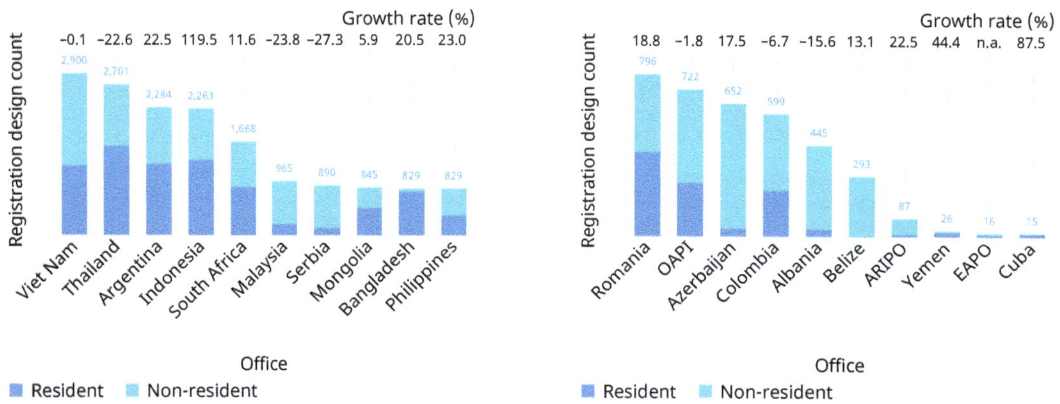

Note: ARIPO is the African Regional Intellectual Property Organization, EAPO is the Eurasian Patent Organization and OAPI is the African Intellectual Property Organization. The selected offices are from different world regions and income groups (low-income, lower middle-income and upper middle-income). Where available, data for all offices are presented in statistical table C37 at the end of this section.

n.a. indicates not applicable.

Source: WIPO Statistics Database, September 2022.

C15. Non-resident application design counts by filing route, 2007–2021

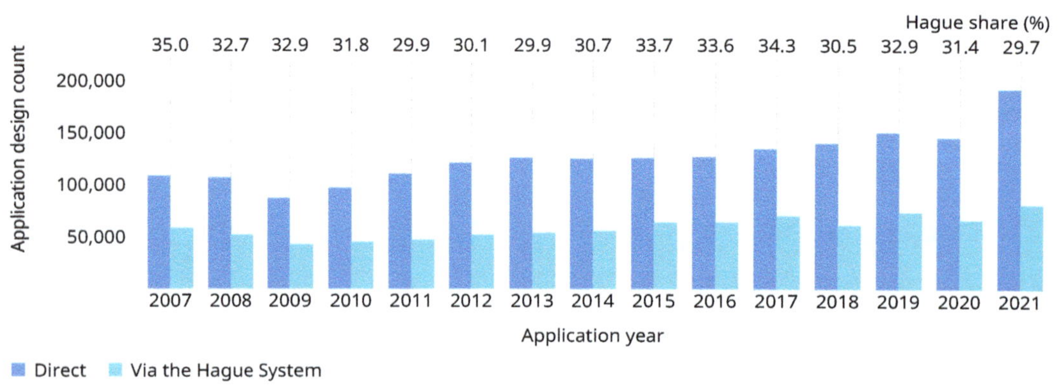

Source: WIPO Statistics Database, September 2022.

Application design counts by origin

C16. Equivalent application design counts for the top 20 origins, 2021

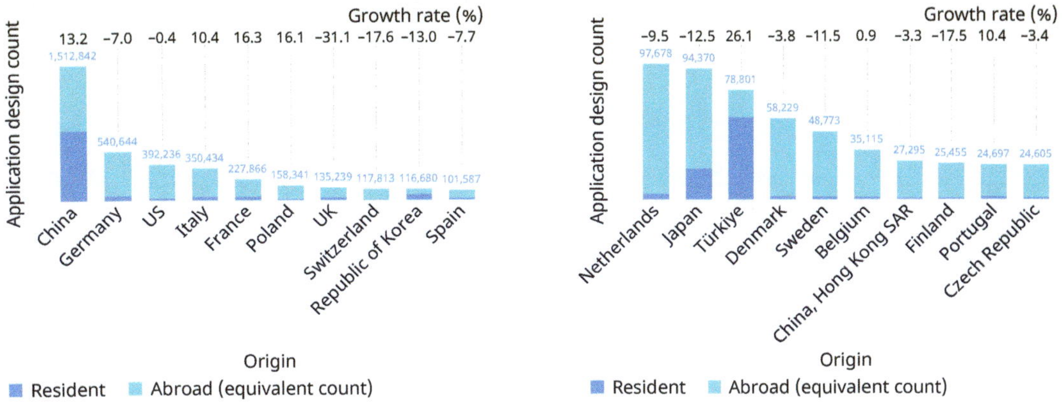

Note: The origin of an industrial design application is determined by the residence of the first named applicant. An application filed at a regional office is considered to be a resident filing, if the applicant is a resident of one of that office's member states. Applications filed at some regional offices are considered equivalent to multiple applications in the member states of those offices. See the glossary for the definition of equivalent application and design count.

Source: WIPO Statistics Database, September 2022.

C17. Application design counts for the top 20 origins, 2021

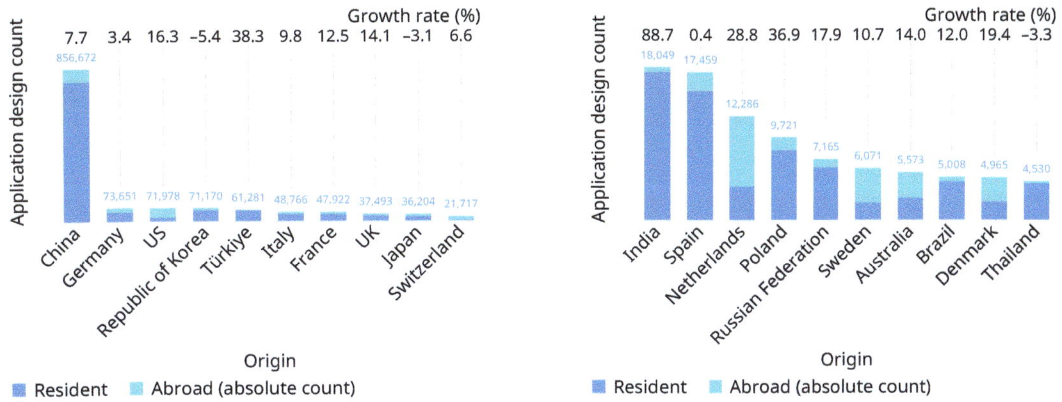

Note: Data are based on an absolute not an equivalent count. The origin of an industrial design application is determined by the residence of the first named applicant. An application filed at a regional office is considered to be a resident filing, if the applicant is a resident of one of that office's member states.

Source: WIPO Statistics Database, September 2022.

C18. Equivalent application design counts for selected low- and middle-income origins, 2021

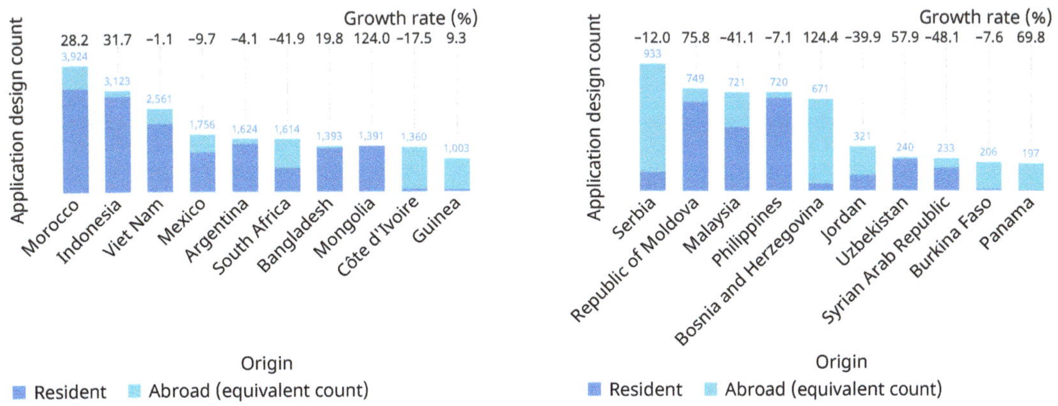

Note: The selected origins are from different world regions and income groups (low-income, lower middle-income and upper middle-income). Where available, data for all origins are presented in statistical table C36 at the end of this section. The origin of an industrial design application is determined by the residence of the first named applicant. An application filed at a regional office is considered to be a resident filing, if the applicant is a resident of one of that office's member states. Applications filed at some regional offices are considered equivalent to multiple applications in the member states of those offices. See the glossary for the definition of equivalent application and design count.

Source: WIPO Statistics Database, September 2022.

C19. Application design counts for selected low- and middle-income origins, 2021

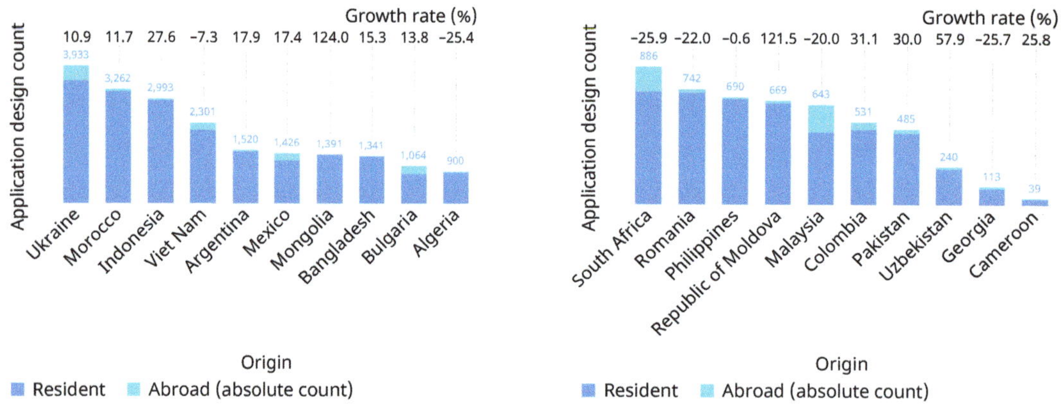

Note: Data are based on an absolute count not an equivalent count. The selected origins are from different world regions and income groups (low-income, lower middle-income and upper middle-income). Where available, data for all origins are presented in statistical table C36 at the end of this section. The origin of an industrial design application is determined by the residence of the first named applicant.

Source: WIPO Statistics Database, September 2022.

C20. **Flows of non-resident application design counts for the top five origins and the top 10 offices of high-income economies, 2021**

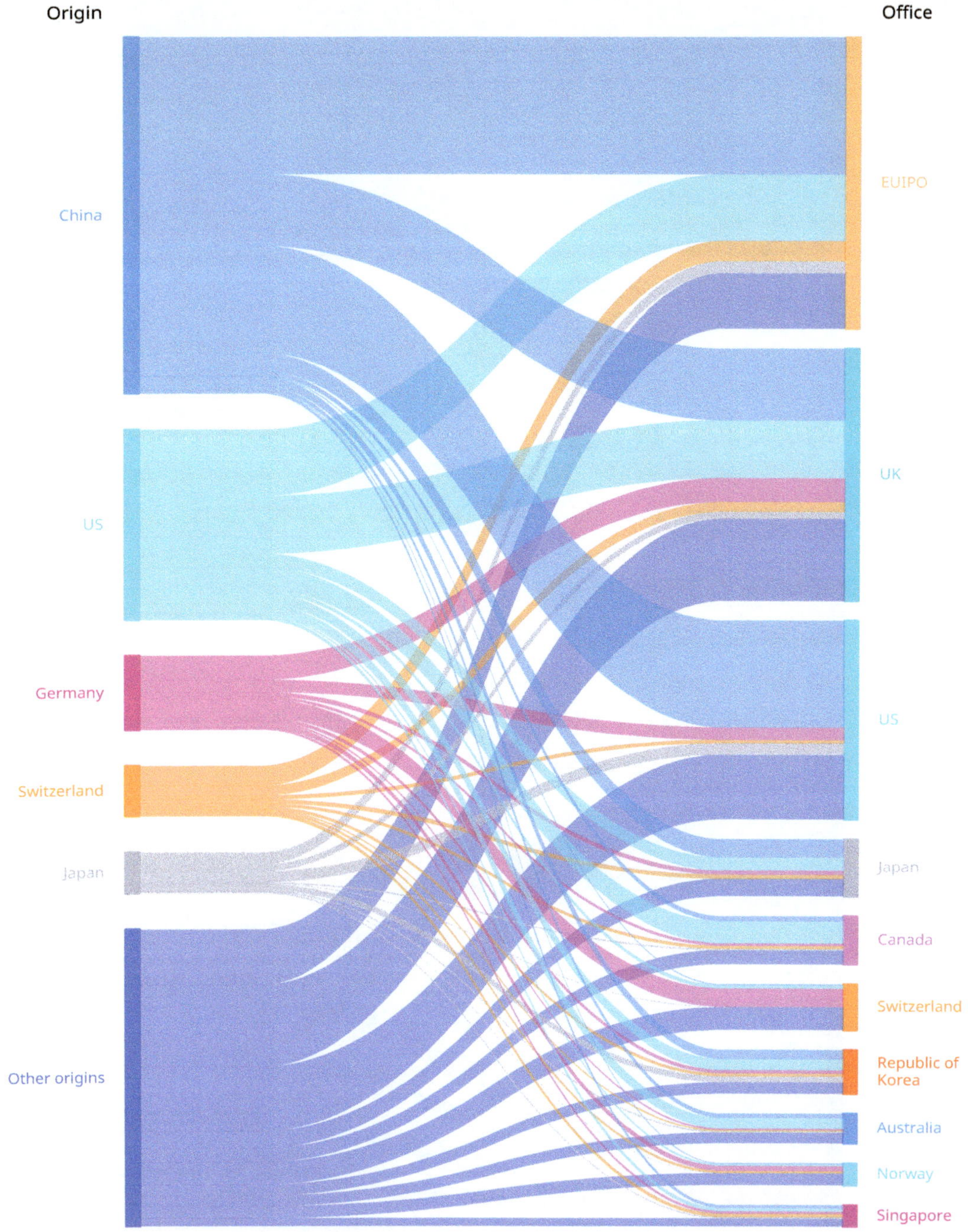

Note: EUIPO is the European Union Intellectual Property Office.
Source: WIPO Statistics Database, September 2022.

C21. Flows of non-resident application design counts for the top five origins and the top 10 offices of low- and middle-income economies, 2021

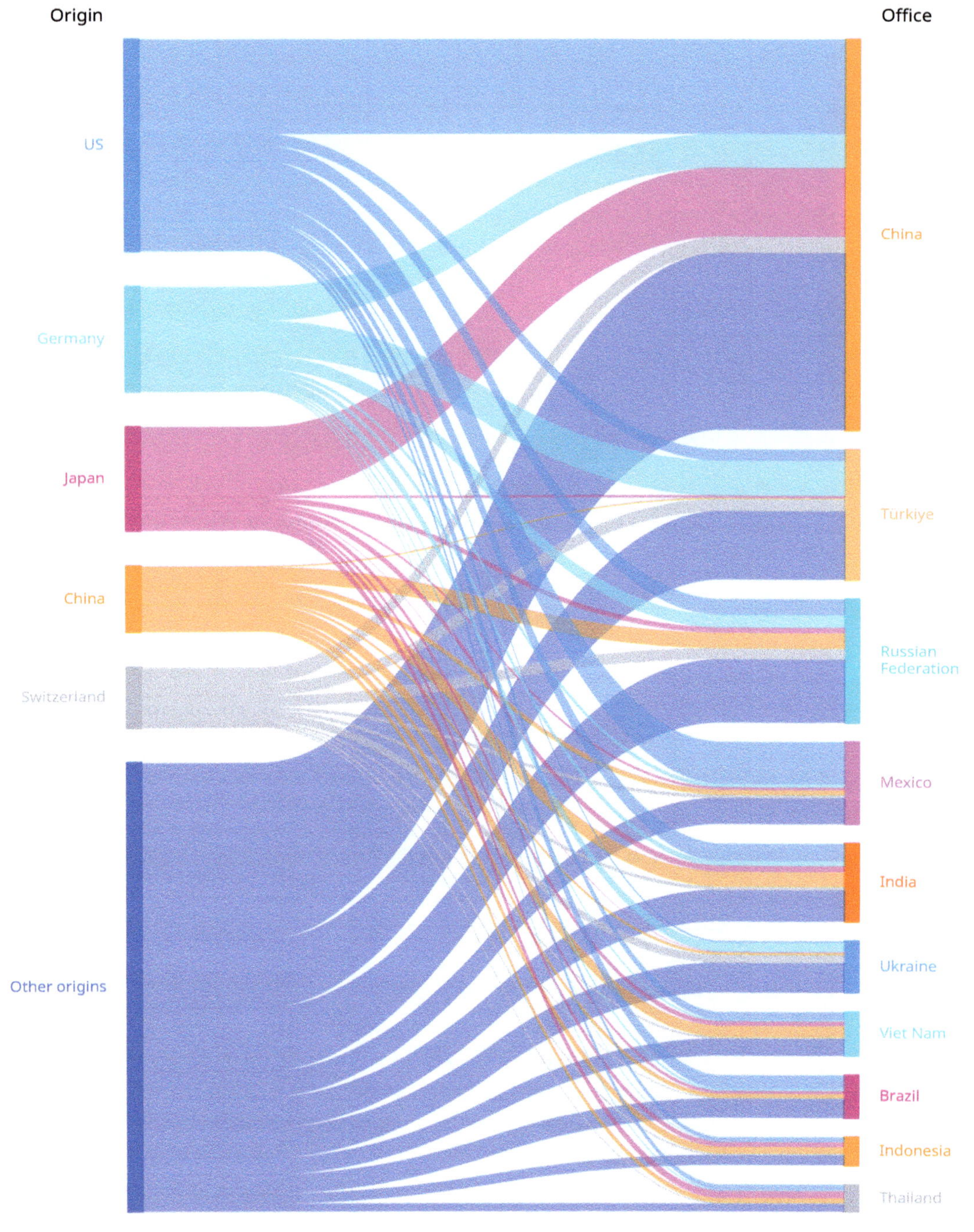

Source: WIPO Statistics Database, September 2022.

Application design counts by Locarno class and industry sector

C22. Application design counts for the top 10 Locarno classes, 2021

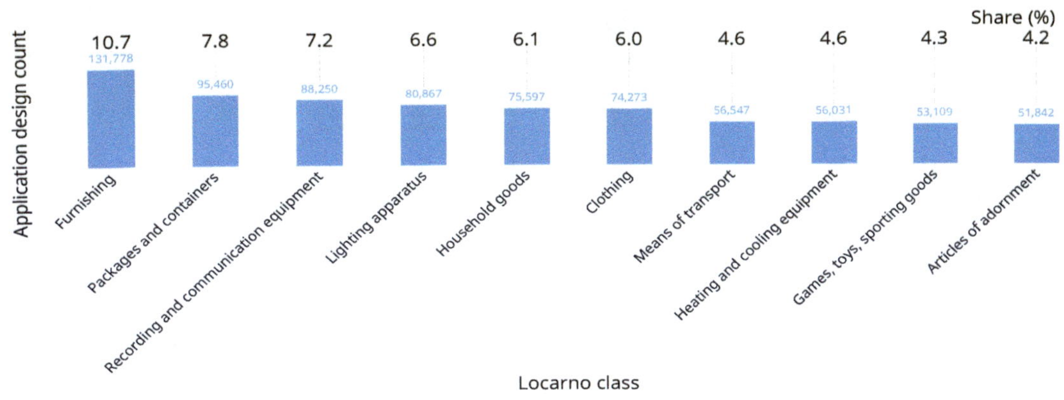

Note: See annex C for class numbers. These figures are based on data from 118 IP offices. Data for several of the larger offices are either not available or incomplete, including for the offices of Japan and the US.

Source: WIPO Statistics Database, September 2022.

C23. Application design counts by industry sector, 2021

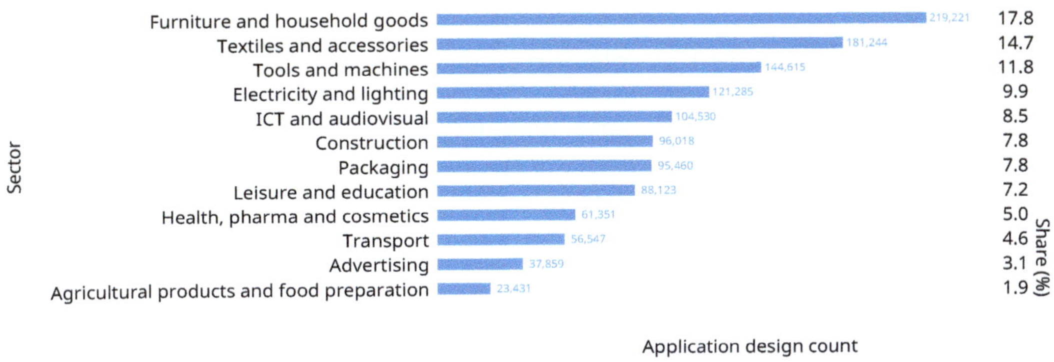

Note: A concordance table produced by the Organisation for Economic Co-operation and Development (OECD) was used to convert the 32 classes into 12 industry sectors (see annex C for definitions). These figures are based on data from 118 IP offices. Data for several of the larger offices are either not available or incomplete, including for the offices of Japan and the US.

Source: WIPO Statistics Database, September 2022.

C24. Distribution of application design counts by the top three sectors for the top 10 offices, 2021

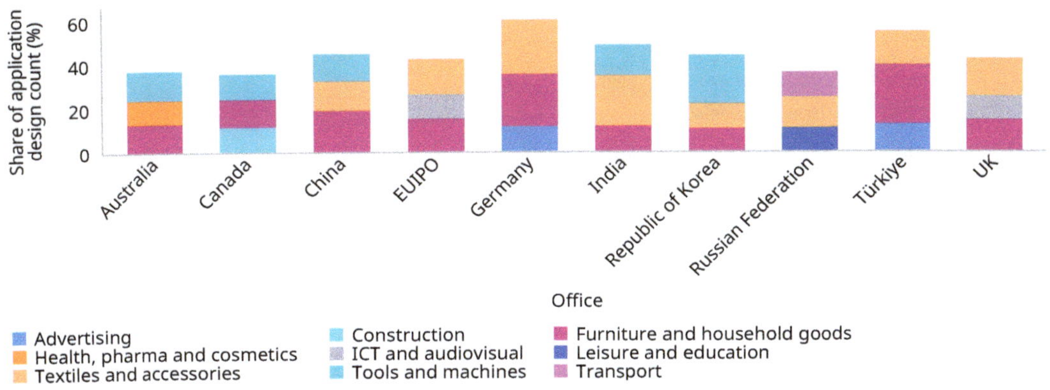

Note: EUIPO is the European Union Intellectual Property Office. A concordance table produced by the Organisation for Economic Co-operation and Development (OECD) was used to convert the 32 classes into 12 industry sectors (see annex C for definitions). The top three sectors and top 10 offices were selected based on 2021 totals. Data for several of the larger offices are either not available or incomplete, including for the offices of Japan and the US.

Source: WIPO Statistics Database, September 2022.

C25. Distribution of application design counts by the top three sectors for the top 10 origins, 2021

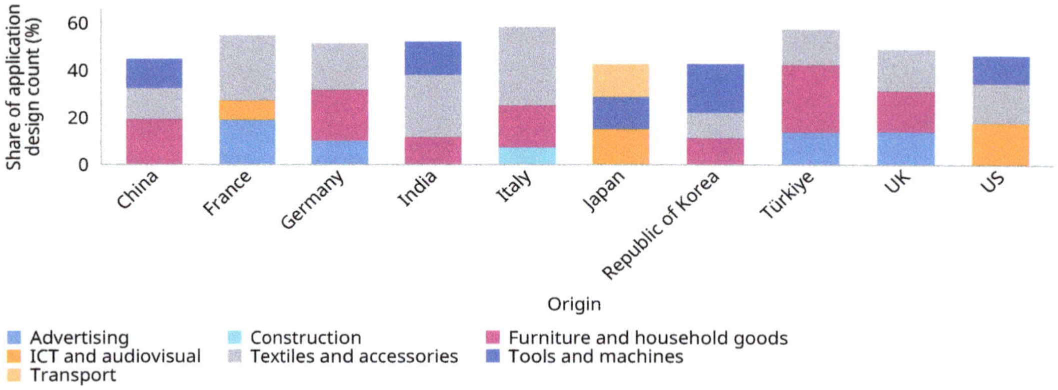

Note: A concordance table produced by the Organisation for Economic Co-operation and Development (OECD) was used to convert the 32 classes into 12 industry sectors (see annex C for definitions). These figures are based on data from 118 IP offices. Data for several of the larger offices are either not available or incomplete, including for the offices of Japan and the US.

Source: WIPO Statistics Database, September 2022.

Application design count in relation to GDP and population

C26. Resident application design count per USD 100 billion of GDP for the top 20 origins, 2011 and 2021

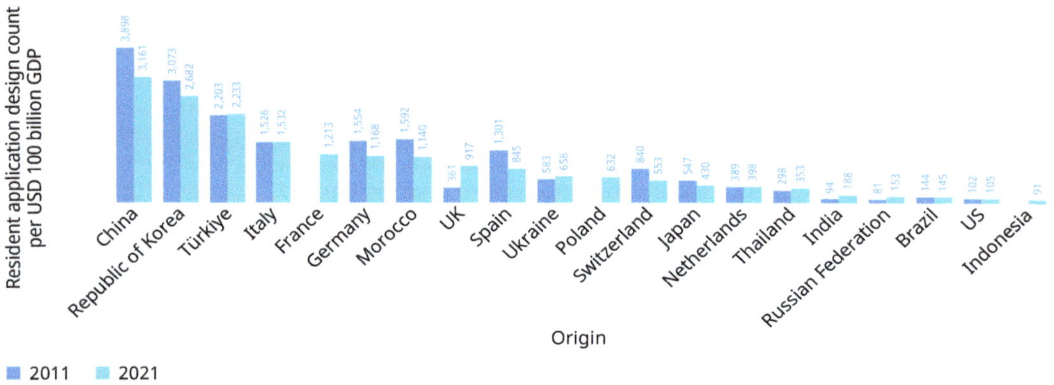

Note: GDP data are in constant 2017 US PPP dollars. Origins were selected based on the top origins list in terms of application design count and on GDP data availability.

Sources: WIPO Statistics Database and World Bank, September 2022.

C27. Resident application design count per million population for the top 20 origins, 2011 and 2021

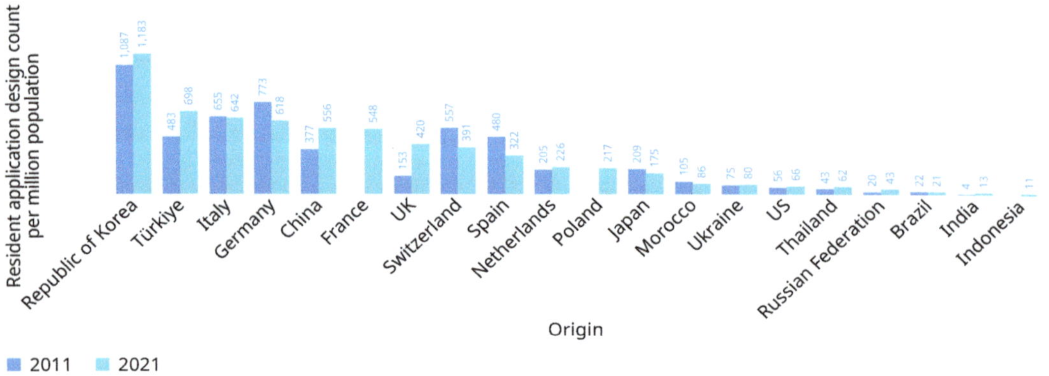

Note: Origins were selected based on the top origins list in terms of application design count and on population data availability.

Sources: WIPO Statistics Database and World Bank, September 2022.

Industrial design registrations in force

C28. Trend in industrial design registrations in force worldwide, 2011–2021

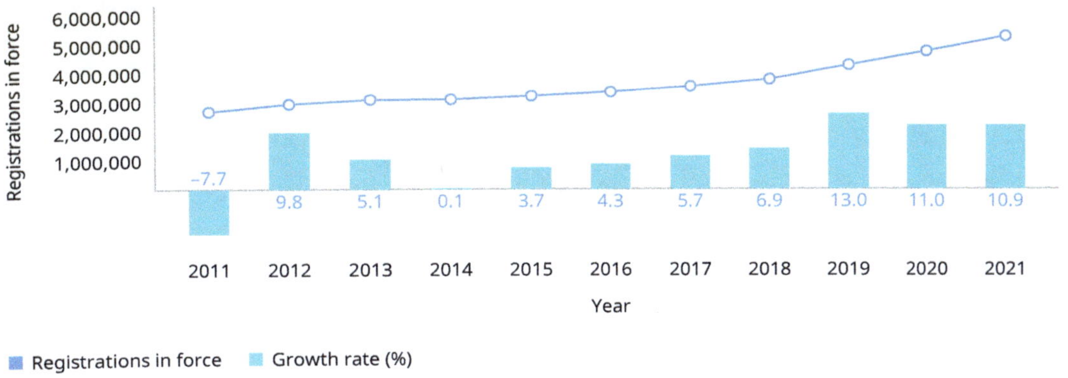

Note: WIPO estimates cover 129 IP offices and include direct national and regional applications, as well as designations received via the Hague System. Data refer to the number of industrial design registrations in force and not the number of designs contained in registrations in force.

Source: WIPO Statistics Database, September 2022.

C29. Industrial design registrations in force for the top 20 offices, 2021

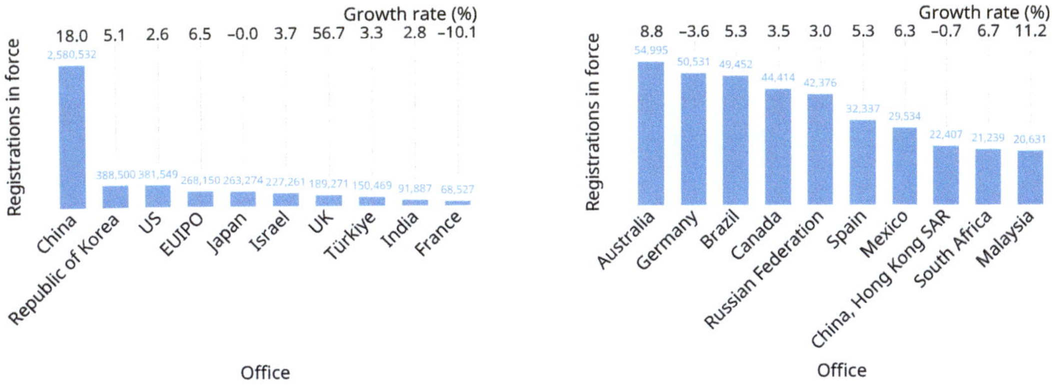

Note: EUIPO is the European Union Intellectual Property Office. Data refer to the number of industrial design registrations in force and not the number of designs contained in registrations in force.

Source: WIPO Statistics Database, September 2022.

C30. Industrial design registrations in force in 2021 as a percentage of total registrations

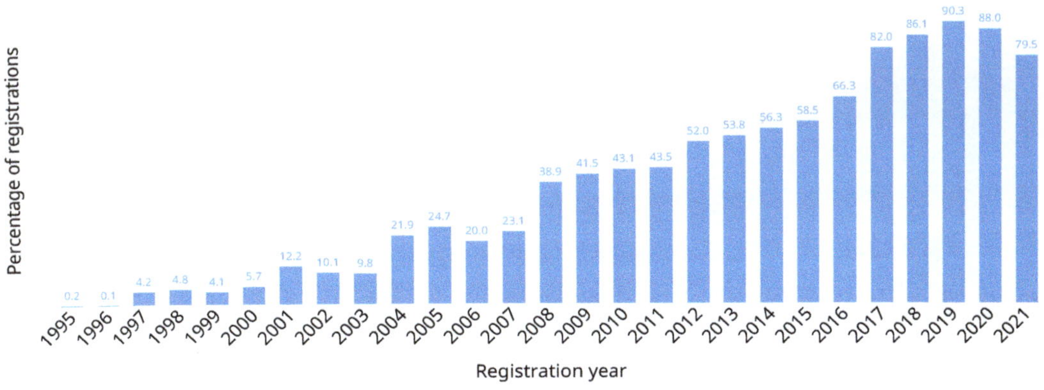

Note: Percentages are calculated using the number of industrial designs registered in year *t* and in force in 2021 divided by the total number of industrial designs registered in year *t*. The graph is based on data from the 92 offices (including most of the larger offices) for which a breakdown of industrial design registrations in force by year of registration was available.

Source: WIPO Statistics Database, September 2022.

C31. Average age of industrial design registrations in force at selected offices, 2016 and 2021

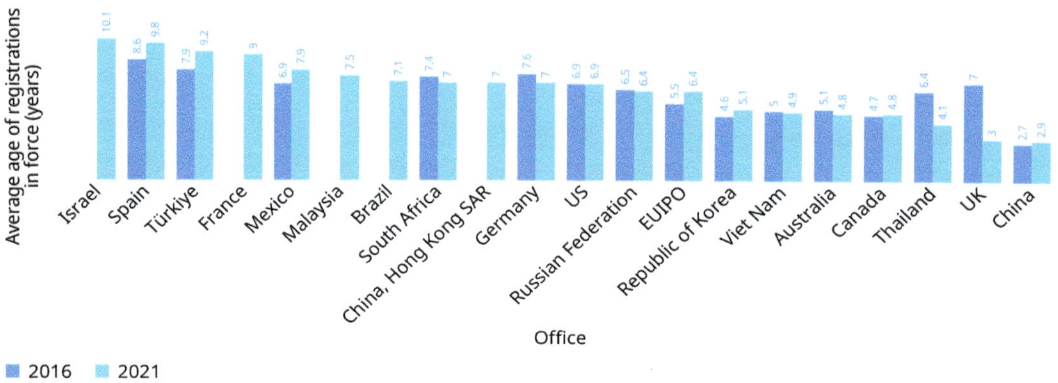

Note: EUIPO is the European Union Intellectual Property Office. Percentages are calculated using the number of industrial designs registered in year *t* and in force in 2021 divided by the total number of industrial designs registered in year *t*.

Source: WIPO Statistics Database, September 2022.

Industrial design office procedural data

C32. Distribution of industrial design examination outcomes for selected offices, 2021

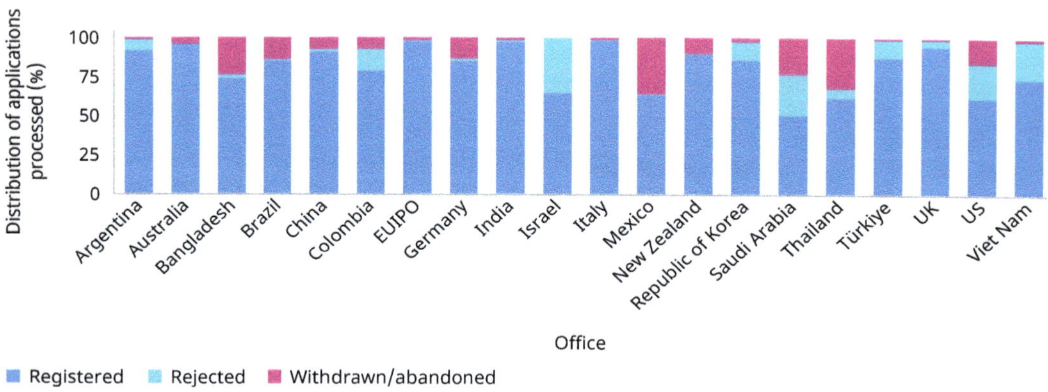

Note: EUIPO is the European Union Intellectual Property Office. WIPO collects data from IP offices using a common questionnaire and methodology. However, due to differences in industrial design procedures between offices, data cannot be fully harmonized. Therefore, caution should be exercised when making comparisons across offices.

Source: WIPO Statistics Database, September 2022.

C33. Potentially pending applications for selected offices, 2021

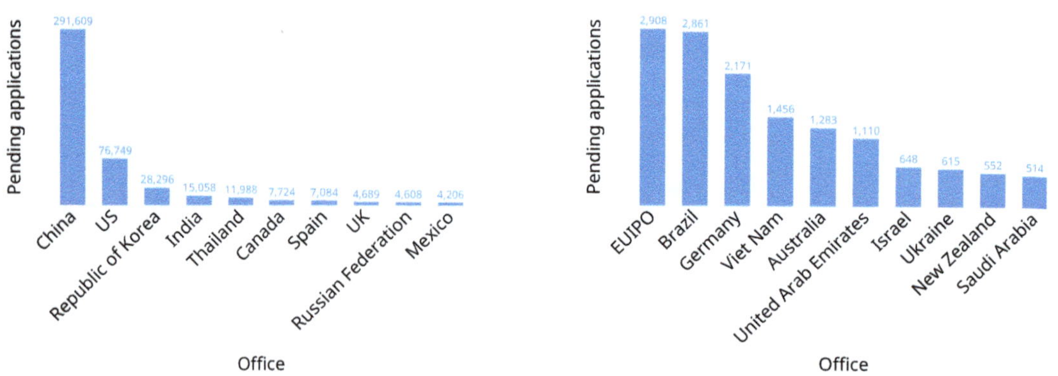

Note: EUIPO is the European Union Intellectual Property Office. WIPO collects data from IP offices using a common questionnaire and methodology. However, due to differences in industrial design procedures between offices, data cannot be fully harmonized. Therefore, caution should be exercised when making comparisons across offices.

Source: WIPO Statistics Database, September 2022.

C34. Average pendency times from filing date to first office action and to final decision at selected offices, 2021

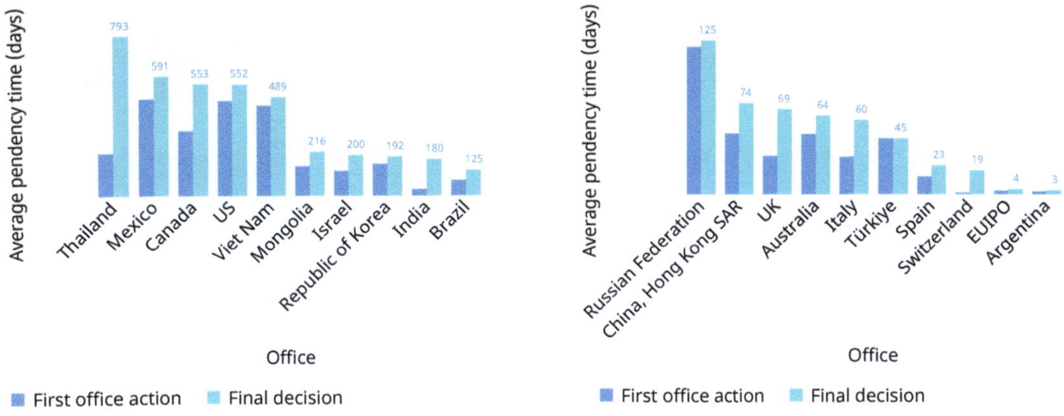

Note: EUIPO is the European Union Intellectual Property Office. WIPO collects data from IP offices using a common questionnaire and methodology. However, due to differences in industrial design procedures between offices, data cannot be fully harmonized. Therefore, caution should be exercised when making comparisons across offices.

Source: WIPO Statistics Database, September 2022.

C35. Number of industrial design examiners for selected offices, 2021

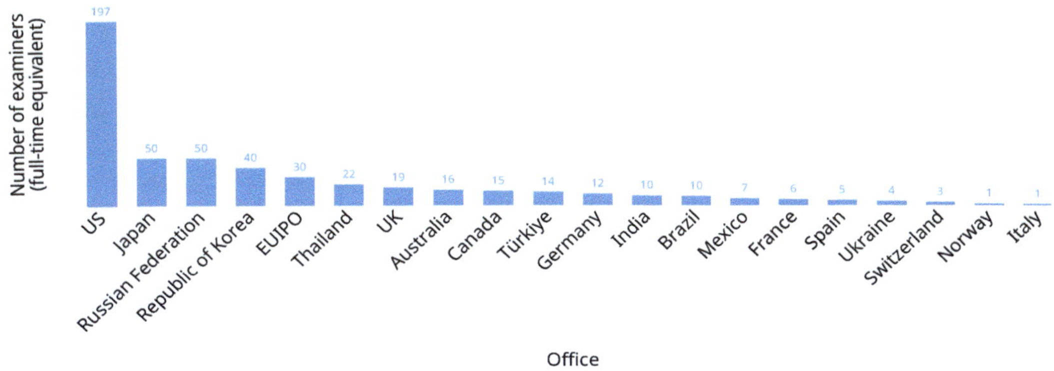

Note: EUIPO is the European Union Intellectual Property Office.

Source: WIPO Statistics Database, September 2022.

C36. Industrial design applications by office and origin, 2021

Name	Application design count by office: Total	Resident	Non-resident	Change over previous year	Application design count by origin: Total (a)	Equivalent application design count by origin: Total (a)	Change over previous year
Afghanistan (b)	..	..	..	..	7	7	..
African Intellectual Property Organization	774	258	516	-87	n.a.	n.a.	n.a.
African Regional Intellectual Property Organization	85	16	69	-2	n.a.	n.a.	n.a.
Albania	490	57	433	-58	58	58	-81
Algeria	1,161	879	282	-311	900	900	-307
Andorra (b)	..	..	..	..	11	63	..
Antigua and Barbuda	1	1	0	0	2	2	+1
Argentina	2,372	1,479	893	+273	1,520	1,624	-70
Armenia	360	78	282	-47	81	81	-170
Australia	8,120	2,584	5,536	+761	5,573	18,049	+2,369
Austria (b)	..	..	..	..	5,553	81,953	..
Azerbaijan	660	63	597	+77	81	81	+45
Bahamas (b)	..	..	..	..	7	7	..
Bahrain	124	10	114	+51	15	15	-55
Bangladesh	1,424	1,338	86	+183	1,341	1,393	+230
Barbados (b)	..	..	..	..	152	1,608	..
Belarus	784	273	511	+375	344	462	+198
Belgium	n.a.	n.a.	n.a.	n.a.	2,693	35,115	+330
Belize	299	5	294	+29	7	59	+53
Benelux Office for Intellectual Property	1,195	989	206	-104	n.a.	n.a.	n.a.
Benin (b,c)	n.a.	n.a.	n.a.	n.a.	5	85	0
Bhutan	3	3	0	-6	3	3	-6
Bosnia and Herzegovina	730	52	678	-113	125	671	+372
Botswana	70	18	52	..	18	18	..
Brazil	6,711	4,520	2,191	+448	5,008	7,920	+2,503
Brunei Darussalam	72	0	72	-100	..	..	..
Bulgaria	474	388	86	-308	1,064	13,014	+2,224
Burkina Faso (b,c)	n.a.	n.a.	n.a.	n.a.	14	206	-17
Cambodia (b)	..	..	..	..	2	2	..
Cameroon (b,c)	n.a.	n.a.	n.a.	n.a.	39	631	+152
Canada	9,491	715	8,776	+1,961	3,349	17,985	+2,871
Chad (b,c)	n.a.	n.a.	n.a.	n.a.	7	119	-544
Chile	388	42	346	-71	85	189	-175
China	805,710	785,857	19,853	+35,348	856,672	1,512,842	+176,609
China, Hong Kong SAR	3,858	946	2,912	-20	4,155	27,295	-943
China, Macao SAR	264	29	235	+57	89	245	-994
Colombia	952	486	466	+160	531	635	+230
Congo (b,c)	n.a.	n.a.	n.a.	n.a.	1	17	-17
Costa Rica	75	9	66	-3	13	13	+2
Côte d'Ivoire (b,c)	n.a.	n.a.	n.a.	n.a.	80	1,360	-289
Croatia	713	285	428	-235	869	5,867	+2,475
Cuba	15	14	1	-8	14	14	-6
Cyprus	20	20	0	-62	770	9,184	+4,696
Czech Republic	608	522	86	-68	2,375	24,605	-872
Democratic People's Republic of Korea (b)	..	..	..	..	7	59	..
Denmark	320	135	185	-111	4,965	58,229	-2,329
Dominican Republic	21	4	17	+5	18	44	+37
Ecuador	161	78	83	+45	81	107	+52
Egypt (b)	..	..	..	..	24	24	..
El Salvador	40	16	24	+6	16	16	+7
Equatorial Guinea (b,c)	n.a.	n.a.	n.a.	n.a.	1	1	+1
Estonia	126	36	90	-14	471	5,773	+344

Name	Application design count by office				Application design count by origin	Equivalent application design count by origin	
	Total	Resident	Non-resident	Change over previous year	Total (a)	Total (a)	Change over previous year
Eswatini (b)	..	..	..	..	1	1	..
Ethiopia (b)	..	..	..	..	6	6	..
Eurasian Patent Organization	190	110	80	..	n.a.	n.a.	n.a.
European Union Intellectual Property Office	117,049	63,053	53,996	+3,854	n.a.	n.a.	n.a.
Finland	224	150	74	-15	1,878	25,455	-5,384
France	31,344	30,120	1,224	+145	47,922	227,866	+31,967
Gabon (b,c)	n.a.	n.a.	n.a.	n.a.	12	204	+85
Georgia	482	103	379	-120	113	113	-39
Germany	36,997	33,448	3,549	-3,644	73,651	540,644	-40,686
Ghana (b)	..	..	..	..	15	28	..
Greece	883	721	162	-192	1,342	11,758	+985
Guatemala	92	35	57	-45	57	83	+76
Guinea (b,c)	n.a.	n.a.	n.a.	n.a.	59	1,003	+85
Guinea-Bissau (b,c)	n.a.	n.a.	n.a.	n.a.	3	51	0
Guyana	1	1	0	..	1	1	..
Hungary	907	868	39	+303	1,114	5,132	-1,915
Iceland	464	7	457	+50	12	38	+26
India	21,446	17,497	3,949	+8,653	18,049	19,763	+7,914
Indonesia	4,368	2,959	1,409	+848	2,993	3,123	+751
Iran (Islamic Republic of) (b)	..	..	..	..	8	34	..
Ireland	114	95	19	-134	1,325	15,625	-1,920
Israel	1,955	626	1,329	+193	2,129	10,163	-2,806
Italy	26,694	26,386	308	+1,330	48,766	350,434	+32,906
Jamaica	100	94	6	-117	94	94	-117
Japan	32,747	22,051	10,696	+1,097	36,204	94,370	-13,439
Jordan	129	114	15	+40	165	321	-213
Kazakhstan	330	134	196	..	166	283	..
Kuwait (b)	..	..	..	..	41	67	..
Kyrgyzstan	321	7	314	-21	30	30	-851
Latvia	127	84	43	-85	240	2,504	-1,526
Lebanon (b)	..	..	..	..	74	672	..
Libya (b)	..	..	..	..	20	20	..
Liechtenstein	692	25	667	-179	597	3,215	+245
Lithuania	344	132	212	-266	361	5,327	+1,027
Luxembourg	n.a.	n.a.	n.a.	n.a.	910	8,992	-4,259
Madagascar	328	328	0	+108	328	328	+93
Malaysia	1,739	468	1,271	+38	643	721	-503
Mali (b,c)	n.a.	n.a.	n.a.	n.a.	14	206	0
Malta	17	17	0	-19	2,106	13,822	+7,000
Mauritius	27	24	3	-59	28	60	-45
Mexico	5,353	1,225	4,128	+1,486	1,426	1,756	-188
Monaco	643	28	615	-87	93	431	-420
Mongolia	1,749	1,391	358	+732	1,391	1,391	+770
Montenegro (b)	..	..	..	..	..	..	..
Morocco	4,386	3,208	1,178	+478	3,262	3,924	+863
Mozambique	81	40	41	+5	40	40	-2
Myanmar (b)	..	..	..	..	1	1	..
Namibia (b)	..	..	..	..	5	57	..
Netherlands	n.a.	n.a.	n.a.	n.a.	12,286	97,678	-10,276
New Zealand	1,431	320	1,111	+64	1,338	5,992	-270
Niger (b,c)	n.a.	n.a.	n.a.	n.a.	..	..	..
Nigeria (b)	..	..	..	..	3	19	..
North Macedonia	622	67	555	-43	94	172	-142
Norway	4,404	452	3,952	+1,090	1,559	8,501	-681
Oman	562	17	545	+70	17	17	-4
Pakistan	572	463	109	+108	485	485	+112
Palau (b)	..	..	..	..	1	1	..
Panama	85	5	80	+43	15	197	+81

Name	Application design count by office: Total	Resident	Non-resident	Change over previous year	Application design count by origin: Total (a)	Equivalent application design count by origin: Total (a)	Change over previous year
Paraguay (b)	..	..	..	..	2	2	..
Peru	389	97	292	+113	98	98	+3
Philippines	1,372	682	690	+79	690	720	-55
Poland	2,755	2,489	266	+675	9,721	158,341	+22,014
Portugal	1,129	1,008	121	-635	2,371	24,697	+2,336
Qatar (b)	..	..	..	..	184	548	..
Republic of Korea	69,248	61,233	8,015	-1,573	71,170	116,680	-17,432
Republic of Moldova	1,132	654	478	+267	669	749	+323
Romania	681	378	303	-231	742	9,686	-958
Russian Federation	12,543	6,128	6,415	+1,954	7,165	11,772	-607
Rwanda (b)	..	..	..	..	..	..	..
Samoa (b)	..	..	..	..	7	7	..
San Marino	86	0	86	-53	18	486	-101
Sao Tome and Principe (b)	..	..	..	..	..	..	..
Saudi Arabia	1,400	853	547	+452	914	1,096	+448
Senegal (b,c)	n.a.	n.a.	n.a.	n.a.	25	425	-136
Serbia	895	137	758	-170	333	933	-127
Seychelles (b)	..	..	..	..	27	27	..
Sierra Leone	4	4	0	..	4	4	..
Singapore	4,594	683	3,911	+1,028	3,236	15,300	+7,076
Slovakia	408	262	146	+40	621	6,497	+664
Slovenia (b)	..	..	..	..	541	4,425	..
South Africa	1,561	728	833	-147	886	1,614	-1,165
Spain	12,294	12,010	284	-82	17,459	101,587	-8,516
Sri Lanka	139	112	27	-142	227	227	-232
Sudan (b)	..	..	..	..	1	1	..
Suriname (b)	..	..	..	..	1	3	..
Sweden	419	390	29	+122	6,071	48,773	-6,316
Switzerland	11,808	3,403	8,405	+1,648	21,717	117,813	-25,212
Syrian Arab Republic	259	166	93	-315	181	233	-216
Tajikistan (b)	..	..	..	..	1	1	..
Thailand	5,687	4,323	1,364	-131	4,530	4,764	-540
Togo (b,c)	n.a.	n.a.	n.a.	n.a.	5	85	-17
Trinidad and Tobago	59	58	1	+40	60	60	+44
Tunisia (b)	..	..	..	..	22	22	..
Türkiye	65,924	59,353	6,571	+18,271	61,281	78,801	+16,332
Turkmenistan (b)	..	..	..	..	..	..	..
Uganda (b)	..	..	..	..	1	1	..
Ukraine	6,122	3,526	2,596	+503	3,933	6,149	+552
United Arab Emirates	972	103	869	+286	266	1,260	+636
United Kingdom	74,781	28,299	46,482	+42,048	37,493	135,239	-60,919
United Republic of Tanzania (b)	..	..	..	..	1	2	..
United States of America	59,477	21,913	37,564	+8,735	71,978	392,236	-1,492
Uruguay (b)	..	..	..	..	21	21	..
Uzbekistan	273	231	42	+93	240	240	+88
Venezuela (Bolivarian Republic of)	291	..	..	+265	5	5	+4
Viet Nam	4,310	2,107	2,203	-67	2,301	2,561	-29
Yemen	80	77	3	+16	79	79	+20
Zimbabwe (b)	..	..	..	..	3	5	..
Others/Unknown	..	..	..	..	2,933	16,193	-8,461
Total (2021 estimates)	**1,515,200**	**1,241,800**	**273,400**		**1,515,200**		

(a) Design count by origin data are incomplete, because some offices do not report the origin of applications.

(b) Only Hague designation data are available and/or this office has not reported the origin of applications therefore the design count by office and origin data may be incomplete.

(c) The African Intellectual Property Organization (OAPI) is the competent office for processing applications.

n.a. indicates not applicable.

.. indicates not available.

Source: WIPO Statistics Database, September 2022.

C37. Industrial design registrations by office and origin, and registrations in force, 2021

	Registration design count by office			Registration design count by origin	Equivalent registration design count by origin	In force by office	
Name	Total	Resident	Non-resident	Total (a)	Total (a)	Total	Change over previous year
Afghanistan (b)	..	..	..	4	4	..	..
African Intellectual Property Organization	722	261	461	n.a.	n.a.	1,930	-43
African Regional Intellectual Property Organization	87	11	76	n.a.	n.a.	580	+9
Albania	445	33	412	34	60	75	+22
Algeria	601	491	110	491	491	1,613	-46
Andorra (b)	..	..	..	6	58	..	..
Argentina	2,284	1,279	1,005	1,307	1,359	..	..
Armenia	302	48	254	51	51	262	+77
Australia	7,945	2,543	5,402	4,988	16,132	54,995	+4,436
Austria (b)	..	..	..	5,117	78,177	..	..
Azerbaijan	652	38	614	43	43	1,676	+72
Bahamas (b)	..	..	..	20	20	..	..
Bahrain	108	4	104	8	8	758	+59
Bangladesh	829	780	49	782	834	5,321	-1,616
Barbados (b)	..	..	..	185	1,277	12	0
Belarus	662	241	421	308	386	1,439	-55
Belgium	n.a.	n.a.	n.a.	2,474	34,298	n.a.	n.a.
Belize	293	2	291	4	56	2	-3
Benelux Office for Intellectual Property	1,240	1,012	228	n.a.	n.a.	3,291	+7
Benin (b,c)	n.a.	n.a.	n.a.	7	119	..	..
Bhutan	1	1	0	1	1	33	+1
Bolivia (Plurinational State of) (b)	..	..	..	1	1	..	..
Bosnia and Herzegovina	717	63	654	112	762	505	+22
Botswana (b)	..	..	..	..	..	222	-204
Brazil	5,468	3,467	2,001	3,796	5,044	49,452	+2,480
Brunei Darussalam (b)	..	..	..	..	..	376	+29
Bulgaria	493	334	159	1,004	13,330	1,945	+19
Burkina Faso (b,c)	n.a.	n.a.	n.a.	13	221	..	..
Cabo Verde	4	4	0	7	7	4	+1
Cambodia (b)	..	..	..	2	2	1,018	..
Cameroon (b,c)	n.a.	n.a.	n.a.	35	595	..	..
Canada	6,928	425	6,503	2,339	14,767	44,414	+1,508
Chad (b,c)	n.a.	n.a.	n.a.	7	119	..	..
Chile	371	27	344	55	185	2,674	-429
China	785,521	767,078	18,443	819,825	1,482,157	2,580,532	+393,176
China, Hong Kong SAR	4,206	1,062	3,144	4,092	27,258	22,407	-162
China, Macao SAR	177	22	155	89	349	1,425	+35
Colombia	599	224	375	260	364	5,204	+289
Congo (b,c)	n.a.	n.a.	n.a.	1	17	..	..
Costa Rica	36	5	31	8	8	565	-64
Côte d'Ivoire (b,c)	n.a.	n.a.	n.a.	83	1,411	..	..
Croatia	651	182	469	614	4,234	3,321	-251
Cuba	15	14	1	16	16	138	+75
Cyprus	20	20	0	770	8,924	50	+8
Czech Republic	1,020	744	276	2,437	22,717	2,379	-58
Democratic People's Republic of Korea (b)	..	..	..	16	68	..	..
Denmark	371	108	263	4,661	58,133	1,745	-48
Dominican Republic	23	4	19	4	4	188	..
Ecuador	116	38	78	40	40	881	+37
Egypt (b)	..	..	..	24	24	..	..
El Salvador	42	12	30	12	12	..	..
Estonia	146	41	105	455	5,783	1,234	-265
Ethiopia (b)	..	..	..	1	1	..	..
Eurasian Patent Organization	16	9	7	n.a.	n.a.	..	..

Name	Registration design count by office: Total	Registration design count by office: Resident	Registration design count by office: Non-resident	Registration design count by origin: Total (a)	Equivalent registration design count by origin: Total (a)	In force by office: Total	In force by office: Change over previous year
European Union Intellectual Property Office	115,613	62,028	53,585	n.a.	n.a.	268,150	+16,458
Finland	191	110	81	1,814	25,656	1,615	-181
France	9,773	8,857	916	26,370	199,846	68,527	-7,676
Gabon (b,c)	n.a.	n.a.	n.a.	12	204	..	..
Georgia	471	101	370	109	109	2,749	+21
Germany	31,636	28,421	3,215	65,098	525,399	50,531	-1,882
Ghana (b)	..	..	..	1	2	..	..
Greece	928	782	146	1,395	12,045	1,243	+68
Guatemala	34	1	33	12	38	302	-52
Guinea (b,c)	n.a.	n.a.	n.a.	55	935	..	..
Guinea-Bissau (b,c)	n.a.	n.a.	n.a.	7	119	..	..
Guyana	1	1	0	1	1	1	..
Holy See (b)	..	..	..	1	1	..	..
Hungary	437	390	47	611	4,459	2,505	-593
Iceland	374	14	360	26	52	1,332	+196
India	13,013	9,885	3,128	10,362	11,950	91,887	+2,490
Indonesia	2,263	1,348	915	1,391	1,469	..	..
Iran (Islamic Republic of) (b)	..	..	..	5	31	..	..
Iraq (b)	..	..	..	8	8	..	..
Ireland	117	98	19	1,209	15,535	1,576	-65
Israel	1,893	579	1,314	1,951	10,073	227,261	+8,113
Italy	24,912	24,533	379	45,229	336,259	9,002	-128
Jamaica	76	70	6	70	70	1,363	+66
Japan	28,289	19,361	8,928	32,520	89,296	263,274	-33
Jordan	104	91	13	139	295	1,058	+43
Kazakhstan	177	56	121	65	91	3,740	+2,483
Kenya (b)	..	..	..	3	6	..	..
Kuwait (b)	..	..	..	32	58	..	..
Kyrgyzstan	301	16	285	161	499	56	-15
Latvia	150	94	56	245	2,379	371	-17
Lebanon (b)	..	..	..	76	674	..	..
Liechtenstein (b)	..	..	..	367	2,593	..	..
Lithuania	346	121	225	333	4,831	290	-21
Luxembourg	n.a.	n.a.	n.a.	2,166	13,374	n.a.	n.a.
Madagascar	246	233	13	233	233	1,278	+138
Malaysia	965	199	766	340	470	20,631	+2,077
Mali (b,c)	n.a.	n.a.	n.a.	15	207	..	..
Malta	16	16	0	1,305	7,821	138	+6
Marshall Islands (b)	..	..	..	1	1	..	..
Mauritius	24	23	1	29	61	148	-17
Mexico	4,797	656	4,141	749	1,061	29,534	+1,756
Monaco	618	28	590	131	469	215	-17
Mongolia	845	486	359	487	487	646	-118
Montenegro (b)	..	..	..	..	..	..	..
Morocco	4,295	3,158	1,137	3,193	3,787	..	..
Mozambique	68	28	40	29	30	1,501	+21
Myanmar (b)	..	..	..	1	1	..	..
Namibia (b)	..	..	..	6	75	..	..
Nepal (b)	..	..	..	1	1	..	..
Netherlands	n.a.	n.a.	n.a.	11,103	103,063	n.a.	n.a.
New Zealand	1,240	254	986	1,027	4,615	11,956	+148
Niger (b,c)	n.a.	n.a.	n.a.	..	..	..	..
Nigeria (b)	..	..	..	6	74	..	..
North Macedonia	513	25	488	64	194	2,314	-153
Norway	3,760	473	3,287	1,528	9,068	11,735	+429
Oman	564	12	552	13	13	..	..
Pakistan	330	252	78	263	263	..	..
Panama	113	9	104	24	232	633	-134

	Registration design count by office			Registration design count by origin	Equivalent registration design count by origin	In force by office	
Name	Total	Resident	Non-resident	Total (a)	Total (a)	Total	Change over previous year
Paraguay (b)	..	..	..	7	7	..	..
Peru	347	87	260	88	88	3,035	+42
Philippines	829	353	476	360	388	..	..
Poland	2,453	2,267	186	9,113	155,393	8,655	+155
Portugal	1,077	911	166	2,008	24,524	3,370	-311
Qatar (b)	..	..	..	137	657	..	..
Republic of Korea	57,796	50,863	6,933	60,427	107,207	388,500	+18,974
Republic of Moldova	670	225	445	239	319	2,923	-8
Romania	796	412	384	765	9,709	2,990	-288
Russian Federation	10,638	4,678	5,960	5,535	8,936	42,376	+1,215
Rwanda (b)	..	..	..	..	..	..	..
Saint Vincent and the Grenadines (b)	..	..	..	..	..	2	0
Samoa (b)	..	..	..	2	2	102	0
San Marino	82	0	82	26	494	..	..
Sao Tome and Principe (b)	..	..	..	..	..	..	..
Saudi Arabia	996	530	466	578	812	4,838	+481
Senegal (b,c)	n.a.	n.a.	n.a.	25	425	..	..
Serbia	890	130	760	335	1,171	5,470	+952
Seychelles (b)	..	..	..	12	12	..	..
Sierra Leone	4	4	0	4	4	4	..
Singapore	4,064	575	3,489	2,445	12,845	13,238	-318
Slovakia	486	320	166	635	6,485	1,005	+57
Slovenia (b)	..	..	..	592	5,148	..	..
South Africa	1,668	861	807	1,006	1,662	21,239	+1,341
Spain	13,145	12,865	280	18,206	105,040	32,337	+1,640
Sri Lanka	97	52	45	61	113	1,467	-657
Sudan (b)	..	..	..	2	2	..	..
Suriname (b)	..	..	..	1	3	..	..
Sweden	353	325	28	5,258	46,530	3,102	-494
Switzerland	10,846	3,297	7,549	20,585	110,621	9,545	+333
Syrian Arab Republic	377	..	..	15	67	134	-421
Tajikistan (b)	..	..	..	..	..	..	..
Thailand	2,701	1,599	1,102	1,764	1,946	19,159	+2,015
Togo (b,c)	n.a.	n.a.	n.a.	4	68	..	..
Trinidad and Tobago	24	24	0	26	26	76	..
Tunisia (b)	..	..	..	1	17	..	..
Türkiye	50,172	44,269	5,903	45,894	59,862	150,469	+4,813
Turkmenistan (b)	..	..	..	..	..	..	..
Uganda (b)	..	..	..	1	2	..	..
Ukraine	5,533	3,070	2,463	3,379	5,827	13,626	-997
United Arab Emirates	721	57	664	190	1,492	4,417	+180
United Kingdom	62,312	24,066	38,246	32,410	132,882	189,271	+68,493
United States of America	36,347	15,439	20,908	59,721	375,923	381,549	+9,679
Uruguay (b)	..	..	..	15	15	..	..
Uzbekistan	152	152	0	157	157	567	-10
Venezuela (Bolivarian Republic of) (b)	..	..	..	1	1	246	..
Viet Nam	2,900	1,249	1,651	1,384	1,644	14,067	+487
Yemen	26	21	5	22	22	121	+32
Zimbabwe (b)	..	..	..	4	8	..	..
Others/Unknown	..	..	..	2,352	15,820	..	..
Total (2021 estimates)	**1,354,700**	**1,121,200**	**233,600**	**1,354,700**		**5,276,400**	

(a) Design count by origin data are incomplete, because some offices do not report the origin of registrations.

(b) Only Hague designation data are available and/or the office has not reported the origin of registrations therefore design count by office and origin data may be incomplete.

(c) The African Intellectual Property Organization (OAPI) is the competent office for registering applications.

n.a. indicates not applicable.

.. indicates not available.

Source: WIPO Statistics Database, September 2022.

C38. Industrial design office procedural data, 2021

Office	Total applications processed	Registered	Rejected	Withdrawn or abandoned	Applications pending	Number of examiners (FTE)	First office action from filing date (days)	Final office decision from filing date (days)
African Intellectual Property Organization	..	..	..	..	30	2.0	..	..
Albania	..	14	..	..	35	1.0	30.0	180.0
Algeria	..	255	139	..	148	2.0	180.0	365.0
Argentina	2,455	2,258	172	25	..	4.0	2.0	3.0
Armenia	47	40	2	5	10	1.0	10.0	108.0
Australia (a)	..	9,407	..	384	1,283	16.1	48.6	63.7
Azerbaijan	31	23	1	7	5	2.0	60.0	180.0
Bangladesh	1,118	829	27	262	306	2.0	90.0	270.0
Belarus	231	223	4	4	35	1.0	58.0	73.0
Bhutan	..	..	1	..	..	1.0	1.0	240.0
Bosnia and Herzegovina	..	22	2	..	..	1.0	1.0	120.0
Botswana	..	7	6	..	5	4.0	3.0	30.0
Brazil	6,402	5,468	55	879	2,861	9.5	73.6	125.3
Brunei Darussalam	..	..	..	2	4	1.0	2.0	90.0
Bulgaria	..	105	..	5	23	2.0	1.0	30.0
Cabo Verde	..	..	..	..	14	3.0	..	..
Canada	3,944	3,652	1	291	7,724	15.0	319.1	553.1
China	861,379	785,521	12,814	63,044	291,609	..	..	87.0
China, Hong Kong SAR	4,249	4,206	2	41	306	2.0	49.2	74.2
China, Macao SAR	..	177	54	..	290	1.0	48.9	48.9
Colombia	760	599	108	53	381	1.0	4.0	204.0
Croatia	..	89	..	..	31	2.0	14.0	72.0
Cuba	..	24	..	..	15	1.0	127.0	475.0
Cyprus	..	8	..	..	..	1.0	20.0	30.0
Czech Republic	339	261	45	33	193	3.0	..	447.0
Denmark	112	98	5	9	14	3.0	1.0	22.1
Ecuador	143	115	13	15	50	1.0	30.0	180.0
El Salvador	..	42	..	..	..	3.0	5.0	180.0
Estonia	..	42	..	8	10	1.0	7.0	43.0
France	..	..	..	..	..	6.0	..	..
Georgia	202	183	2	17	38	2.0	10.0	210.0
Germany	5,606	4,775	92	739	2,171	11.7	..	125.6
Guatemala	..	34	..	1	316	1.0	600.0	1,100.0
Guyana	..	1	..	..	..	1.0	5.0	5.0
Hungary	146	75	10	61	48	2.0	5.0	254.0
Iceland	..	136	..	..	48	0.2	4.0	25.0
India	13,308	13,013	128	167	15,058	10.0	30.0	180.0
Israel	..	1,387	749	..	648	4.0	120.0	200.0
Italy	1,091	1,072	8	11	..	1.0	30.0	60.0
Jamaica	100	76	19	5	..	2.0	45.0	90.0
Japan	..	27,490	..	..	..	50.0	..	..
Jordan	..	104	36	..	55	2.0	30.0	180.0
Kazakhstan	222	198	10	14	55	5.0	213.0	213.0
Kyrgyzstan	..	6	..	3	6	7.0	60.0	180.0
Latvia	..	53	..	7	49	1.0	3.0	10.0
Lithuania	..	30	..	12	..	2.0	7.0	63.0
Madagascar	..	246	50	..	46	3.0	210.0	210.0
Mexico	4,649	2,964	21	1,664	4,206	7.0	480.0	591.0
Monaco	..	12	2	..	..	2.0	53.0	66.0
Mongolia	166	108	57	1	153	2.0	144.0	216.0
Mozambique	..	..	..	..	..	4.0	..	..
New Zealand	1,379	1,240	1	138	552	1.0	13.3	83.9
North Macedonia	35	22	11	2	39	1.0	2.0	150.0
Norway	450	390	1	59	131	1.4	90.0	..
Oman	43	23	18	2	5	..	..	..
Panama	..	53	..	..	129	1.0	60.0	60.0
Peru	..	346	13	..	254	7.0	269.0	269.0
Philippines	..	1,230	..	276	426	6.0	71.0	219.0

Office	Total applications processed	Registered	Rejected	Withdrawn or abandoned	Applications pending	Number of examiners (FTE)	First office action from filing date (days)	Final office decision from filing date (days)
Poland	1,163	1,025	30	108	..	..	..	..
Portugal	271	243	17	11	2	2.0	15.0	120.0
Republic of Korea	66,897	57,545	7,864	1,488	28,296	40.0	156.0	192.0
Republic of Moldova	78	60	6	12	141	3.0	4.0	240.0
Romania	509	477	25	7	101	5.0	2.9	170.0
Russian Federation	6,639	5,990	145	504	4,608	50.0	120.0	125.0
Saint Vincent and the Grenadines	..	..	..	..	..	2.0	..	..
Saudi Arabia	1,962	996	518	448	514	3.0	1.0	32.0
Serbia	132	103	23	6	30	1.0	30.0	150.0
Sierra Leone	..	4	..	..	..	3.0	1.0	3.0
Singapore	1,656	1,613	6	37	6	..	..	..
Slovakia	132	121	1	10	7	2.0	..	60.0
Spain	2,124	1,921	93	109	7,084	5.0	14.0	23.0
Sri Lanka	742	97	40	605	189	2.0	7.0	60.0
Sweden	..	205	..	36	31	2.0	70.0	156.0
Switzerland	875	811	13	51	28	3.0	1.0	19.0
Thailand	4,360	2,701	271	1,388	11,988	22.0	210.0	793.0
Trinidad and Tobago	..	..	..	..	74	6.0	..	..
Türkiye	13,730	12,030	1,599	101	364	14.0	45.0	45.0
Ukraine	..	1,494	..	173	615	4.0	..	90.0
United Arab Emirates	1,097	1,072	23	2	1,110	6.0	593.0	593.0
United Kingdom	53,345	50,639	2,401	305	4,689	18.6	31.0	69.0
United States of America	50,444	31,308	11,104	8,032	76,749	197.0	471.4	552.4
Uzbekistan	246	175	19	52	65	1.0	10.0	190.0
Venezuela (Bolivarian Republic of)	809	737	41	31	..	1.0	365.0	365.0
Viet Nam	2,849	2,114	689	46	1,456	12.0	446.0	489.0
Zimbabwe	..	..	..	..	2	1.0	..	..

Note: FTE is full time equivalent. WIPO collects data from IP offices using a common questionnaire and methodology. Every effort has been made to compile procedural data based on common definitions and concepts, but procedural differences make it extremely difficult to fully harmonize such data. Therefore caution should be exercised when making comparisons across offices. The total number of applications processed for any given office may be incomplete due to the omission of one or several elements by the office.

(a) data are for formalities examinations only.

.. indicates not available.

Source: WIPO Statistics Database, September 2022.

Plant varieties

Highlights

Plant variety applications sustain strong growth

Around 25,340 plant variety applications were filed worldwide in 2021, up +12% on 2020 – a sixth consecutive year of growth (figure 4.1). China contributed the most to global growth, followed by the United States of America (US) and the United Kingdom (UK).

Applications grew by +12% in 2021

4.1. Plant variety applications worldwide, 2007–2021

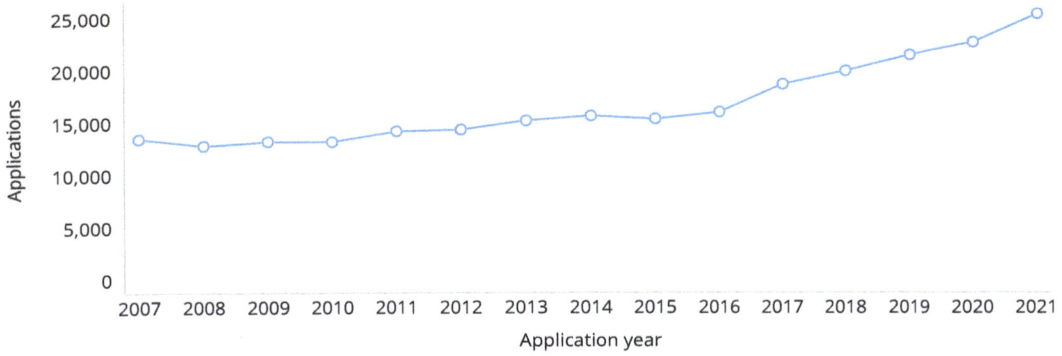

Source: Figure D1.

China received 44.2% of all plant variety applications filed worldwide

China remained the top destination in 2021, receiving 11,195 plant variety applications. China accounts for over two-fifths of the plant varieties filed worldwide. The Community Plant Variety Office of the European Union (CPVO) received 3,480 applications, accounting for 13.7% of global filings. Following the CPVO are the US (1,902), Ukraine (944) and the Netherlands (836) (figure 4.2). Filings in China grew for an eighth straight year of sizeable growth, and represented a +24.9% year-on-year increase, driven almost entirely by resident filings. Likewise, resident filings were largely responsible for a big increase in filings in the US (+32.8%), despite a slight decline in non-resident filings (figure D6). Among the other top five destinations, Ukraine (–25.1%) and the Netherlands (–0.1%) experienced an overall decline in filings. A fall in both resident and non-resident applications drove a decline in the Ukraine, whereas the drop in non-resident filings in the Netherlands was almost compensated for by a nearly equivalent growth in resident filings.

In 2021, the combined share of applications received at the top five jurisdictions worldwide grew by 1.7 percentage points to 72.4%, due to a large growth in filings in China and the US.

The CPVO and the UK deserve a closer look, as 2021 was the first year when the UK was no longer a member of the European Union. Filings at the CPVO increased by +1.5%, driven by growth in non-resident filings; however, the impact of the UK's withdrawal from the CPVO was minimal. A drop in resident filings received by the CPVO was due in large part to a drop in filings originating from France, the Netherlands and Spain, whereas the increase in non-resident filings was driven by applications originating from Switzerland and the US, despite UK applicants being now classified as non-resident. By contrast, filings in the UK increased by +214.6%, as applicants seeking to protect plant varieties within the UK now only have the option of filing directly at the UK office, rather than via the CPVO system.

Seven of the top 10 jurisdictions received more applications from residents than from non-residents. China's resident share (94.1%) was the highest among the top 10 offices. In contrast, Canada, the UK and Ukraine received a majority of their filings from non-resident applicants.

China continues to be the top destination for plant variety applications

4.2. Plant variety applications for the top 10 offices, 2021

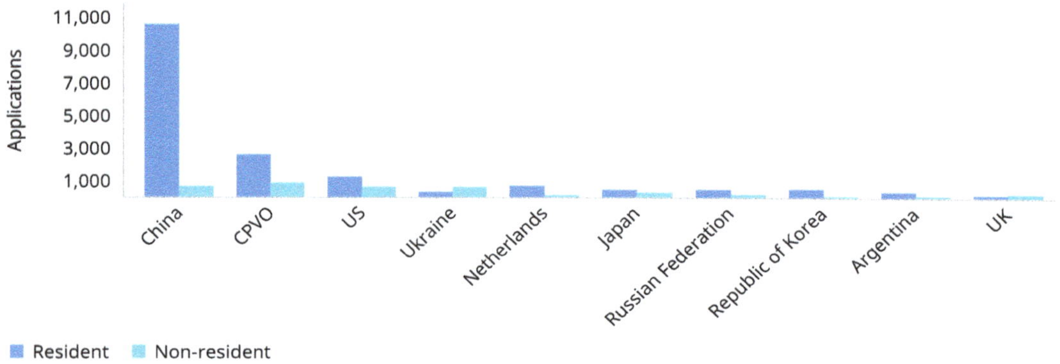

Source: Figure D5.

Asia is the top region, with 52.3% of all applications

4.3. Plant variety applications by region, 2011 and 2021

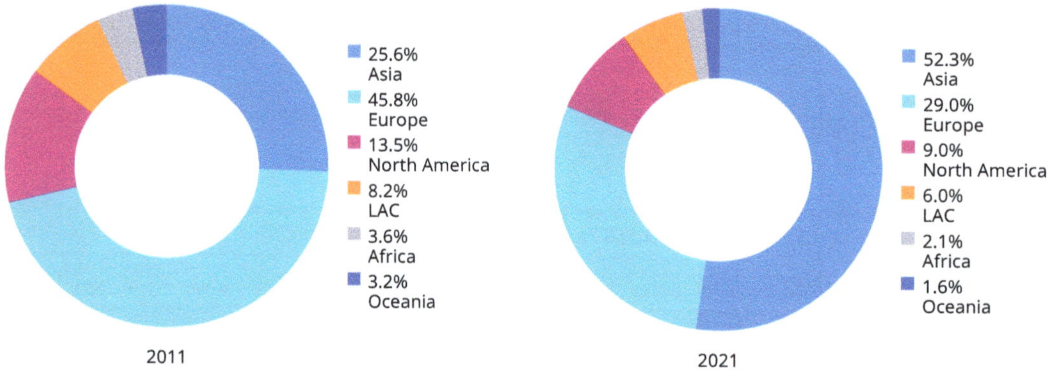

Note: LAC is Latin America and the Caribbean

Source: Figure D3.

Asia received the most filings, representing 52.3% of all plant variety applications in 2021. Filings in Asia have more than doubled compared to 2011, when the region's share was a fraction over a quarter (25.6%) (figure 4.3). Europe represented the second largest region in terms of total plant filings, accounting for roughly 29% of the world total in 2021. However, due to the large growth of filings in Asia during the period, Europe's overall share was down from 45.8% of total filings in 2011. In addition to Asia (+13.8%), Latin America and the Caribbean (LAC) (+2.6%), North America (+1.7%), Europe (+1.3%) and Africa (+0.6%) have all experienced positive average annual growth over the 10 years from 2011 to 2021. Unlike 2020, when three regions experienced a decline, only one region, namely Oceania, had filings lower in 2021 than in 2011, recording an average annual decline of -0.8% between 2011 and 2021.

Applicants from China were the most active filers worldwide

Applications received by offices from resident and non-resident applicants are referred to as office data, whereas applications filed by applicants at a national or regional office (resident applications) or at foreign offices (applications abroad) are referred to as origin data. Here, plant variety statistics based on the origin of residence are reported in order to complement the global picture. Note that for applicants domiciled in European Union (EU) member states, filing at the CPVO regional office is regarded as a resident filing.

Applicants from China were the most active applicants in the world in 2021, filing 10,574 plant variety applications (figure 4.4). This represents +26.5% growth on the previous year driven by resident filings. China-based applicants were followed by applicants from the Netherlands, who filed 3,212 applications, a -6.6% decrease from 2020. The US (2,781), Germany (1,101) and France (1,060) were the next three largest origins, respectively. Applicants from the US (+27%), Germany (+17.3%) and France (+9.3%) recorded a strong growth in applications compared to a year earlier. Similar to China, the large growth in filings by applicants in the US was driven by resident applications. For German and French applicants, growth was primarily due to non-resident filings. The Netherlands (-6.6%) was the only top five origin to experience a drop in applications. At the same time as filing more applications in their home jurisdiction, applicants from the Netherlands decreased their filings at foreign offices and at the CPVO. Combined, the top five origins represented 73.9% of total filings globally in 2021, with China (41.7% of the total) and the Netherlands (12.7%) contributing the majority.

Whereas applicants from four of the top five origins filed most of their applications either abroad or at a regional office, applicants from China filed almost exclusively at home. Like with those in China, applicants from Japan, the Republic of Korea and Argentina also filed predominantly at home.

Applicants from China filed primarily at their home office

4.4. Plant variety applications for the top 10 origins, 2021

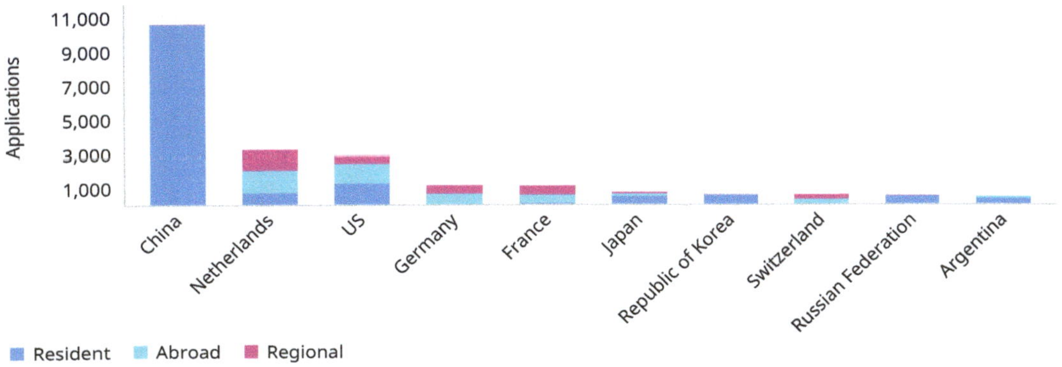

Source: Figure D11.

Equivalent count

Origin data are compiled using two different counting methods - absolute counts and equivalent counts. The difference between the two lies in the treatment of regional office data (the CPVO and the African Intellectual Property Organization (OAPI)). For absolute counts, an application received by a regional office is counted only once. For the equivalent count, a single application filed at a regional office is equivalent to multiple applications. To calculate the number of equivalent applications at a regional office in 2021, each application has been multiplied by the corresponding number of member states for the regional office. For CPVO applications, if the applicant resided in one of the 27 EU member states, the application was counted as one resident filing and 26 filings abroad. If the applicant did not reside in an EU member state, the application was counted as 27 filings abroad. The same methodology was applied to OAPI member states.

Equivalent counts take multiple members of the regional office into account. One would expect to see those country origins whose applicants filed intensively at the CPVO move up the ranking when this counting method is applied (figure D12). Not surprisingly therefore European countries and the US topped the list of origins based on equivalent counts. Applicants from the Netherlands once again ranked first, with 34,048 equivalent applications filed worldwide. They were followed by applicants from France (13,488), the US (13,203) and Germany (12,957). Rounding out the top five origins by equivalent count was China, with 10,682 applications.

China was the only non-European country to be found among the top five origins by equivalent count, despite only 1.3% of its applicants' filings being equivalent filings abroad. This is in marked contrast to the Netherlands, for which the abroad share was 94.5%.

Plant variety titles issued increased by +8.2%

4.5. Plant variety titles issued worldwide, 2007–2021

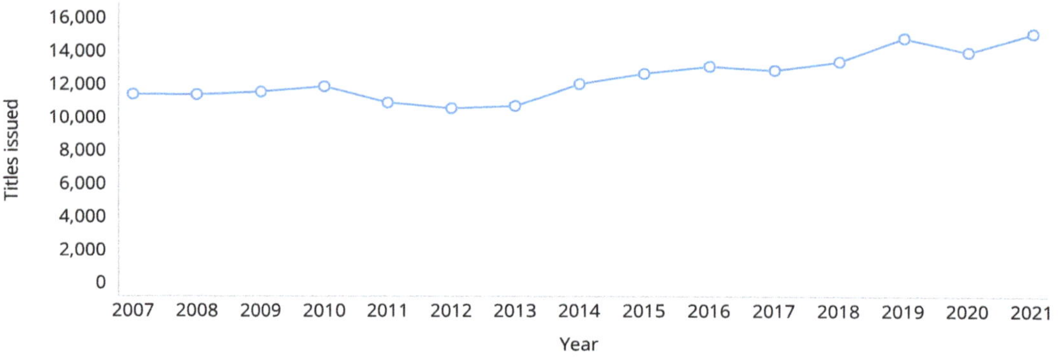

Source: Figure D2.

Titles issued returned to growth in 2021

The total number of plant variety titles issued increased by +8.2% in 2021, more than reversing last year's contraction. The 15,090 plant variety titles issued in 2021 is the largest number ever recorded, and 2.0% higher than the previous peak recorded in 2019 (figure 4.5). China issued the most titles, with 3,979, up +33.1% on the previous year. China was followed by the CPVO (2,853), the US (1,609), Ukraine (1,161) and the Netherlands (624) (figure D9). Similarly to China, Ukraine also experienced a large increase in titles issued, with an increase of +41.8% on the year. China and Ukraine were the primary drivers of global growth in titles issued. In contrast, the US (–17.1%), the CPVO (–4.2%) and the Netherlands (–2.7%) all experienced a decline in titles issued compared to 2020.

The grant or registration process takes time, so fluctuations in the volume of plant variety titles granted may be a consequence of changes in processing capacity or procedural delay.

Steady growth in plant varieties in force continues

Around 154,800 plant variety titles were in force at the end of 2021, up +4.5% on 2020. The CPVO (29,578), the US (28,210) and China (19,696) were the three offices with the highest number of active titles (figure D17). Other offices maintaining at least 5,000 active titles included Ukraine (12,100), the Netherlands (9,460), Japan (8,090), the Russian Federation (6,418) and the Republic of Korea (5,999).

Plant variety statistics

Plant variety applications and titles issued worldwide

D1. Trend in plant variety applications worldwide, 2007-2021

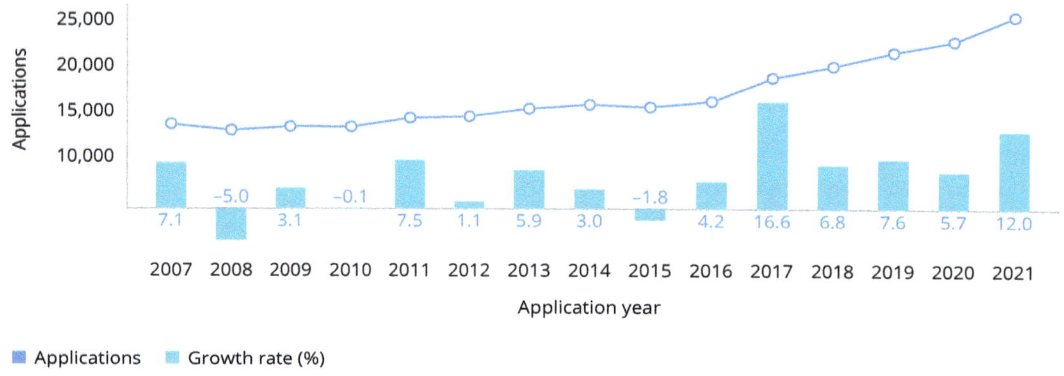

Note: World totals are WIPO estimates using data covering 71 offices.
Source: WIPO Statistics Database, September 2022.

D2. Trend in plant variety titles issued worldwide, 2007-2021

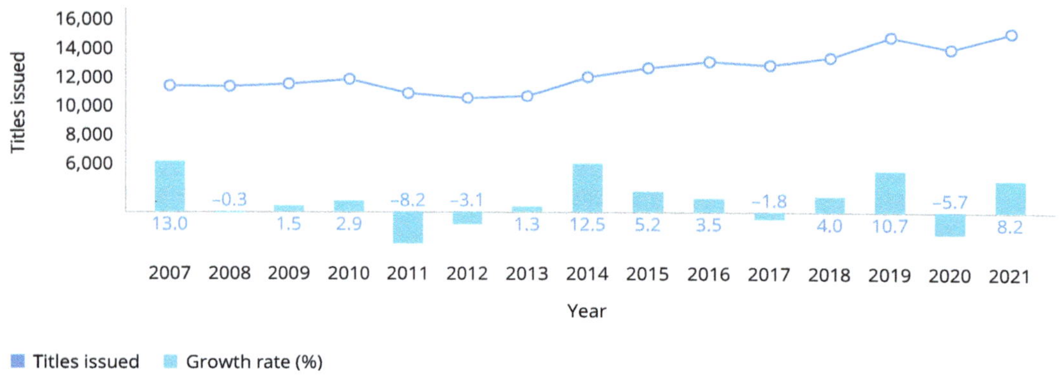

Note: World totals are WIPO estimates using data covering 71 offices.
Source: WIPO Statistics Database, September 2022.

Plant variety applications and titles issued by office

D3. Plant variety applications by region, 2011 and 2021

	Number of applications		Resident share (%)		Share of world total (%)		Average growth (%)
Region	**2011**	**2021**	**2011**	**2021**	**2011**	**2021**	**2011-2021**
Africa	508	538	24.6	9.7	3.6	2.1	0.6
Asia	3,631	13,252	78.8	90.1	25.6	52.3	13.8
Europe	6,484	7,357	69.1	66.4	45.8	29.0	1.3
Latin America and the Caribbean	1,168	1,509	41.0	43.6	8.2	6.0	2.6
North America	1,918	2,268	45.8	59.0	13.5	9.0	1.7
Oceania	451	416	52.1	39.2	3.2	1.6	-0.8
World	**14,160**	**25,340**	**64.0**	**75.1**	**100.0**	**100.0**	**6.0**

Note: Totals by geographical region are WIPO estimates using data covering 71 offices. Each region includes the following number of offices: Africa (7), Asia (12), Europe (33), Latin America and the Caribbean (14), North America (3) and Oceania (2).

Source: WIPO Statistics Database, September 2022.

D4. Trend in plant variety applications for the top five offices, 2000–2021

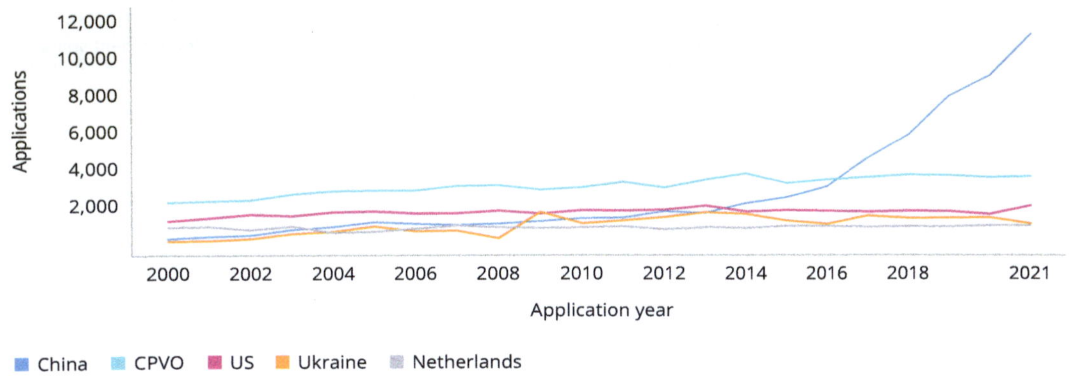

Note: CPVO is the Community Plant Variety Office of the European Union. The top five offices were selected based on their 2021 totals.

Source: WIPO Statistics Database, September 2022.

D5. Plant variety applications for the top 20 offices, 2021

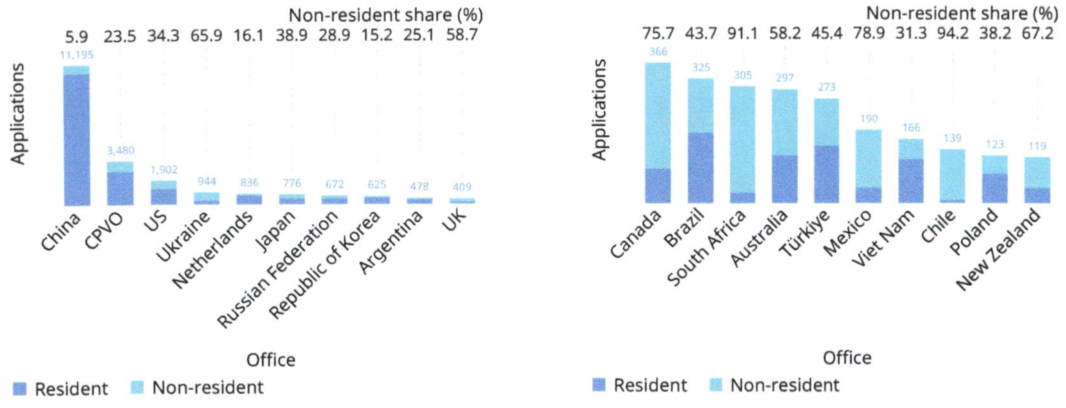

Note: CPVO is the Community Plant Variety Office of the European Union. In general, the national offices of CPVO member states receive lower volumes of applications, because applicants may choose to apply via the CPVO when seeking protection within any CPVO member state.

Source: WIPO Statistics Database, September 2022.

D6. Contribution of resident and non-resident applications to total growth for the top 20 offices, 2020–2021

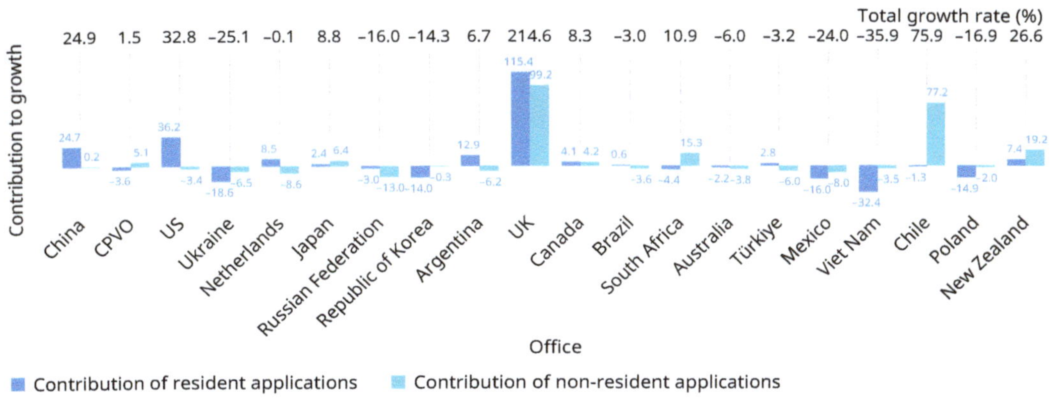

Note: CPVO is the Community Plant Variety Office of the European Union. This figure shows total growth in plant variety applications broken down by the respective contributions of resident and non-resident filings. For example, applications in Japan grew by +8.8%, with resident applications contributing 2.4 percentage points to total growth and non-resident applications accounting for the other 6.4 percentage points.

Source: WIPO Statistics Database, September 2022.

D7. Plant variety applications for offices of selected low- and middle-income countries, 2021

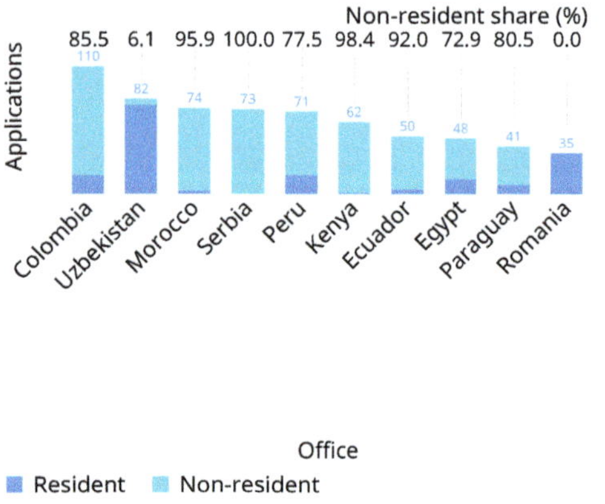

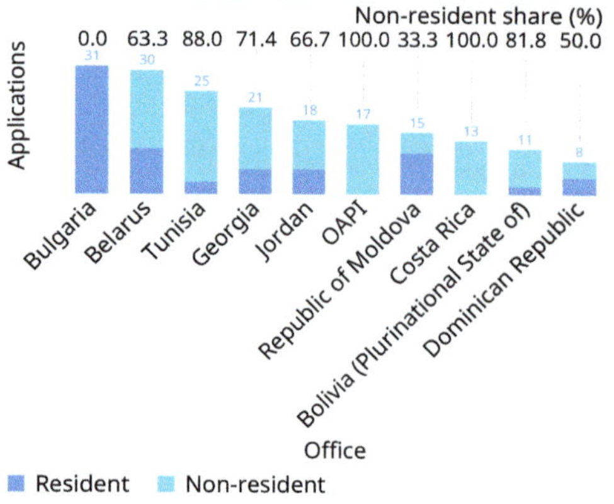

Note: OAPI is the African Intellectual Property Organization. The selected offices are from different world regions and income groups. Where available, data for all offices can be found in the statistical table at the end of this section.

Source: WIPO Statistics Database, September 2022.

D8. Flow of non-resident applications for the top offices, 2021

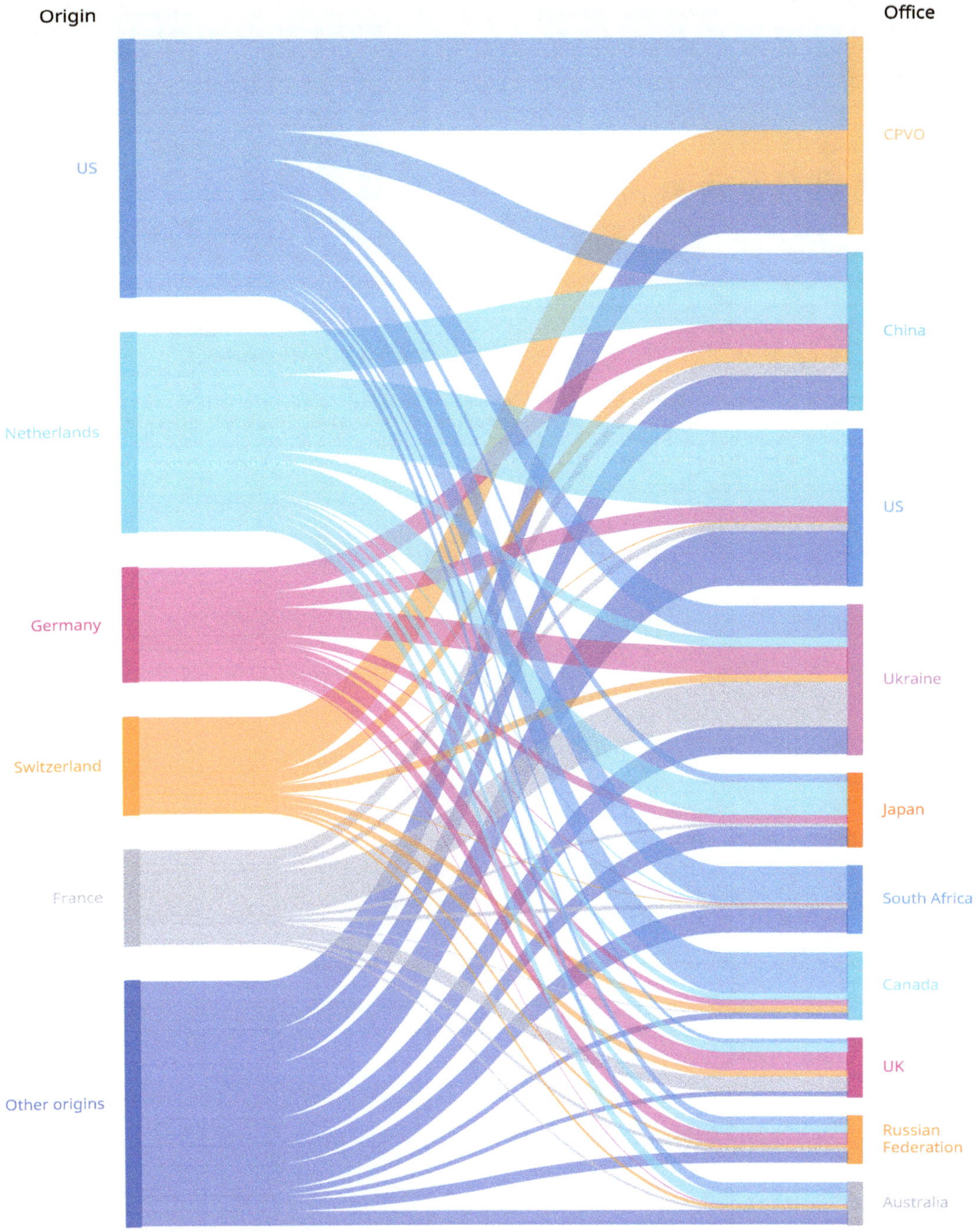

Note: CPVO is the Community Plant Variety Office of the European Union.
Source: WIPO Statistics Database, September 2022.

D9. Plant variety titles issued by the top 20 offices, 2021

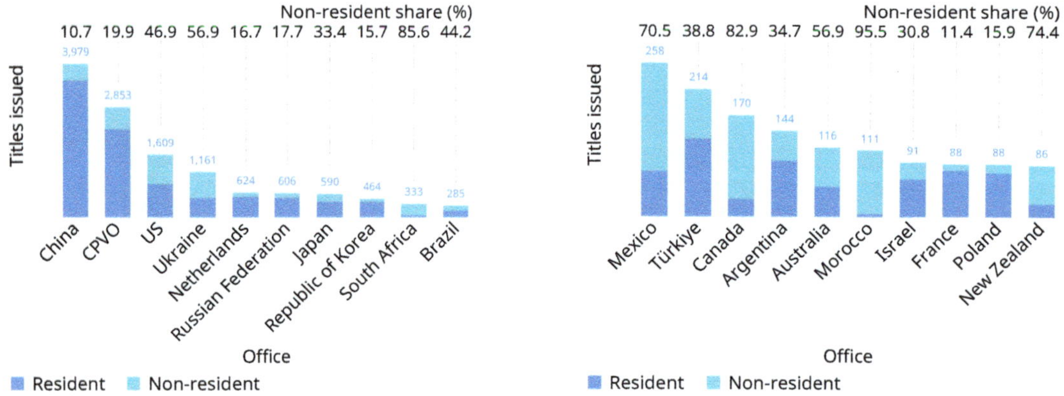

Note: CPVO is the Community Plant Variety Office of the European Union. The procedure for issuing titles varies across offices, and factors such as examination capacity and procedural delays mean there are differences in the time lag between application and title issue dates. For this reason, data on applications for any given year should not be compared with data on titles issued that same year.

Source: WIPO Statistics Database, September 2022.

D10. Trend in plant variety titles issued for the top five offices, 2000–2021

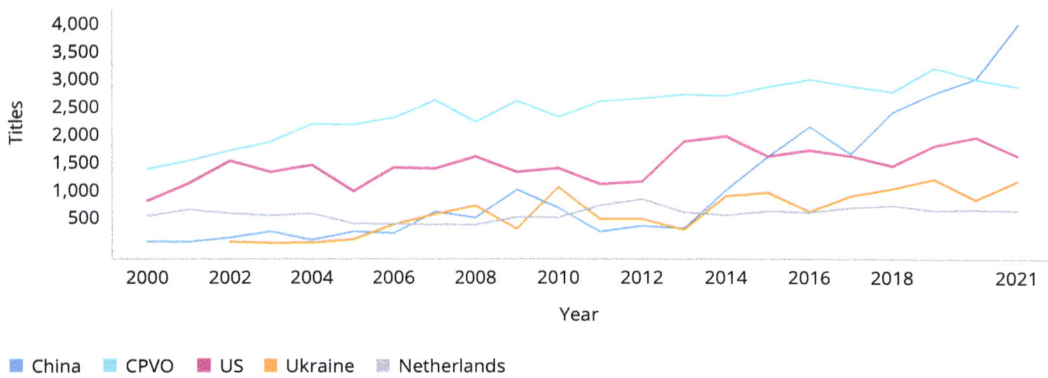

Note: CPVO is the Community Plant Variety Office of the European Union. The top five offices were selected based on their 2021 totals.

Source: WIPO Statistics Database, September 2022.

Plant variety applications and titles issued by origin

D11. Plant variety applications for the top 20 origins, 2021

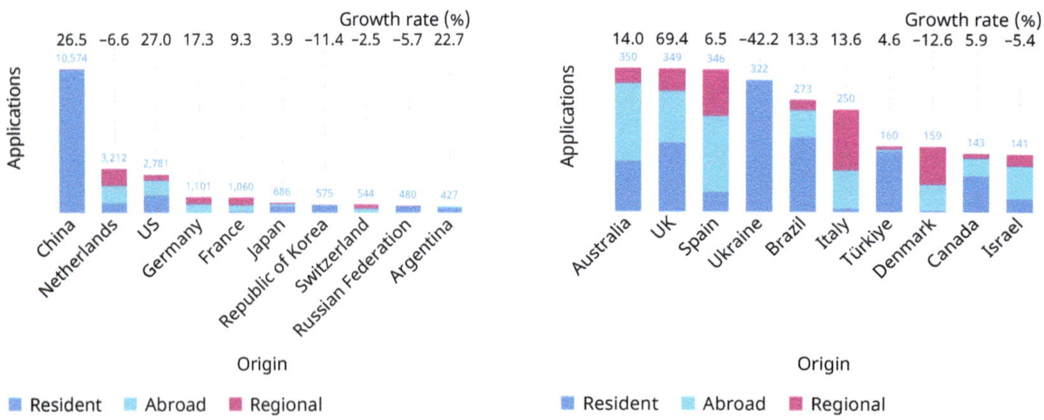

Note: Data are based on absolute count, not equivalent count. Applications by origin include resident applications and applications filed abroad. The origin of an application is determined by the residence of the applicant. Regional refers to applications filed at the Community Plant Variety Office of the European Union.

Source: WIPO Statistics Database, September 2022.

D12. Plant variety equivalent applications for the top 20 origins, 2021

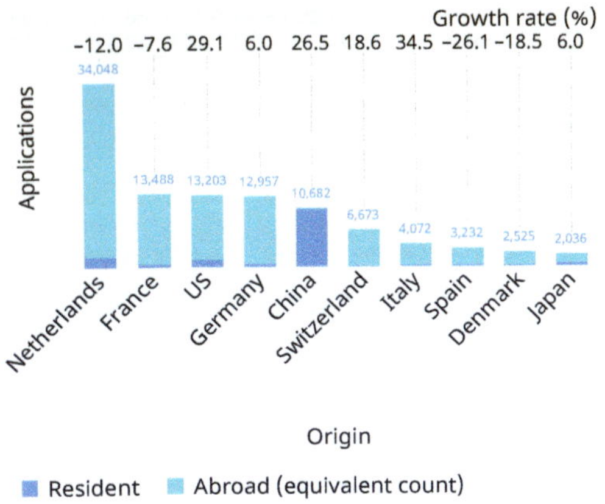

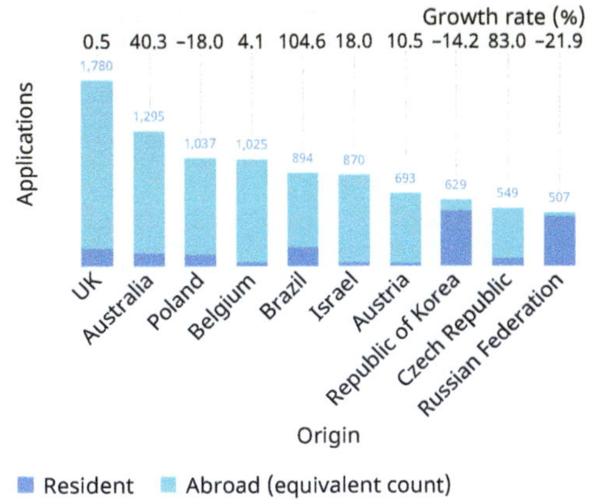

Note: Data are based on equivalent count (see the glossary for the definition of equivalent applications). Applications by origin include resident applications and applications filed abroad. The origin of an application is determined by the residence of the applicant.

Source: WIPO Statistics Database, September 2022.

D13. Plant variety applications abroad for the top 20 origins, 2021

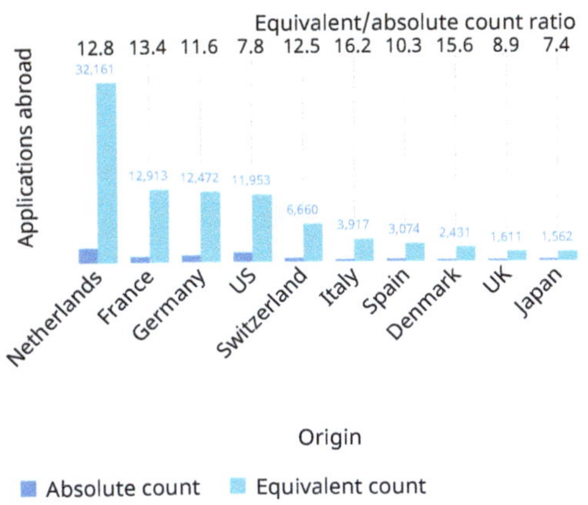

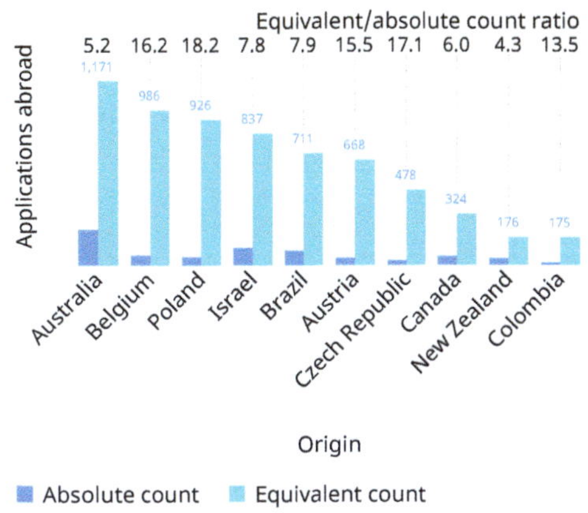

Note: The origin of an application is determined by the residence of the applicant. Applications filed at regional offices are considered equivalent to multiple applications in the relevant member states. See the glossary for the definition of equivalent applications.

Source: WIPO Statistics Database, September 2022.

D14. Plant variety titles issued for the top 20 origins, 2021

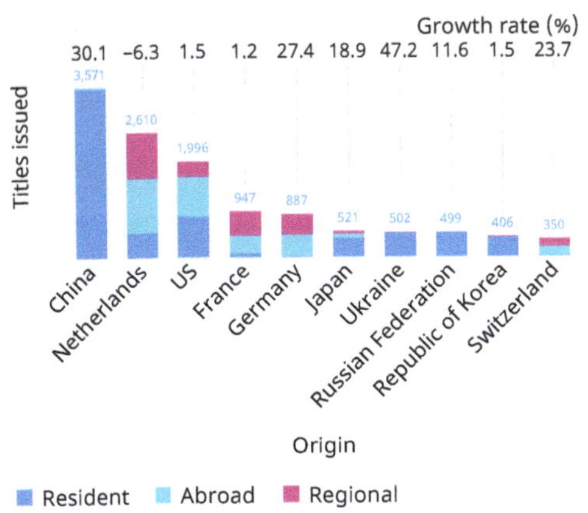

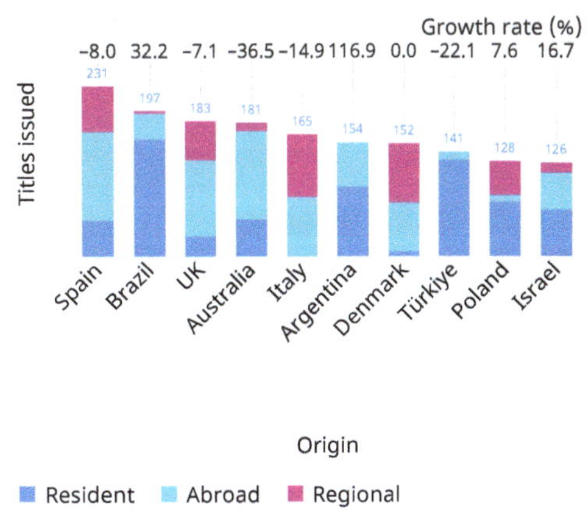

Note: Data are based on an absolute count not an equivalent count. The origin of titles issued is determined by the residence of the applicant. Regional refers to titles issued by the Community Plant Variety Office of the European Union.

Source: WIPO Statistics Database, September 2022.

D15. Plant variety titles issued abroad for the top 20 origins, 2021

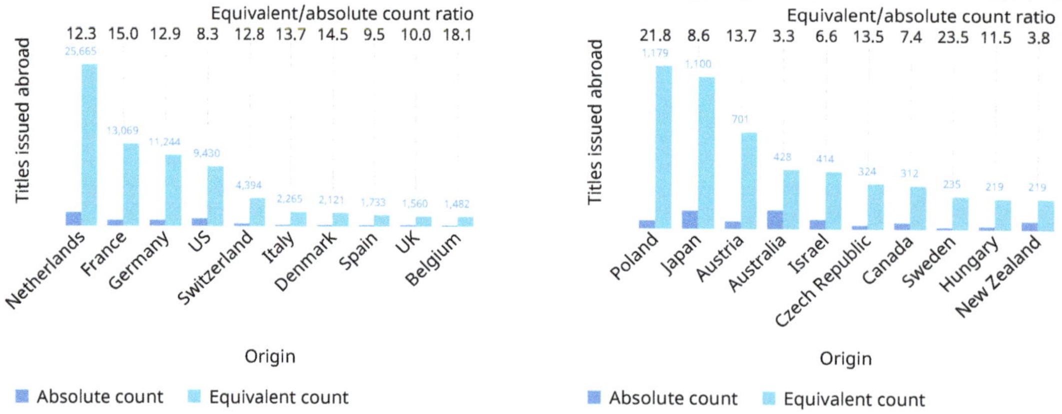

Note: The origin of titles issued is determined by the residence of the applicant. Titles issued by regional offices are considered equivalent to multiple titles in the relevant member states. See the glossary for the definition of equivalent count.

Source: WIPO Statistics Database, September 2022.

Plant varieties in force

D16. Trend in plant varieties in force worldwide, 2007–2021

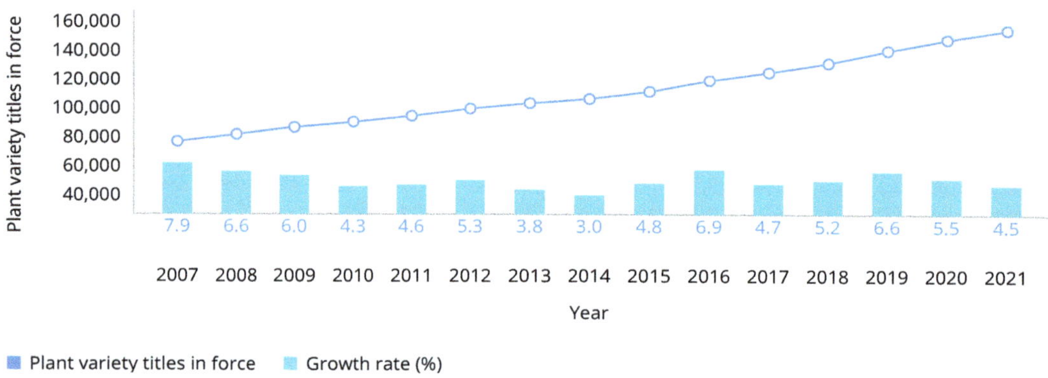

Note: World totals are WIPO estimates using data covering 70 offices.

Source: WIPO Statistics Database, September 2022.

D17. Plant varieties in force at selected offices, 2021

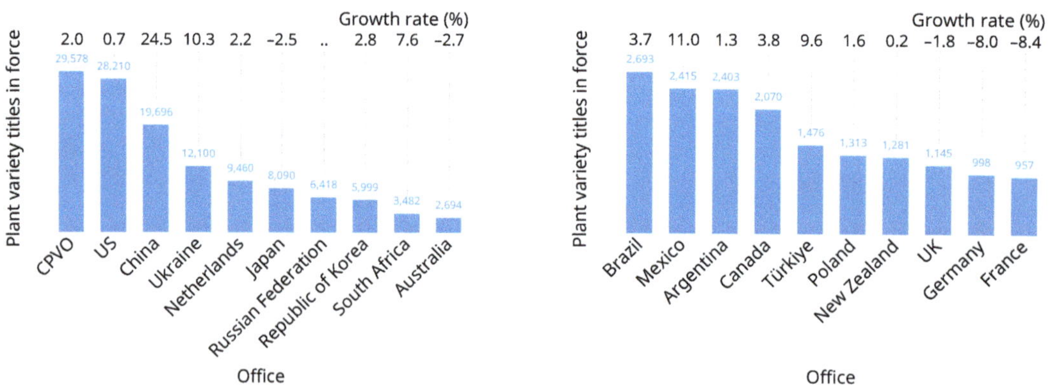

Note: CPVO is the Community Plant Variety Office of the European Union.

.. indicates not available.

Source: WIPO Statistics Database, September 2022.

Statistical table

D18. Plant variety applications and titles issued by office and origin, and plant variety titles in force by office, 2021

	Applications by office			Applications by origin	Equivalent applications by origin	Titles issued by office			Plant varieties in force
Name	Total	Resident	Non-resident	Total	Total	Total	Resident	Non-resident	Office
African Intellectual Property Organization	17	3	14	..	..	..	..	..	10
Argentina	478	358	120	427	427	144	94	50	2,403
Australia	297	124	173	350	1,295	116	50	66	2,694
Austria (a)	..	..	..	43	693	..	..	..	15
Belarus	30	11	19	19	19	18	11	7	255
Belgium	2	2	0	63	1,025	1	1	0	34
Bolivia (Plurinational State of)	11	2	9	2	2	11	2	9	70
Brazil	325	183	142	273	894	285	159	126	2,693
Bulgaria	31	31	0	31	31	24	24	0	298
Canada	366	89	277	143	413	170	29	141	2,070
Chile	139	8	131	19	46	69	8	61	910
China	11,195	10,539	656	10,574	10,682	3,979	3,555	424	19,696
Colombia	110	16	94	29	191	83	0	83	754
Community Plant Variety Office	3,480	2,609	871	n.a.	..	2,853	2,234	619	29,578
Costa Rica	13	0	13	24	24	2	2	0	21
Croatia	13	13	0	13	13	24	24	0	67
Cyprus (b)	..	..	..	2	2	..	..	..	..
Czech Republic	63	53	10	81	549	51	41	10	796
Denmark	10	3	7	159	2,525	6	6	0	43
Dominican Republic	8	4	4	4	4	5	3	2	18
Ecuador	50	4	46	7	34	23	5	18	388
Egypt	48	13	35	13	13	76	42	34	480
Estonia	6	0	6	1	27	8	2	6	99
Finland	6	1	5	20	150	10	9	1	204
France	112	97	15	1,060	13,488	88	78	10	957
Georgia	21	6	15	6	6	2	0	2	207
Germany	48	29	19	1,101	12,957	21	18	3	998
Greece (b)	..	..	..	3	81	..	..	..	..
Hungary	30	30	0	39	169	22	21	1	196
India (b)	..	..	..	3	84	..	..	..	..
Indonesia (b)	..	..	..	1	1	..	..	..	..
Ireland	1	1	0	6	84	1	1	0	52
Israel	62	33	29	141	870	91	63	28	791
Italy	9	8	1	250	4,072	..	..	..	44
Jamaica (b)	..	..	..	1	1	..	..	..	..
Japan	776	474	302	686	2,036	590	393	197	8,090
Jordan	18	6	12	6	6	8	0	8	59
Kazakhstan (b)	..	..	..	4	4	..	..	..	..
Kenya	62	1	61	1	1	76	9	67	504
Kyrgyzstan	4	0	4	..	..	..	..	..	6
Latvia	11	3	8	6	58	9	3	6	188
Lithuania	17	17	0	17	17	17	17	0	129
Mexico	190	40	150	60	168	258	76	182	2,415
Monaco (b)	..	..	..	1	1	..	..	..	..
Morocco	74	3	71	3	3	111	5	106	643
Netherlands	836	701	135	3,212	34,048	624	520	104	9,460
New Zealand	119	39	80	80	215	86	22	64	1,281
Nicaragua	1	1	0	1	1	3	3	0	17
Norway	25	1	24	10	118	24	3	21	242
Panama	6	0	6	..	..	..	..	..	19
Paraguay	41	8	33	13	13	28	3	25	214
Peru	71	16	55	16	16	29	1	28	312
Poland	123	76	47	127	1,037	88	74	14	1,313

	Applications by office			Applications by origin	Equivalent applications by origin	Titles issued by office			Plant varieties in force
Name	Total	Resident	Non-resident	Total	Total	Total	Resident	Non-resident	Office
Portugal (a)	..	..	..	2	2	..	..	..	9
Republic of Korea	625	530	95	575	629	464	391	73	5,999
Republic of Moldova	15	10	5	10	10	28	27	1	288
Romania	35	35	0	52	52	47	47	0	474
Russian Federation	672	478	194	480	507	606	499	107	6,418
Senegal (b)	..	..	..	3	51	..	..	..	..
Serbia	73	0	73	8	62	71	3	68	473
Singapore	4	0	4	..	..	5	1	4	12
Slovakia	5	5	0	9	61	4	4	0	303
Slovenia (a)	..	..	..	..	..	..	..	..	9
South Africa	305	27	278	61	196	333	48	285	3,482
Spain	59	47	12	346	3,232	51	48	3	433
Sweden	7	5	2	11	115	1	0	1	84
Switzerland	106	13	93	544	6,673	56	6	50	646
Tunisia	25	3	22	3	3	20	0	20	229
Türkiye	273	149	124	160	322	214	131	83	1,476
Ukraine	944	322	622	322	322	1,161	500	661	12,100
United Kingdom	409	169	240	349	1,780	57	27	30	1,145
United Republic of Tanzania	7	2	5	2	2	6	0	6	121
United States of America (PPA) (c)	1,429	874	555	n.a.	..	1,085	404	681	19,871
United States of America (PVPA)	473	376	97	2,781	13,203	524	451	73	8,339
Uruguay	66	18	48	24	51	66	18	48	631
Uzbekistan	82	77	5	81	81	66	64	2	227
Viet Nam	166	114	52	114	114	82	79	3	620
Others/Unknown	..	..	..	47	452	..	..	..	..
Total (2021 estimates)	**25,340**	**19,100**	**6,240**	**25,340**	**n.a.**	**15,090**	**9,000**	**3,010**	**154,800**

(a) This office did not report data; therefore, applications by origin data may be incomplete.

(b) This office is not a member of the International Union for the Protection of New Varieties of Plants (UPOV).

(c) Applications by origin are reported under United States of America Plant Varieties Protection Act (PVPA).

n.a. indicates not applicable.

.. indicates not available.

Source: WIPO Statistics Database, September 2022.

Geographical indications

Highlights

Introduction

A geographical indication (GI) is a sign identifying a good as originating from a specific geographical area and possessing a given quality, reputation or other characteristic essentially attributable to that geographical origin. Thus, the main function of a GI is to identify goods whose quality, reputation or other characteristics are strongly connected to the territory of origin.

GIs can be protected through a variety of legal means (e.g., *sui generis* systems, trademark laws, regional system, international agreements, other national legal means, etc.). In addition, the protection of GIs at a national level is often shared among several agencies. WIPO has made a major effort to gather data from all sources, but in many instances it has not been possible to obtain data from every source. For instance, many countries are unable to identify GIs protected through the trademark system. Nonetheless, the statistics gathered afford a valuable insight into how this form of intellectual property (IP) is being used in different parts of the world.

How many GIs are in force worldwide?

Data received by WIPO from a total 93 national and regional authorities show there were an estimated 63,600 protected GIs in existence in 2021.[1] To minimize double counting, GIs in force through the European Union (EU) (5,076 GIs in force) regional system and the Lisbon System (1,052) are counted once only, rather than multiplied by the number of member states party to each system. That notwithstanding, the overall total of around 63,600 will inevitably include a degree of double counting, as GIs in force through bilateral, plurilateral or multilateral agreements could potentially be included multiple times. If GIs in force through various international agreements are excluded, then around 20,600 GIs were in force in 2021.

Of the 63,600 GIs in force in 2021, high-income (45.1%) and upper middle-income (45.3%) economies reported a similar share of around 45% each, while lower middle-income economies (9.5%) accounted for almost one-tenth of the total.[2] In terms of regional distribution, Europe had the most GIs in force among regions, amounting to 58.1%, followed by Asia (31.7%), Latin America and the Caribbean (4.5%), Oceania (3.3%), North America (2.3%) and Africa 0.1%.[3]

Figure 5.1 shows the total number of GIs in force for selected national and regional authorities, while figure 5.2 reports data on GIs in force for EU member states. In 2021, China (9,052) had the most GIs in force within its territory, followed by Hungary (7,743), the Czech Republic (6,272), Slovakia (6112) and Bosnia and Herzegovina (6,087). The high rankings achieved by EU countries is explained by the fact that the 5,076 GIs in force through the EU regional system are in force in every member state. In addition, some EU member states, such as the Czech Republic, are party to the Lisbon System; therefore GIs in force via the Lisbon System (1,052 appellations of origin and geographical indications, excluding domestic and refusals) are also included in the total. Several middle-income economies had a high number of GIs in force within their jurisdiction in 2021; for example, there were 6,087 GIs in force in Bosnia and Herzegovina, 5,888 in Bulgaria and 4,600 in the Republic of Moldova. Again, these

1 Of the 93 responses received from authorities worldwide, eight – Angola, Bhutan, Dominica, Iraq, Liberia, Saint Vincent and the Grenadines, Uganda and Uruguay – replied saying there were no GIs in force within their respective jurisdictions in 2021.

2 Each category includes the following number of offices: high-income economies (43), upper middle-income (28), lower middle-income (16) and low-income (3). European Union data are allocated to the high-income group, because most of its member states are high-income countries. Venezuela is unclassified pending release of revised national accounts statistics.

3 Regions include the following number of offices: Africa (7), Asia (23), Europe (41), Latin America and the Caribbean (16), North America (2) and Oceania (2).

countries' high ranking in terms of GIs in force is due to their being party to the Lisbon System. In contrast, India (417) and Thailand (170) had considerably fewer GIs in force, which could be explained by them having no GIs protected through international agreements in 2021 (see table 5.7).

China had over 9,000 GIs in force in 2021, up 6.8% on the previous year

5.1. Geographical indications in force for selected national and regional authorities, 2021

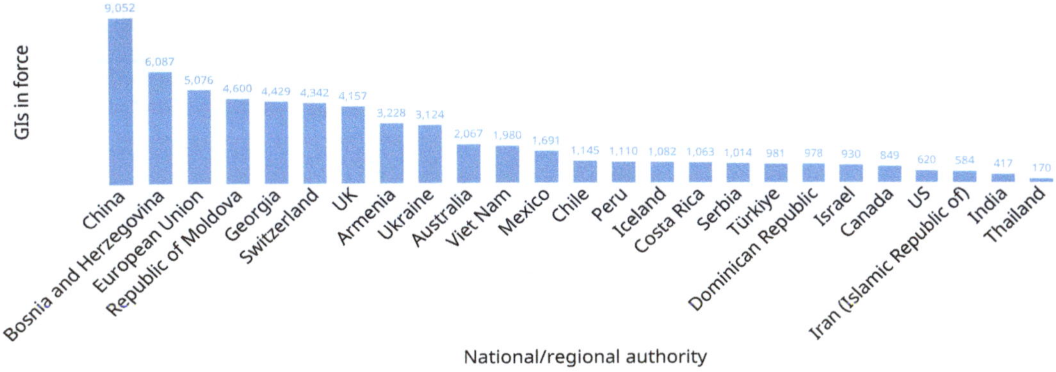

Source: Table 5.7.

A majority of EU member states protect nearly all their GIs through the EU regional system

5.2. Geographical indications in force for EU member states, 2021

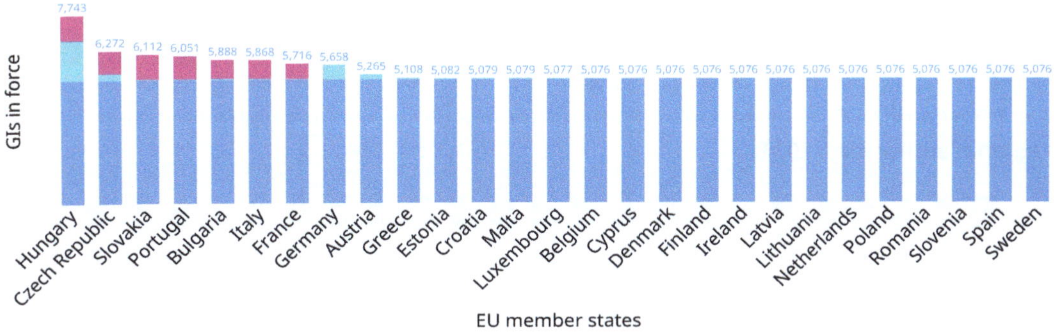

Note: The EU's regional systems for the protection of GIs cover agricultural and foodstuff products, wines and spirits.
Source: Table 5.7.

Figure 5.3 shows the total number of GIs in force broken down by legal means of protection for selected national and regional authorities. All GIs in force in Brazil and India, Malaysia and the United States of America (US) were protected through national systems, whereas the bulk of GIs in force in Dominican Republic (97.5%), Israel (99.2%) and Peru (87.7%) were protected through the Lisbon System.

Most GIs in force in Dominican Republic, Israel and Peru were protected by the Lisbon System

5.3. Distribution of geographical indications in force by legal means of protection for selected national and regional authorities, 2021

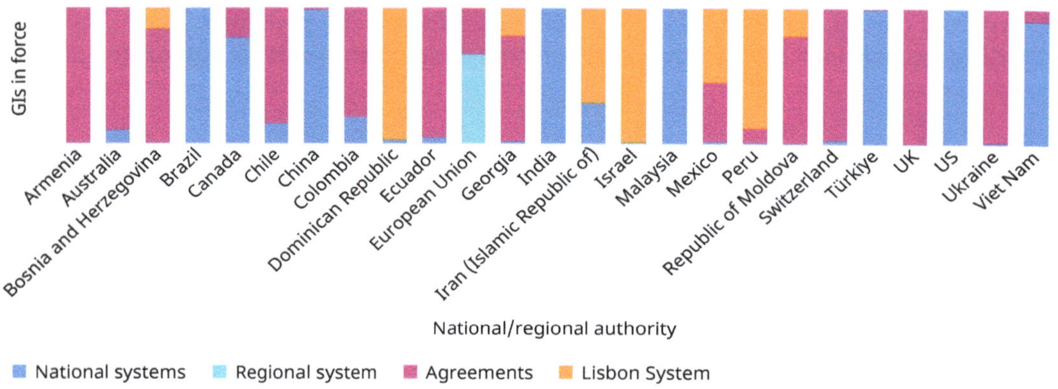

Source: Table 5.7.

A number of authorities provided GIs data broken down according to source (i.e., national or foreign GIs). Figure 5.4 shows data for selected national and regional authorities. The share of national GIs ranged from as low as 2.2% in the United Kingdom (UK) to up to 100% in Argentina. More than 90% of the GIs in force in Brazil (90.7%), China (94.4%), India (93.5%), Indonesia (91.7%) and Türkiye (99.7%) were national GIs, whereas almost all those in force in Germany (97%), Switzerland (97.4%) and the UK (97.8%) were foreign GIs.

National GIs among a selection of national and regional authorities ranged from 2.2% in the UK to 100% in Argentina

5.4. Distribution of geographical indications in force by source for selected national and regional authorities, 2021

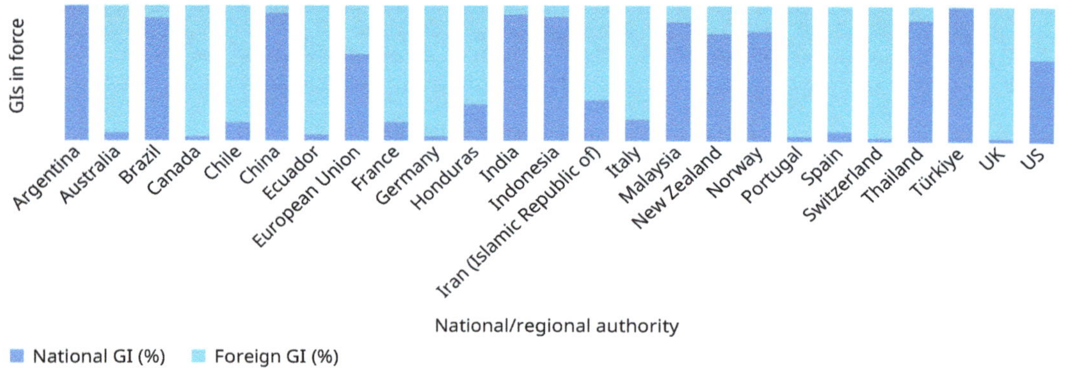

Source: WIPO Statistics Database, September 2022.

GIs in force relating to wines and spirits (51%) accounted for just over half of the 2021 global total, while agricultural products and foodstuffs accounted for 43.6% and handicrafts 3.9% of the total (figure 5.5). In terms of absolute numbers, Bosnia and Herzegovina (6,070) had the highest number of GIs in force for agricultural products, followed by Portugal (2,052), Bulgaria (2,028) and Germany (1,919). When it comes to the category of wines and spirits, Portugal had the most GIs in force (3,846), followed by Bulgaria (3,730), Germany (3,650) and Greece (3,290). Switzerland (425), India (231) and the Republic of Moldova (136) each had a considerable number of GIs in force for handicrafts in 2021. Data for EU member states include GIs in force through the EU regional system.

Wines and spirits accounted for just over half of GIs in force globally

5.5. Geographical indications in force by product category, 2021

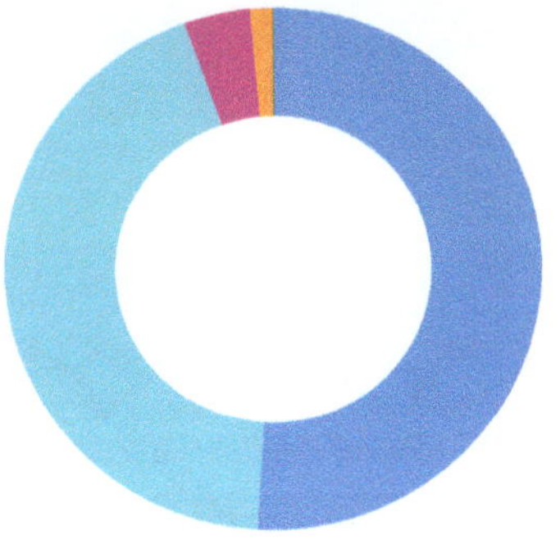

Note: The global total by product category is based on data from the 63 national jurisdictions plus the EU regional system for which 2021 data by product category are available. GIs in force through regional systems like the EU were counted once rather than multiple times, as they were in force in all the respective member states. This is so as to minimize double counting. China's 2021 product category data – the country with the greatest number of GIs in force – are unavailable.

Source: WIPO Statistics Database, September 2022.

The GIs in force data reported here are partial and incomplete and therefore ought to be interpreted with caution. The questionnaire underlying the data collection requested information from respondents regarding GIs protected through *sui generis* systems, trademark systems, other national legal means, regional systems and international agreements (including GIs in force under the Lisbon System and the Madrid System). As table 5.7 indicates, many countries did not provide statistics on the number of GIs protected through the trademark system. This might be because the countries concerned do not use the trademark system to protect GIs or else some countries that do use it have difficulty separating GIs from other trademarks (most commonly, collective and certification trademarks). In addition, several countries could not provide data on how many GIs were protected through international agreements.

China (2,350) reported the highest number of GIs protected via the *sui generis* system, followed by Türkiye (978) and Canada (665).[4] The most GIs protected via the trademarks system were in China (6,562), followed by Viet Nam (1,696) and the US (344), whereas Bosnia and Herzegovina (5,138), Switzerland (4,230) and the UK (4,154) reported high volumes of GIs protected through international agreements.

Appellations of origin and GIs in force via the Lisbon System grew by 3.4% in 2021 to reach 1,052

As of 2021, the Lisbon System consisted of 36 Contracting Parties. Lao People's Democratic Republic, Oman and Switzerland acceded to the Lisbon System in 2021.

In 2021, there were 1,052 appellations of origin (AOs) and geographical indications in force via the Lisbon System (figure 5.6). This is 35 more than in the previous year and the biggest increase since 2017. Despite a 16.5% decrease, France remains the primary user of the Lisbon System. It accounted for two-fifths (40.4%) of the 2021 total, followed by Italy (16.6%), the European Union (11%), the Czech Republic (7.1%) and the Islamic Republic of Iran (6.4%). The 2021 shares for Czech Republic, Italy and the Islamic Republic of Iran were similar to what they were in 2020. While the share of France declined from 50% in 2020 to 40.4% in 2021. The EU is a recent member of the Lisbon System.

4 Although the EU regional system is a *sui generis* system, GIs in force via the EU are reported under the regional system category rather than the *sui generis* category.

France remains the main user of the Lisbon System

5.6. Appellations of origin in force by origin, 2021

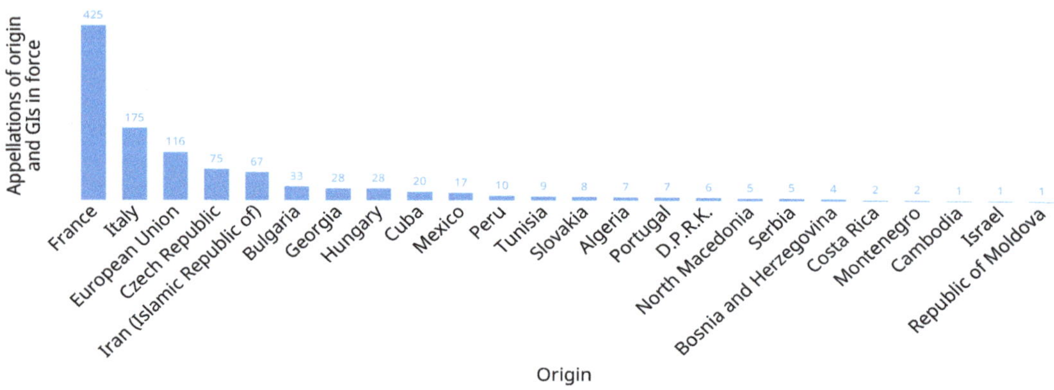

Note: D.P.R.K. is the Democratic People's Republic of Korea.
Source: WIPO Statistics Database, September 2022.

5.7. Geographical indications in force in 2021

National/regional authority	Total	*Sui generis*	Trademarks	Other national legal means	Regional system	Agreements	Lisbon System (a)
Andorra	7	4	2	..	..	1	..
Albania	1,064	..	16	..	..	..	1,048
Argentina	114	114	..	..	..	..	..
Armenia	3,228	8	..	..	..	3,220	..
Australia	2,067	116	79	..	..	1,872	..
Austria	5,265	..	..	..	3,348	1,916	1
Azerbaijan	42	..	42	..	..	..	..
Bangladesh	6	6	..	..	..	..	..
Belarus	35	35	..	..	..	..	..
Belgium	5,076	..	..	..	3,348	1,727	1
Bosnia and Herzegovina	6,087	15	..	..	..	5,138	934
Botswana	1	1	..	..	..	..	..
Brazil	97	97	..	..	..	..	..
Bulgaria	5,888	42	..	..	3,348	1,727	771
Cabo Verde	2	2	..	..	..	..	..
Cambodia	7	7	..	..	..	..	..
Canada	849	665	..	..	..	184	..
Chile	1,145	43	..	123	..	979	..
China	9,052	2,350	6,562	44	..	96	..
China, Hong Kong SAR	52	..	52	..	..	..	..
China, Macao SAR	22	3	19	..	..	..	..
Colombia	157	30	..	..	..	127	..
Costa Rica	1,063		33				1,030
Côte d'Ivoire	10	..	..	..	8	2	..
Croatia	5,079	3	..	..	3,348	1,727	1
Cyprus	5,076	..	..	..	3,348	1,727	1
Czech Republic	6,272	62	..	..	3,348	1,935	927
Denmark	5,076	..	..	..	3,348	1,727	1
Dominican Republic	978	..	24	..	..	..	954
Ecuador	141	6	..	..	..	135	..
El Salvador	29	29	..	..	..	..	..
Estonia	5,082	6	..	..	3,348	1,727	1
Ethiopia	11	..	11	..	..	..	..
European Union (b)	5,076	..	..	..	3,348	1,727	1
Finland	5,076	..	..	..	3,348	1,727	1
France	5,716	12	..	4	3,348	1,727	625
Georgia	4,429	57	..	..	..	3,471	901
Germany	5,658	..	1	..	3,448	2,208	1
Greece	5,108	16	..	16	3,348	1,727	1
Honduras	45	..	45	..	..	..	..

National/regional authority	Total	*Sui generis*	Trademarks	Other national legal means	Regional system	Agreements	Lisbon System (a)
Hungary	7,743	10	..	..	3,348	3,368	1,017
Iceland	1,082	2	..	..	..	1,080	..
India	417	417	..	..	..	..	..
Indonesia	108	108	..	..	..	..	..
Iran (Islamic Republic of)	584	174	..	..	..	..	410
Ireland	5,076	..	..	..	3,348	1,727	1
Israel	930	7	..	..	..	..	923
Italy	5,868	36	..	..	3,348	1,727	757
Jamaica	4	3	1	..	..	..	..
Jordan	6	..	6	..	..	..	..
Lao People's Democratic Republic	8	8	..	..	..	..	..
Latvia	5,076	..	..	..	3,348	1,727	1
Lithuania	5,076	..	..	..	3,348	1,727	1
Luxembourg	5,077	1	..	..	3,348	1,727	1
Malaysia	104	104	..	..	..	..	..
Malta	5,079	..	..	3	3,348	1,727	1
Mexico	1,691	18	..	..	..	744	929
Mongolia	39	39	..	..	..	..	..
Mozambique	4	..	..	4	..	..	..
Netherlands	5,076	..	..	..	3,348	1,727	1
New Zealand	24	24	..	..	..	..	..
Norway	37	30	..	..	..	7	..
Pakistan	1	1	..	..	..	..	..
Panama	121	..	121	..	..	..	..
Peru	1,110	10	..	..	..	115	985
Poland	5,076	..	..	..	3,348	1,727	1
Portugal	6,051	25	..	..	3,348	1,727	951
Republic of Moldova	4,600	24	..	..	..	3,648	928
Romania	5,076	..	..	..	3,348	1,727	1
Russian Federation	376	272	..	..	..	104	..
Serbia	1,014	85	..	..	..	..	929
Singapore	142	142	..	..	..	..	..
Slovakia	6,112	23	..	..	3,348	1,727	1,014
Slovenia	5,076	..	..	..	3,348	1,727	1
Spain	5,076	..	..	..	3,348	1,727	1
Sweden	5,076	..	..	..	3,348	1,727	1
Switzerland (c)	4,342	110	..	2	..	4,230	..
Thailand	170	170	..	..	..	..	..
Trinidad and Tobago	1	1	..	..	..	..	..
Türkiye	981	978	..	..	..	3	..
United Kingdom (d)	4,157	3	..	..	..	4,154	..
Ukraine	3,124	33	..	..	..	3,091	..
United States of America (e)	620	..	344	276	..	..	..
Venezuela (Bolivarian Republic of)	8	8	..	..	..	..	..
Viet Nam	1,980	115	1,696	..	..	169	..

Note: Identifying GIs protected via the trademark system (certification and collective marks) is extremely time consuming and requires extensive manual intervention. For this reason, a number of authorities like the United Kingdom were unable to report on GIs protected via the trademark system.

(a) Lisbon System data reported here refer to foreign GIs and appellations of origin in force based on the Lisbon System.

(b) The EU's regional system for the protection of GIs covers agricultural and foodstuff products, wines and spirits. Although the EU regional system is a *sui generis* system, GIs in force via the EU are reported under the regional system category rather than the *sui generis* category.

(c) There is no registration requirement for the *sui generis* protection of GIs in Switzerland. Only those denominations subject to registration or recognition on the basis of the instruments provided for in the Law on Agriculture and the Law on the Protection of Trademarks and Indications of Source, or of a court decision or special legislation, are counted under the national systems of protection.

(d) The United Kingdom created a new GI scheme after Brexit. This new UK GI scheme includes all GI's directly registered by the EU prior to December 31, 2022. The UK GI scheme covers England, Wales and Scotland.

(e) The United States of America protects geographical indications through its trademark system as certification marks, collective marks or trademarks. Complementary protection is provided under the Federal Alcohol Administration Act and its implementing regulations for wines and distilled spirits of both domestic and foreign origin.

.. indicates zero/not available.

Source: WIPO Statistics Database, September 2022.

Creative economy

Highlights

Introduction

Publishing industry data are not unified under a single authority. For this reason, data are drawn from three different surveys for an overview of the global publishing industry worldwide. This Creative economy section begins by presenting data from a publishing industry survey, followed by data from a legal deposits survey and then International Standard Book Number (ISBN) registrations data.[1]

Publishing survey data

This first subsection presents publishing industry data provided by the 37 countries that responded to the global publishing industry survey undertaken in 2022. In total, 35 national publishers' associations and copyright authorities agreed to share their 2021 data, while Canada and the Republic of Korea provided their latest available 2020 data. Publishing industry revenue and the number of titles published are presented below.

Publishing industry revenue

The 2021 sales and licensing revenue data covering the trade and the educational sectors are available for 22 countries. An additional country provided revenue data for the trade sector only. Combined publishing industry revenue for these 23 countries was USD 71.6 billion in 2021. The United States of America (US) (USD 26.8 billion) reported the largest sales revenue, followed by Germany (USD 11.4 billion), Japan (USD 11.3 billion), the United Kingdom (UK) (USD 5.4 billion) and Italy (USD 4.1 billion) (figure 6.1).[2] The 2021 revenue data for the Republic of Korea are unavailable; however, in 2020, revenue of USD 5.4 billion was generated in the Republic of Korea from books sales, which would place it among the top five countries for sales revenue. Among the top five countries, the US (+13.6%) and Italy (+12.2%) both had strong revenue growth in 2021. Japan (+7.5%), the UK (+5.1%) and Germany (+3.5%) also reported a healthy growth in revenue.

Trade sector revenue accounted for 50% or more of total revenue for 13 of the 19 countries for which 2021 data by sector are available - ranging from 50.4% in Norway up to 94.3% in Hungary. Educational sector revenue accounted for over three-fifths of total revenue in Brazil (61.4%), the Netherlands (63.4%) and Mexico (75.1%) (table F16).

1 The publishing industry survey was conducted by the World Intellectual Property Organization (WIPO), Centro Regional para el Fomento del Libro en América Latina y el Caribe (CERLALC) and the Federation of European Publishers (FEP). The legal deposits survey was conducted by WIPO and the ISBN data compiled by CERLALC and the International ISBN Agency.

2 Germany reported a slightly higher volume of sales revenue than Japan. However, Japan's revenue data covers only print edition sales revenue with data for digital sales unavailable.

6.1. Publishing industry revenue (USD million), 2021

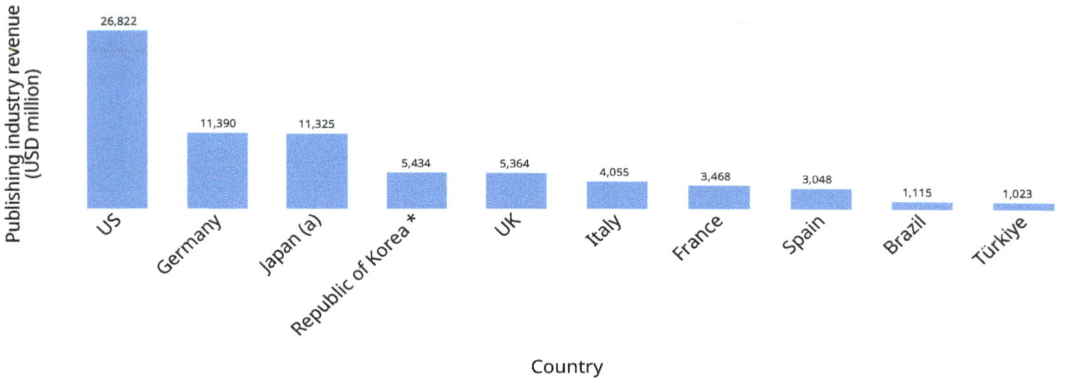

Note: Data for Germany, Italy and Spain are at market value calculated from retail prices.
(a) print format only.
* 2020 data.
Source: Table F16.

Publishing industry survey

The publishing industry survey was established in 2017 as a collaboration between the World Intellectual Property Organization (WIPO) and the International Publishers Association (IPA). WIPO has strengthened its cooperation with Centro Regional para el Fomento del Libro en América Latina y el Caribe (CERLALC) and the Federation of European Publishers (FEP) in order to reduce the burden on respondents and extend the geographical coverage of the survey. CERLALC provided data for several Latin America and the Caribbean (LAC) countries, while the FEP compiled and shared 2021 data relating to 14 European countries (FEP members). WIPO is grateful to CERLALC and the FEP for sharing their data.

The scope of the publishing industry survey is limited to (a) the trade and educational sectors and (b) those published materials (i.e., books, monographs, and so on) issued with an ISBN, a Digital Object Identifier (DOI) or any other book identifier.

Every effort has been made to compile statistics based on the same definitions to facilitate international comparison. However, caution should be exercised when interpreting data, as some data points are incomplete or partial. For example, several countries provided only data on print format revenue and/or number of titles published, meaning any digital components are missing. Similarly, a few countries reported revenue data at market value calculated from retail prices rather than net revenue. Furthermore, for most countries, respondents were national publishers associations (NPAs), with the share of the overall publishing industry represented by NPAs varying between countries.

The 2021 revenue by format data - print, digital and audio formats - are available for 15 countries. The digital/audio formats share ranged from 3% in Brazil to 37.8% in Japan (figure F2). Digital/audio formats generated around a third of total revenue in Finland (33.2%), Japan (37.8%) and Sweden (32.9%). The 2021 digital/audio formats share for those three countries is slightly higher than it was in 2020. For example, Japan's digital/audio formats share increased from 33.1% in 2020 to 37.8% in 2021. Similarly, Finland saw a five percentage points increase over the same period.

Only 13 countries were able to provide publishing industry revenue by destination (domestic or foreign markets) for 2021, while Canada and the Republic of Korea provided their latest (2020) data. Of these countries, the UK generated 40.7% of total revenue from foreign markets, followed by New Zealand (11.6%), Colombia (8%) and Portugal (7.5%). Foreign market share for the remainder was below 5% (figure F3). Although the US generated only 4.9% of total revenue from foreign markets, in absolute terms it generated USD 1.3 billion in 2021.

Revenue data by sales channel - brick and mortar, online and others - are available for 14 countries for 2021. Online sales generated more than two-thirds of total publishing industry revenue in the UK (67.4%) in 2021 (figure F4). Italy (53.2%) generated more the half of total revenue through online sales. Finland (35.1%), Sweden (38.4%), Türkiye (36.0%) and the US (33.3%) also had a large proportion of total revenue generated through online sales. Brick and mortar, however, continued to generate the bulk of total revenue in Japan (69.6%), Malta (67.9%) and New Zealand (64.6%).

The total revenue generated from children's books sales is available for 18 countries and amounted to USD 9.8 billion in 2021. The US reported revenue of USD 5.3 billion from children's books in 2021, followed by Germany (USD 2.1 billion), the UK (USD 584 million), Spain (USD 511 million) and France (USD 487 million) (figure F5). Revenue from children's books represented more than a third of trade sector revenue in Colombia (34.4%), Denmark (36.5%), Malta (44.3%) and New Zealand (37.7%) (figure F6). For a majority of the countries children's books revenue as a share of total trade revenue was around 20–25%.

Number of titles published

Data on the total number of titles published in 2021 covering both the trade and educational sectors are available for 29 countries. The UK reported a combined total of 167,267 titles published in 2021. Brazil (140,187), Italy (135,126) and France (109,480) reported more than 100,000 published titles in 2021 (figure 6.2). Among the top five countries, France (+12.5%), Brazil (+10%), Italy (+7.3%) and Türkiye (+6.9%) reported a strong growth in titles published between 2020 and 2021. In contrast, the UK saw a 10% decrease.

The trade sector share of titles published ranged from 25.3% in New Zealand up to 97.9% in Japan. In all countries where data was reported by sector, the trade sector accounted for more than half of all titles published, the exceptions being Belarus (44.8%), Mexico (42.7%) and New Zealand (25.3%). Like in Japan, the trade sector accounted for the vast bulk of titles published in Cuba (92.1%), Estonia (97.1%) and Italy (97.6%) (table F17).

6.2. Total number of titles published, 2021

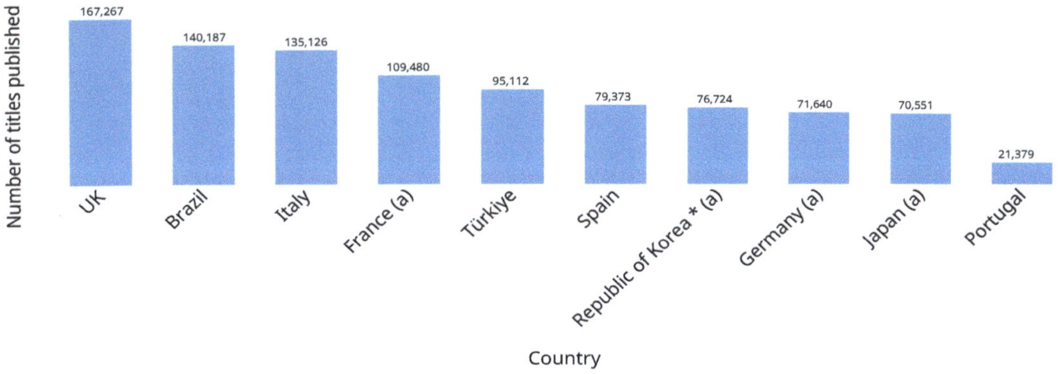

(a) print format only.
* 2020 data.
Source: Table F17.

In total, 18 countries reported data on the number of titles published by format (print, digital and audio) in 2021. The share of digital/audio formatted titles ranged from 2.1% in Croatia up to 65.9% in Brazil (figure F8). Shares were largest in Brazil (65.9%), Finland (62%) and Sweden (55%), where more than half of titles were in digital/audio formats. In contrast, only around 2% of all titles published in Croatia and Serbia were in digital/audio format.

Data on children's books published by the trade sector in 2021 is available for 22 countries. France (19,357) reported the highest number of children's books titles published in 2021, followed by the UK (17,389), Türkiye (12,540), Italy (10,951) and Germany (7,206) (figure F9). Children's books represented the largest share of trade sector published titles in New Zealand (39.1%), Mexico (30.4%), Norway (27.7%), Ukraine (27.5%) and Sweden (27.1%) (figure F10).

Legal deposits in recognized repositories

This second subsection presents data on legal deposits. In total, 66 national repositories shared their 2021 data with WIPO.[3] WIPO's legal deposits survey covers four categories of deposit,

3 In addition, China and Montenegro shared their 2020 data, while Trinidad and Tobago, and Zimbabwe did not receive any legal deposits in 2021. Due to the impact of the COVID-19 pandemic, Brazil was unable report legal deposits data for books. Nepal indicated that it does not have a legal deposits system. In total, 72 national repositories responded to the survey.

namely (a) books, (b) music sheets and music audio files, (c) films and videos, and (d) periodicals (journals, e-series, etc.).

Despite a decrease, Germany's legal repository received the most books of any repository in 2021

The highest number of books published and deposited in a national repository in 2021 was recorded by Germany (413,158), followed by the US (197,931), the UK (152,355), Japan (116,914) and the Republic of Korea (100,242) (figure 6.3). China's 2021 data are unavailable, but in 2020 the National Library of China received 414,409 books, similar in magnitude to Germany. Data for all countries where available are presented in table F18.

6.3. Number of books in legal repositories, 2021

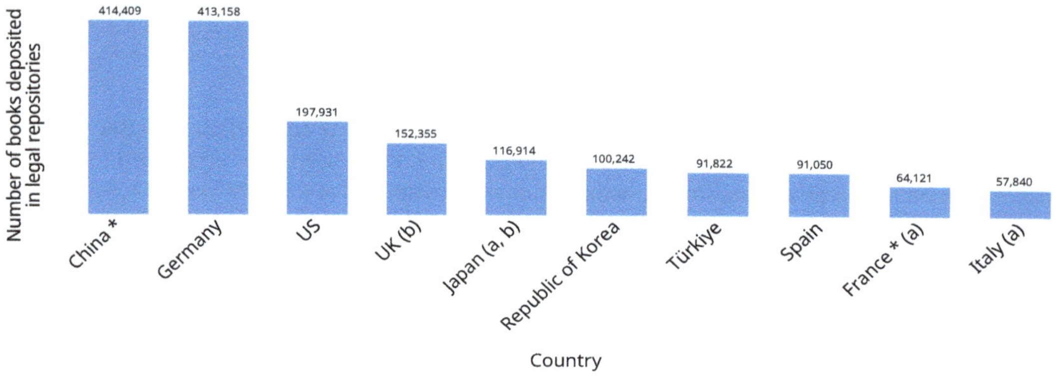

(a) print format only.
(b) 2020–2021 fiscal year
* 2020 data.
Source: Table F18.

The top five national repositories – for which 2020 and 2021 data are available – received fewer book deposits in 2021 compared to 2020. The US saw the largest decrease in deposits, which fell from 263,674 in 2020 down to 197,931 in 2021 (figure F11). The UK (–17,141) and Germany (–12,166) also received substantially fewer book deposits in 2021 compared to the year before. Japan (–6,948) and the Republic of Korea (–1,076) reported a smaller decrease over the same period. Among the 66 countries or territories for which data for 2020 and 2021 are available, 44 reported an increase in books deposited in 2021, while the remaining 22 saw a decrease.

Data on the books deposited by format – print, digital and other – are available for 44 countries or territories. More than two-thirds of all books deposited in Finland (72.9%), Germany (71.4%), Mexico (86.5%), the UK (68.7%) and the US (91.9%) in 2021 were in a digital format (figure F12). In contrast, print format constituted the bulk of the books deposited in Belgium (92.6%), Greece (95.4%) and Sweden (93.8%). The high shares reported for books in a print format could in part be due to the fact that data coverage for digital formats is not comprehensive in some countries.

Legal deposits

Legal deposit is a statutory obligation at the national level requiring publishers to deposit a certain number of copies of published documents at a repository, that is, a recognized place of legal deposit. Ordinarily, national legal provisions require at least two copies to be submitted, although this varies across countries/ territories.

In some countries/ territories, legal deposits are required only for printed books, while in others digital publications and other formats are required also. Moreover, a number of countries reported items as having undergone a process of digitization recently, which has resulted in a more comprehensive data coverage, but also a significant increase in digital publications. In some countries, there is no legal obligation to deposit e-books, although this may be done on a voluntary basis. For this reason, care should be exercised when making cross-country comparisons.

Denmark and Germany reported the most music item deposits in 2021

Thirty-one national repositories reported data on music sheets and music audio (hereafter referred to as music items) deposited in 2021. Denmark received 61,022 music item deposits in 2021, followed by Germany (43,267), Spain (14,259), Japan (10,697) and Poland (6,276) (figure F13).[4] Among the top five countries, Denmark saw a substantial growth in music items, from 1,728 in 2021 to 61,022 in 2021, driven by an improved data coverage for digital music audio. Germany also recorded a substantial increase (+13,985 additional music items). In contrast, Japan reported -2,714 fewer music items in 2021 compared to 2020. Poland saw a modest increase (+743), Spain (-631) a slight decline over the same period.

Music audio constitutes almost all the music items deposited in Denmark (99.4%) and Iceland (99.1%). Italy (90.3%), Poland (89%) and Sweden (91.2%) also had a high percentage of music audio within total music items (figure F14). In fact, music audio accounted for more than two-thirds of total music items in 13 of the 20 countries reported in figure F14.

Denmark received the largest number of films and videos deposited in 2021

Data on the number of films and videos deposited are available for 25 countries. It should be noted that some data on the visual or audiovisual items in legal deposits are collected by agencies other than national libraries. Such is the case in Finland and Italy, for example. Despite a 30% decrease, Denmark reported the highest number of films and videos deposited in legal repositories, amounting to 118,651 items - almost all deposits were in digital format (mp4, flv, avi, etc.). Denmark was followed by the Republic of Korea (17,382), Japan (4,477), Poland (3,032) and Sweden (2,134) (figure F15). A word of caution: a number of countries reported data for physical format only, meaning digital components are missing.

International Standard Book Number (ISBN) data

This third subsection presents data on ISBN registrations. An ISBN is a permanent international standard book identifier assigned to a publication and administered by the International ISBN Agency and national or regional ISBN agencies throughout the world. ISBN data gives a good indication as to the size of the publishing market in different countries and is a means of validating data from other sources. For 2021, the International ISBN Agency shared data for 36 countries provided by national ISBN agencies. In addition, CERLALC shared data for 14 countries covering the LAC region.

Table F19 presents data on (a) the lifetime ISBNs registered and (b) the number of ISBNs registered in 2021. The US, with 2.9 million registered ISBNs in 2021, was by far the biggest user of the ISBN identifier in 2021, followed by the Republic of Korea (340,506), Germany (284,000), Poland (220,042) and Japan (184,985). China's 2021 data - one of the top five users of the ISBN identifier - are unavailable. Registrations data for 2020 and 2021 are available for 49 countries, of which 37 reported an increase in the number of ISBN registrations in 2021 compared to 2020. Japan (+70,713), the Netherlands (+22,146), Spain (+15,281) and Indonesia (+14,537) recorded the largest increases. In contrast, the US (-1 million) and the UK (-19,593) reported considerably fewer ISBN registrations in 2021 compared to the year before. For both countries, 2021 was a second consecutive year of decline. This could be partly due to the negative impact of COVID-19-related restrictions imposed in these two countries.

Although ISBN data represents the number of publications, there will be some double counting, as alternative formats for the same publication (e.g., e-book, paperback and hardcover editions) will have been assigned a separate ISBN.

4 The Republic of Korea reported 10,936 music audio deposited in 2021. However, data on music sheets are unavailable therefore not included.

ISBN as an identifier

The International Standard Book Number (ISBN) is the most common publication identifier in use. The ISBN system has a three-tier administrative structure – the International ISBN Agency, the national and regional registration agencies, and publishers. The International ISBN Agency is the official registration authority appointed by the International Organization for Standardization (ISO) to supervise the global use of the ISBN Standard. There are around 150 registration agencies assigning unique registrant elements and ISBNs to publishers. Publishers are then responsible for assigning unique ISBNs to individual publications from within the registrant elements they have been allocated.

Publishers do, however, also use other identifiers, such as an Amazon Standard Identification Number (ASIN), a Digital Object Identifier, and others.

Creative economy statistics

Publishing industry sales revenue

F1. Publishing industry revenue (USD million), 2021

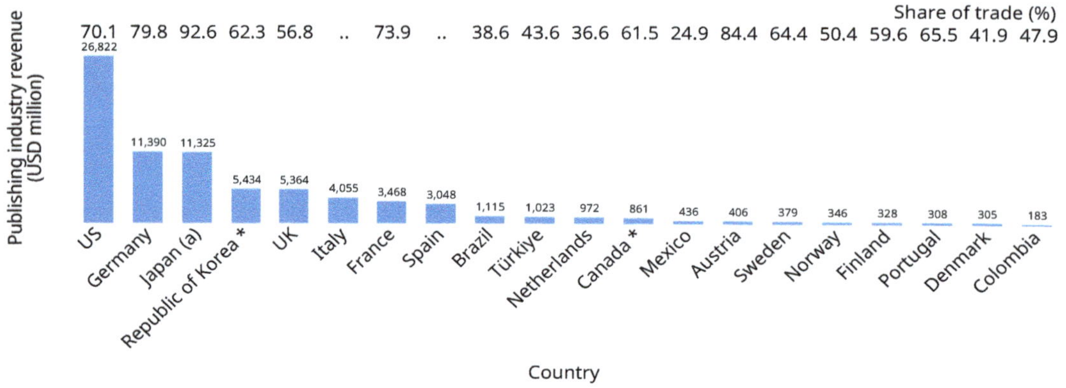

Note: Data for Austria, Germany, Italy, Portugal and Spain are at market value calculated from retail prices.
(a) print format only.
* 2020 data.
.. indicates not available.
Source: WIPO Statistics Database and Federation of European Publishers (FEP), September 2022.

F2. Distribution of publishing industry revenue by format, 2021

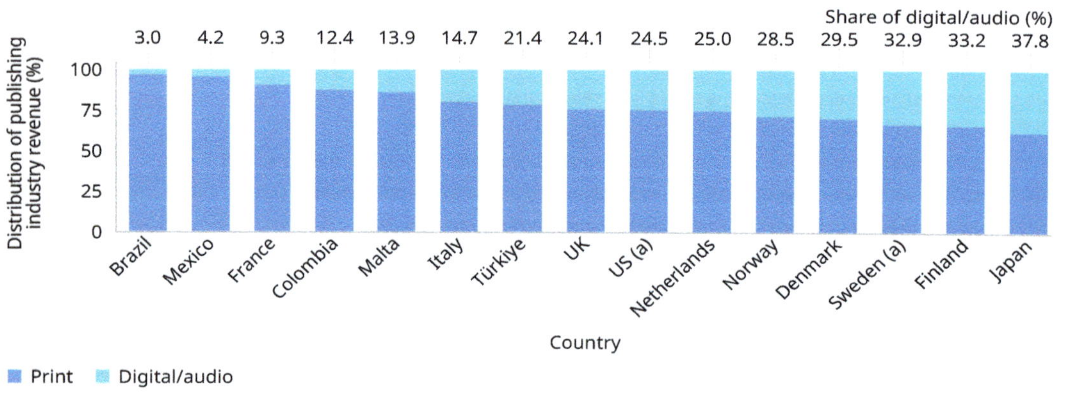

Note: Data for Italy are at market value calculated from retail prices.
(a) trade sector only.
Source: WIPO Statistics Database and Federation of European Publishers (FEP), September 2022.

F3. Distribution of publishing industry revenue by destination, 2021

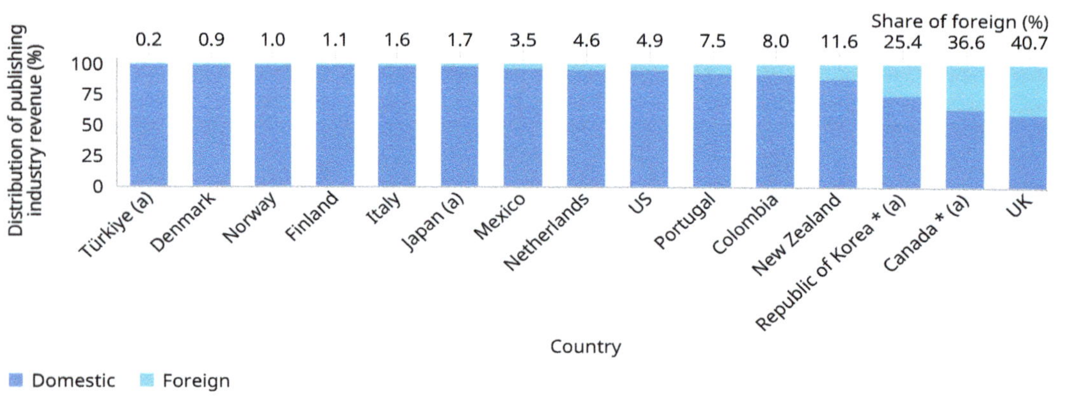

Note: Data for Italy and Portugal are at market value calculated from retail prices.
(a) trade sector only.
* 2020 data.
Source: WIPO Statistics Database and Federation of European Publishers (FEP), September 2022.

F4. Distribution of publishing industry revenue by sales channel, 2021

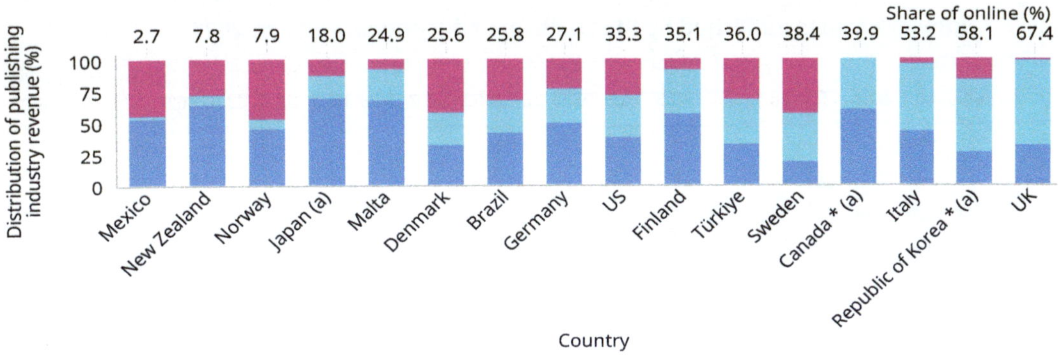

Note: Data for Germany and Italy are at market value calculated from retail prices. Online category includes digital sales.
(a) trade sector only.
* 2020 data.
Source: WIPO Statistics Database and Federation of European Publishers (FEP), September 2022.

F5. Children's books revenue (USD million), 2021

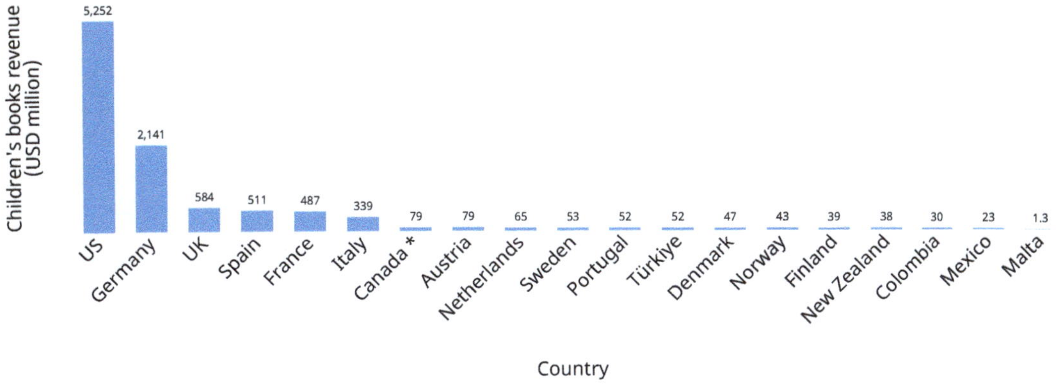

Note: Data for Austria, Germany, Italy, Portugal and Spain are at market value calculated from retail prices.
* 2020 data.
Source: WIPO Statistics Database and Federation of European Publishers (FEP), September 2022.

F6. Share of children's books within trade sector revenue, 2021

Note: Data for Austria, Germany and Portugal are at market value calculated from retail prices.
* 2020 data.
Source: WIPO Statistics Database and Federation of European Publishers (FEP), September 2022.

Titles published

F7. Number of titles published by the trade and educational sectors, 2021

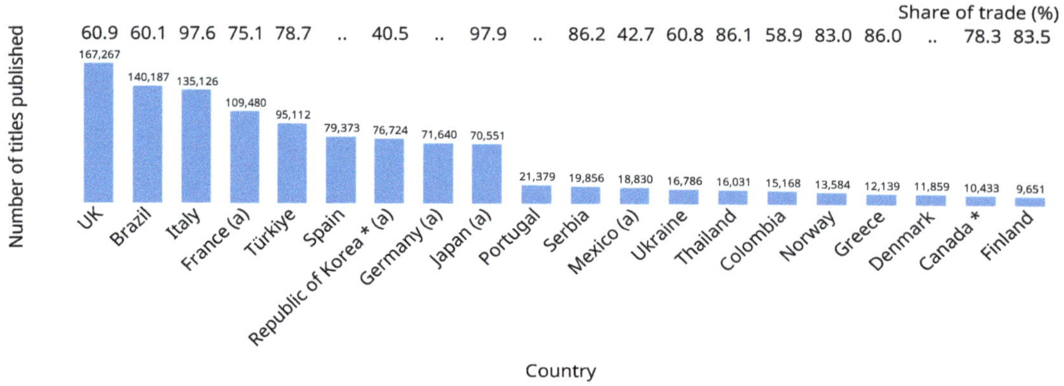

(a) print format only.

* 2020 data.

.. indicates not available.

Source: WIPO Statistics Database and Federation of European Publishers (FEP), September 2022.

F8. Distribution of titles published by the trade and educational sectors by format, 2021

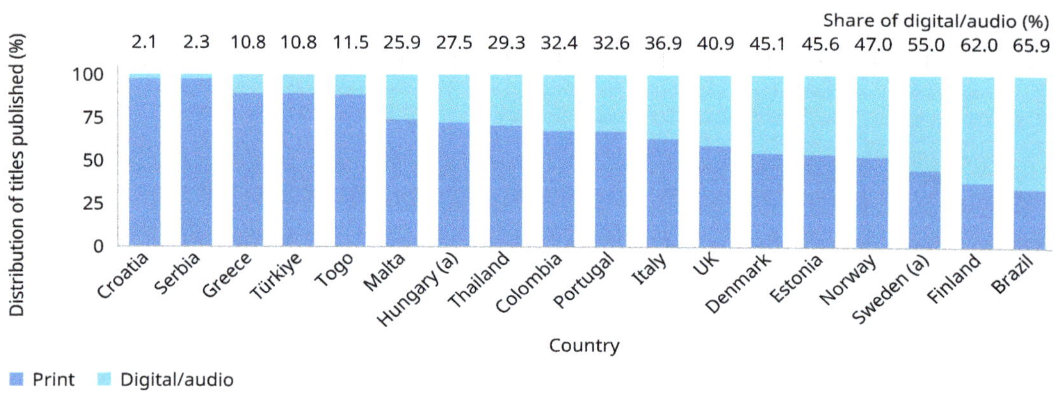

(a) trade sector only.

Source: WIPO Statistics Database and Federation of European Publishers (FEP), September 2022.

F9. Number of children's books titles published by the trade sector, 2021

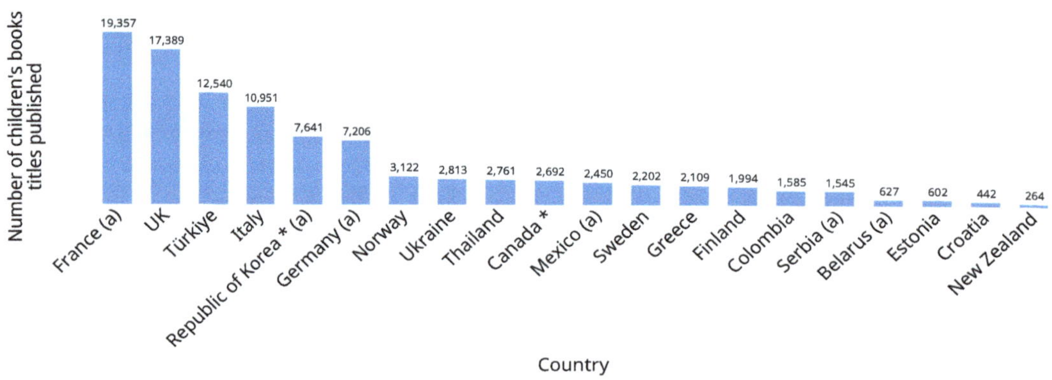

(a) print format only.

* 2020 data.

Source: WIPO Statistics Database and Federation of European Publishers (FEP), September 2022.

F10. Share of children's books in the number of titles published by the trade sector, 2021

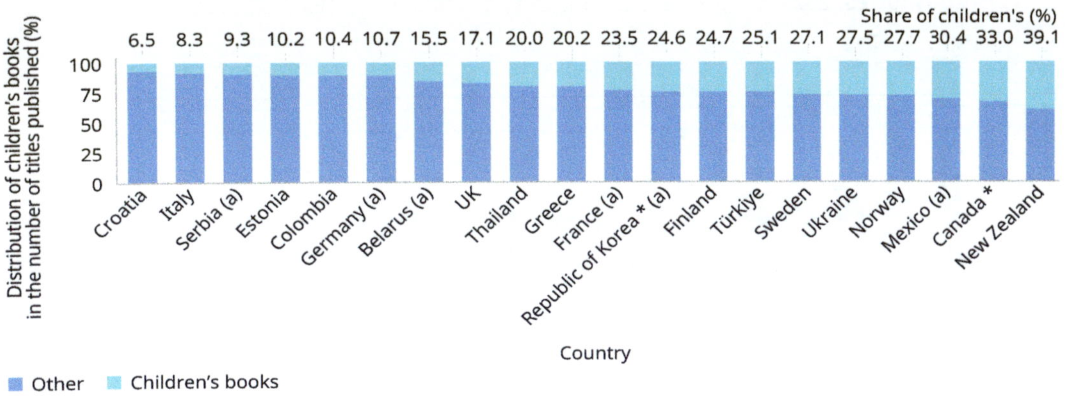

(a) print format only.

* 2020 data.

Source: WIPO Statistics Database and Federation of European Publishers (FEP), September 2022.

Legal deposits in recognized repositories

F11. Number of books deposited at the top 20 legal repositories, 2021

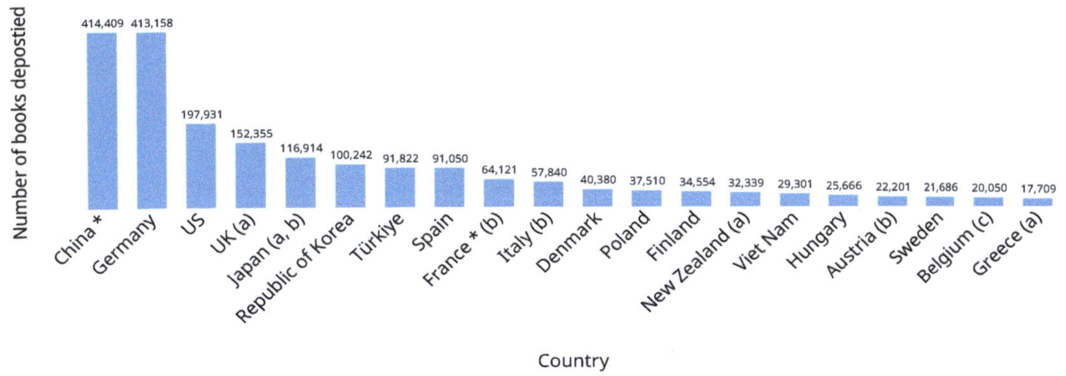

(a) 2020-2021 fiscal year.

(b) print format only.

(c) digital deposits are collected on a voluntary basis.

* 2020 data.

Source: WIPO Statistics Database, September 2022.

F12. Distribution of books deposited at selected legal repositories by format, 2021

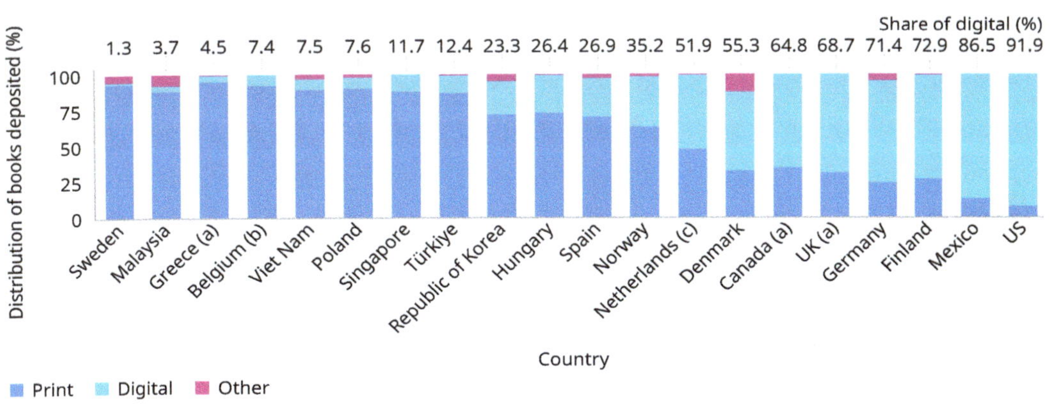

(a) 2020-2021 fiscal year.

(b) digital deposits are collected on a voluntary basis.

(c) deposits are on voluntary basis as deposits are not covered by legislation.

Source: WIPO Statistics Database, September 2022.

F13. Total number of music sheets and music audio deposited at selected legal repositories, 2021

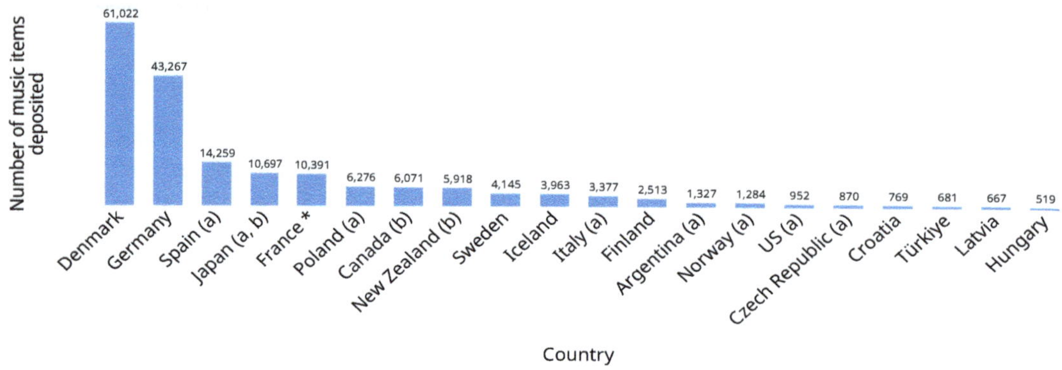

(a) physical format only.
(b) 2020–2021 fiscal year.
* 2020 data.
Source: WIPO Statistics Database, September 2022.

F14. Distribution of music sheets and music audio deposited at selected legal repositories, 2021

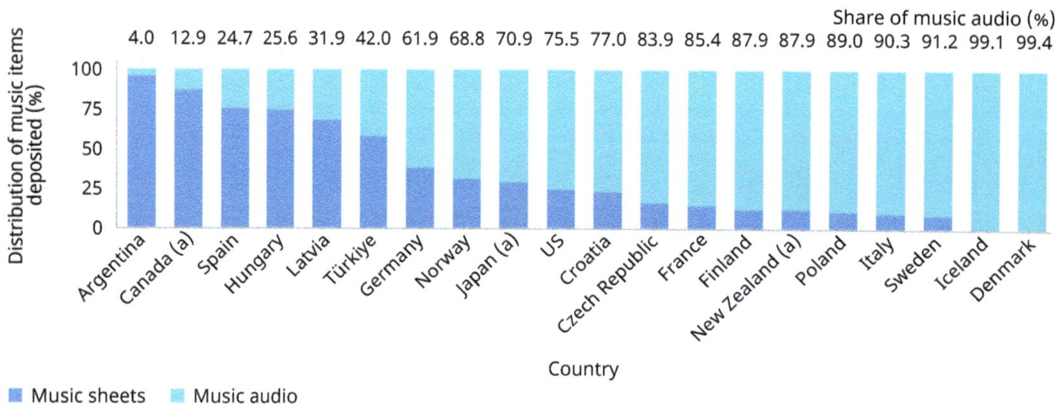

(a) 2020–2021 fiscal year.
Source: WIPO Statistics Database, September 2022.

F15. Total number of films and videos deposited in a recognized repository, 2021

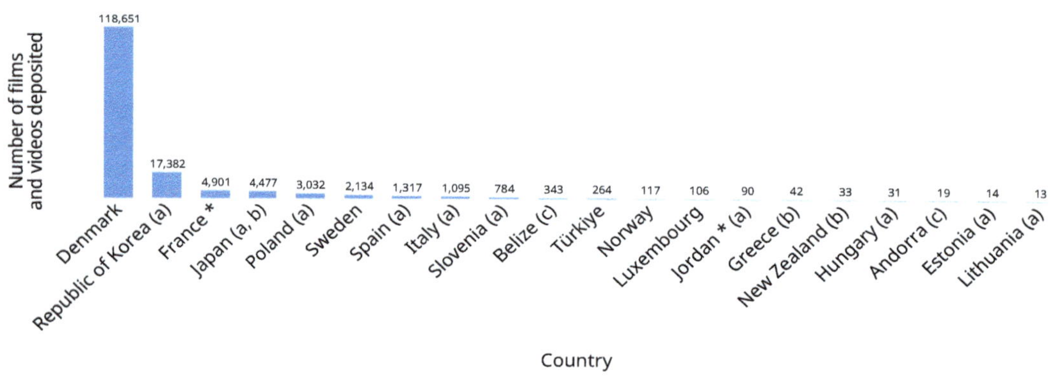

(a) physical format only.
(b) 2020–2021 fiscal year.
(c) digital format only.
* 2020 data.
Source: WIPO Statistics Database, September 2022.

F16. Total publishing industry revenue by sector (USD million), 2021

Country	Total	Trade	Educational	Share of total (%) Trade	Share of total (%) Educational
Austria	405.8	342.6	63.3	84.4	15.6
Azerbaijan (a)	22.6	22.6	..	..	..
Brazil	1,115.0	430.8	684.2	38.6	61.4
Canada *	860.9	529.4	331.5	61.5	38.5
Colombia	183.1	87.8	95.4	47.9	52.1
Czech Republic *	33.4	21.3	12.2	63.6	36.4
Denmark	305.4	127.9	177.5	41.9	58.1
Finland	327.6	195.2	132.5	59.6	40.4
France	3,467.8	2,562.8	905.0	73.9	26.1
Georgia * (a)	6.2	6.2	..	..	..
Germany	11,389.8	9,089.1	2,300.7	79.8	20.2
Hungary	156.5	147.6	8.9	94.3	5.7
Iceland	34.9	..	..	..	..
Italy	4,055.1	..	..	..	..
Japan (b)	11,324.7	10,484.3	840.3	92.6	7.4
Malta	4.3	2.9	1.4	68.1	31.9
Mexico	436.0	108.7	327.3	24.9	75.1
Netherlands	972.2	356.3	616.0	36.6	63.4
New Zealand	124.1	99.6	24.5	80.2	19.8
Norway	345.8	174.4	171.5	50.4	49.6
Portugal	308.1	201.7	106.4	65.5	34.5
Republic of Korea *	5,433.8	3,386.3	2,047.6	62.3	37.7
Spain	3,047.6	..	..	..	..
Sweden	378.5	244.0	134.6	64.4	35.6
Türkiye	1,023.1	446.5	576.7	43.6	56.4
United Kingdom	5,363.5	3,048.7	2,314.8	56.8	43.2
United States of America	26,822.0	18,791.0	8,031.0	70.1	29.9

Note: Data for Austria, Germany, Italy, Portugal and Spain are at market value calculated from retail prices.
(a) trade sector only.
(b) print format only.
* 2020 data.
.. indicates not available.
Source: WIPO Statistics Database and Federation of European Publishers (FEP), September 2022.

F17. Total number of titles published by sector, 2021

Country	Total	Trade	Educational	Share of total (%) Trade	Share of total (%) Educational
Australia *	19,241	..	..	..	..
Austria	8,686	..	..	..	..
Belarus (b)	9,055	4,058	4,997	44.8	55.2
Brazil	140,187	84,253	55,934	60.1	39.9
Canada *	10,433	8,164	2,269	78.3	21.7
Chile *	7,058	6,085	973	86.2	13.8
Colombia	15,168	8,938	6,230	58.9	41.1
Croatia	7,538	6,776	762	89.9	10.1
Cuba	1,554	1,431	123	92.1	7.9
Czech Republic *	16,474	6,174	10,300	37.5	62.5
Denmark	11,859	..	..	..	..
Ecuador *	4,153	2,318	1,835	55.8	44.2
Estonia	6,085	5,906	179	97.1	2.9
Finland	9,651	8,058	1,593	83.5	16.5
France (b)	109,480	82,258	27,222	75.1	24.9
Georgia * (a, b)	1,542	1,542	..	..	..
Germany (b)	71,640	..	..	..	..
Greece	12,139	10,442	1,697	86.0	14.0
Hungary (a)	8,424	8,424	..	..	..

Country	Total	Trade	Educational	Share of total (%) Trade	Educational
Ireland (b)	2,101	1,781	320	84.8	15.2
Italy	135,126	131,818	3,308	97.6	2.4
Japan (b)	70,551	69,052	1,499	97.9	2.1
Kyrgyzstan (b)	1,003	800	203	79.8	20.2
Latvia *	2,375	2,191	184	92.3	7.7
Lebanon	3,000	..	..	..	..
Malta	530	436	94	82.3	17.7
Mexico (b)	18,830	8,048	10,782	42.7	57.3
New Zealand	2,672	675	1,997	25.3	74.7
Norway	13,584	11,272	2,312	83.0	17.0
Peru *	6,885	5,699	1,186	82.8	17.2
Portugal	21,379	..	..	..	..
Republic of Korea * (b)	76,724	31,057	45,667	40.5	59.5
Republic of Moldova *	4,559	2,635	1,924	57.8	42.2
Serbia	19,856	17,121	2,735	86.2	13.8
Spain	79,373	..	..	..	..
Sweden (a)	8,118	8,118	..	..	..
Thailand	16,031	13,805	2,226	86.1	13.9
Togo	78	61	17	78.2	21.8
Türkiye	95,112	74,895	20,217	78.7	21.3
Ukraine	16,786	10,213	6,573	60.8	39.2
United Kingdom	167,267	101,812	65,455	60.9	39.1

(a) trade sector only.
(b) print format only.
* 2020 data.
.. not available.
Source: WIPO Statistics Database and Federation of European Publishers (FEP), September 2022.

F18. Total number of books deposited in recognized repositories, 2021

Country/territory	Total	Print	Digital	Other formats
Andorra	108	74	34	..
Argentina (a)	1,505	1,505	..	..
Armenia (a)	3,736	3,736	..	..
Austria (a)	22,201	22,201	..	..
Azerbaijan	6,543	6,364	179	..
Belgium (b)	20,050	18,562	1,488	..
Belize (a)	26	26	..	..
Canada (c)	15,169	5,328	9,837	4
China *	414,409	408,860	..	5,549
China, Hong Kong SAR (a)	14,559	14,559	..	..
Colombia (d, e)	16,860	..	..	..
Costa Rica	1,996	1,102	894	..
Croatia	8,437	7,433	477	527
Cyprus (a)	42	42	..	..
Czech Republic	14,462	14,134	..	328
Denmark	40,380	13,167	22,313	4,900
Ecuador (a)	670	670	..	..
Estonia	6,228	3,208	3,011	9
Finland	34,554	9,329	25,180	45
France * (a)	64,121	64,121	..	..
Georgia	2,537	2,505	32	..
Germany	413,158	100,689	295,140	17,329
Ghana	1,056	1,039	17	..
Greece (c)	17,709	16,898	798	13
Hungary	25,666	18,853	6,778	35
Iceland	7,104	4,341	798	1,965
Ireland (a)	1,744	1,744	..	..
Israel *	10,954	8,845	2,109	..
Italy (a)	57,840	57,840	..	..
Jamaica	367	359	8	..
Japan (a, c)	116,914	116,914	..	..

Country/territory	Total	Print	Digital	Other formats
Jordan	6,712	6,004	708	..
Latvia	3,466	2,698	688	80
Lithuania	8,646	7,614	1,032	..
Luxembourg	1,828	1,421	407	..
Malaysia	13,305	11,827	492	986
Maldives (a)	106	106	..	..
Malta (a)	521	521	..	..
Mauritius (a, c)	1,027	1,027	..	..
Mexico	15,034	2,026	13,007	1
Monaco * (a)	109	109	..	..
Montenegro * (a)	1,338	1,338	..	..
Mozambique (a)	141	141	..	..
Myanmar (a)	2,047	2,047	..	..
Namibia (a, c)	288	288	..	..
Netherlands (e)	32,339	15,504	16,789	46
New Zealand (c)	9,680	3,369	6,309	2
Norway	14,508	9,222	5,108	178
Pakistan (a)	1,895	1,895	..	..
Panama	526	491	35	..
Paraguay (e)	841	693	120	28
Peru	7,653	7,113	540	..
Philippines	930	845	85	..
Poland	37,510	33,957	2,865	688
Portugal (a)	13,293	13,293	..	..
Republic of Korea	100,242	72,381	23,406	4,455
Republic of Moldova	3,118	2,900	218	..
Serbia	11,508	11,500	..	8
Seychelles (a)	215	215	..	..
Singapore	14,852	13,111	1,741	..
Slovakia	6,086	5,361	695	30
Slovenia	10,028	8,070	1,842	116
South Africa * (c)	5,758	5,455	303	..
Spain	91,050	64,385	24,524	2,141
Sri Lanka (a)	2,425	2,425	..	..
Sweden	21,686	20,336	286	1,064
Thailand	10,098	9,400	698	..
Türkiye	91,822	80,199	11,352	271
Uganda (a)	1,483	1,483	..	..
United Kingdom (c)	152,355	47,755	104,600	..
United States of America	197,931	16,000	181,931	..
Viet Nam	29,301	26,287	2,203	811

(a) print only.
(b) digital deposits are collected on a voluntary basis.
(c) 2020-2021 fiscal year.
(d) it is not feasible to separate data for books, audio, film and video. Hence data are not comparable to other countries.
(e) deposits are on a voluntary basis as deposits are not covered by legislation.
.. not available.
* 2020 data.
Source: WIPO Statistics Database, September 2022.

F19. Total number of ISBN registrations, 2021

Country	Lifetime ISBNs registered	ISBNs registered in 2021
Argentina (a)	633,092	34,256
Australia	749,897	34,299
Bolivia (Plurinational State of)	24,335	1,544
Brazil *	..	114,114
Bulgaria	263,207	13,085
Canada (French) (b)	517,714	19,317
Chile	128,886	8,528
China *	..	263,066
Colombia	355,938	20,347
Costa Rica	39,709	2,007
Croatia (a, c)	179,427	7,260
Cuba (a)	58,655	2,361
Czech Republic	661,471	26,597
Denmark	740,842	39,183
Dominican Republic	14,777	1,853
Ecuador	74,827	4,477
El Salvador	11,156	661
Estonia (b)	139,982	13,342
Germany (a)	5,886,569	284,000
Ghana (b)	102,000	2,200
Guatemala	18,774	1,258
Indonesia (a)	816,644	159,330
Iran (Islamic Republic of)	855,610	89,888
Italy	2,387,482	142,267
Japan (a)	2,709,133	184,985
Latvia (b)	94,220	3,541
Lithuania	145,190	5,187
Malawi	15,514	311
Malta	15,501	1,032
Mexico	..	23,304
Mongolia	..	3,916
Netherlands	1,931,923	62,251
Nigeria	493,328	18,300
Norway	461,232	9,324
Panama	27,571	1,596
Paraguay	16,952	1,112
Peru	113,286	7,885
Philippines (a)	190,525	9,497
Poland	..	220,042
Portugal (b)	460,218	21,379
Republic of Korea	4,149,615	340,506
Russian Federation *	2,084,160	124,454
Slovakia	299,853	12,065
Spain	2,679,310	95,985
Sweden (a)	818,228	34,984
Syrian Arab Republic	29,200	1,900
Thailand	464,706	18,225
Türkiye	1,010,090	87,231
Ukraine	477,219	25,722
United Kingdom (a)	8,065,000	168,960
Uruguay	22,741	2,697
United States of America	42,827,156	2,884,609
Venezuela (Bolivarian Republic of)	52,037	3,050

Note: The starting year for lifetime data varies. For example, lifetime data for Costa Rica starts from 1998, whereas for Indonesia it is from 2021 onwards.

(a) statistics are believed by the relevant ISBN Agency to be possibly underestimated, especially in terms of the lifetime figures owing to a lack of or insufficient data.

(b) figures are estimates provided by the relevant ISBN Agency.

(c) ebooks that are chargeable or for which registration is needed are not included.

* 2020 data.

.. not available.

Source: International ISBN Agency and Centro Regional para el Fomento del Libro en América Latina y el Caribe (CERLALC), September 2022.

Additional information

Data description

Data sources

Intellectual property (IP) data are taken from the WIPO Statistics Database and based primarily on WIPO's annual IP statistics surveys (see below) and on data compiled by WIPO in processing international applications/registrations through the Patent Cooperation Treaty (PCT) and the Madrid and Hague Systems. Data are available from WIPO's Statistics Data Center at *www.wipo.int/ipstats.*

Patent family and technology data are extracted from the WIPO Statistics Database and from the 2022 spring edition of the European Patent Office's PATSTAT database.

Gross domestic product and population data are from the World Bank's World Development Indicators database.

This report uses the World Bank's income classifications. Economies are classified according to 2021 gross national income per capita, calculated using the World Bank Atlas method. The classifications are low-income (USD 1,085 or less), lower middle-income (USD 1,086 to USD 4,255), upper middle-income (USD 4,256 to USD 13,205) and high-income (over USD 13,205).[1]

This report uses United Nations (UN) definitions of regions and sub-regions, whereas the geographical terms used may differ slightly from the ones defined by the UN.

WIPO's annual IP statistics surveys

WIPO collects data from national and regional IP offices, other competent authorities and publishers' associations from around the world through annual surveys consisting of multiple questionnaires. These data are then entered into the WIPO Statistics Database.

Continuous efforts are being made to improve the quality and availability of IP statistics and to gather data from as many IP offices and countries as possible.

WIPO's long-established and regular IP survey covers patents, utility models, trademarks, industrial designs and plant varieties. It consists of 27 questionnaires, all of which are available in Arabic, Chinese, English, French, Russian and Spanish at *www.wipo.int/ipstats/en/data_collection/questionnaire.*

In 2017, WIPO started to collect data on geographical indications (GIs) through an annual survey. This simple questionnaire seeks to collect data on GIs in force broken down by legal means of protection (e.g., *sui generis* systems, trademarks, international agreements, and so on) and products types (e.g., wines and spirits, agricultural products, and so on). This 2022 edition reports data for 93 authorities - a considerable improvement upon the 54 responses that WIPO received in 2017.

Global publishing industry survey

WIPO's survey of the global publishing industry was established in collaboration with the International Publishers Association (IPA) in 2017. In addition, WIPO has strengthened its cooperation with Centro Regional para el Fomento del Libro en América Latina y el Caribe (CERLALC) and the Federation of European Publishers (FEP) in order to reduce the burden

1 Venezuela is unclassified pending release of revised national accounts statistics.

on respondents and extend the geographical coverage of the survey. This year, the FEP compiled and shared data with WIPO for 14 European countries (FEP members). In addition, CERLALC provided data for several Latin America and the Caribbean (LAC) countries. WIPO is grateful to CERLALC and the FEP for sharing data. The scope of the publishing industry survey is limited to (a) the trade and educational sectors, and (b) published materials (i.e., books, monographs, and so on) issued with an International Standard Book Number (ISBN), a Digital Object Identifier (DOI) or any other book identifier (e.g., ASIN, and so on). This edition includes publishing industry data for the 37 associations and authorities who shared their latest data with WIPO.

To validate the data collected through the global publishing survey, WIPO has begun to collect data on legal deposit. Legal deposit is a statutory obligation at the national level requiring publishers to deposit a certain number of copies of published documents at a repository, that is, a recognized place of legal deposit. In 2019, WIPO conducted a pilot survey among national legal repositories, to which 51 countries responded. This 2022 edition reports data for 66 authorities.

IP office survey coverage

Intellectual property offices are requested to report data by the origin (country or territory) of applications, grants or registrations. Offices unable to provide this detailed breakdown instead report either an aggregate total or a simple breakdown by total resident and total non-resident counts. For this reason, the totals for each origin are underreported. However, shares of the 2021 totals where the origin is unknown are low – only 1.3% for patent applications, 0.4% for trademark application class counts and 1.6% for application design counts.

IP applications data coverage by IP type

IP type	Number of offices on which 2021 world totals are based	Number of offices for which 2021 data are available	Data coverage (%)
Patents	160	117	99.2
Utility models	82	62	99.9
Trademarks (a)	169	115	95.7
Industrial designs (b)	151	127	98.3
Plant varieties	71	69	99.2

(a) Refers to the number of trademark applications based on class count (i.e., the number of classes specified in applications).

(b) Refers to the number of industrial design applications based on design count (i.e., the number of designs contained in applications).

Estimating world totals

World totals of applications for, and grants/registrations of, patents, utility models, trademarks, industrial designs and plant varieties are WIPO estimates. Data are not available for every IP office each year. Missing data are estimated using methods such as linear extrapolation and averaging adjacent data points. The estimation method chosen depends on the year and the office in question. When an office provides data that is not broken down by origin, WIPO estimates the resident and non-resident counts using the historical shares recorded at that office. Data are available for most of the larger offices; only small shares of world totals are estimated. For example, the estimated total number of patent applications worldwide covers 160 offices; data are available for 117 of these, which together account for 99.2% of the estimated world total.

National and international data

Application and grant/registration data include data on both direct filings and filings made through WIPO-administered international systems (where applicable). For patents and utility models, data comprise direct filings at national patent offices, as well as PCT national phase entries. For trademarks, data comprise filings at national and regional offices and designations received by relevant offices through the Madrid System. For industrial designs, data comprise national and regional applications combined with designations received by relevant offices through the Hague System.

International comparability of indicators

Every effort has been made to compile IP statistics based on the same definitions in order to facilitate international comparison. Although data are collected from offices using questionnaires from WIPO's harmonized annual IP survey, national laws and regulations for filing IP applications or for issuing IP rights, as well as statistical reporting practices, may vary between jurisdictions. Due to the continual updating of data and the revision of historical statistics, data in this report may differ from data in previous editions and from data available on WIPO's website.

Change in method of counting IP applications by CNIPA in 2017

Due to a change in the method by which the National Intellectual Property Administration of the People's Republic of China (CNIPA) calculates how many patent, utility model and industrial design applications are filed, data on the number of such applications filed in China in 2017 and 2018 are not comparable with data for previous years. Prior to 2017, these data included all applications received; from 2017 onwards they include only those applications for which the necessary application fees were paid. As a result, it is not meaningful to report growth rates in the number of patent, utility model and industrial design applications filed in China in 2017 compared to 2016. Moreover, since China accounts for such a large proportion of IP applications globally, it is not meaningful to report growth rates in the numbers of such applications filed worldwide in 2017 compared to 2016. For the reason of this break in the data series, figures A1 (page 22), A48 (page 44), C1 (page 104) and C2 (page 104) do not report 2017 growth.

IP systems at a glance

The patent system

A patent is a set of exclusive rights granted in law to applicants for an invention that meets the standards of novelty, non-obviousness and industrial applicability. It is valid for a limited period (generally 20 years), during which time the patent holder may commercially exploit the invention on an exclusive basis. In return, applicants are obliged to disclose their inventions to the public, so that they may be replicated by others skilled in the art. The patent system is designed to encourage innovation by providing innovators with time-limited exclusive legal rights, thus enabling them to appropriate returns from their innovative activity.

The procedures for acquiring patent rights are governed by the rules and regulations of national and regional patent offices. These offices are responsible for issuing patents and rights limited to the jurisdiction of the issuing authority. To obtain patent rights, applicants must file an application describing the invention with a national or regional office.

Applicants can also file an international application through the Patent Cooperation Treaty (PCT) System, an international treaty administered by WIPO that facilitates the acquisition of patent rights in multiple jurisdictions. The PCT System simplifies the process of multiple national patent filings by delaying the requirement to file a separate application in every jurisdiction in which protection is sought. However, the decision on whether to grant a patent remains the prerogative of national or regional patent offices and patent rights limited to the jurisdiction of each patent-granting authority.

The PCT application process begins with the international phase, during which an international search and optional preliminary examination and supplementary international search are performed. It concludes with the national phase, during which national (or regional) patent offices decide on the patentability of an invention according to national law. Further information about the PCT System is available at *www.wipo.int/pct*.

The utility model system

Like a patent, a utility model (UM) confers a set of rights to an invention for a limited period, during which time the UM rights holder can commercially exploit their invention on an exclusive basis. The terms and conditions for granting a UM differ from those for granting a traditional patent. For example, UMs are issued for a shorter period (6–10 years) and at most offices protection is granted without substantive examination. As with patents, procedures for granting UM rights are governed by the rules and regulations of national IP offices and rights limited to the jurisdiction of the issuing authority. In this report, the term "utility model" refers to UMs and other types of protection similar to UMs, such as short-term patents in Ireland.

Microorganisms under the Budapest Treaty

The Budapest Treaty on the International Recognition of the Deposit of Microorganisms for the Purposes of Patent Procedure plays an important role in relation to biotechnological inventions. Disclosing an invention is a generally recognized requirement for receiving a patent. When an invention involves microorganisms, national laws in most countries require the applicant to deposit a sample at a designated International Depositary Authority (IDA).

To eliminate the need to deposit a microorganism in every country where patent protection is sought, under the Budapest Treaty the deposit of a microorganism with any IDA is sufficient for the purposes of patent procedures at the national patent offices of all contracting states and at any regional patent office that recognizes the Treaty. An IDA is a scientific institution – typically a "culture collection" – capable of storing microorganisms. As of September 2022, there were

48 IDAs around the world. Further information about the Budapest Treaty is available at *www.wipo.int/treaties/en/registration/budapest.*

The trademark system

A trademark is a sign used to distinguish the goods or services of one enterprise from those of another and is protected as an intellectual property (IP) right. Trademarks can be registered for both goods and services. In the latter case, the term "service mark" is sometimes used. For simplicity, this report uses "trademark," regardless of whether the registration concerns goods or services. The holder of a registered trademark has the exclusive right to use the mark in relation to the goods or services for which it is registered and can block unauthorized use of the trademark, or a confusingly similar mark, to prevent consumers from being misled. Unlike patents, trademark registrations can be maintained indefinitely, provided that the trademark holder pays the required renewal fees.

The procedures for registering trademarks are governed by the legislation and procedures of national and regional IP offices. Therefore, trademark rights are limited to the jurisdiction of the authority that has registered the trademark. Trademark applicants can file an application with a relevant national or regional IP office or an international application through the Madrid System. However, when an applicant files internationally via the Madrid System, the decision to issue a trademark registration remains the prerogative of the national or regional IP office concerned and trademark rights remain limited to the jurisdiction of the authority issuing that registration.

Between December 1995 and October 2016, two treaties administered by the World Intellectual Property Organization (WIPO) governed the Madrid System for the International Registration of Marks – the Madrid Agreement Concerning the International Registration of Marks, adopted in 1891, and the Protocol Relating to the Madrid Agreement, adopted in 1989. As of October 11, 2016, following a decision by the Madrid Union Assembly that no country could accede only to the Agreement, the Protocol is now the sole governing treaty of the Madrid System. The Madrid System offers many advantages to trademark holders and IP offices compared with the alternative method of obtaining international protection for marks called the Paris route or the direct route. The Paris route involves filing separate applications directly at the IP office in the countries or regions where protection is sought (under the Paris Convention for the Protection of Industrial Property). In contrast, by paying a single set of fees in a single currency (Swiss francs), the Madrid System allows trademark holders to submit a single application in one language (English, French or Spanish) indicating the Madrid members where protection is sought (designations).

The Madrid System also simplifies managing the mark once it has been registered by making it possible to request centrally the recording of further changes or to renew the registration through a single procedural step. A registration recorded in the International Register has the same effect as a registration made directly with every designated Contracting Party (Madrid member), if the competent authority of that jurisdiction has not issued a refusal within a specified time period. Further information about the Madrid System is available at *www.wipo.int/madrid.*

The industrial design system

Industrial designs are applied to a wide variety of industrial products and handicrafts.[2] They refer to the ornamental or aesthetic aspects of a useful article, including compositions of lines or colors or three-dimensional forms that give a special appearance to a product or handicraft. The holder of a registered industrial design has exclusive rights over the design and can prevent unauthorized copying or imitation of the design by others.

The procedures for registering industrial designs are governed by national or regional laws. An industrial design can be protected if it is new or original and rights are limited to the jurisdiction of the issuing authority. Registrations can be obtained by filing an application with a relevant national or regional IP office or by filing an international application through the Hague System. Once a design is registered, the term of protection is generally five years and may be renewed for

2 The products and handicrafts to which industrial designs are applied range from technical and medical instruments to watches, jewelry and other luxury items, and from homeware, electrical appliances, vehicles and construction materials to textile designs and leisure goods.

additional five-year periods up to a total of 15 years, in most cases. In some countries, industrial designs are protected through the delivery of a design patent rather than design registration.

The Hague System comprises two international treaties – the Hague Act and the Geneva Act. The System makes it possible for an applicant to register industrial designs in multiple territories by filing a single application with the International Bureau of WIPO, thus simplifying the multinational registration process. Moreover, by allowing the filing of up to 100 different designs per application, the System offers considerable opportunities for efficiency gains. It also streamlines the subsequent management of industrial design registration, since it is possible to record changes or renew a registration through a single procedure for all territories. Further information about the Hague System is available at *www.wipo.int/hague.*

Plant variety protection

To obtain protection, a plant breeder must file an individual application with every authority entrusted with granting breeders' rights. A breeder's right is granted only when a variety is new, distinct, uniform and stable, and has a suitable denomination.

In the United States of America (US), two legal frameworks protect new plant varieties: the Plant Patent Act (PPA) and the Plant Variety Protection Act (PVPA). Under the PPA, whoever invents or discovers and asexually reproduces any distinct and new variety of plant – including cultivated sports, mutants, hybrids and newly-found seedlings, other than a tuber-propagated plant (in practice, Irish potato and Jerusalem artichoke) or a plant found in an uncultivated state – may obtain a patent. Under the PVPA, the United States of America protects all sexually-reproduced plant varieties and tuber-propagated plant varieties, excluding fungi and bacteria.

The geographical indication system

A geographical indication (GI) is a sign identifying a good as originating in a specific geographical area and possessing a given quality, reputation or other characteristic essentially attributable to that geographical origin. Thus, the main function of a GI is to indicate a connection between the quality, characteristics or reputation of the good and its territory of origin.

World-renowned examples of GIs include "Café de Colombia" (Colombia), "Bordeaux" (France), "Kampot Pepper" (Cambodia), "Penja Pepper" (Cameroon) and "Scotch Whisky" (United Kingdom).

Geographical indications are mainly used for agricultural and food products, which typically tend to have a close natural link with their place of origin. However, there are many GIs for other kinds of products, whose specific characteristics may derive from traditional manufacturing skills or from a combination of local know-how and natural resources. Examples of GIs for handicraft and manufactured goods include "Bohemia Crystal" (Czech Republic), "Solingen" for cutlery (Germany), "Isfahan Handmade Carpet" (Islamic Republic of Iran) and "Swiss Made" for watches (Switzerland).

Although GIs are commonly names of places, they may also consist of non-geographical terms with a traditional geographical connotation (traditional denominations); for example, "Argane" (Morocco) serves as a GI, although it is not a geographical name.

Geographical indications can only be used on goods that conform to the applicable requirements concerning the area of origin, processing method and typicity of the product. Goods from production sites located outside the area of origin and goods that do not meet the applicable requirements are prohibited from using the protected indication.

Appellations of origin

An appellation of origin is a special kind of geographical indication. It generally consists of a geographical name or a traditional denomination that serves to designate a product as originating in a defined geographical area, where the quality or characteristics of the product are due exclusively or essentially to that geographical environment, including natural and human factors, and which have given the good its reputation. The most important difference between appellations of origin and other GIs is that the link with the geographical area should be stronger in the case of an appellation of origin; in other words, appellations of origin are a more restrictive sub-category of GI.

Protection of GIs

At the national and regional levels, GIs are protected through a variety of legal means. These include *sui generis* systems – that is, laws specifically designed to protect geographical indications,[3] often based on a registration procedure. *Sui generis* systems generally provide protection against any direct and indirect commercial use of a GI, as well as against its imitation. *Sui generis* systems for GI protection are used in many countries and also by two regional intergovernmental organizations: namely, the African Intellectual Property Organization (OAPI) and the European Union (EU).

Geographical indications can also be protected on the basis of trademark law, commonly through the use of collective and certification marks. Because trademarks incorporating geographical terms are typically not recorded by IP offices as a separate category of trademark, and because not all trademarks incorporating geographical terms can be considered to be GIs, it may be difficult to determine the exact number of registered GIs within jurisdictions. It is also worth noting that GI protection via *sui generis* or trademark systems are not mutually exclusive, but often coexist under many legal frameworks and are available for the benefit of GI holders.

Finally, GIs are typically also protected under unfair competition regulations, consumer protection laws and administrative and judicial decisions, as well as under specific laws or decrees recognizing individual GIs.

As for other IP rights, the effects of a GI right obtained in a particular jurisdiction are limited to the territory of that jurisdiction. Thus, where a right over a GI is obtained in one jurisdiction, it is protected there but not abroad. In order to obtain protection in a foreign jurisdiction, GI holders must, in principle, seek protection under the relevant national or regional laws of the jurisdiction in question. However, international agreements can facilitate the acquisition of GI rights abroad. In particular, bilateral and regional agreements have incorporated lists of GIs that are to be protected within the jurisdiction of the relevant parties to the agreement. The listed GIs may relate to existing or subsequent GI rights, but protection may also emanate from the trade agreements themselves.

Another way of obtaining protection for GIs abroad is through two international registration systems administered by WIPO: namely, the Lisbon System and the Madrid System.

The Lisbon System

The Lisbon System was established in 1958 to facilitate the international protection of appellations of origin through a single registration procedure.[4] Registration with the WIPO International Bureau ensures protection in all Lisbon contracting parties, without the need for renewal and for as long as the appellation of origin remains protected within its contracting party of origin. However, the decision as to whether to protect a newly registered appellation of origin at the national or regional level remains the prerogative of each contracting party and each Lisbon member can refuse protection based on any ground foreseen at national or regional level within one year of being notified of a new appellation of origin by the WIPO International Bureau.

Globally-renowned examples of appellations of origin protected under the Lisbon System include "Tequila" for spirits (Mexico), "Chianti" for wines (Italy), "Habanos" for cigars (Cuba) and handicrafts such as "Chulucanas" for ceramics (Peru) and "Herend" for porcelain (Hungary). The scope of the System extends to non-geographical traditional names, such as "Reblochon" for cheese (France) and "Vinho Verde" for wines (Portugal).

3 The terminology used at national and regional levels to refer to *sui generis* rights over GIs is not uniform. Different terms, such as appellations of origin, controlled appellations of origin, protected designations of origin, protected geographical indications, (qualified) indications of source, or simply geographical indications are used in different legislations. Despite the different terminology, however, the common denominator remains the link between the specific quality, characteristics or reputation of the product and its territory of origin. For simplicity, the present text generally uses "geographical indication (GI)," regardless of differences in national and regional terminology.

4 The Lisbon System is administered by WIPO and comprises the Lisbon Agreement for the Protection of Appellations of Origin and their International Registration (1958), as revised at Stockholm in 1967 and amended in 1979, and the Geneva Act of the Lisbon Agreement on Appellations of Origin and Geographical Indications (2015), which entered into force on February 26, 2020.

In 2015, with the adoption of the Geneva Act of the Lisbon Agreement on Appellations of Origin and Geographical Indications – which entered into force on February 26, 2020 – Lisbon contracting parties modernized the System in order to attract a wider membership, while preserving its principles and objectives. The Geneva Act formally extends the scope of the Lisbon System to the general category of GIs in addition to appellations of origin. The new Act also opened the Lisbon System to accession by intergovernmental organizations, such as the EU and OAPI. It also made the Lisbon System more flexible so as to secure a wider recognition for, and inclusion of, the various means by which countries may protect appellations of origin and GIs at a national or regional level (e.g., *sui generis* systems, trademark laws or specific ad hoc decrees, as well as judicial and administrative decisions).

Protection of GIs abroad through the Madrid System

Geographical indications can be protected in several countries as trademarks (most commonly collective and certification marks) through the Madrid System, an international registration system legally governed by the Madrid Agreement (1891) and the Madrid Protocol (1989) and administered by WIPO. A famous example of a collective/certification mark registered under the Madrid System is Napa Valley for wines from the United States of America.

Glossary

This glossary provides definitions of key technical terms and concepts. Many are defined generically (for example, "application"), but apply to several or all of the various forms of intellectual property (IP) covered by this report.

Applicant
An individual or other legal entity that files an application for a patent, utility model, trademark or industrial design. There may be more than one applicant in an application. For the statistics in this publication, the name of the first named applicant is used to determine the origin of the application.

Application
The procedure for requesting IP rights at an office, which then examines the application and decides whether to grant protection. Also refers to a set of documents submitted to an office by the applicant.

Application abroad
For statistical purposes, an application filed by a resident of a given state or jurisdiction with the IP office of another state or jurisdiction. For example, an application filed by an applicant domiciled in France with the Japan Patent Office (JPO) is considered an application abroad from the perspective of France. This differs from a "non-resident application," which describes an application filed by a resident of a foreign state or jurisdiction from the perspective of the office receiving the application: the example above would be a non-resident application from the JPO's point of view.

Application date
The date on which an IP office receives an application that meets the minimum requirements. Also referred to as the filing date.

Book
A book represents informational content in the form of many pages of text or images published in print and/or digital format in all their manifestations.

Budapest Treaty
Disclosure of an invention is a requirement for granting a patent. Normally, an invention is disclosed by means of a written description. Where an invention involves a microorganism or the use of a microorganism, disclosure is not always possible in writing and can sometimes only be effected by depositing a sample of the microorganism with a specialized institution. To eliminate the need to deposit a microorganism in every country where patent protection is sought, under the Budapest Treaty the deposit of a microorganism with any International Depositary Authority (IDA) is sufficient for the purposes of patent procedure at the national patent offices of all contracting states and at any regional patent office that recognizes the Treaty.

Certification trademark
Certification marks are usually awarded for compliance with defined standards, but are not confined to any membership. They may instead be used by anyone able to certify that the products involved meet certain established standards. In many countries, the main difference between collective marks and certification marks is that collective marks may only be used by a specific group of enterprises – for example, members of an association – while certification marks may be used by anybody who complies with the standards defined by the owner of the certification mark.

Class
May refer to the classes defined in either the Locarno Classification or the Nice Classification. Classes indicate the categories of goods and services (where applicable) for which industrial design or trademark protection is requested. See "Locarno Classification" and "Nice Classification."

Class count
The number of classes specified in a trademark application or registration. In the international trademark system, and at certain national and regional offices, an applicant can file a trademark application specifying one or more of the 45 goods and services classes of the Nice Classification. Offices use either a multi-class or a single filing system. For example, the offices of Japan, the Republic of Korea and the United States of America (US), as well as many European IP offices, have multi-class filing systems. On the other hand, the offices of Brazil, Mexico and South Africa follow a single-class filing system, requiring a separate application for each class in which an applicant seeks trademark protection. To capture the differences in application and registration numbers across offices, it is useful to compare their respective application and registration class counts.

Collective trademark
Collective marks are usually defined as signs that distinguish the geographical origin, material, mode of manufacture or other common characteristics of goods or services of different enterprises using the collective mark. The owner may be either an association of which those enterprises are members or any other entity, including a public institution or a cooperative.

Community Plant Variety Office (CPVO) of the European Union (EU)
An EU agency that manages a system of plant variety rights covering all EU member states.

Design count
The number of designs contained in an industrial design application or registration. Under the Hague System for the International Registration of Industrial Designs, it is possible for an applicant to obtain protection for up to 100 industrial designs for products belonging to one and the same class by filing a single application. Some national or regional IP offices allow applications to contain more than one design for the same product or within the same class, while others allow only one design per application. In order to capture the differences in application and registration numbers across offices, it is useful to compare their respective application and registration design counts.

Designation
A request made in an international application or registration by which the applicant/international registration holder specifies the jurisdiction(s) in which they seek to protect their industrial designs (Hague System) or trademarks (Madrid System).

Direct filing
See "National route."

Educational publishing
Educational publishing refers to books intended for teaching in schools and educational institutions. This includes the following two sub-sectors: (a) school textbooks (K-12) are books for schools and (b) higher education publishing are books for colleges, universities, and other higher education institutions. Educational books should include books sold to educational institutions, governments or through specialist academic vendors and outlets, and so on.

Equivalent application

Applications at regional offices are equivalent to multiple applications, one in each of the member states of those offices. To calculate the number of equivalent applications for the Benelux Office for Intellectual Property (BOIP), the Eurasian Patent Organization (EAPO), the African Intellectual Property Organization (OAPI), the Patent Office of the Cooperation Council for the Arab States of the Gulf (GCC Patent Office) and the European Union Intellectual Property Office (EUIPO), each application is multiplied by the corresponding number of member states. For European Patent Office (EPO) and African Regional Intellectual Property Organization (ARIPO) data, each application is counted as one application abroad, if the applicant does not reside in a member state, or as one resident application and one application abroad, if the applicant resides in a member state. The equivalent application concept is used for reporting data by origin.

Equivalent grant (registration)

Grants (registrations) at regional offices are equivalent to multiple grants (registrations), one in each of the member states of those offices. To calculate the number of equivalent grants (registrations) for BOIP, EAPO, the EUIPO, the GCC Patent Office or OAPI, each grant (registration) is multiplied by the corresponding number of member states. For EPO and ARIPO data, each grant is counted as one grant abroad, if the applicant does not reside in a member state, or as one resident grant and one grant abroad, if the applicant resides in a member state. The equivalent grant (registration) concept is used for reporting data by origin.

European Patent Office (EPO)

The EPO is the regional patent office created under the European Patent Convention (EPC), in charge of granting European patents for EPC member states. Under Patent Cooperation Treaty (PCT) procedures, the EPO acts as a receiving office, an International Searching Authority and an International Preliminary Examining Authority.

European Union Intellectual Property Office (EUIPO)

The EUIPO is the office responsible for managing the EU trademark and the registered community design. The validity of these two IP rights extends across the jurisdictions of the 27 EU member states.

Filing

See "Application."

Foreign-oriented patent families

A special subset of patent families that comprises foreign-oriented patent families, this includes only those patent families with at least one filing office that differs from the office of the applicant's country of origin. Some foreign-oriented patent families include only one filing office, because applicants may choose to file directly with a foreign office. For example, if a Canadian applicant files a patent application directly with the United States Patent and Trademark Office (USPTO) without having first filed at the patent office of Canada, that application will form a foreign-oriented patent family.

Geographical indication

A geographical indication (GI) is a sign identifying a good as originating in a specific geographical area and possessing a given quality, reputation or other characteristic essentially attributable to that geographical origin. The main function of a GI is to identify goods while informing about a connection between the quality, characteristic or reputation of the good and its territory of origin.

Grant

A set of exclusive rights legally accorded to the applicant when a patent or utility model is granted or issued.

Gross domestic product (GDP)

The total unduplicated output of economic goods and services produced within a country as measured in monetary terms.

Hague System

The abbreviated form of the Hague System for the International Registration of Industrial Designs. The System comprises two international treaties: the Hague Act of 1960 and the Geneva Act of 1999. The Hague System makes it possible for an applicant to register up to 100 industrial designs in multiple jurisdictions by filing a single application with the International Bureau of WIPO. It simplifies multinational registration by reducing the requirement to file separate applications at each IP office. The System also simplifies the subsequent management of the industrial design, since it is possible to record changes or renew a registration through a single procedural step for all designated Hague members.

Industrial design
Industrial designs are applied to a wide variety of industrial products and handicrafts. They refer to the ornamental or aesthetic aspects of a useful article, including compositions of lines or colors or any three-dimensional forms that give a special appearance to a product or handicraft. The holder of a registered industrial design has exclusive rights against unauthorized copying or imitation of the design by third parties. Industrial design registrations are valid for a limited period. The term of protection is usually 15 years in most jurisdictions. However, differences in legislation exist, notably in China (which provides for a 10-year term from the application date).

In force
Refers to IP rights that are currently valid or, in the case of trademarks, active. To remain in force, IP protection must be maintained.

Intellectual property (IP)
Refers to creations of the mind: inventions, literary and artistic works, and symbols, names, images and designs used in commerce. IP is divided into two categories: industrial property – which includes patents, utility models, trademarks, industrial designs and geographical indications of source – and copyright, which includes literary and artistic works (such as novels, poems, plays, films), musical works, artistic works (such as drawings, paintings, photographs and sculptures) and architectural designs. Rights related to copyright include those of performing artists in their performances, those of producers of sound recordings in their recordings and those of broadcasters in their radio and television programs.

International Depositary Authority (IDA)
A scientific institution – typically a culture collection – capable of storing microorganisms that has acquired the status of an International Depositary Authority under the Budapest Treaty and provides for the receipt, acceptance and storage of microorganisms and the furnishing of samples thereof. As of September 2022, 48 such authorities were in existence around the world.

International Patent Classification (IPC)
An internationally recognized patent classification system, the IPC has a hierarchical structure of language-independent symbols and is divided into sections, classes, sub-classes and groups. IPC symbols are assigned according to the technical features in patent applications. A patent application that relates to multiple technical features can be assigned several IPC symbols.

International Union for the Protection of New Varieties of Plants (UPOV)
An intergovernmental organization established by the International Convention for the Protection of New Varieties of Plants (the UPOV Convention) that was adopted on December 2, 1961. UPOV provides and promotes an effective system of plant variety protection aimed at encouraging the development of new varieties of plants for the benefit of society.

Invention
A new solution to a technical problem. To qualify for patent protection, the invention must be novel, involve an inventive step and be industrially applicable, as judged by a person skilled in the art.

Lisbon System
The Lisbon System was established in 1958 and revised first in 1967 and then again in 2015 in order to facilitate the international protection of appellations of origin and geographical indications through a single registration procedure. Registration with the WIPO International Bureau ensures protection in all Lisbon contracting parties, without the need for renewal and for as long as the appellation of origin or the GI remains protected in its contracting party of origin. However, the decision on whether to protect a newly registered appellation of origin or GI at the national or regional level remains the prerogative of each contracting party, and each Lisbon member can refuse protection based on any ground foreseen at national or regional level within one year of being notified of a new appellation of origin or GI by the WIPO International Bureau. The Lisbon System is flexible with regard to the means by which countries may provide protection

at national or regional level for their appellations of origin or GIs (e.g., *sui generis* systems, trademark laws or specific ad hoc decrees, as well as judicial and administrative decisions).

Locarno Classification
The abbreviated form of the International Classification for Industrial Designs under the Locarno Agreement used for registering industrial designs. The Locarno Classification consists of 32 classes and their respective subclasses with explanatory notes, plus an alphabetical list of the goods in which industrial designs are incorporated and an indication of the classes and subclasses into which they fall.

Madrid System
An abbreviation describing the system for the international registration of trademarks, originally established by the Madrid Agreement Concerning the International Registration of Marks and later also governed by the Protocol Relating to the Madrid Agreement. Following a decision by the Madrid Union Assembly in October 2016, the Protocol is now the sole governing treaty of the Madrid System. The Madrid System is administered by the International Bureau of WIPO.

Maintenance
An act by the applicant to keep an IP grant/registration valid (in force), primarily by paying the required fee to the IP office of the state or jurisdiction providing protection. That fee is also known as a "maintenance fee." A trademark can be maintained indefinitely by paying renewal fees; however, patents, utility models and industrial designs can be maintained for only a limited number of years.

Microorganism deposit
The transmittal of a microorganism to an International Depositary Authority (IDA), which receives and accepts it, the storage of such a microorganism by the IDA, or both transmittal and storage.

National phase under the PCT
The phase that follows the international phase of the PCT procedure and which consists of the entry and processing of the international application in the individual countries or regions in which the applicant seeks protection for an invention.

National route
Applications for IP protection filed directly with the national office of, or acting for, the relevant state or jurisdiction (see also "Hague route," "Madrid route" and "PCT route"). The national route is also called the direct route or Paris route.

Nice Classification
The abbreviated form of the International Classification of Goods and Services for the Purposes of Registering Marks, an international classification established under the Nice Agreement. The Nice Classification consists of 45 classes, which are divided into 34 classes for goods and 11 for services. (See "Class.")

Non-resident
For statistical purposes, a "non-resident" application refers to an application filed with the IP office of, or acting for, a state or jurisdiction in which the first named applicant in the application is not domiciled. For example, an application filed with the Japan Patent Office (JPO) by an applicant residing in France is considered to be a non-resident application from the perspective of the JPO. Non-resident applications are sometimes referred to as foreign applications. A non-resident grant or registration is an IP right issued on the basis of a non-resident application.

Origin (country or region)
For statistical purposes, the origin of an application means the country or territory of residence of the first named applicant in the application. In some cases (notably in the United States of America), the country of origin is determined by the residence of the assignee rather than that of the applicant.

Paris Convention
The Paris Convention for the Protection of Industrial Property, signed on March 20, 1883, is one of the most important treaties, as it establishes general principles applicable to all IP rights. It establishes the "right of priority" enabling an IP applicant, when filing an application in

countries other than the original country of filing, to claim priority of an earlier application filed up to 12 months previously for patents and utility models, and up to six months previously for trademarks and industrial designs.

Paris route
An alternative to the Hague, Madrid or PCT routes, the Paris route (also called the direct route or national route) enables individual IP applications to be filed directly with an IP office of a country/territory that is a signatory to the Paris Convention.

Patent
A set of exclusive rights granted by law to applicants for inventions that are new, non-obvious and commercially applicable. A patent is valid for a limited period (generally 20 years), during which time patent holders can commercially exploit their inventions on an exclusive basis. In return, applicants are obliged to disclose their inventions to the public in a manner that enables others skilled in the art to replicate the invention. The patent system is designed to encourage innovation by providing innovators with time-limited exclusive legal rights, thus enabling them to appropriate returns from their innovative activity.

Patent family
Applicants often file patent applications in multiple jurisdictions, meaning some inventions are recorded more than once. To take this into account, WIPO has indicators related to patent families, defined as patent applications interlinked by one or more of: priority claim, Patent Cooperation Treaty national phase entry, continuation, continuation-in-part, internal priority, and addition or division. WIPO's patent family definition includes only those patent families associated with patent applications for inventions and excludes those associated with utility model applications.

PCT System
The PCT, an international treaty administered by WIPO, facilitates the acquisition of patent rights in a large number of jurisdictions. The PCT System simplifies the process of multiple national patent filings by reducing the requirement to file a separate application in each jurisdiction. However, the decision on whether to grant patent rights remains the prerogative of national and regional patent offices, and patent rights remain limited to the jurisdiction of the patent granting authority. The PCT application process starts with the international phase, during which an international search and, possibly, a preliminary examination are performed, and concludes with the national phase, during which a national or regional patent office decides on the patentability of an invention according to national law.

Pending patent application
In general, this refers to a patent application filed with a patent office for which a patent has yet to be either granted or refused, and for which the application has not been withdrawn. In jurisdictions where a request for examination is required in order to begin the examination process, a pending application may refer to an application for which a request for examination has been received or one for which a patent has neither been granted nor refused, and for which the application has not been withdrawn.

Plant Patent Act (PPA) of the United States of America
Under the law commonly known as the "Plant Patent Act," whoever invents or discovers and asexually reproduces any distinct and new variety of plant, including cultivated sports, mutants, hybrids and newly-found seedlings, other than a tuber-propagated plant or a plant found in an uncultivated state, may obtain a patent therefor.

Plant variety
According to the UPOV Convention, plant variety means a plant grouping within a single botanical taxon of the lowest known rank which, regardless of whether the conditions for the granting of a breeder's right are fully met, can be defined by the expression of the characteristics resulting from a given genotype or combination of genotypes, distinguished from any other plant grouping by the expression of at least one of the said characteristics and considered as a unit with regard to its suitability for being propagated unchanged.

Plant variety title
Under the UPOV Convention, the breeder's right is granted (title of protection is issued) only when the variety is new, distinct, uniform, stable and has a suitable denomination.

Plant Variety Protection Act (PVPA) of the United States of America
Under the PVPA, the United States of America protects all sexually reproduced plant varieties and tuber-propagated plant varieties, excluding fungi and bacteria.

Prior art
All information disclosed to the public about an invention, in any form, before a given date. Information on prior art can assist in determining whether the claimed invention is new and involves an inventive step (i.e., is non-obvious) for the purposes of international searches and international preliminary examination.

Priority date
The filing date of the application on the basis of which priority is claimed. (See "Paris Convention.")

Publication date
The date on which an IP application is disclosed to the public. On that date, the subject matter of the application becomes prior art.

Publishing industry revenue
Total revenue refers to net revenue generated by sales and licenses excluding value-added and/or local sales tax. The net revenue calculation should exclude discounts offered to retailers and distributors. Whereas, revenue at market value is calculated from retail prices, including deductions for discounts, value-added tax, and so on.

Regional application/grant (registration)
An application filed with or granted (registered) by an IP office having regional jurisdiction over more than one country. There are currently seven regional offices: the African Intellectual Property Organization (OAPI), the African Regional Intellectual Property Organization (ARIPO), the Benelux Office for Intellectual Property (BOIP), the Eurasian Patent Organization (EAPO), the European Patent Office (EPO), the European Union Intellectual Property Office (EUIPO) and the Patent Office of the Cooperation Council for the Arab States of the Gulf (GCC Patent Office).

Registered Community Design
A registration issued by the EUIPO based on a single application filed directly with the office by an applicant seeking protection within the EU as a whole.

Registration
An exclusive set of rights legally accorded to the applicant when an industrial design or trademark is registered or issued. See "Industrial design" or "Trademark." Registrations are issued to applicants allowing them to make use of and exploit their industrial designs or trademarks for a limited period of time and can, in some cases (particularly in the case of trademarks), be renewed indefinitely.

Renewal
The process by which the protection of an IP right is maintained (kept in force). This usually consists of paying renewal fees to an IP office at regular intervals. If renewal fees are not paid, the registration may lapse. See also "Maintenance."

Resident
For statistical purposes, a resident application refers to an application filed with the IP office of, or acting for, the state or jurisdiction in which the first named applicant in the application is resident. For example, an application filed with the Japan Patent Office (JPO) by a resident of Japan is considered a resident application from the perspective of the JPO. Resident applications are sometimes referred to as "domestic applications." A resident grant/registration is an IP right issued on the basis of a resident application.

Trademark
A sign used to distinguish the goods or services of one undertaking from those of another. A trademark may consist of words and combinations of words (for instance, names or slogans),

logos, figures and images, letters, numbers, sounds, or, in rare instances, smells or moving images, or a combination thereof. The procedures for registering trademarks are governed by the legislation and procedures of national and regional IP offices and WIPO. Trademark rights are limited to the jurisdiction of the IP office that registers the trademark. Trademarks can be registered by filing an application at the relevant national or regional office(s), or by filing an international application through the Madrid System.

Trade publishing

Trade publishing refers to books intended for the consumer market and distributed through various channels. It includes a wide variety of genres in fiction, non-fiction, children's and young adult books.

Utility model

A special form of patent right granted by a state or jurisdiction to an inventor or the inventor's assignee for a fixed period of time. The terms and conditions for granting a utility model are slightly different from those for normal patents (including a shorter term of protection and less stringent patentability requirements). The term "utility model" can also describe what are known in certain countries as "petty patents," "short-term patents" or "innovation patents."

World Intellectual Property Organization (WIPO)

A United Nations specialized agency dedicated to the promotion of innovation and creativity for the economic, social and cultural development of all countries through a balanced and effective international IP system. WIPO was established in 1967 with a mandate to promote the protection of IP throughout the world through cooperation between states and in collaboration with other international organizations.

Abbreviations

ARIPO	African Regional Intellectual Property Organization
BOIP	Benelux Office for Intellectual Property
CNIPA	National Intellectual Property Administration of the People's Republic of China
CPVO	Community Plant Variety Office of the European Union
EAPO	Eurasian Patent Organization
EPO	European Patent Office
EU	European Union
EUIPO	European Union Intellectual Property Office
GCC Patent Office	Patent Office of the Cooperation Council for the Arab States of the Gulf
GDP	gross domestic product
GI	geographical indication
IDA	International Depositary Authority
IP	intellectual property
IPA	International Publishers Association
IPC	International Patent Classification
JPO	Japan Patent Office
KIPO	Korean Intellectual Property Office
LAC	Latin America and the Caribbean
NPA	national publishers' association
OAPI	African Intellectual Property Organization
PPA	Plant Patent Act of the United States of America
PRO	public research organization
PVPA	Plant Variety Protection Act of the United States of America
UK	United Kingdom
UM	utility model
UN	United Nations
UPOV	International Union for the Protection of New Varieties of Plants
US	United States of America
USPTO	United States Patent and Trademark Office
WIPO	World Intellectual Property Organization

Annexes

Annex A. Definitions for selected energy-related technology fields

Energy-related technologies	International patent classification (IPC) symbols
Solar energy technology	E04D 1/30, E04D 13/18, F03G 6/06, F24J 2/00, F24J 2/02, F24J 2/04, F24J 2/05, F24J 2/06, F24J 2/07, F24J 2/08, F24J 2/10, F24J 2/12, F24J 2/13, F24J 2/14, F24J 2/15, F24J 2/16, F24J 2/18, F24J 2/23, F24J 2/24, F24J 2/36, F24J 2/38, F24J 2/42, F24J 2/46, F24S%, G02B 5/10, G02F 1/136, G05F 1/67, H01L 25/00, H01L 31/00, H01L 31/04, H01L 31/042, H01L 31/048, H01L 31/052, H01L 31/18, H01L 33/00, H02J 7/35, H02N 6/00, H02S
Fuel cell technology	H01M 4/00, H01M 4/86, H01M 4/88, H01M 4/90, H01M 8/00, H01M 8/02, H01M 8/04, H01M 8/06, H01M 8/08, H01M 8/10, H01M 8/12, H01M 8/14, H01M 8/16, H01M 8/18, H01M 8/20, H01M 8/22, H01M 8/24
Wind energy	B60L 8/00, F03D
Geothermal energy	F03G 4/00, F03G 7/05, F24J 3/08, F24T
Hydro	B63H 19/02, B63H 19/04, E02B 9/00, E02B 9/02, E02B 9/04, E02B 9/06, F03B, F03C

Note: For definitions of IPC symbols, see *www.wipo.int/classifications/ipc*. The correspondence between IPC symbols and technology fields is not always clear-cut, therefore it is difficult to capture all patents in a specific technology field. Nonetheless, the IPC-based definitions of the four technologies presented above are likely to capture the vast majority of related patents.

Source: WIPO.

Annex B. Composition of industry sectors by Nice goods and services classes

Industry sector	Abbreviation (where applicable)	Nice classes
Agricultural products and services	Agriculture	29, 30, 31, 32, 33, 43
Management, communications, real estate and financial services	Business services	35, 36
Chemicals	..	1, 2, 4
Textiles – clothing and accessories	Clothing and accessories	14, 18, 22, 23, 24, 25, 26, 27, 34
Construction, infrastructure	Construction	6, 17, 19, 37, 40
Pharmaceuticals, health, cosmetics	Health	3, 5, 10, 44
Household equipment	..	8, 11, 20, 21
Leisure, education, training	Leisure & Education	13, 15, 16, 28, 41
Scientific research, information and communication technology	Research & Technology	9, 38, 42, 45
Transportation and logistics	Transportation	7, 12, 39

Source: Edital®.

Annex C. Industry sectors by Locarno classes

Sector	Locarno classes
Advertising	20, 32
Agricultural products and food preparation	1, 27, 31
Construction	23, 25, 29
Electricity and lighting	13, 26
Furniture and household goods	6, 7, 30
Health, pharma and cosmetics	24, 28
ICT and audiovisual	14, 16, 18
Leisure and education	17, 19, 21, 22
Packaging	9
Textiles and accessories	2, 3, 5, 11
Tools and machines	4, 8, 10, 15
Transport	12

Source: Organisation for Economic Co-operation and Development (OECD).

www.ingramcontent.com/pod-product-compliance
Ingram Content Group UK Ltd.
Pitfield, Milton Keynes, MK11 3LW, UK
UKHW052153041026
15590UKWH00007B/2053

9 789280 534627